The History and Antiquities of the Hundred of Willey in the county of Bedford. [With plates and maps.]

William Marsh Harvey

The History and Antiquities of the Hundred of Willey in the county of Bedford. [With plates and maps.]
Harvey, William Marsh
British Library, Historical Print Editions
British Library
1872-8
xxi. 570 p. ; 4°.
L.R.41.d.11.

The BiblioLife Network

This project was made possible in part by the BiblioLife Network (BLN), a project aimed at addressing some of the huge challenges facing book preservationists around the world. The BLN includes libraries, library networks, archives, subject matter experts, online communities and library service providers. We believe every book ever published should be available as a high-quality print reproduction; printed on- demand anywhere in the world. This insures the ongoing accessibility of the content and helps generate sustainable revenue for the libraries and organizations that work to preserve these important materials.

The following book is in the "public domain" and represents an authentic reproduction of the text as printed by the original publisher. While we have attempted to accurately maintain the integrity of the original work, there are sometimes problems with the original book or micro-film from which the books were digitized. This can result in minor errors in reproduction. Possible imperfections include missing and blurred pages, poor pictures, markings and other reproduction issues beyond our control. Because this work is culturally important, we have made it available as part of our commitment to protecting, preserving, and promoting the world's literature.

GUIDE TO FOLD-OUTS, MAPS and OVERSIZED IMAGES

In an online database, page images do not need to conform to the size restrictions found in a printed book. When converting these images back into a printed bound book, the page sizes are standardized in ways that maintain the detail of the original. For large images, such as fold-out maps, the original page image is split into two or more pages.

Guidelines used to determine the split of oversize pages:

- Some images are split vertically; large images require vertical and horizontal splits.
- For horizontal splits, the content is split left to right.
- For vertical splits, the content is split from top to bottom.
- For both vertical and horizontal splits, the image is processed from top left to bottom right.

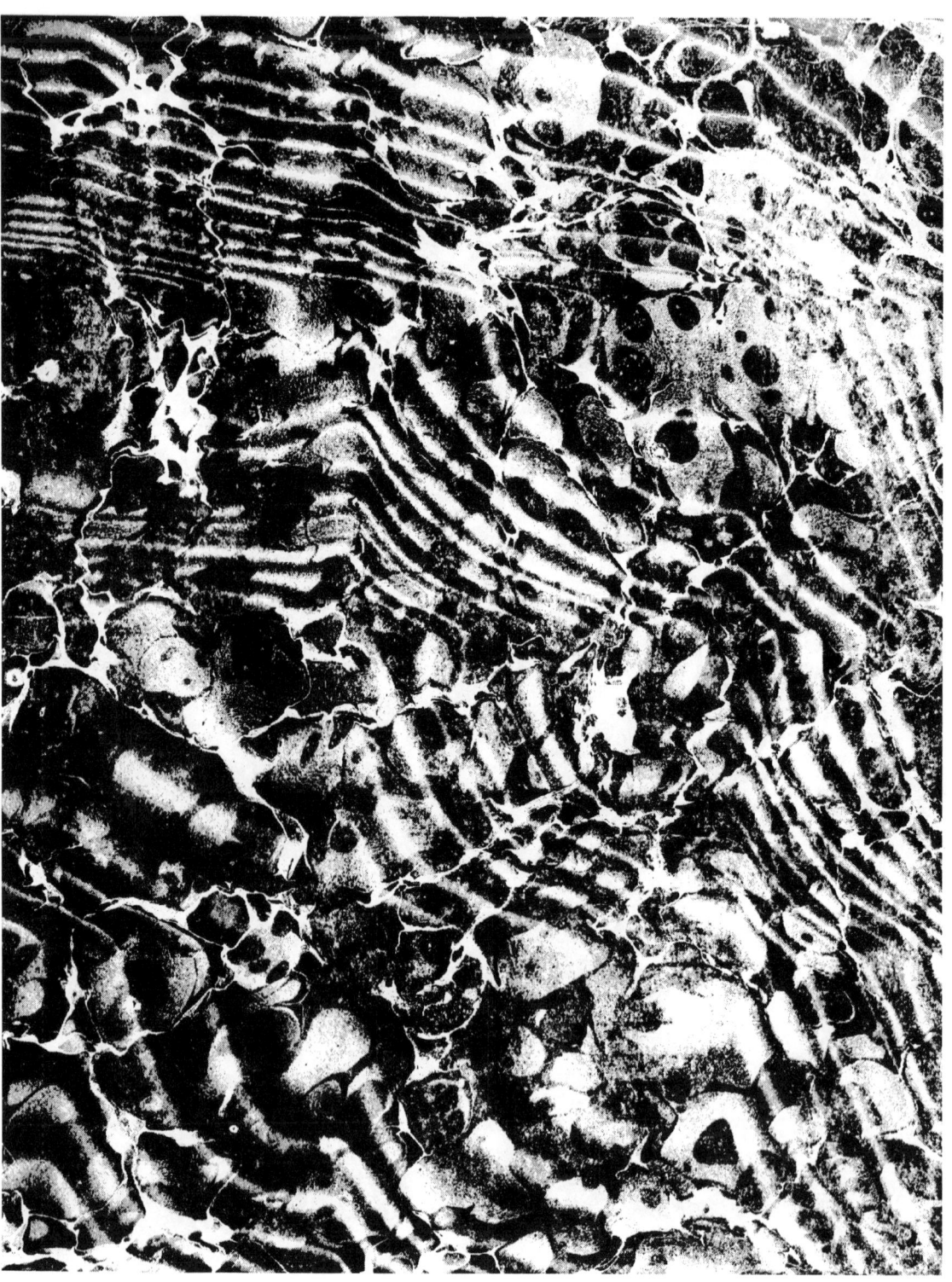

THE HISTORY AND ANTIQUITIES

OF

THE HUNDRED OF WILLEY,

IN THE

COUNTY OF BEDFORD.

BY

WILLIAM MARSH HARVEY, ESQ., F.R. Hist. Soc.,

OF THE MIDDLE TEMPLE, BARRISTER-AT-LAW.

LONDON:
PRINTED BY NICHOLS AND SONS, 25, PARLIAMENT STREET.

1872—8.

TO THE RIGHT HONORABLE

ST. ANDREW,

15TH BARON ST. JOHN OF BLETSOE,

&c., &c., &c.,

THIS WORK IS, WITH MUCH RESPECT,

INSCRIBED.

ADVERTISEMENT.

The Author of the History and Antiquities of the Hundred of Willey cannot allow his now completed work to go forth to the public without acknowledging his obligations to the Clergy and Gentry of the County who have contributed materials to, and otherwise assisted in, the undertaking; and in particular to the Rev. Canon Haddock, Vicar of Clapham, Beds., the Rev. William Sweet Escott, R.D., Vicar of Stagsden, and the President and Committee of the Bedford General Library. To these, and the many friends who have kindly aided him in his researches, he takes this opportunity of returning his very grateful thanks.

Parishes Described.

	PAGE		PAGE
Biddenham	1	Pavenham	301
Bletsoe	481	Poddington	379
Bromham	29	Sharnbrook	455
Carlton	239	Souldrop	447
Chellington	263	Stagsden	113
Farndish	411	Stevington	141
Felmersham	275	Thurleigh	501
Harrold	315	Turvey	169
Odell	345	Wymington	421

Plates and Engravings.

Map of the Hundred of Willey	*Frontispiece*	Turvey Abbey (2)	190
Ford End, Biddenham	11	Turvey House	191
Biddenham Church	20	Rectory	197
Plan	20	Church	201
Font	21	Font	205
Bromham Hall (2)	49	Plan	205
Miller's House, Biddenham Bridge	51	Interior of Church	207
Bromham Vicarage	56	Part of Village	219
The Church (1866)	59	Old Rectory-house	237
Church (north-west)	61	Carlton Rectory	253
Font	62	Church	256
Plan	65	Font	257
Stagsden Vicarage	131	Plan	257
School	131	Chellington Church	270
Church	132	Church	271
Interior of the Church	133	Plan	271
Font	135	Font	272
Plan	135	Felmersham Grange	282
Brass of John Cocke	137	Radwell Hall and Ancient Glass	286
Stevington, manor-house (2)	149	Felmersham Church and Parsonage House	290
Vicarage	156	School	299
Church (1866)	158	Pavenham Church	308
Church	159	Plan	308
Details and Plan	160	Font	314
Interior of Church (nave)	160	Harrold Hall	324
Interior of Church (aisles) (2)	161	Staircase, Harrold Hall	324
Font	161	Harwold Priory	326

Plates and Engravings.

	PAGE		PAGE
Harrold Church (2)	335	Sharnbrook Church (2)	470
Plan	336	Plan	471
Odell Castle (1860)	362	Font	500
Odell Church	367	Colworth House	479
Plan	368	Mansion House, Bletsoe (2)	486
Hinwick House	394	Bletsoe Church	490
Poddington Church	398	Plan	490
Plan	399	Font	500
Farndish Church	413	Monuments to the St John Family in Bletsoe Church (2)	492
Farm House at Farndish	413		
Plan of Church	417	Farm House on Site of Thurleigh Hall	512
Font	500	Blackbourne Hall Farm	516
Plan of Wymington Church	438	Thurleigh Vicarage	523
Font	446	Church (2)	526
Souldrop Rectory	450	Font	527
Church (2)	452	Plan	528
Plan	453	Interior of the Church	528
Font	500	Old Farm House near the Church	534
The Toft, Sharnbrook	462		

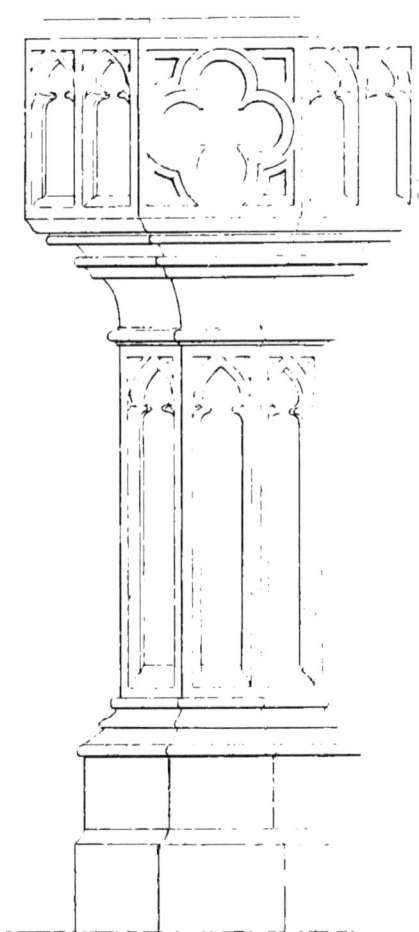

INTRODUCTION.

The modern Hundred of Willey, comprising nearly the whole of the ancient Hundred of the same name, together with part of the half-hundred of Bucklai,[a] probably takes its denomination from the winding course of the river Ouse through and round a great portion of this district.

Bedfordshire anciently formed part of the extensive diocese of Dorchester.[b] Until a few years ago, when it was transferred to Ely, it was included in that of Lincoln. The eighteen parishes[c] of the Hundred of Willey are in the Archdeaconry of Bedford,[d] and, with two exceptions, in the Rural Deanery of

---

[a] The regular establishment of parishes is attributed to King Alfred, who, to check the disposition to plunder which his own subjects in their conflicts with the Danes had too much practised, wisely instituted parishes, vills, or tithings. We are informed they were denominated tithings because every such division consisted originally of ten families. Ten of these parishes or vills constituted a hundred, as consisting of ten times ten families.

The half-hundred of Bochelai, or Bucklai, contained, at the time of the great survey, the manors of Biddenham, Bletsoe, Bromham, Stagsden, and Stevington, now included in Willey Hundred, and Renhold and Goldington, in Barford Hundred; parts of the borough of Bedford and Newenham Abbey were formerly taken to be within the limits of Willey, but are not included in later surveys.

[b] From maps published in Freeman's *Norman Conquest* it appears that this Hundred formed part of the following subdivisions of Britain at various times:—

A.D.
597. Bedfordshire, included in Mercia, inhabited by Teutons (Angles).—Vol. i. pp. 34, 35.
    10th and 11th centuries. The Hundred of Willey, in the Earldom of Mercia. North of river Ouse, *Middle Angles;* south of river Ouse, *Hwiccas.*—*Ib.* p. 284, 285.
    Under Edward the Confessor, Beds. (Ely and Lincoln), in the diocese of Dorchester (Oxon.)—*Ib.* vol. ii. pp. 82, 83.
1045. Willey, in the Earldom of Beorn. } *Ib.* pp. 568, 569.
1065.   ,,   ,,   Yrth. }

Of the ancient inhabitants and government of Bedfordshire, Lysons and other writers give an account somewhat as follows:—

When the Romans invaded Britain Bedfordshire was inhabited by the Cassii, or "Catieucblani," a tribe mentioned by Dio Cassius. During the government of the Romans it formed part of Britannia Superior, afterwards Britannia Prima, and upon the last Roman division of the island it was included in the district of Flavia. After the establishment of the Saxon Heptarchy it became part of the kingdom of Mercia. When two kingdoms of the Heptarchy were abolished, as related by Bromton, the Kings of Mercia retained one moiety of Bedfordshire, the Kings of Essex became possessed of the other. After the whole of England was united into one monarchy this county was comprised within the district called Denelege, or the Danish jurisdiction; it may, however, be doubted whether the *whole* county was within the Denelege, and particularly part of the hundred with which we are more immediately concerned.

[c] Of these, Poddington, Farndish, and Wymington are included in the Wellingborough Poor-law Union, the remainder are in that of Bedford.

[d] ARCHDEACONS OF BEDFORD:

[N.B.—The names down to about the year 1728 are from a list by Browne Willis.—Add. MS. 21,067, ff. 135, 136.]

Year.	Year.
1095. Osbert.	1180. Laurence.
1105. Ralph.	
1112. Hugh.	[14th Sept. 1186, Laurence, Archdeacon of Bedford, Bernard, Prior of *Novo Burgo*, and Roger Harundel, or Arundel, were candidates for the see of York, but the King rejected them all. The first of these and Roger Arundel were actually the two farmers of the see of York at this time.—*Chron. Benedict* (Stubbs), i. 352.]
1145-72. Nicholas.	

Clapham,—Thurleigh being in Eaton Socon, and Biddenham (formerly part of the half-hundred of Bucklai) in Bedford Deanery.

This Hundred was farmed by bailiffs or lessees of the Crown; the office of bailiff appears to have been hereditary in a family, surnamed De Willey, for several generations.[a] The Hundred continues, it is presumed, to belong to the Crown. As to its civil government, it is under the same jurisdiction as the rest of the county of Bedford.

In the year 1176, Hugo de Cressi, Walter FitzRobert, and Robert Mantel were itinerant justices in Bedfordshire and other counties;[b] and John, Bishop of Norwich, Hugo Murdac *Clericus Regis*, Michael Belet, Richard de Peck, and Radulfus Brito, in 1179.[c]

Until the year 1574 the sheriffs exercised jurisdiction over the counties of Bedford and Buckingham conjointly. Lists of the Sheriffs of Beds. and Bucks. from 1135 to 1574, have already been printed in Lipscomb's *History of Buckinghamshire* and in Berry's *County Genealogies (Bucks)*.

ARCHDEACONS OF BEDFORD, continued:

Year.
1203. Geoffrey.
1217. Alexander, ob. 1218.
1218. John Octon.
1228-31. John Hauton.
1231-41. Almaricus de Buggeden.
1245-59. John de Crakehale, R. Kiblington.
1259-69. Peter de Aldeham, or Audham.
1270-3. John de Maydeston.
1275. Nicholas.
1280-2. Richard de Dradwelle.
1282. John Hook.
1291-1327. Roger de Rowele.
1327-33. Edmund de London.
1333. John Daubeny.
1333-49. Philip de Daubeny.
1333(?). John de Wottesden.
1351-66. Thomas de Compton.
1373. John de Irthlingberry.
1385-1405. Thomas Stow.
1405-22-3 William Aughton.
1423-31. Richard Caudray.
1431-8. William Derby.
1438-50. Robert Thornton.
1450-60. Thomas Salisbury.
1460-8. John Ruding, LL.B., buried at Biggleswade.
1468. John Collynson.
1471-89. Henry Sharpe.
1489. Thomas Hutton.
1493-1524. William Cosyn.
1524-49. John Chambre, or Chamber.
1549-54. Gilbert Bourne.
1554-8. Thomas Cope.
1558. Michael Dunning.
1558-60 Richard Barber.
1560-74. William Forde.
1574-98. John Robinson.
1598. Roger Parker.

Year.
1599-1631. George Eland.
1631-62. John Hacket.
1662-7. Frederick Wilford.
1667-8. Theophilus Dillingham, D.D.
1678-1704. John Skelton.
1704. Thomas Franke, ob. 1731.
1731-44. John Dudley, M.A.
1745-50. John Taylor, M A.
1756. Charles Jenner, D.D.
1771. Richard Grey, D.D., ob. 1771.
1773. William Stafford Donne, D.D., buried at St. Mary's church, Bedford.
1776. Hadley Cox, M.A.
1803. Richard Shepherd, D.D., died 1809.
1809. Samuel Vince, M.A., 1st visitation 1811, charge published.[1]
1822. Henry Kaye Bonney, D.D., appointed Archdeacon of Bedford 1822; Archdeacon of Lincoln 1844; died 24 Dec., 1862, aged 82. He was author of a "Life of Bishop Jeremy Taylor;" "The Life and Remains, with Correspondence, of Bishop Middleton;" "Illustrated History of Fotheringhay;" and some charges and sermons.[2]
1844. Henry Tattam,[3] LL.D., D.D., F.R.S. Rector of Stanford Rivers, Essex, 1849, formerly (1822) Rector of St. Cuthbert's, Bedford, and (1831) of Great Wolstone, Bucks. Died at Stanford Rivers 8th Jan. 1868, having sometime previously resigned his Archdeaconry.
1866. Henry John Rose,[4] B.D., Rector of Houghton Conquest, died 31st Jan. 1873.
1873. Frederick Bathurst, M.A., Vicar of Biggleswade.

---

[1] Add. MS. 21,967, fo. 35b.
[2] Cooper's *Biographical Dictionary*. London: George Bell and Sons, York Street, Covent Garden. 1873.
[3] A brief memoir of Dr. Tattam will be found in "The Bedfordshire Times" newspaper of 14th Jan. 1868.
[4] "The Bedford Times and Independent" newspaper for 8th Feb. 1873, contains a short notice of Archdeacon Rose.

[a] Inquisitions post mortem.   [b] *Chron. Benedict.* (Stubbs), i. 107.   [c] *Ibid.* 239.

INTRODUCTION.

Appended to this Introduction will be found a supplemental list of the sheriffs of Bedfordshire from the latter date down to the present time.

We do not find this district conspicuously associated with any notable historical incidents. A glimpse at the state of the neighbourhood during the troublous times of the usurpation[a] is presented in the following warrants and summary of taxes, &c., copied from MSS. in the possession of Richard Orlebar, esq., of Hinwick.

To ye Constables of Harrold,

 I have receiued and other letter from Sr Samuell Luke Knight wherein you are desired to giue notice to some of your chiefe inhabitants of your p^rish yt they in   doe bring ye numbers and names of all those who are to serue as dragoones and foote souldiers for defence of his Ma:^{ttes} person ye parliament and kingdom and ye same to deliuer unto Willm. Haston gent. at ye Redd Lyon in Bedd' on Tuesday next wch will be taken as an ecceptable seruice. Dated 22th of January, 1642.

Ro: TAPP.

(To the same.)

 Wheras theire is certaine informacon giuen yt there are great forces aduanceinge towards Northampton yt beinge a towne and place neere unto us we cannot be free from p'ill and danger but be exposed to yer plunderings and violences as they haue needs in other places. These are therefore by vertue of a warrant from Sr Thomas Alston Knight and Barronet, Sir John Burgoyne Knight Barronet, Thomas Rolt Esq. Doe require you y^t you warne all mayridd men, Supplies and Voluntrees wthin your P^{ish} wth their arms to attend tomorrow by 8 of ye clock in ye morneinge et Bedd. to receive such dirrections as shall be fit for ye securringe of our Countie and herof faile you not at your P'ill. Dated ye 1st of Sept. 1642.

ROBT. TAPP.

(To the same.)

 By order of a warrant from Sr Thomas Alston Knight Sr Beauchamp St. John Knight Sr Oliver Luke Knight and Thomas Rolt Esqr. doe require you to warne and enjoine all ye trainord Souldiors and Supplies with in your P'ish that they appear at Bedd. in their arms compleat on Saturday next by 8 of ye Clock in ye morneinge there to be trained and excercised and to receive such further instructions and directions as there and then shall be enjoynned them, as you will answer ye contempt thereof and herof faile not. Dated 20th of October, 1642.

ROBT. TAPP.

(To the same.)

 By virtue of a Command from ye right wor^{sh} ye Deputy Leiut for the Countie doe require you y^t you charge those trained Souldiers wthin your Pⁱsh wch did not appeare uppon ye last Warninge y^t they faile not to appeare at Bedd. on Thursday next by 9 of ye Clocke in ye Morninge in their Arms Compleat to goe to ye Rendevouz under ye Command of Captaine Bokler and Also y^t you then and there show one horse for a dragoone according to former directions if you have not showed one uppon ye last Summons and hereof faile you not. Dated this 1st of November 1642.

ROBT. TAPP.

(To the same.)

 You are req^{ed} by virtue of an ordinance of pa'lmt to warn 4 of y^r ablest inhabitants of your P'ish to appear at ye Swan in Bedd. on Tuesday next by 9 of ye clock to be assessed of such sums as shall be weekely charged uppon your said P'ish by virtue of ye said ordinance and under such penalties as is in ye said ordinance mentioned. And y^t you be then and there present to make returne of this service, and to bringe in your leuies for ye second half of y^e £400,000 wth ye assessare thereof were lately enioyned to doe. Dat. ultio die Aprilis 1643.

---

[a] Cannon balls have been found in the meadows below Odell Castle and other places, but, so far as I am aware, there is no authentic record of any battle or skirmish of importance having been fought within the limits of this hundred. Lord Clarendon observes that Bedfordshire was one of the counties in which the King had not any visible party, nor one fixed quarter, and this remark seems true, for the only very prominent supporter of the Royal cause in this county was the renowned and gallant Sir Lewis Dyve, of Bromham.

INTRODUCTION.

To ye Constables of Harrold.

I am reqrd by Sr Sammuell Luke Kt to warne you to bringe in unto Layton to morrow by 8 of ye clocke ye number of ye dragoones raised wthin your P'ish wth y^{re} names, horses, and arms and a months pay for every one of them together wth ye returne of all those y^t refuse to pay those taxes for ye same and if you shall neglect so to doe you will be taxed for malignitie and p'ceeded against accordingly. Dated this 22th of May 1643.

ROBERT TAPP.

Whereas all cannot but be sensible of ye great miseryes and calamities y^t this kingdom hath a long time groaned under, and is likely by inevitable necessity to be totally waisted and consumed by a long and tedious warre, through the desperate malice of our most wicked and blood thirstye enemies who hunger after the ruine and confusion of us and all others well affected to ye publike ; haveinge noe other ends in their counsells, and actions, but to swallow our estates, and the very bread, breath, and livelyhood of us, our parliament, wives, and children, unlesse some speedy and desperate cure be applyed to ye allmost unmedecinable disease, The wise and serious considerations of these things hath caused our parliament for our present cure to move a generall risinge of all well affected persons and counties through the kingdome, for theire present aide and assistance, and of this have given the lord generall information, whose letters and commands are now come to signifie his and their pleasure herein.

By vertue therof a warrant received from Sr Samuell Luke Knight and Richard Edwards esqr doe will and require yow y^t you summon all men from to 60 years of age to appeare before them at Layton to morrow by 9 of ye clocke. And you uppon your oath bringe in a true list of ye names of all persons fitteinge to serve in so great and weighty expedicion, and y^t they come all wth armes and weapons they can provide and also y^t yow make returnes of all those y^t are malignants and refractory and w^t their abilities are, y^t ye ready for warre and well affected to serve may be supplied wth all things necessary for theire journey. And y^t likewise provisions be made by your parish for such numbers they send first for theire present sustenances in theire march and lastly ye souldiers under your pay be provided for one months pay : And hereof fayle not as you will answere ye contrary at your perille. Dated this 2^d of June 1643. To ye Constables of Harrold.

RO : TAPP.

I have received an order from ye last generall sessions y^t you cause sufficient watch and ward to be dayly kept wthin your parish.

To ye Constables of Oakley Keysoe Clapham Milton and Puddington and to everie of them. Thes are to will and require you uppon y^{re} sight hereof to bringe unto us wthout any more delay one month's pay for all your dragoones and foote in everie one of your p'ishes and if any shall refuse to pay ye taxe layed uppon him by y^r p'ish By vertue hereof we doe authorise you to seize their horses armes plate and other goodes to ye same value and we doe hereby authorise those souldiers whose names here underwritten to be aideinge and assistinge to you therein and to make sale of y^m to y^r best advantage of ye state and owners giveinge us a just accompt for ye same You are alsoe further to send in all y^r horses men and armes allotted uppon your severall p'ishes to appeare before us at Layton wth all speed and diligence ye 8^m day of this instant month hereof faile you not or you will answere ye contrary at y^r p'ill given under our handes this 7th day of June 1643.

SAMUEL LUKE.

To Clement Johnson, Daniel Cooper, Edmund Cozen,
  John Russell, and to anie one of them and alsoe
  to John Tapp, Richard Russell.

9th of July (? June) 1643. To ye Constables of Harrold or to either of them.

Whereas some charge and trouble hath beene to many well affected p'sons and p'ishes in this county by severall warrants cominge to y^{em} for their appearance, and being in a redines wth horse and foote for ye most spedy and likeliest way of putinge an end to all ye trouble and miseries y^t threaten this kingdome by a long and lingering warre, but by some after intelligence and orders they have beene again discharged till some other warninge for ye more ease of ye said p'ishes and p'sons. But it now beinge well knowne and perceived both by ye inclosed letter from his excellency ye Earle of Essex and alsoe by divers other advertisements of ye certayne march of ye whole army ye last night to Nettelfed, and so forwarde to ye designe intended, wherin ye generall aydes of this county, as also of buckingha^m, and hereford are desired and expected. These are therfore to desire all p'sons y^t have any care or sence of ye miseries of their country in every p'ish through this county to come unto us to laighton by to-morrow at 12 of ye clocke wth armes they can p'cure, and to bringe wth y^m p'visions for y^{ir} journey and marchinge y^t such a considerable strength may appeare wth all accommodations wth them both for man and horse to stay for some time abroad to p'forme somewh^t worthy of us and our country, and we shall be reddy to venture our lives and march along wth them. If any of our dragoons remayne wthin your p'ishes pray bringe y^m wth you and alsoe making the full number if any defect be, charged on your p'ishes.

SAM. LUKE.
RICHARD EDWARDS.

Laighton this 8th of June 1643.

INTRODUCTION.

Rec this ye 9th of June.

If any p'son or p'ish shall be dischouraged by reason of any malignant p'son y^t will remayne behind and refractory you shall bringe such p'sons to laighton wth you where such order shall be taken for their security y^t ye country may be in safety in your absence.

SAM. LUKE.

I am this night wth my army at Wittlef'rd and heare y^t you are not yet advanced towards me. I would have you come on as fast as you can. And if it may be wth convenience you may doe well to joyne wth Buckinghamshire forces y^t I have written to to be about or at Slisbury tomorrow night, let me heare w^h way you march y^t you may have new directions.

Your assured friend,
ESSEX.

This is a true coppy,
SAM : LUKE.
RICHARD EDWARDS.

Wheras warn^{ts} and let^{res} have issued out into this country to stirre up my country men for a generall riseinge to dispatch this great businesse now in hand but such fruites hath not proceded from this way as was in so faire a manner and for so great a good desired and expected. Theis are therefore to signifye unto you and my Desire is it may be published in every parish wthin your Devisions wth all speed that I will noe longer dally wth or by more faire wayes and meanes my country men seeinge it is allmost altogethere vaine and fruite lesse, but I am resolved y^t if all persons in every parish betweene 16 and 60 beinge able to carry armes shall not severally and speedily appeare wth all provisions wth them and armes and weapons for ye service of ye state and theire owne safety I will proceede against such cold insensible persons and parishes of this county wth ye rigor and severity as is done in other places y^t ye good may not all wayes remayne scoft and derided at but y^t they shall and may receive such ease and comfort by such my proceedinge as is agreable to all manner of equitie, and give confidence and y[?] let them know w^t all such as doe come are to march away presently and therefore desire them to come provided for ye purpose June ye 7 1643. SAM. LUKE.

To ye high Constables of ye hundred of Willy and to either of them, this on saterday 10 June 1643.

To ye Constables of Harrold.

Whereas I have read a warrant from Sr Samuell Luke K^t intimating y^t divers warrants hath been sent for ye bringing in of a proportion of able men for ye service of ye state in these times of eminent danger and as yet little fruit hath proceeded thereby, whereby ye kingdome is in distress by ye neglect of such means as may be in due time used for prevention thereof. These are therefore by virtue thereof you require uppon sight hereof everie person being betweene ye ages of 16 and 60 wthin your parish to appear at Layton tomorrow by 9 in ye morning to March along wth ye saide Sr Samuell Luke to ye armie wth such arms and provisions as they can possibly get or otherwise to send out 9 foote souldiers with provision and armes to march to ye Rendevons of ye parliaments armed for the service of ye King parliaments and kingdome. hereof faile not or you will answere ye contrary at your perills and undergoe such seueritie as ye malign^{ts} in Buckshire have done in ye like case for theire refusall Dated June the 14th 1643.

RO. TAPP.

If you have allreddy brought in any number you shall be accordingly.

To ye Constables of Harrold.

His Excellencie ye Earle of Essex hath directed his warrant to Colonell Thompson from whom y (I) have received warrant and by vertue thereof doe require you to summon all such persons wthin your p'ish as are able to baire armes to appeare at ye Swan in Bedd. to morrow by 8 of ye cloke in the morneinge for ye service of ye Kinge parliament and kingdome, and hereof you and every of them not to faile at the^{ir} p'rills

RO. TAPP.

Dated this 30th of June, 1643.

The number of p'sons summoned to the workes May 13, 1644. ffrom Willey 83.

The great levy for Bridges as it was layd att michas Sessions 1630.

ll.   s.   d.

Willey, Stod. Barf. 109   18   08

Altered by th^e Bench att the Sessions January 10th 1630.

ll.   s.   d.

Willey Stod. Barf. 090   09   00

Rateable value of property in Willey Hundred 1642-3, *ll.*14,100.

INTRODUCTION.

	Sums levied on the Hundred of Willey.		
	ll.	*s.*	*d.*
The Taxation to the first payment towards raising 400,000 *ll.* May 16, 1642 [a]	227	19	00
A Rate to taxe the county of Bedford, Jan. 18, 1643,[b] Willey Hundred 19*ll.* 07*s.* 01*d.*	19	07	01
The monthly tax to Newport [c]	77	08	06
The Taxe to S\r Thos. ffairfax, monthly 1,000*ll.*	103	04	08
To the maintenance of the Scotch Army, monthly 366*ll.* 00*s.* 08*d.*[d]	37	12	11
The charge of this county to the Easterne Garrison, 173*ll.* 00*s.* 03*d.* Willey Hundred 45*ll.* 17*s.* 9*d.*	17	15	04
(Tho. Battison, of Biddenham, Symon Gale, of Okeley, & Henr. Wagstaffe, of Wilden, High Collectors for the Hundreds of Willey, Stodden, and Barford).			
Willey Hundred, 7 months to the British Army	120	08	09
Charged to the reducing of Newarke	32	08	05
(This tax was laid after 4*s.* 7*d.* per cent.)			
Charged monthly upon Beds. to the Army by order of Parliament, 7 July, 1647, 673*ll.* 13*s.* 11*d.* Willey division 6 months [e]	422	07	06
Three monthes taxe to S\r Th. ffairfax' Army beginning 25 Dec. 1647. Upon Willey division 538*ll.* 01*s.* 08*d.*, distributed 22 Feb. 1647. by Sir T. Alston, Sir W. Boteler, Mr. Rolt, and Mr. Hervy, on 13,950*ll.* ann. value	209	13	01
25 April, 1648. The monthly taxe to Ireland,[f] p. ordinance of 16 Feb. 1647, 224*ll.* 11*s.* 04*d.* Willey Hundred 6 months	139	15	05
The Aid of 1651 70*2ll.* 18*s.*[g] Paid quarterly. Willey Hundred 12 months	2,241	04	02
To the Army for 3 months ending 24 June, 1649	313	07	08
To the Army from June 24, 1649 to Michaelmas following [h]	124	04	06

---

a The provision for Bedfo.
The Agreement with Mr. Backwell, Easter Sessions, 1641, and Backwell's demands in particular.
May 16th, 1642, charged upon the County of Bedford by the Act of Parliament for raising of £400,000 . . . £4,372 1*s.* 0*d.*
Whereof charged upon the Hundreds of Wiley, Stodden, and Barford £1,165 6*s.* 11*d.*

WM. BOTFLER.	ROBT. BANFORD, mayor.
THOMAS ROALT.	FFR. BANISTER.
OLI BOTELER	TH. PABADINE.
HUM. FFYSH.	THO. HAWES.
	RO HAWFS.

The Taxation of the Townes of W. S. and B. (Willey, Stodden, and Barford Hundreds) to the one payment being 582*ll.* 13 shillings. Sumr.: 582*ll.* 13*s.* 05*d.* This y\ls charged after the rate of 01*ll.* 12*s.* 04*d.* p. cent. excepting that there is 8*s.* set upon Bolnehurst, and 5*s.* 4*d.* more upon Knotting then the proporcion ; and there is 8*d.* more then the propor'ion sett upon Colmorth by mistake wch shd have been upon Shilton.

b A Rate to Tax the County of Bedford Jan. 18, 1643. Wiley, Stoden, and Barford may bear their proportions as in the great subsidy without any considerable Inequality.

c Jan. 18, 1643, Charged Weekley upon Beds. to the Garrison of Newport £187 10*s.*
This Tax is laid after 2*s.* 9*d.* per cent. only there is 6*s.* 6*d.* abated in the whole Hundred of Willy upon several Towns, and Odell is layde but after the rate of 800*ll.* p. an.

d This Tax comes to 5*s.* 5*d.* in the Hundred (pounds) In Wiley division after our Valuation. In the great subsidy only in a month's Tax there is overplus 13*s.* 07*d.*

e 1647, W. Boteler, T. H. Rolt, Ed. Osborne, Armigers.

	ll.	*s.*	*d.*		*ll.*	*s*	*d.*
f To the Irish monthly	166	13	4	Willey Division	44	4	4

Agreed forthwith to Assess six months and collect 3 presently and the other 3 months upon farther order, W. Boteler, W. Briers, Tho. Alston, Tho Rolt, T Daniell, Ed. Osbourne.

g Total for Beds. 3,031 *ll.* 12*s.* 11*d.* 9.
Mr. John Spencer ordered to be Receiver General.

h Total for town and county 1,200 *ll.*

The priory of Harwold or Harrold was the only monastery established within the limits of the modern Hundred of Willey. The templars and hospitalers had preceptories, commandries, granges, or farms in several parishes. Part of the rectory and advowson of Turvey with an estate in that parish belonged to the priory of St. Neots. At Felmersham was a cell or grange under Lenton Priory, Notts. The church of Sharnbrook was given to the abbey of St. Mary de Pratis at Leicester. The priory of Canons Ashby, Northamptonshire, possessed an interest in Poddington and Thurleigh. The monastery of Denny, in Cambridgeshire, presented to the church of Biddenham; the priory of Cauldwell, Beds, to that of Bromham; and Newenham priory to that of Stagsden. Several other religious houses in various counties were also seised of small estates in some of the parishes hereafter to be described.

The author of *Domestic Architecture in England*[a] under the heading "Domestic Architecture, Fourteenth Century," says,

"In Bedfordshire no remains of domestic work of this period have been observed beyond mere foundations; and at Stevington a large plain barn of this date." This barn no longer exists.

"There were licences to crenellate houses at Stevington 9 Edward I., and Bletsoe 1 Edward III., but both have been destroyed."

The principal river of Bedfordshire, the Ouse, enters this Hundred, on its course from Bucks, in the parish of Turvey, from whence it passes between Carlton and Harrold, between Odell and Chellington, near Felmersham, Sharnbrook, Bletsoe (Milton-Ernest and Oakley in Stodden hundred), and between Bromham and Biddenham to Bedford, where it becomes navigable.

The bridges over the Ouse in this Hundred are at Turvey, Harrold, Felmersham, Radwell, Pavenham (Oakley Bridge), and Bromham. The fish of the Ouse are pike, perch, tench, bream, chub, bleak, cray-fish, dace, roach, gudgeon, and fine eels.[b] The Ouse is esteemed a good river for trolling; the average depth is about ten feet; at Sharnbrook it is not less than twenty-five, in few places less than four; there are notwithstanding several fords, as at Odell, Pinchmill in Sharnbrook, and Radwell in Felmersham. The river is at all seasons subject to sudden inundations. The Cambridgeshire proverb, "the bailiff of Bedford is coming," mentioned by Fuller, alludes to the inundations of the Ouse, a most rapacious distrainer of hay and cattle.[c]

Important public meetings for the purpose of considering schemes for the

---

[a] Vol. ii. p. 275, by the editor of the *Glossary of Architecture*, Oxford, John Henry Parker, 1853.

[b] River lampreys and salmon-trout have been taken in the Ouse. Mr. Marsh mentions that two of the former were taken at Pavenham on the 30th April, 1807, and one at Milton Mill in the same month; on the same authority a salmon-trout was shot at Felmersham, in the water by Gad Meadow, at the end next Odell. [c] Lysons's *Magna Britannia* (*Beds.*)

drainage of the Ouse valley were held at Huntingdon on the 22nd December, 1876, and at Bedford on the 9th January, 1877, the proceedings at which were fully reported in the local newspapers.

The road from London to Higham Ferrers and Kettering passes through Bletsoe, leaving Sharnbrook, Souldrop, and Wymington on the left, and Thurleigh on the right. In 1802 an Act was passed for making a new turnpike road from Brown's Lane in Great Staughton to the Bedford turnpike road in the parish of Lavendon, Bucks; this is now one of the best roads in the county, it crosses the Kettering road near Stoke Mill, and passes through Sharnbrook, Odell, and Harrold. The turnpike road from Bedford to Olney passes over Biddenham bridge through Bromham to Turvey, where it leaves the county. The old road from Bedford to Buckingham passes through Stagsden.

The principal manufactures of this district are straw plaiting and thread-lace, otherwise bone-lace; matting at Pavenham, Stevington, Carlton, and Sharnbrook; basket and other wicker-work at Harrold.

This Hundred is intersected by two lines of railway, the Midland main line running in a northerly direction through the parishes of Biddenham, Bromham, Pavenham, Felmersham, Sharnbrook, Souldrop, and Wymington, with a station at Sharnbrook;[a] and the Bedford and Northampton line running nearly due west through the parishes of Bromham, Stevington, and Turvey, with a station at the last-named place. The Act for the Bedford and Northampton received the royal assent 15 July, 1867, and the line was opened for traffic in June, 1872.

As regards the Geology and Produce of the district, its Natural History, Roman Remains, and conjectures respecting the derivation or meaning of names of places, I fear it is not in my power to add anything very material to what has already been written concerning those matters.[b] The late lamented Mr. James Wyatt, F.G.S.,

---

[a] The Midland Railway crosses the river Ouse six times between Bedford and Sharnbrook, within a distance of about as many miles.

[b] Lysons's *Magna Britannia, Bedfordshire*, 17-28.
Abbot's *Flora Bedfordiensis*, Bedford, 1798. As this work does not contain an index of Places, the following references to its pages may be found useful.
    Biddenham (Ford End), 7, 14, 35, 38, 72, 96, 102, 131, 150, 160, 163, 164, 181, 188, 335, 337.
    Bletsoe, 152, 194.
    Bromham, 6, 8, 9, 11, 23, 24, 31, 56, 75, 86, 94, 124, 137, 156, 160, 162, 179, 225, 282.
    Pavenham, 9 (Stafford Bridge), 225.
    Sharnbrook, 94, 99.
    Stagsden, 124.
    Stevington, 3, 9, 33, 47, 85, 99, 103, 120, 124, 183, 193, 196, 198, 202, 204, 229, 247.
    Thurleigh, 27, 42, 58, 68, 76, 77, 83, 88, 109, 181, 194, 195, 196, 212, 293, 309, 347.
    Turvey, 56.
Bibliotheca Topographica Britannica (Bedfordshire).
Lewis's *Topographical Dictionary*, &c.
Etymologies of Bedfordshire. By the Rev. W. Monkhouse, B.D., F.S.A., vicar of Goldington, and fellow of Queen's College, Oxford. Bedford, 1857, 8vo.

of Bedford, had kindly undertaken to contribute a paper for this work on the geological peculiarities of the Hundred of Willey, but death, alas, frustrated the design. That learned and accomplished antiquary has, fortunately, however, left on record a very admirable treatise on "Flint Implements in the Drift, found in Bedfordshire,"[a] which, together with a paper by the late Rev. W. Monkhouse, B.D., "On the Well at Biddenham,"[b] will be found to contain much that may interest the general reader as well as the archæologist.

The late Rev. Thomas Orlebar Marsh, of Felmersham, gives the extent, in his time, of woods and spinneys in the following parishes and places:

		A.	R.	P.	Soil.
Turvey	about	80	0	0	
Odell	,,	590	0	0	
Chellington	,,	19	0	15	
Carlton Wood		43	0	0	
Carlton	about	30	0	0	
Stagsden	,,	86	0	0	
Sharnbrook	more than	150	0	0	
Bletsoe	about	100	1	11	
Poddington	,,	100	0	0	
Stevington		0	0	0	Stone scale.
Pavenham		0	0	0	Some blue clay in a close of Lady Lucas's.
Farndish		0	0	0	Clay.

Coal of an inferior description has been found at Poddington, and was supposed to exist also at Harrold.[c] At the former place, in ground about 100 yards from the church; Mr. Marsh, who, with a party, visited the pits at Poddington in October or December, 1826, made the following notes:[d]—

"27 Dec. 1826, went with a party to see the coal pits at Poddington."

"23 Oct. 1826, ground where coal is, 300 yards from church. Pyrites 4 inches thick over the coal; strata of coal, 9 inches thick, Mr. Orlebar says 8; mouth of pit, 12 feet square; 80 bushels of coal have been dug. Horn Close; depth of pit, 65½ feet. Hogs Close, 12 (or 17) feet; original pit: 2 feet earth, 6 feet white clay, 4 feet blue clay. Mr. James White discovered the coal."

In 1823 pottery (probably Roman) was found in a close of six acres, called "Potter's," at Harrold; in fine mould, two feet below the surface.[e]

At Farndish Mr. Marsh mentions a part of a complete petrified bone having been found, and in 1827 a fossil stag's horn was dug up.

Writing of Bromham, the Rev. Oliver St. John Cooper says:—"The soil also produces several curiosities in the fossil and vegetable kingdoms. In the veins of clay are found selenites, or moon-stones,

---

[a] Read at the general meeting of the Bedfordshire Architectural and Archæological Society. Published in the Associated Architectural Societies' (York, Lincoln, Northampton, Bedford, Worcester, and Leicester) *Reports and Papers*, 1861, vol. vi. part i. pp. 71-93.

[b] Read at the Annual Meeting of the Bedfordshire Architectural and Archæological Society, Nov. 10, 1857. "Associated Architectural Societies' *Reports and Papers*," 1858, vol. iv. part ii. pp. 283-90.

[c] It was supposed that coal might be found at Harrold Moor, Dungee Fox, Hole Close, and particularly at a place called The Bottoms. In the yard of Carlton Hall farm (Mr. Eyles') lead ore was discovered; a specimen was formerly in the possession of one Mr. Robert Adams, a surgeon.—MS. Marsh (from the information of Mr. W. Falkner, of Carlton Moor, who lived many years at Harrold).

[d] Additional MSS. in the British Museum, No. 21,067, ff. 32, 34.   [e] MS. Marsh.

not only of the common sorts, but of the more curious and rhomboidical forms." Mr. Marsh was in possession of several large bucardites from the pits of limestone; and also two fragments of an elephant's tusk, which together measured two feet four inches; they were found near the road, a quarter of a mile from the river.

In Lewis's *Topographical Dictionary*, article "Podington," we read that there is in that parish "a petrifying spring; and small shells of the ostroites, belemnitæ, and turbunitæ species are found imbedded in the clay and gravel-pits."

In the spring of 1792 a hen belonging to a labourer, at Bromham, hatched a chicken with three legs. A Scoter, or Anas Niger, was shot in October (probably in the same year) near Biddenham Bridge.[a] This fowl is allowed in the Romish Church to be eaten in Lent.[b]

Mr. Marsh mentions a custom the children have, of going round the villages on St. Thomas' day, "a gooding," as they call it. A few halfpence from the farmers in the parish is expected on the occasion.

I have been favoured by Captain Robe, of Biddenham, with the subjoined account of a curious custom practised in olden times at that village, on Sept. 22:—

"A little procession of villagers carry a white rabbit, decorated with scarlet ribbons, through the village singing a hymn in honour of St. Agatha. All the young unmarried women who chance to meet the procession extend the first two fingers of the left hand pointing towards the rabbit, at the same time repeating the following doggerel:—

     Gustin, Gustin, lacks a bier,
     Maidens, maidens, bury him here.

This ceremony is said to date from the year of the first crusade."

[a] MS. Cooper. [b] Tennant's *British Zoology*.

SHERIFFS OF BEDFORDSHIRE[a] FROM 1574.

[Lansd. MS. 887 ; Harl. MS. 1097, fo. 37 b, &c.]

Year.
1574. Ralph Astry, esq., of Harlington.
1575. John Barnardiston, esq., of Ickwell Bury.
1576. George Kenesham (John Kensham, *Harl.* 1097, f. 37), esq., of Tempsford.
1577. John Spencer, esq. of Cople (of Newenham, Harl. 1097).
1578. Nicholas Luke, esq., of Woodend.
1579. Henry Butler, esq., of Biddenham.
1580. John Thompson, esq., of Crawley.
1581. Richard Conquest, esq., of Houghton Conquest.
1582. Lewis Dive, esq., of Bromham.
1583. John Rowe, esq., of Clapham, and Richard Charnock, esq., of Hulcot.
1584. Oliver St. John, esq.
1585. Richard Charnock, esq.
1586. William Butler, esq.
1587. Ralphe Astry, esq., of Westoning.
1588. Oliver St. John, esq.
1589. George Rotherham, esq.
1590. C. Hoddesdon, esq. (Christopher Hoddesdon, of Leighton Beaudesert).
1591. William Duncomb, esq., of Battlesden.
1592. Nicholas Luke, esq.
1593. John Dive, esq.
1594. William Gostwick, esq., of Willington.
1595. Richard Conquest, esq.
1596. Thomas Cheney, esq., of Sundon.
1597. Sir Edward Ratcliffe, knt., of Elstow.
1598. William Butler, esq.
1599. Sir John Croft, knt.
1600. Richard Charnock, esq.
1601. George Francklyn, esq., of "Malvern" (Maverns in Bolnhurst).
1602. John Dive, arm.
1603. Sir John Dive, knt.
1604. John Leigh, esq., of Leighton Beaudesert.
1605. Sir Edward Sands, knt., of Eaton Bray.
1606. Sir Francis Anderson, knt., of Eyworth.
1607. Sir Thomas Snagge. knt., of Marston.
1608. Edward Mordant, esq., of Oakley.
1609. Thomas Ancell, esq., of Barford.
1610. Sir Francis Ventris, knt., of Campton.
1611. Robert Sandy, esq. (Robert Napier, knt., Luton Hoo).
1612. William Beecher, esq., of Hooberry.
1613. Richard Sanders, esq., of Marston.
1614. Edward Duncombe, esq.
1615. William Plomer, esq., of Holme, Beds. and Radwell, Herts.
1616. Roger Burgoyne, esq., of Sutton.
1617. Sir Oliver Luke, knt.

Year.
1618. Sir Edward Conquest, knt.
1619. George Keynsham, esq., of Tempsford.
1620. Francis Stanton, esq., of Birchmoor.
1621. William Bryers, esq., of Woodbury (or Upbury, in Polluxhill).
1622. William (Admiral ?) Hawkins, esq., of Tilbrook.
1623. Sir Francis Clerke, knt., of The Grove, in Houghton Conquest.
1624. Matthew Wenton, esq., of Barton.
1625. John Wingate, esq., of Harlington.
1626. Sir Edward Gostwick, knt.
1627. John Moore, esq.
1628. Sir Anthony Chester, bart., of Litlington.
1629. Michael Grigg, esq., of Dunstable.
1630. William Cator, esq., of Kempston.
1631. Edward Anderson, esq.
1632. James Beverly, esq., of "Clapmell."
1633. Onslow Winch, esq., of Everton.
1634. Humphrey Monoux, esq., of Wootton.
1635. Richard Gery, esq., of Bushmede.
1636. Henry Chester, esq.
1637. William Boteler, esq.
1638. William Plomer, esq.
1639. Richard Child, esq., of Puddington.
1640. John Burgoyne, esq.
1641. Sir Thomas Alston, knt. and bart., of "Wodhill" (Odell).
1642.
1643.
1644. Humphrey Fyche (Fyshe), esq., of Ickwell Green.
1645. Nicholas Denton, esq.
1646.
1647. Matthias (Michael) Taylor, esq., of Eaton Socon.
1648. { William Allen, arm.
       { William Duncombe, esq.
1649. Robert Lovet, esq.
1650. Sir William Boyer.
1651.
1652. Thomas Bromsall, esq., of Northill.
1653. John Huxley, esq., Eaton Bray.
1654. H. Pygot, esq.
1655. Robert Staunton, esq.
1656. John Wells, esq., of Heath.
1657.
1658.
1659.
1660. John Wells, esq.
1661. Edmund Wylde, esq., of The Grove, in Houghton Conquest.
1662. George Wynne, esq.

[a] The names of a few sheriffs in the 17th century are wanting.

INTRODUCTION.

Year.	
1663.	
1664.	
1665.	
1666.	Thomas Snagge, esq., of Marston.
1667.	John Huxley, esq., of Eaton Bray.
1668.	Sir Henry Massingberd, bart.
1669.	.... Delanoy, esq.
1670.	Sir R. Bovey, bart., of Warden Abbey.
1671.	Richard Wagstaff, esq., of Colworth House.
1672.	Henry Brandreth, esq., of Houghton Regis.
1673.	Thomas Bromsall, esq., of Blunham.
1674.	Matthew Dennis, esq., of Kempston.
1675.	Robert Bell, esq., of Bedford.
1676.	Samuel Reynardson, esq., of Polluxhill.
1677.	John Arnold, esq., of Ampthill.
1678.	Samuel Reynardson, esq.
1679.	Thomas Snagge, esq.
1680.	Sir William Gostwick, bart.
1681.	Sir Villiers Chernocke, bart.
1682.	George Abbott, esq., of Stepingly Park.
1683.	Sir James Astry, knt.
1684.	William Daniel, esq., of Newbury, in Flitton.
1685.	Humphrey Fyshe, esq., of Ickwell.
1686.	Thomas Halfpenny, esq., of Faldo, in Heigham Gobion.
1687.	Thomas Cross, esq , of Bramingham, Beds.
1688.	John Wagstaffe, esq., of Colworth.
1689.	Ralph Bromsall, esq., of Blunham.
1690.	Samuel Cater, esq., of Kempston.
1691.	William Boteler, esq.
1692.	John Neal, of Dean, esq.
1693.	Sir Samuel Thomson, knt., of Wootton.
1694.	John Eston, esq., of Bedford.
1695.	Sir S. Anderson, bart., of Egworth.
1696.	Sir William Millard, knt., of Houghton Regis.
1697.	Robert Bell, esq., of Bedford.
1698.	John Spencer, esq., of Cople.
1699.	John de la Fountain, esq.
1700.	Sir John Burgoyne, bart., of Sutton.
1701.	William Hillersden, of Elstow and Colmworth, esq.
1702.	Thomas Bromsall, of Roxton, esq.
1703.	Thomas Johnson, of Milton Bryant, esq.
1704.	Sir Samuel Ongley, of Warden.
1705.	Edward Duncombe, esq. (? Sir Pynsent Chernock).
1706.	John Snagg, esq., of Marston.
1707.	John Huxley, esq., of Eaton Bray.
1708.	John Clark, of Rugemont, esq.
1709.	John Wright, esq.
1710.	William Crewe, of Dunstable, esq.
1711.	Ralph Bromsall, of Blunham, esq.
1712.	William Nicholls, esq.
1713.	John Vaux, of Whipsnade, esq.
1714.	Thomas Everton, esq.
1715.	Thomas Boswell, of Dean, esq.
1715.	Thomas Bromsall, esq., of Blunham.
1716.	John Livesay, of Hinwick Hall, esq.
1717.	Sir Thomas Napier, bart. of Luton Hoo.

Year.	
1718.	Sir William Smith, knt., of Old Warden.
1719.	Nicholas Luke, esq., of Wood End.
1720.	Robert Hynde, of Wotton, esq.
1721.	Richard Orlebar, of Hinwick House, esq.
1722.	Henry Brandreth, esq., of Houghton Regis.
1723.	Robert Abbot, esq., of Steppingley Park. (The Houghton MS. designates him a "Pocket Sheriff.")
1724.	Thomas Aynscombe, of Shillington, esq.
1725.	Thomas Garth, of Harrold, esq. (Joseph Johnson, esq.)
1726.	Theophilus Dillingham, of Shelton, esq.
1727.	William Coleman, of Cranfield, esq.
1728.	Benjamin Rhodes, esq., of Flitwick.
1729.	Sir John Napier, bart., of Luton Hoo.
1730.	William Lamb, esq., of Farndish.
1731.	George Blundell, esq., of Cardington.
1732.	Henry Southouse, of Ravensden, esq., excused, and Edmund (or Edward) Morgan, esq., of Cardington, served.
1733.	Hillersdon Franks (or Frankish), esq., of Stoke Hammond, and of Heath, in Leighton.
1734.	Thomas Groom, esq., of Dunstable.
1735.	Thomas Crawley, esq., of Stockwood.
1736.	Francis Jessop, esq., of Bedford.
1737.	Oliver Edwards, esq., of "Carrington" (Cardington).
1738.	David Williams (Guiliaume), esq., of Tingrith.
1739.	John Franklin, esq , of Great Barford.
1740.	John White, esq., of Ewe or Hoo Green, in Flitwick.
1741.	John Lawson, jun., esq., of Barton.
1742.	John Coppin, esq., of Markyate Street. John Miller, jun., esq., of Dunstable.
1743.	Richard Browne, esq., of Eggington.
1744.	Richard Bell, esq., of Bedford.
1745.	Robert Ashwell, esq., of Leighton Buzzard.
1746.	William Gery, esq., of Bushmead.
1747.	John Hill, esq., of Bedford.
1748.	Thomas Crawley, esq., of Dunstable.
1749.	(John or Thomas) Cave, esq., of Bedford.
1750.	Harry Johnson, esq., of Milton Bryant.
1751.	Thomas Gilpin, esq., of Hockliffe.
1752.	Francis Herne, esq., of Luton.
1753.	David James, esq., of Ampthill.
1754.	Thomas Vaux, esq., of Whipsnade.
1755.	James Smith, esq., of Streatley.
1756.	J. Casson, or Capon, esq., of Leighton Buzzard.
1757.	William Coles, esq., of Sundon.
1758.	Dennis Farrer Hillersdon, esq., of Elstow.
1759.	Baker Coleman, esq., of Cranfield.
1760.	Baker Coleman, esq., again.
1761.	Robert Butcher, esq., of Cople.
1762.	Simon Taylor, esq., of Woburn.
1763.	Sir Philip Monoux, bart., of Sandy.
1764.	William Pym, esq., of Hasells Hall.
1765.	Richard Edwards, esq., of Arlsey.
1766.	Philip Field, esq., of Barton.
1767.	(Charles Pye, esq., of "Wadley") (Charles Chester, esq., of Tillesworth.)

INTRODUCTION. xxi

Year.
1768. John Cater, esq., of Kempston.
1769. William Farrer, esq., of Kempston.
1770. John Franklin, esq., of Northill.
1771. Charles Barnett, esq., of Stratton.
1772. Sir Gillies Payne, of Tempsford, bart.
1773. John Howard, esq., of Cardington.
1774. John Crawley, esq , of Stockwood.
1775. George Paunceford, esq., of Ampthill.
1776. Philip Field, esq.
1777. John Gager Weal Regnal, esq., of Eggington.
1778. John Beecher, esq., of Howbury.
1779. Sir Rowland Alston, bart., of Odell.
1780. William Thornton Astell, esq., of Everton.
1781. John Harvey, esq., of Northill.
1782. Robert Thornton, esq.. of Moggerhanger.
1783. John Willey, esq , of Southill.
1784. William Goldsmith, esq., of Stretley.
1785. William Gibbard, esq., of Sharnbrook.
1786. Matthew Rugeley, esq., of Potton.
1787. Joseph Partridge, esq., of Cranfield.
1788. William Lee-Antonie, esq , of Colworth.
1789. Samuel Boyden, esq., of Milton Ernest.
1790. James Metcalfe, esq , of Roxton.
1791. Francis Pym, esq., of Hasells Hall.
1792. Sir John Buchanan Riddell, of Sundon bart.
1793. Thomas Crosse, esq., of Bramlingham.
1794. Edward Nicholl, esq., of Studham.
1795. John Harvey, esq., of Ickwell.
1796. George Brooks, esq., of Flitwick.
1797. John Higgins, sen., esq., of Turvey.
1798. John Fox, esq., of Dean.
1799. Robert Trevor, esq.
1800. John Everitt, esq., of Westoning.
1801. Stephen Raymond, esq., of Potton.
1802. John Higgins, jun., esq., of Turvey.
1803. Godfrey Thornton, esq., of Moggerhanger.
1804. George Edwards, esq., of Henlow.
1805. John Polhill, esq., of Renhold.
1806. Sir William Long, knt., of Kempston.
1807. Sir Philip Monoux, bart., of Sandy.
1808. Richard Orlebar, esq., of Poddington.
1809. Robert Garstin, esq., of Harrold.
1810. Sir Gregory Osborn Page Turner, bart., of Battlesden.
1811. Joseph Howell, esq., of Markyate Street.
1812. John Cooper, esq., of Toddington.
1813. { George Parkes, esq., of Luton ; or Richard Parker, esq.
1814. Stephen Thornton, esq., of Moggerhanger.
1815. Robert Hibbert, esq., of East Hide.
1816. Henry Brandreth, esq., of Houghton Regis.
1817. Samuel Crawley, esq., of Stockwood.
1818. John Pedley, esq., of Eaton Bray.
1819. Honourable Samuel Ongley, of Sandy.
1820. Sir John Burgoyne, bart. In his place Charles Barnett, esq., of Stratton.
1821. John Thomas Brooks, esq., of Flitwick.
1822. Peter Augustus Lautour, esq., of Staughton Parva.
1823. Thomas Charles Higgins, esq., of Turvey.

Year.
1824. Sir B. H. Inglis, bart., of Milton Bryan.
1825. Samuel Bedford Edwards, esq., of Arlsey.
1826. Robert Elliot, esq., of Goldington.
1827. George Nigel Edwards, esq., of Henlow.
1828. George Musgrave, esq., of Shillington.
1829. William Dodge Cooper Cooper, of Toddington, esq.
1830. John Thomas Dawson, esq., of Clapham.
1831. Samuel Charles Whitbread, esq., of Cardington.
1832. Abram Edward Gregory, esq.
1833. George Pearse, esq., of Harlington.
1834. Joseph Morris, esq., of Ampthill.
1835. Charles James Metcalfe, esq., of Roxton.
1836. Francis Green, esq., of Bedford.
1837. William Henry Whitbread, of Southill, esq.
1838. John Harvey, esq., of Ickwell.
1839. L. Ames, esq., of East Hide.
1840. William Frederick Brown, esq., of Dunstable.
1841. Arthur Macnamara, esq., of Eaton Bray.
1842. Robert Lindsell, esq., of Biggleswade.
1843. William Sutcliffe, of Great Bramingham, esq.
1844. George James Sullivan, of Leegrave, esq.
1845. W. B. Higgins, esq., of Picts Hill.
1846. William Stuart, esq., of Aldenham Priory.
1847. Robert Newland, of Kempston, esq.
1848. Thomas Abbot Green, of Pavenham, esq.
1849. Humphrey Brandreth, esq., of Houghton Regis.
1850. R. T. Gilpin, esq., of Hockliffe.
1851. Sir C. G. Payne, of Blunham.
1852. Sir J. M. Burgoyne, of Sutton.
1853. Henry Littledale, esq., of Kempston.
1854. F. C. Polhill-Turner, of Howbury, esq.
1855. J. S. Leigh, esq., of Luton.
1856. Talbot Barnard, esq., of Kempston.
1857. Sir G. R. Osborn, bart., of Chicksands.
1858. J. S. Crawley, esq., of Stockwood.
1859. R. L. Orlebar, esq., of Hinwick.
1860. C. L. Higgins, esq., of Turvey.
1861. Joseph Tucker, esq., of Pavenham.
1862. Crewe Alston, esq., of Odell.
1863. B. H. Starey, esq., of Milton Ernest.
1864. Robert Henry Lindsell, of Biggleswade, esq.
1865. Lionel Ames, esq., of East Hide.
1866. Charles Livius Grimshawe, of Aspley Guise, esq.
1867. William Cooper Cooper, esq., of Toddington.
1868. Sir J. M. Burgoyne, bart., of Sutton.
1869. Henry Francis Cockayne-Cust, esq., of Cockayne Hatley.
1870. John Nathaniel Foster, esq., of Sandy.
1871. Edw. Henr. Frederick Dawkins, esq., of Moggerhanger.
1872. William Francis Higgins, esq., of Turvey.
1873. Harry Thornton, esq., of Kempston.
1874. John Gerard Leigh, esq., of Luton Hoo.
1875. Lieut.-Col. William Stuart, of Tempsford.
1876. George Sowerby, esq., of Putteridge Bury.
1877. Charles Magniac, esq., of Colworth.
1878. James Howard, esq., of Clapham.

BIDDENHAM.

The parish of Biddenham, or (as it is written in Domesday Book) *Bidenham*, is situated in the extreme south of the Hundred of Willey, and is in the Deanery of Bedford.

The village is about a mile and a half distant from the town of Bedford in a westerly direction. The parish contains 1,760 acres of very rich arable and pasture land. It is bounded on the east by the parish of St. Paul, Bedford; and on the north-east by the road leading from Bedford to Clapham, and by a small portion of the parish of Clapham; the Ouse circumscribing it on the north, west and south. The Ouse enters the boundary of the parish from Clapham, and proceeds in a south-westerly direction, dividing it from Bromham and Kempston on the north and west. As it approaches Kempston church it takes an easterly course till it arrives at Bedford, separating the parish of Biddenham from Kempston, and from St. Mary's, Bedford, on the south.

There is a tradition that a balk called Gallows Balk, extending along the boundaries of the manor of Bedford from the Bromham to the Clapham Road, was for a considerable time unclaimed. But in consequence of a person being found dead there, and neither the officers of the parish of Biddenham nor of St. Paul, Bedford, being willing to bear the expenses of the funeral, the case was brought into court and the land decided to belong to Biddenham.

The soil on the northern side of the parish is a strong clay, inclining to loam, where there is also found very excellent lime and building stone. The depth of the stratum of clay is considerable in some parts. A field near the confines of the parish of Bromham contains numerous excavations from which much excellent building stone has been taken; and it is conjectured, with much appearance of truth, that the neighbouring churches were built with this material, as they are constructed of the same kind of stone. The soil inclines to gravel in the other parts of the parish, and in several places excellent gravel is obtained for repairing the roads.

The manor of Biddenham was in possession of William Speck or Le Espec at the time of the Domesday Survey, in the hands of Ralph and Serlo de Ros, and had been held by eleven socmen in the Confessor's time.

"The land of William Speck. Ralph and Serlo de Ros hold, in Bidenham, of William, four hides, one virgate and less than a half. There is land for four plough-teams.[a] In the demesne there are two plough-teams and six villans; they have two ploughs. There are two bordars and two servi, and one mill[b] of 10s. value. There is pasture for four plough-teams. It is worth 40s.—when he received it 20s.; in the time of King Edward, 40s. Eleven yeomen held this manor, and could give or sell it to whom they would. The said William obtained this land in exchange for Toddington."—See Domesday, p. 218.

ESPEC.[c] (Harl. MS. 1233, fo. 71b.)

Arms: Gules, three Katherine wheels or.

William Speck or Le Espec, Lord of Biddenham, had three virgates of land in Wimentone.[d]

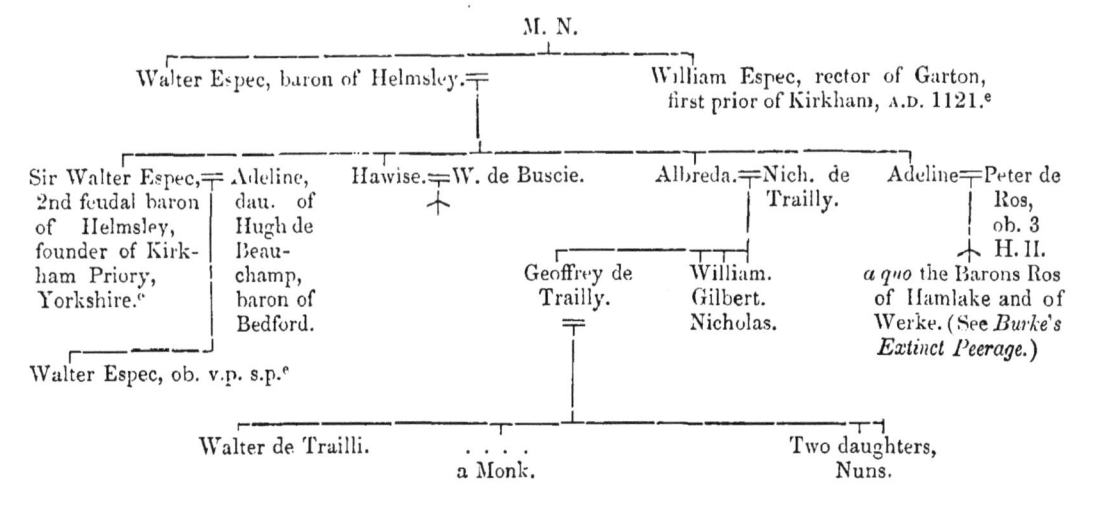

```
                                    M. N.
                ┌───────────────────┴───────────────────┐
    Walter Espec, baron of Helmsley.=      William Espec, rector of Garton,
                │                              first prior of Kirkham, A.D. 1121.[e]
  ┌─────────────┼──────────────┬──────────────┬──────────────┐
Sir Walter Espec,=Adeline,  Hawise.=W. de Buscie.  Albreda.=Nich. de   Adeline=Peter de
  2nd feudal baron  dau. of                           Traily.          Ros,
  of Helmsley,      Hugh de           │                                ob. 3
  founder of Kirk-  Beau-         Geoffrey de    ┌────┬────┐           H. II.
  ham Priory,       champ,        Traily.     William. Gilbert.  a quo the Barons Ros
  Yorkshire.[e]     baron of         =        Nicholas.          of Hamlake and of
  │                 Bedford.                                     Werke. (See Burke's
  │                                                              Extinct Peerage.)
Walter Espec, ob. v.p. s.p.[e]
  ┌──────────────────┬──────────────────┐
Walter de Trailli.    . . . .         Two daughters,
                      a Monk.         Nuns.
```

The manor became parcel of the Honor of Gloucester, and was held by the De Trailys, Passelews, and others, under the superiority of the De Clares, Audleys, and Staffords in succession.

[a] A hide of land has been represented as 96 acres; and, again, as 100 acres. A virgate, Holme states, was in some places 20 acres, and in other places from 24 to 30. Plough (Car.) as much land as a plough could till in a year, from 60 to 120 acres.

[b] Mills were anciently manorial appendages, and if the tenants neglected or refused to grind at the lord's mill he might amerce them in his court or sue them at common law. The tenant was also obliged to bake all his household bread at the bakehouse and ovens belonging to his liege lord.—MS. Tattam.

[c] Nichols, Leicestershire, v. ii. p. 27. Blore's Rutland, p. 15.

[d] Domesday.

[e] See legend of the foundation of Kirkham Priory, Dugd. Monast. vol. vi. p. 207.

Gilbert de Clare, Earl of Gloucester and Hertford, died seised of two fees in Holecote and Biddenham in the 8th King Edward II. (1315).[a] Hugh de Audle married Margaret, one of the daughters and co-heirs of Gilbert de Clare Earl of Gloucester, widow of Piers de Gaveston Earl of Cornwall, and niece to the King. He was created Earl of Gloucester in 1338; and died in 1348, seised of leet in Bidenham which he held in right of his wife, leaving an only daughter, Margaret, then the wife of Ralph Lord Stafford. In 1348 Lord Stafford obtained special livery of all those lands which descended to his wife as daughter and heir of Hugh de Audley, Earl of Gloucester, his homage being respited on account of his military services in France. He died in 1373, leaving two sons and four daughters. Ralph died without issue. Hugh succeeded his father in his honours as third Baron Stafford and second Earl, and died 1386.[b] His second but eldest surviving son, Thomas, fourth Baron and third Earl, was sixteen years old at his father's death; he died without issue, seised of one carucate of land and view of frank-pledge in Bidenham, together with two fees in Bidenham and Holcote,[c] and bequeathed his estate to his brother and successor William fourth Earl of Stafford. This nobleman was but fourteen years of age when he came to the title, and in ward to the Duke of Gloucester. He died without issue in three years after, when the two fees just mentioned were in the hands of John Trailly.[d] The next brother, Edmond de Stafford, fifth Earl, possessed two knight's fees in Bydenham and Holcote, with view of frank-pledge in this parish, and also held a court here.[e] His son, Humphrey, was created Duke of Buckingham, 14th Sept. 1444, whose grandson Henry, second Duke, was beheaded 2nd Nov. 1483, having entered into a conspiracy to place the Earl of Richmond upon the throne, when his estates were forfeited to the crown, but for the most part restored by King Henry VII. to Edward de Stafford, the renowned Duke of Buckingham. The Staffords' interest in this manor appears to have been excepted and to have remained in the Crown.[f]

---

[a] (1316), 9 Edw. II. Bromham and Biddenham were rated as one village, of which John de Botetourt, John de Mowbray, John de Pateshull, Walter Trye (Traly), John Pirot, William Passelew of Warrington, and the Prior of Newenham, were lords.—Nomina Villarum.

[b] Cal. Inq. p m. 20 Ed. III. 10 Ric. II.   [c] Ib. 16 Ric. II. nu. 27.

[d] Ib. 22 Ric. II. nu. 46.   [e] Ib. a. 4 Hen. IV.

[f] MS. Tattam. In a list of freeholders of the county of Bedford, made early in the reign of Queen Elizabeth, the name of the then lord of the manor of Biddenham, as such, does not occur, William Malcott being the only one named in this parish.—Lansd. MS. 5, fo 27. 1547.—Will of Thomas Malcot of Bidenham. Testator devised his "indentures of fermes in Bidenham" to his son William Malcot, and left

Serlo de Ros, one of the mesne lords of the manor, as before stated, also held Hugh de Beauchamp's land[a] in this parish, which was annexed to the barony of Bedford. In the fourteenth century, Elizabeth wife of John de Mowbray of Axholme,[b] and after her John de Neville of Raby, Knt. and Elizabeth his wife[c] were possessors of Beauchamp's fee here.

The Passelews appear to have succeeded the de Ros as tenants of a considerable portion of this fee as well as of the manor; they were seated at Drayton Passelew, in Buckinghamshire, and were great benefactors to the Abbey of Woburn. William de Passelewe held two knight's fees under Simon de Beauchamp, and Gilbert de Passelewe, who presented twice to the church between the years 1235 and 1257, held one hide of land in Biddenham of the barony of William de Beauchamp of Bedford.[d]

The annexed pedigree of the Beauchamps will elucidate the descent of the barony of Bedford, to which the seigniory of this and many neighbouring estates and manors was appendant.

Ralph Passelewe held one knight's fee under Ralph de Beauchamp, and he of Walter Traily, who was feudatory of the honour of Gloucester, and of kin to the Especs; the same Ralph Passelewe presented to the living soon after 1258, but in 1278 the advowson and some land belonged to John de Kerkeby, and of him Gilbert Goze held in villanage, the rector possessing half a virgate. The Passelewes had one water-mill, and right of fishery in the river Ouse; their estate was occupied by twenty-five tenants, not including the religious houses of Caldewell, Newenham, and Harewold, each of which possessed small

---

money for repairs of the bridge. In the year 1536, among the witnesses to the will of Thomas Negus of Bidenham are Thomas Malcott, William Malcot, and S[r] Thomas Cowper, "paryssh preste of Bedenham."—Bedfordshire Wills in Court of Probate, Northampton District Registry.

[a] The land of Hugh de Beauchamp, in the half-hundred of Bochelai.[1] Serlo de Ros holds in Bidenham one hide of Hugh. There is land for one plough-team, and there it is, and one bordar and one servus. There is pasture for one plough-team. It is worth, and always has been, ten shillings. Alsi of Brumham, a freeman of Queen Eddith, held this land, and could dispose of it to whom he would.—Domesday.

[b] Cal. Inq. p. m. nu. 44.

[c] Ib. nu. 12.

[d] Testa de Nevill, Hen. III., Ed. I., p. 248; Harl. 313, fo. 46.

---

[1] The half-hundred of Bochelai or Buchelai is now distributed to the hundreds of Willey and Stodden.

A Map of the Hundred of WILLEY in the County of BEDFORD.

BEAUCHAMP.

Dugd. Bar. Harl. MS. 313, fo. 46.

Arms: Quarterly or and

Hugh de Beauchamp, the Norman. Lord paramount of Bletsoe, Bromham, and Stagsden, had lands, &c., in Biddenden, Turvey, Sharnbrook, and Thurleigh, in the Hundred of Willey, and many other estates in this and the neighbouring counties.

Simon de Beauchamp, called "the elder," lord of Bedford, supposed to have died s. p.

Paganus or Pain, had the castle and barony of Bedford given to him by King Wm. Rufus. He rebuilt and defended the castle against K. Stephen. The tenure of the barony was by performing the office of Almoner to the Sovreign on the Coronation Day. = **Rohese,** da. of Alberic de Vere, Justice of England, widow of Geoffrey de Mandeville, Earl of Essex.

Walter, ancestor of the Beauchamps, Earls of Warwick. (Sir H. Nicolas stating him to have been "supposed of this family.")

Roger de Beauchamp, relationship uncertain, gave the church of Stagsden to Newenham Priory. (Rot. Hundr. 7 E. I.)

Walter de Beauchamp, descended from Walter of Powyke and Alcester, younger brother of Wm. de Beauchamp, 1st Earl of Warwick of that name. The said Walter of Powyke was also ancestor of the Beauchamps of Bletsoe. = **Elizabeth,** da. and coh. Sir John Roche, Kt., Bromham, II. IV. and V. (Extinct Peerage.)

Simon de Beauchamp, steward to K. Stephen, sheriff of Beds and Bucks 1194 to 1197, ob. 9 K. John, bur. in the Church of St. Paul at Bedford.

Willm. de Beauchamp, Baron of St. Amand, 2 Jan. 1449 to 26 May 1455. 1st h. *Arms:* A fesse between six martlets within a bordure. (Dingley.) = **Elizabeth,** eldest da. and coh. of Gerard de Braybrooke, grandson and eventually heir of Almaric of St. Amand, 3rd and last Baron St. Amand of that family. Bur. in Bromham Church, Wilts, 1492. (Dingley's Papers, printed for the Camden Society an. 1866, nu. 94, fo. 34.)

Richard de B...

William de Beauchamp, Baron of Bedford, received the rebellious barons into his castle there, 17 K. Joh. Sheriff of Beds and Bucks 1235. Died an old man, 44 H. III. 1260. Almoner at the nuptials of K. Henry III. = **Avicia, or Idonea,** da. of Willm. Longespée, Earl of Salisbury.

The arms of... in Bromham Ch...

Simon de Beauchamp, Baron of Bedford, ob. 47 H. III. (1262). = **Isabella,** da. of Hugh Wake, Lord of Chesterfield, sister of Baldwin Lord Wake.

William, Baron of Bedf., d. in London 1262 "by witchcraft as some suppose." (Annal. Dunstap.)

John, last Baron, slain at the battle of Evesham, 49 H. III. (1265). His estates confiscated and given to Prince Edward. (Beauties of Eng. and Wal. vol. i. p. 13.)

Roger de Beauchamp, ob. 1266, 1st husb. = **Maud** = Sir Reg. Baron... Ellesmere II. (1314)... of a ... Bromham p. m.)

Joan de Beauchamp, only da. and heir, m. John de Mansell, and ob. s.p.

Ralph de Beauchamp (relationship uncertain) held the manor of Bidenham, 7 E. I., under Walter Trayley, of the Honour of Gloucester. (Rot. Hundr.)

Roger, 1st Lord Mowbray, ob. 1298. = **Rose de Clare.**

John, 2nd Ld. Mowbray, b. 2 Nov. 1286; had land and tens. in Bromham. He was hanged at York, and his lands seized for the Crown 1321. = **Aliva,** da. and coh. of Willm. de Braose, Ld. Braose of Gower, m. 2ndly, Sir R. de Peshale, Knt., ob. 5 E. III.

Ida Wake, coh. of her mother. = **John de Steingreve,** de com. Ebor. ob. 1295. Seised of land and rent in Stagsden, Bromham, and the manor of Caisho, Beds., with other premises in Essex, Linc. and Yorkshire. (Inq.p.m. 23 E.I.) Summoned to Parliament 1294, Baron Steingrave.

Eliz. Wake, coh. of her mother. = **John de Horbey** or Hoobury, dead 1315.

A qu...

At the coronation of... Blundell, and Thomas... Barony of Bedford, r... Almoner. The claim b... Earl pro hâc vice, with... England and Wales, r...

Lady Joane, da. of Henry Earl of Lancaster. = **John, 3rd Baron Mowbray,** Lord of Bromham, ob. 1361, when by Inq. p.m. taken in the 35th Edw. III. he was found to be seised as follows:— Bedford, sect. cur., Ouse, aqua piscar., Wyllington m., Haunes m., Bromham m., Bedf., and other lands and manors in Bucks, Yorks., Linc., Sussex, and Northants.

Walter de Tey. 2nd husb. Walter de... Teye and Isabella seised of one vill., grant 18 acr. of land, 1 acr. and 1 rood of ... pasture, and 10s. rent in Bromham and part of Bedford barony. (Inq. p.m. 7 E. II.)

John de Mowbray, 4th Baron. Killed 1368 in a conflict with the Turks nr. Constantinople. = **Elizabeth,** da. and h. of John Ld. Segrave, d. seised of Bedford Cas., &c., and the manors of Wyllington, Hawens, and Stotfold, of land or rent in Wyllinton, Maldon, Kerdington, Bromham, Cowpoll, Berford, and Bydenham in this co.; and of divers lands in Lynchlade Bucks, as of the barony of Bedford; together with three manors in Yorksh. (Inq. p. m. 50 Edw. III., no. 44.)

Sir John de Pateshull = Mab... summoned 1342 as d. of Baron Pateshull. Bar...

Mabel de Pateshull, m. Walter de Fauconberg.

Kath. de Pateshull, m. Sir Robert de Tudenham, Knt., bu. at Thetford, Norf. (Arms of Tudenham, Lozengy arg. and gu.)

A quo Tudenham of Heyford, Northants. The heiress m. Sir Edm. Bedingfield, who d. 1451. (Baker's Northants, v. 1 p. 186.)

Sir Wm. de Pateshull, Baron, ob. 1359, s.p.

Alice de Pateshull. = **Thomas Wake,** of Blyseworth, great-grandson of Bald. Ld. Wake and Hawise de Quincy, seised of land and rent in Bromham. (Inq. p. m. 34 and 46 E. III.) In the 6th Hen. VI. their grandson, Thomas, son and heir of Thos.,‡ son and heir of Thos. Wake, had 38s. rent in Bromham, divers lands and tens. in Kerdington, and a small portion of the barony of Bedford. (MS. Goodhall.) = **Margaret Philpot.**

Sybil de Pateshull. = ...

BEAUCHAMP OF BLETSOE.

Thos. Wake, armiger, ... manors of Bromham and ... Bucks, Northants, and S...

* Adam Picot suffered a fine of certain tenements in Bromholm and Linslade. Abbr...
† Sir Roger Beauchamp, Knt., of Eaton Soken, sheriff of Beds and Bucks 1401...

NS OF BEDFORD.

887, fo. 40. Im Hoff, cap. 26, fo. 123.

er all a bend of the last.

;d his father's es- | Adelino, m. Walter le Espec,
andy, yet was one | Ld. of Kirkham and Helmesley,
o held Bedford | co. York.
t K. Stephen; he
aton, co. Beds.

Walter Le Espec, died in his father's lifetime, without issue. See pedigree of ESPEC.

nchet, or Tockets,
Wilts, bur. there.
gley.)
me way connected
m in Bedfordshire.
3, ff. 121-124.)

2nd Baron St. Amand,
. 1508.
np quartering Braybrooke
s. (Dingley.)

DE MUNCHENSI, or DE MONTE CANISO. *Arms*: Or, three escutcheons barry of six vaire and gules.

Baldwin, Lord Wake,=Ela de Beauchamp,= | Thomas Fitz Other=Beatrice de Beauchamp.=William de Monchensie, of
1st husb. M. Hawise | ob. seis. of two nativi | Quincy. | or Oto. He and the | Edwardston, ob. 1286,
de Quincy, da. and h. | in Bromham. (Inq. | said Beatrice were | younger brother of Warine
of Robert de Quincy, | p. m. 7 E. II.) | seised of rent in | de M., seised of the manor
by whom he had issue. | Bromham. (Inq. p. m. | and of rent in Bromham as
(See pedigree of WAKE | 2 E. I.) | the inheritance of his wife.
under Stevington.) | (Inq. p. m. temp. Edw. I.)

Pickot=Joane Wake,=Rafe Paynell, | Otto or Otho | Matilda, sist.=John, 1st Baron de Botetourt. He and | William de Monchensi, ob. 1302.=
t,* 1st. | coh. of her 2nd husb. | Fitz Thomas, | and h. of Otho | his wife were seised of a mill, 4 virg.
∧mother. (Lansd. 887.) | ob. s.p. | Fitz Thomas. | and 30 acr. in Bromham and part | William de Monchensi.=
| | | of Bedf. barony. (Inq. p. m. 7 E. II.)

e of Cardington, whose coheirs | William, 3rd Lord Latimer, 1st. husb., ob. 1335, seised of=Elizabeth de=Sir Robert | Joan de Munchensi,
Blundell and Harvy. | land and tenements in Bromham, and the manors of Sutton, | Botetourt, | Ufford, | m. Sir Wm. Walde-
II. the Earl of Exeter, Sir George | Dylewyke, Ronhale, and Kerdington, with lands or rent in | elder da. | 2nd. husb. | grave.
being seised of several parts of the | Pottou, Wrastlingworth, and Wotton, co. Beds., with other
claimed to execute the office of | manors and lands in the cos. of Surrey, Linc., Northants,
red to the King he appointed the | Bucks. Cumbr., Northumb., Ebor., and Cantab. (Inq. p. m.
ars to the other two. (Beauties of | 9 E. III., no. 51.)

teyn=Sir Simon de | William, 4th Lord Latimer of Danby=Lady Eliz. Fitz Alan.
h. of | Pateshull,
| of
| Pateshull,
| Northants,

Eliz. Latimer, da. and h., Lady of the=John Lord Neville of Raby, ob. 17 Oct.,=Maud, d. of Henry Ld. Percy, 1st wife.
manor of Bromham, 2nd wife. (In | 1388, seised of the manor of Bromham
Harl. 1233, fo. 162, called Eleanor da. | and of a fee in Hinwick and Bidden-
and h. of Ralph Lord Latimer. | ham. (Inq. p. m. 12 R. II.) | Ralph, Earl of West-=2nd
| merland. | wife.

ndison,
f Wm.
m.

Sir John de Neville or Latimer, Baron Latimer, claimed and had the
office of Almoner at the coronation of K. Hen. IV., Lord of Bromham,
ob. s. p. (Beaut. Eng. and Wales, 1, p. 13.) "Sold the Barony of | Sir Geo. Neville, Baron Latimer,
Latimer to his brother Ralph, E. of Westmerland; hee left a sister | Ld. of Bromham.
Elizabeth, whose great-grandchild, Sir Robt. Willoughby Ld. Brooke,
made challeng to y^e Barony of Latimer, temp. Hen. VII., but went
without it." (Harl. 1233, p. 162.)

lamp,† younger son of Giles and grand-
e Beauchamp of Powyke and Alcester.
a Walter, supposed to have been a
Hugh de Beauchamp, the Norman.
w in Bidenham.

10 Dec. 1458, seised of the=Agnes
co. Bedf., and of others in | Lovell.
. p. m. 37, 38, 39 H. VI.)

9 E. II. Adam Picot de Wooton, and Amabilla his wife, seised of land in Bromham. Inq. p. m. 9 E. III.

rs lands in Kerdington, of a messuage, &c., in Bromham, and of estates in Herts and Bucks. (Inq. p. m. 3 H. VI.)

BIDDENHAM.

portions by the gift of William Passelew, in the time of King Henry III., as also the master of the Hospital of St. John at Bedford, by grant of the ancestors of the said Ralph, during the reign of King John.ª

Out of these, and the other minor fees in this parish,ᵇ grew the estates which were afterwards in the families of Boteler, St. John, and Dyve.

ª Rot. Hun. 7 Ed. I.

ᵇ The land of the Bishop of Lincoln in the half-hundred of Buchelai. Ernuin the presbyter holds one hide and one virgate of land in Bidenham of the Bishop Remigius. There is land for one plough, and there is one; and a mill at the yearly rent of 25s. Pasture for one plough-team. It is worth, and has been, 40s. Laurie, a man of the Bishop of Lincoln, held this land, but he could not give it away, nor sell it without leave of the Bishop.—Domesday, p. 210. In the thirteenth century this land was occupied by six tenants, one of whom was William Fitz Henry.—Hundred Rolls, temp. K. Henry III. and Edward I.

Land here belonged to Dunstable Priory, the gift of King William the Conqueror, though it does not appear in Domesday-book; four tenants occupied it in the thirteenth century, and the Priory of Newenham appears to have held a portion.[1]

In the year 1299 (27 Edw. I.) Matthew Donstaple died seised of lands, &c. in Bidenham, Bromham, and other places in the county of Bedford, which he held for the chanters in the chapel of the Blessed Mary in Bedford.[2]

Wardon Abbey possessed a close of pasture called "Kingesmede," containing twenty-five acres; the Abbess of Elstowe, thirteen acres of land, held by John de Pateshulle;[3] and the Prior of Cauldewell, five acres of pasture, by the gift of William the Conqueror. The Taxation of Pope Nicholas gives the value of land and rents belonging to the last-named foundation in Bidenham, Schelton, and Kempston as iij li. x s iiij½ d., and in fruits, flocks, and animals, ij li. viij s. viij d.[4]

The land of St. Paul of Bedford, in the half-hundred of Bochelai. The Canon Osmond of St. Paul of Bedford holds of the King in Bidenham three virgates of land; there is land for one plough-team, and it is there, and one villan and one bordar. Pasture for one plough-team. It is worth, and has been worth, 10s. Leviet the priest held this land in pure alms of King Edward, and afterwards of King William, which priest dying, granted one virgate of this land to the Church of St. Paul. One Ralph Talbois added other two virgates to the same church in pure alms.

---

[1] Rot. Hundr. Hen. III. Ed. I.

[2] Calend. Inq. p. m. nu. 141.

[3] 3 Rich. II. 1380. Sir Roger de Beauchamp, Knt. (de Bletsoe) died seised of ten acres of meadow in Bidenham.—Inq. p. m. nu. 5.

[4] Abbrev. Rot. Orig.

At the time of the dissolution of monasteries, the priory of—

	£	s.	d.
Newenham had rents, &c. in Biddenham to the annual amount of	7	0	0
Cauldwell Priory ,, ,, ,,	2	12	2
Harwold Priory ,, ,, ,,	0	18	0
Woburn Monastery ,, ,, ,,	0	15	0

Abstract of the Roll 28 Hen. VIII. Augmentation Office.

The manor of Biddenham was in the possession of the Botelers,[a] who resided in the parish as early as the time of King Edward II., in the sixth year of whose reign Thomas Botyler of Bydenham occurs in a deed or charter afterwards (1586) in possession of William Boteller of Kyrtons, in this parish. From a drawing of the seal of this Thomas in the Harl. MS. 245, fo. 27, the arms appear to be very similar to those borne by the Botelers, Barons of Wemme, viz., a fesse

---

The Canon Ansfrid holds in the same one virgate of land. There are two ox-gangs, and they are kept there. Pasture for two oxen. Now worth, and hath been, 3s. Mauven held this. He might sell it to whom he would. Ralph Tallbose appropriated this to the church of St. Paul in pure alms.—v. Domesday, p 211.

The Prior of Newenham possessed three virgates, holden of the Prebendary of St. Paul's, Bedford, the gift of King William I.; of this Isold Blancoste held half a virgate at a certain rent, and three other tenants the remainder —Hundred Rolls, Hen. III., Edw. I.

The Prior of Newnham died possessed of lands in Biddenham in the 9th of Richard II. 1386.—Calend. Inq. post mortem, nu. 41. The Priory of Newnham had lands and tenements in Biddenham granted to the priory by Simon de Passelewe, and confirmed by his descendants.—Chartulary of the Priory of Newnham, Brit. Mus.

The Prior of Newnham also claimed of the Abbess of Denny 20s. in Biddenham.—Roll 28 Hen. VIII. Augmentation Office.

The land of St. Edmund, in the half-hundred of Bocheleia. The Abbot Baldwin of St. Edmund's hath in Bidenham half a hide of land, and Ordin of Bedford holds it under him. There is land for half a plough-team, and it is there, and two servi. Pasturage for half a plough-team; it is worth, and hath been worth, 6s. Ulmar the priest held this land of King Edward; he could give it to whom he would, but Ordin, when he was major of the borough, took it from him for a certain forfeiture, and now says that he holds it of the Abbot of St. Edmund, but the men of the hundred say that he seized it unjustly. —Domesday.

This Abbot Baldwin had been a monk at St. Denis, near Paris, and Prior of Derehurst in Gloucestershire, a cell to St. Denis. He was made Abbot of St. Edmund's Bury, on the death of Abbot Leofston in 1065. He is called "Medicus Edwardi Regis" (Harl. MS. 447), and is said by Lidgate to have been "gretly expert in crafft off medycyne." He was particularly favoured by the Confessor, who granted him the privilege of a mint. He was greatly esteemed by King William the Conqueror, and Pope Alexander. He died in 1097 or 1098.—MS. Tattam, and from the Register of Laking-heth.

The land of the Burgesses of Bedford in the half-hundred of Bochelai. Osgar of Bedford holds in Bidenham one virgate of land of the King. There are two oxgangs of land, which are worth 11s. and always have been. He who now holds it held it in the time of King Edward, and could give it to whom he would.

---

[a] MS. Tattam.

The Messrs. Lysons say "the mesne lordship seems to have been held for several generations by the St. Johns, who were in possession of it till 1582, and perhaps later;" it is probable that they inherited some interest in this parish through the Beauchamps.

componée between six cross-crosslets, with a crescent for difference, and various pedigrees indicate some connection with that ancient house.

John, son of Thomas Boteler of Bidenham, had an estate in Stagsden,[a] by the

In the same place, Godwin the Burgess holds of the King one hide and the fourth part of one virgate of land; there is land for one plough-team, and there is one. There is pasture for one plough-team. It is worth 10s. and always has been. Half a hide of this land—he who now holds it held it in the time of King Edward, which he could give to whom he would. One half a hide and the fourth part of one virgate he bought after King William came into England, but neither to the King nor to any other person did he do service, nor had livery of it. William Speck reclaimed of the same man one virgate and the fourth part of a virgate which had been released to himself, and he afterwards lost it.

In the same place Ordwun the Burgess holds of the King one hide, and the third part of half a hide. There is land for one plough-team, and it is there. There are two villans and one bordar, and pasture for one plough-team. It is and always has been worth 10s. Half a hide and the fourth part of one virgate of this land, the same that now holds it held it in the time of King Edward, and could give it to whom he would, but one virgate in mortgage he held in the time of King Edward, and so holds it, as the men of this hundred testify. The same bought one virgate and the fourth part of one virgate after King William came into England, and neither to the King nor to any one rendered service.

In the same place Ulmar the Burgess holds of the King two parts of one virgate. There is land for one ox. It is worth, and always has been, twelvepence He himself held it in the time of King Edward, and could give it to whom he would.—v. Domesday, p. 218.

William Fitz Ralph, in the time of King Henry III. held one hyde and half a hyde of land in this parish of John de Burgo, by serjeanty.[1] Hamund FitzWalter had three virgates and sixty acres in demesne about the same time.[2]

Sir William de Morley, Knt. (Lord M.) died possessed of one knight's fee in Biddenham anno 1370, his grandmother was Christiana daughter and co-heir of Robert FitzWalter by Devorgulla, daughter and co-heir of John de Burgh.[3]

In 1232 Nicholas de Neville held a grant of a meadow in Biddenham called Martinesholm.[4]

---

[1] Nomina Villarum. Harl. MS. 313, f. 38b.

[2] Rot. Hund. vol. ii. p. 326.

[3] See Morley's descent from Mareschal and De Rie in Baker's Northants, vol. ii. p. 59. The Morleys of Glynde in Sussex, a cadet branch, intermarried with the families of Wylde and Trevor.—V. Bromham. Horsfield's Hist. Lewes, vol. ii. p. 117.

[4] Cal. Rot. Chart.

---

[a] This is very remarkable, because the *manor* of Stagsden is mentioned in an inquisition post mortem, in connection with a John Boteler, who died 1415, lord of Mapertyshal and Pulhanger, Beds; but who, if the arms assigned to him (Harl. 1428, fo. 3) are correct, does not appear to have been related to the Biddenham family.—V. Stagsden.

BIDDENHAM.

gift of his father in the twelfth King Edward III., and is described of that place; in the thirty-fifth of the same reign, he married Joane, daughter and heir of

In 1331 John del Hay and Johanna his wife were found to be seised of one messuage and 15 acres in Bidenham, which they held for the hospital of St. Leonard's at Bedford.—Calend. Inq. p.m. nu. 99.

In 1348 Nicholas de Gatesden died seised of four acres of land with appurtenances. In 1374 Robert Bate, a felon, held one cottage and three roods of land; and Simon Bate, a felon, died possessed of one toft, and three acres three and a half rood of land, and one acre one and a half rood of meadow in Biddenham, A.D. 1394.—Cal. Inq. p.m. nu. 39, 63, 64.

In the Hundred Rolls 7 Edward I. a tenement called Bromham Hyde is stated to be in Bidenham.

A younger branch of the Pooleys[1] of Boxted, Suffolk, had estates, or resided in this and the neighbouring parish of Bromham in the sixteenth and seventeenth centuries, as appears in the following pedigree from the Harl. MS. nu. 1531, fo. 125:—

Thomas Pooley, of Boxsted, in com. Suff. . . . =Maude, dau. and heiress of John Gislingham, by Maude, had a 2nd wiffe by whom hee had yssue in Suff. | dau. and heiress of John Gardevile.

Richard Pooley.=Margeret dau of Simon Blyant of Thornham, Essex. | John, a prest. | Anne, m. Myles Lovell. Rose.

Simon Pooley, of Badley, Suff. | John Pooley, of Bidenham, in com. Bedford, 2nd son.=Joanne, dau. of John Hynde, of Harlington, Beds. | Margery. Catherine. } ob. yong.

John Pooley, of Bidenham.=Prudence, dau. of Richard Sheldon. | Thomas, ob. s.p. | Barbara, m. Daniell of Kent. Joane, m. William Ernest of co. Bedford. Jane, m. . . . Baker.

John Pooley, of Bidenham.= | Margerett. Jane. | Thomas Pooley, of Bidenham. | Nicholas.

Robert Pooley, of Bromham, co. Beds.=Jane, dau. of John Carisforth, of Barnesley, co. York.

John Pooley, of , co. Cambridge.=Allice, dau. of John Smyth, of Cambridge.

Thomas Pooley.

---

[1] Edmund Poley, deputy baylie of the manor of Ampthill, baylie of Mylbroke and Malton; collector in Flytwycks, anno 4 Elizabeth.—Lansd. MS. 5, fol. 30. Johanna Poley, widow, by her will (*circa* 1500), desired to be buried in St. James' church, Bidenham, and gave money for repairs of the church and bridge, Testatrix names John Poley her son, Thos. Poley, Margaret Poley de Chicksand, Robert Poley, and John Gyre.

Anno 1506. Will of John Poley of Bydenham. Testator desired to be buried in the chancel of St. James' church, Bidenham; gave money to the high altar of the same, and to the Priories of Newnham and Caldwell: names Agnes Fitz-Gefferey, Caterine Fitzhugh, William Grueys, and his son John Poley. (From a book in the Northampton District Registry, containing copies of Bedfordshire wills, beginning with the year 1496.)

Walter Mullesworth,[a] and in the year last-mentioned granted land in "Southfeld" to Richard Davy of Bydenham.[b] He was succeeded in the estate by another John,[c] said to have died without issue. William, another son of John Boteler of Stagsden, in the sixth King Henry V. granted a messuage and cottage (formerly held by Agnes Downes) to Robert Godlok and Alice his wife, and John their son, for a term of four years, at six shillings, and rendering suit twice a year at the court of the said William.[d] His son, Richard Boteler, enjoyed the estate of Kirton's in this parish through his wife Grace, daughter and heir of Alan Kyrton or Kirketon. The Botelers resided in the mansion-house of Kyrtons, otherwise Biddenham-Ford, for several generations.[e]

Sir William Boteler, Knight, Lord Mayor of London in 1515, was a grocer. Fuller calls him "Wm. Butler, son of Richard Butler of Biddinham"; he bore a difference in his coat armour, viz., three annulets or on the fesse.[f] His wife was a daughter of Bussord or Mussord of London, and they had issue five children.

The son and successor William Boteler, Esq., of Biddenham, also received the honour of knighthood;[g] his second wife was Anne, daughter and heir of Thomas Pecocke of Suffolk, Gent., by whom he had four sons and four daughters; one of the latter, Mary Boteler, was the wife of John Newton of Axmouth, Devon, Gent., and their elder son, William Newton, sold his lands in Devon, and planted himself at Lavendon, Bucks, with Humfrey his younger brother. The said William Newton, however, is described "of Bidenham," as also his son William, in 1634.[h]

[a] Several members of the family of Mullesworth served the office of sheriff of Beds and Bucks.—Lipscomb.

[b] Witnesses to this grant, Richard Lorde, Alan Kyrketon,* Wm. Constantine.—Harl. MS. 245, fo. 27.

[c] A Sir John Boteler, of Bidenham, Knt., was sheriff of Beds and Bucks in the time of King Edward IV.

[d] Witnesses, Tho. Wyke, Joh. Flemynge, Tho. Hall, &c.—Harl. MS. 254, fo. 27. The wording of the grant does not indicate whether the messuage and cottage were at Biddenham or Stagsden.

[e] In the Harl. MS. 245, John, son and heir of John Boteler, of Bydenham, is mentioned as living temp. K. Hen. VII.

[f] Lansd. MS. 864. The descendants of this Sir William appear to have been merchants in the City of London.

[g] Monumental Inscription to his grandson, in Biddenham church. MS. Ashmole, No. 1844.—Guillim, p. 78.

[h] Arms of Newton: Argent, three lozenges in fesse azure, each charged with a garb or. Crest: a garb or,

---

* The Kirtons were very early resident in this parish. Arms: Argent, a fesse and chevron in chief gules. Crest: a hawk close or, hooded gules, belled of the first. Seal of Alanus de Kirketon de Bydenhamforde. 1 Hen. IV.—Harl. MS. 245, fo. 27.

William Boteler or Butler, Esq., the eldest son, married Dorothie Sarger, and was father of another William, who, as we learn from the inscription on his monument, founded the north aisle of Biddenham Church; by his wife Ursula, daughter of Thomas Smithe, Esq., "Farmer of the great Custom," he had several children. In all probability this William succeeded Henry Butler of Biddenham, who was sheriff of Bedfordshire in 1579, for we find that a William Butler served as sheriff in 1586.[a]

The son and heir, Sir Thomas Boteler, Knight, married Anne, daughter of Francis Farrar of Harrold, by whom he had five sons and three daughters, viz.:

William, his heir, of Harrold, died 1639, and was buried here; Thomas, James, Francis, and Oliver of Wootton Bourne End, whose son James was of Harrold, and was buried in the chancel of that church 1690. One of Sir Thomas' daughters, viz., Martha, married Sir John Kelynge, Knight, son of John Kelynge of Hertford, Esq., and Alice, daughter of Gregory Waterhouse of Halifax, co. York, Esq. He was of the Inner Temple; a Serjeant-at-Law, 4 July, 1660; knighted 21 Jan. 1661, and M.P. for Bedford the same year; Chief Justice of the King's Bench, 21 Nov. 1665. By his first wife Martha above-mentioned he had, with other issue, Sir John Kelynge of Southill, K.C. and Serjeant-at-Law, who married a daughter of the Resident of the Duke of Tuscany. Sir John, the father, married secondly Mary, daughter of William Jeston of London, by whom he had one daughter; and his third wife was Elizabeth, second daughter of Sir Francis Basset of Cornwall, Knight, by whom he had no issue. His daughter Elizabeth Kelynge married John Orlebar, Esq., of the Middle Temple. He died 9th May, 1671.[b]

The son and heir, as is presumed, of William of Harrold above-mentioned, is described as "William Botiler of Harrauld and Fordend in Bedenham, Esquire," in a list of gentry of the county in the year 1673.

The mansion-house of the Boteler family, called Ford End, about half a mile to the south-east of the village, and, as its name implies, near to the river, was

---

supported by an arm on either side azure, cuffed argent, hands proper.—Harl. MS. 4600, fo. 85, which also contains a pedigree of five descents.

[a] A William Butler, Esq was sheriff of Beds 1598, and William Boteler temp. K. James I.; but whether of the Biddenham family, or of another of the same name, though unconnected, seated at Sharnbrook, does not appear, for it so happens that there was, at the times above mentioned, a William alive at each place, and the surname of each family is often spelt indifferently Boteler and Butler.

[b] Add. MS. 21,067, fo. 11b, Mr. Marsh's Collections.

BOTELER or

Visitations of Beds. Harl. MSS. 4600, 2109, fo. 6; 1390, 1531, 1097, fo. 6, 47b.
Arms: Gules, a fesse chequy arg. and sa. betw. six crosses crosslets or. (Another coat, assigned with three annulets or, betw. six crosses crosslets of the last.) Quarterings, Mullesworth, Esq., also quartered Farrar after Pecocke. (Harl. 5828.)
Crest: Out of a mural coronet or, a boar's head argent. (Ibid.)

Ranfe Boteler, of Wemme and Oversley, temp. H. III.
├── Gawyn,[1] s.p.
└── William of Wemme and Oversley
    └── William of Wemme.[1]
        ├── William, of Wemme, *a quo* the Lords Dacre and Sudley.[1,2]
        └── Thomas Boteler, (Harl. MS. 245, fo. 27.) Copies of two charters, Botyler or Boteler, of Bydenham, one dated ... second deed, by which he gives to John B... lands, &c., in Stacheden, was executed at the feast of the Purification of the Blessed M...
            └── John Boteler, of Biddenham and Stage... (Harl. 245.) His charter of 35 E. III
                └── William Boteler, called "brother and heir to John" (Harl. 4600, fo. 80.) Deed 6 H. IV. or V. (Harl. 245, fo. 27.)
                    └── Richard Boteler, of Biddenham, Esquire, and of Kyrton's, jur. ux. = Grace, da. and h. of Alan Kirt...
                        ├── Sir William Boteler, Knt., major of London, = ..., da. of ... Rufford, of London. (Mussord, Harl. 1097.)
                        │   "7th Hen. VIII. (1515). Wm. Butler, son of Richd. Butler, of Biddenham (grocer), Lord Mayor, London," (Fuller's Worthies), called "cossen and heir to Thomas Kirton." (Harl. 4600, fo. 80.)
                        │   ├── John Boteler, ob. sp.
                        │   ├── Brigit, da. of Sir John Bruges, Knt., Alderman of London 1520. 1st wife. = Sir William Boteler, of Biddenham. (MS. Ashmole, no. 184)
                        │   └── Emme Boteler. m. Arthur Dericot, of London.
                        │   └── William Boteler, or Butler, Esq., of Bidden- = Dorothie, da. of Robt. Sarger, of   Robert.
                        │   ham or Beddingham in com. Bedford.   Moulsey, co. Surrey, gent.   John.
                        │   (Harl. 2109.)[4,12]   Mathew
                        │   ├── Henry Butler, Esq., of Biddenham, sheriff of Beds, 22 Eliz. 1579. (*Relationship uncertain.*)
                        │   └── William Boteler, Esq., of Biddenham.[5] = ...
                        │   Founded the north aisle in Biddenham church, ob. 17 Feb. 1601.[6] 2nd husb.
                        │   ├── Sir Thomas Boteler, Knt., of = Anne, da. of Francis Farrar, of   Oliver, of Felmersham, J.P. = J...
                        │   │   Biddenham.   Harold.
                        │   │   Arms: Arg. on a bend engr.
                        │   │   sable three horse-shoes of the   Thos., bap. 7 Dec. 1636; bur. 9 Jan. 1657.
                        │   │   first.   Robt., bap. 2 Oct. 1642; bur. 29 Nov. 1646.
                        │   │   (Harl. 4108, fo. 77; 5828.)   George. (Harl. MS. 1531, fo. 94.)
                        │   │   Oliver.
                        │   │   ├── William Boteler, Esq., = Helena, da. of Geo. Nodes, of Shephall Bury,   Tho...
                        │   │   │   of Harrold,[12] ob.   Herts, by a da. and coh. of Edw. Docwra, of   Jam...
                        │   │   │   1639.[6]   Hitchin, Esq.[6]   Fran...
                        │   │   │   ├── Eliz. Willson, m. 8 Jan. 1657, 1st wife, = Edward Boteler, relation- = Mary Hull, m. 30 Oct. 1659, 2nd
                        │   │   │   │   ob. July, 1659.[9]   ship uncertain.   wife, bur. 9 Feb. 1670.
                        │   │   │   │   ├── Henry Boteler, b. 1663, ob. same year.[9]   James Boteler, of Harrold, b. 1654 = Jud...
                        │   │   │   │   │   Alderman Boteler, b. 1665.[6]   ob. 8 Jan. 1690. æt. 36.[8]
                        │   │   │   │   └── Oliver Boteler, bap. 13 Jan. 1677, bur.   James Boteler, b. 1685, bap.
                        │   │   │   │   25 Jan. 1687.[7]   Mar. 1712, æt. ...

[1] Harl. 4600, fo. 80.   [2] Arms of Boteler, Barons of Oversley
[3] Kirton of Biddenham. Crest: A hawk close or, hooded gu. belled of the first. (See Baker's Northa...
[4] The following arms, which however do not appear to have been used, were confirmed by Robert Cook, Bedford, Esq., son and heir of Sir William Boteler, the son and heir of Sir William Boteler, of Kyr... 1844. Guillim, p. 78.) Crest: On a wreath, a boar's head party per pale gu. and azure guttée d'or, mu...
[5] The Smithes of Osterhanger quartered Judde, Chiche, Chichele, Mirfine, &c.   Arms on William and v. ii. 291, 336.)
[6] Bur. at Biddenham.   [7] Harrold register.   [8] Bur. in Harrold
[11] It is difficult to assign a proper place in the pedigree to some members of the family. (See ex... Hellen, eldest dau. of Sir William Boteler, of Biddenham, Knt., wife of Thomas Farrer, of Aylesbury, ... dau. of William Boteler, of Biddenham, Esq., wife of William Farrer, of the Inner Temple, Esq., and the... Inscription in chancel of Buckway Church.) Helen, dau. and coh. of William B...

TLER.

Lansd. MS. 864, fo. 6. Parish Registers. Monumental Inscriptions, &c.
Sir William Boteler, Lord Mayor of London. Gules, a fesse chequy arg. and sa. charged
, and Pecocke. (Harl. 1531, fo. 94.) At the Visitation 1699, William Butler, of Kirton,

Ed. I.

Raufe, of Pulesburye and Northbury, younger son.¹

Sir Raufe

of Biddenham.
of this Thomas
, 6 E. II. The
his son, all his
named place on
no 12 E. III.

Rafe, of whom is descended Sir Philip Boteler,
of Herts, 1587.¹

Joane, da. and h. of Walter Mullesworth.
Arms: Gu. an inescutcheon vair, betw.
ight crosses crosslets or.

John Boteler, ob. s. p.

Kirton's in Biddenham, (sister and heir to Thomas Kirton. Harl. 4600, fo. 80.)³
Arms: Arg. a fesse and chev. in chief gu.

Thomas Boteler, 4th son.
(Harl. 1531, fo. 93.)

Chertsey (another)=Margaret, Lady North. (In Harl. MS. 1555, Margaret, d. of Sir Wm.
id to Margaret. Butler, of London, Knt., widow of Sir David Brook, m. Sir Edward North,
1531, fo. 93.) 1st Lord North, of Cartelage, Chanc. of the Court of Augment., 7 Apr., 1554.)

at.=Anne, da. of Thomas Pecocke (Peark, Harl.   Richard, ob. s.p.
    1097) of Suffolk, gent. 2nd wife   Two other
                                                    children.

Martha.
Mary, or Margaret, m. John Newton, of Exmouth, Devon, and had issue William
  Newton, of Biddenham, 1634, m. Frances, d. and h. of John Godfrey, of Bedford.
Anne, m. Job. Elmett, or Esmett, of London (or Joh. Connell, of Lond.—Harl. 2109.)
Margaret, m. Peter Sare, or Sayer, of Hyde, Kent.

la. of Thomas Smithe, Esq., "farmer of the great=Simon Hardinge, 1st husb.
She was sister to Sir Joh. Smythe, Knt., of   (Harl. 4600. f. 6.)
iger and Ashford, Kent, ancestor of Lord Strang-
of kin to Archbp. Chichele.⁵ She died 3 June
in Biddenham church.

la. of Robert H——, alder-   Alice, b. 1586; m. Edward Osborne, Esq., of Northill, and of the
man of Bedford.   Inner Temple. She d. 12 June 1615, æt. 29. Edw. Osborne
                                     m. 2ndly, Frances, da. of James Harvey, of Dagenham, Essex,
., bap. 6 July 1623.⁷ (Harl. 1531.) by whom he had issue; and 3rdly, Ursula, wdw. of Wm.
bap. 18 Dec. 1635; m. 1654, Henry Wol- Burkley, B.D., of London.
m, Esq., of Waltham Abbey, Essex, and Katherine, m. Joh. Kenardesley, of Wardend, co. Warw., Esq.
a dau. Judith, b. and bur. 1657.⁷   Elizabeth, m. Richard Taylor, of Bedford.

                    Oliver, of Wooton Bourne= Martha, 1st wife to Sir John Kelynge,
                    End, b. 1624, ob. 3 June   Knt., Ld. Chf. Just. of the King's
31 Mar. 1618.⁷   1657, æt. 33.⁸   Bench. (Add. MS. 21,067, fo. 11b.)
                                                Anne, bap. 14 Sep. 1623.⁷
                                                Ursula, bap. 16 May 1625.⁷

feo. Orlebar, b. 1656, m. 27 William, b. 1652.¹⁰ ob. 13th, Judith Boteler, relationship uncertain,¹¹
ob. 4 May 1712, æt. 56.⁸   bur. 14th Dec. 1702, æt. 50.⁸   bur. 22 Oct. 1669.⁶⁷

b.   Elizabeth, b. 1682, ob. 23rd, bur. 24th Apr. 1712, æt. 30.⁸
                       Mary, bap. 6 Mar. 1689, m. 12 Feb. 1712, Rev. Wm Bamford, M.A.⁷
                       Judith, bap. 5 June 1681,⁷ m. 25 Aug. 1715 Thomas Orlebar, of
                         Hinwick, gent.⁹ (See Orlebar's pedigree under *Podington*.)

me: Gu., a fesse componée Or and Sa., betw. six crosses patée Arg. (Burke.)
. 719.)
r, 8th May 1585 (27 Eliz.) to William Boteler, of Kyrton's, in the parish of Brdinham, in the county of
l, that is to say: Argent, a fesse chequy or and azure betw. six cross-crosslets sa. (MS. Ashmole,
Iarl. 1531, fo. 94.)
eler's monument in the chancel of Biddenham Church. (Berry's Genealogies of Kent, p. 39. Hasted,

Harrold.   ⁹ Chellington register.   ¹⁰ Carlton register.
parish register.) John, son and heir of John Boteler, of Bydenham, temp. K. Hen. VII. (Harl. 243.)
Aylesbury 30 June, 1696. (From inscription in the chancel of Aylesbury Church, Bucks.) Mary, eldest
u., Mary Farrer, wife of Robert Chester, Esq., of Barkway, Herts, ob. 21 Jan. 1703, æt. 20. (From
at Chernocke, 3rd Bart. of Hulcote, Sheriff of Beds 1703, and M.P. for the county, 4th and 12th Q. Anne.

at one time appropriated as a workhouse; a portion of the old garden wall yet stands, but few traces now remain of its former splendour.[a]

FORD END.

The manor and estate of Biddenham were afterwards in the possession of the Peterborough family, who probably obtained the greater part by purchase, and subsequently disposed of them to the family of the Trevors, of Bromham,[b] from whom they descended to the present proprietors; as to whom further particulars will be found under the parishes of Turvey and Bromham respectively.

Biddenham, or, Bromham Bridge, is a long structure of twenty-six arches; twenty-two of which form a causeway over a large meadow in this parish. It was repaired in 1793, under the direction of Mr. Robert Salmon, architect. This bridge was engraved by Fisher in 1812.

The singular accident, recorded in the *Dunstable Chronicle*, of a woman being carried down the river from Biddenham Bridge to Bedford, on a piece of ice, has given rise to the supposition that the bridge of that day was nearer Bedford than the present one.

The chauntry of Biddenham Bridge had a considerable endowment in lands, in Bromham, Kempston, and in this parish, charged probably with the repairs of

---

[a] Some of the old inhabitants, in Archdeacon Tattam's time, recollected the barrel which was kept full of table beer for the use of all the poor who wished to partake of it, and to which an iron ladle was attached, that they might freely help themselves.—MS. Tattam.

[b] MS. Tattam.

the bridge. Remains of a chapel are visible in the miller's house on the Bromham side of the river.

In the Lincoln Institution books and elsewhere it is called indifferently Bidenham or Bromham Chauntry, though generally the former; but in a certificate in the Augmentation Office the chapel is stated to be situate in the hamlet of Biddenham Bridge End in Bromham, under the account of which parish accordingly further particulars of this Chantry will find a more fitting place.

CHARITIES.[a]

Boteler's Charity.

This is an ancient annual payment of £5 out of an estate in Biddenham, formerly belonging to the family of Boteler, and now the property of the representatives of the Trevors. This annual sum is due and regularly paid on St. Thomas's day to the overseers of the poor, and is applicable by the terms of the original gift (of which, however, no written memorial is now to be found), or by long established usage, to the purchase of a bull, which is killed, and the flesh thereof given away among the poor persons of the parish. For many years past, the annual fund being insufficient to purchase a bull, the deficiency has been made good out of the rents of lands belonging to Mrs. Boteler's charity hereafter mentioned. It was proposed some years ago, by the vicar at the time, that the 5*l.* a year should be laid out in buying meat, but the poor insisted on the customary purchase of a bull being continued, and the usage is accordingly kept up. The churchwardens, overseers, and principal inhabitants assist at the distribution of the meat. The larger portions are given to those poor who have the largest families.

Mrs. Ursula Boteler, by will, directed her executors to purchase land of the yearly value of 20*s.* to be vested in the Corporation of Bedford for the benefit of the poor of that town, to be distributed on Christmas day. And by indenture dated 3 April 1622, Sir Thomas, the son of Mrs. Boteler, granted unto the mayor and other trustees an annuity of 20*s.* issuing out of a messuage and twenty-five acres of land at Biddenham, payable on St. Thomas's day.

[a] Report of the Commissioners for Public Charities.

BIDDENHAM.

Causeway Money.

This is an annual sum of 3*l.* received by the overseers of the poor, at old Michaelmas, from the Grocers' Company in London. The sum of 2*l.*, part of the annual fund which is understood to be applicable to the repairs of the causeway in the parish, is added to and applied with the rents of the premises held under Mrs. Elizabeth Boteler's charity. This mode of applying the 3*l.* a-year has existed as far back as can be traced.

Whitsuntide Beer.

This is an ancient customary donation of a quarter of malt made annually at Whitsuntide by the proprietor of Kempston (Water) Mill near this parish. The malt is always delivered to the overseers of the poor for the time being, and brewed by them into ale, which is distributed among all the poor inhabitants of Biddenham on Whit Tuesday.

Mrs. Elizabeth Boteler's Charity.

Elizabeth Boteler, by will dated 22 July 1706, gave 200*l.* for the use of the poor of Biddenham, and directed her executors to put the same out at interest until land could be bought with the fund, and she directed the profits thereof to be distributed at Christmas and Whitsuntide yearly for ever.

The legacy of 200*l.* was laid out in the purchase of certain copyhold premises held of the manor of Cranfield, in the county of Bedford, containing by estimation 6 acres, surrendered the 15th of May, 1719, to the use of Joseph Field and Thomas Partridge and John Field and their heirs : a cottage in Wharley-end, and a close or pightle of pasture ground thereto adjoining containing 1 acre 1 rood, and a close or pightle of pasture containing 1 acre in Wharley-end, the last surrendered 25th October, 1723, to the use as before. And by a declaration of trust, dated 9th June, 1724, after reciting the above surrenders, &c , it is declared that such surrenders and admittance were made in trust that the said trustees and their heirs should suffer the rents of the premises to be received by the overseers of the parish of Biddenham upon their being due, to be disposed of to such poor people of the said parish and in such proportions as the said overseers, with the consent of the minister of the said parish for the time being should direct. The estate consists of about 8½ acres of land now in one piece at Warley-end. The cottage mentioned in the declaration of trust has long been pulled down. The land is let to a tenant from year to year. The rent is applied partly in making up the price of the bull purchased under Boteler's charity above mentioned, and the remainder, together with the price of the offal of the bull, is distributed by the overseers at or about the time when the bull's flesh is given away, among such poor people as receive portions thereof.

ADVOWSON.

The right of presentation to the rectory, at an early period, was in the Passelewe family. In the year 1278 John de Kerkeby was possessed of the advowson,[a] which descended to Sir William de Kyrkeby, Knight, who presented to this church in 1293 and 1301.[b]

John de Kirkby,[c] or Kerkeby, a person of considerable eminence in the reigns of King Henry III. and Edward I. was on several occasions[d] appointed keeper of the great seal. His mother was Amicia de Gorham,[e] who died in the seventh King Edward I.[f] seised of lands, &c. in the counties of Leicester and Northampton, of which the said John had livery the same year.[g] He was Canon of Wells and York, Lord Treasurer, and Bishop of Ely 1286, and died in the seventeenth of the same reign,[h] being then seised of divers manors and lands in the aforesaid counties, as also in Middlesex, Herts, Cambridgeshire, Beds, Hunts, and including, among others, the advowson of the church of Biddenham with certain lands in this parish.[i]

William de Kirkby, contemporary with John, if not his brother, was one of those great men who in the 22nd King Edward I. had summons[k] to attend a Parliament then appointed to be called together, but of which no place is mentioned for its assembling in the writ of convocation, which is dated at Westminster, 8th July, in the year aforesaid. This William deceased 30th Edward I.[l] (1302), being then seised of the lands, &c. whereof John (de Kirkby) Bishop of Ely

---

[a] Rot. Hund.   [b] Institution Books at Lincoln.

[c] *Arms:* Argent, a cross between two annulets vert.

[d] Pat. Claus. 57 Hen. III. Pat. Rot. 7 Ed. I. nu. 15.

[e] Probably dau. and heir of Sir Hugh de Gorham who (24 Edw. I) was one of those summoned to attend a great council at Newcastle-upon-Tyne, with horse and arms.

[f] Esc. 7 Ed. I. nu. 19.   [g] Orig. 7 Ed. I. Rot. 16 Leic.   [h] Ibid. 17 Ed. I.

[i] Esch. 18 Ed. I. nu. 37.   [k] Dugd.   [l] Esch. 30 Ed. I. nu. 31.

had been possessed, leaving Christian his wife surviving,ᵃ and his four sisters his co-heirs, between whom his great inheritance was divided;ᵇ viz. :—

    1. Margaret, wife of Walter Doseville (called Bosville by Burtonᶜ) who had part of the lands, &c. in Leicestershire, Northants, Middlesex, Herts, and Bucks.

    2. Alice, wife of Peter Prylly, had lands in Leicestershire, Northants, Middlesex, and Cambridgeshire.

    3. Matilda, wife of Walter de Houby, had the manor of Kirkeby, &c. in co. Leicester, and land in Northamptonshire.

    4. Mabill, wife of William Grymbaud, had the manor of Chalvestern,ᵈ the advowson with lands and tenements in Bidenham, co. Bedford, and also lands in Leicestershire, Northants, Bucks, and Middlesex.

William Grymbaud had summons to the before-noticed council at Newcastle; he was called Grimbald de Houghton of Houghton, in Northamptonshire. Robert de Houghton his son and heir had a son William, who together with his son Robert were benefactors to the Priory of St. Andrew's at Northampton.

After Sir William de Kyrkeby—although his sister and coheir, Mabill Grymbaud, was found to be seised of this advowson—the Abbey or Convent of Waterbech in Cambridgeshire, appointed to this living; this convent was founded, A.D. 1293, by the Lady Dionysia de Monchensi,ᵉ for nuns minoresses, "to the honour of the piety of the Blessed Virgin Mary and *S. Clare.*"ᶠ

About the year 1349 the Countess of Pembroke removed the nuns from Waterbech to Denny or Denney, in the same county, a religious house then lately founded by her.ᵍ The convent of Denny presented to the living from the year 1384 until the dissolution of monasteries; shortly before which, in the year 1513, the church was shorn of its rectorial estate.

The parsonage and the advowson of the vicarage were in the Dyves of Bromham before the year 1537,ʰ and passed with a large portion of the estates of that family to the Trevors, in whose representatives they are now vested.

    ᵃ Esch. 31 Ed. I. nu. 118.   ᵇ Orig. 30 Ed. I. Rot. 15.

    ᶜ Burton's Leic. p. 171.

    ᵈ Inq. p. m. 5 Ed. II. Abbrev. Rot. Orig. Ro. 15, p. 123. Chalverstene, now Chawston, in the parish of Roxton.

    ᵉ Grandmother of the Dionysia de Monchensi who married Hugh de Vere. Dugdale, Bar. vol. i. p. 242. Baker's Northamptonshire, vol. ii. p. 315.

    ᶠ Dugdale, Bar. vol. i. 562.

    ᵍ Tanner, Notitia. Camb. xxvii.

    ʰ From the circumstance of several members of the Boteler family having been buried in the chancel, as

BIDDENHAM.

The following estimate of the church property at Biddenham appears to have been made about the year 1345:—

" On the oaths of John de Grendon, Robt. Astell, John de Schelton, Richard Daventry, John Blanncost, and Wm. Joynkeneye the church of the parish of Bidenham is taxed at seven marks and ten shillings and no more, with portions of the prior of Newnham and the prior of Cauldwel in the same, for the fewness of the commodities that pertain to the same church, viz., 30 acres of land which are given to the same church, likewise tithe, hay, mortuary oblations and other small tithes, which indeed comprehend all the commodities in taxes of the same church.

"Also, because the keeper of the Chapel of the Bridge of Bidenham holds 80 acres of land in the same, which have lain uncultivated in that year. Likewise because 27 acres of land, formerly of Thos. Attewal, have laid waste and uncultivated in that year in the same parish. They further say that there are not, neither have been, goods of other burgesses or citizens, nor of others who do not live of agriculture, but poor cottagers who obtain their livelihood by the labour of their hands." [a]

VICARAGE.[b]

The vicarial or small tithes of this parish were also alienated from the Church, and, according to Mr. Lysons, the living, previous to 1723, was only a stipendiary curacy of 8*l*. per annum: about which time Lord Hampden, who was also the owner of the small tithes, by his will gave an annual rent-charge of 12*l*. to the

---

also having erected monuments therein, it may be inferred that, in after years, they possessed some direct interest in the rectory estate, or were lessees thereof under the Dyves. William Boteler was patron of the living in 1605. Lincoln Register.

[a] Nonar Inquis. The origin of these records is this: A grant was made to the King (Edw. III.) of the ninth lamb, fleece, and sheaf, and the ninth part of goods and chattels of cities and boroughs, &c. for two years. Assessors were appointed for every county, and this volume contains the inquisitions taken upon the oath of the parishioners in every parish. MS. Tattam.

[b] In 1219 the institution and endowment of vicarages[1] was in England a new thing. The Abbey at St. Alban's, having the church at Luton with its tithes, had instituted a vicar (instead of sending an occasional preacher) without having fixed the revenue necessary for his support, which led to a long and expensive lawsuit with the Bp. of Lincoln. It was at last decided that his maintenance should be raised from the small tithes and obventions, and that he should be furnished with a suitable mansion and glebe. The living of Biddenham was reduced to a vicarage and endowed in 1513.[2]

---

[1] See also Blackstone, vol. i. p. 387.   [2] Lincoln Register.

minister for the time being, whenever the Governors of Queen Anne's Bounty should have settled on the cure a further augmentation of not less than 10*l*.

The vicarage of Biddenham is partly stipendiary and part arises from several portions of land. From documents in the Augmentation Office it appears that Biddenham vicarage was augmented by 200*l*. from Queen Anne's Bounty, by lot, in 1732, and in 1757 a grant of 200*l*. was made to meet 200*l*. given in land in 1756 by John Lord Trevor and the Hon. Robert Hampden. The vicarage house was enlarged and modernized by the Rev. Thos. S. Grimshawe, soon after he came to the possession of the living. It stands about the middle of the village. A small piece of the glebe is in Oakley parish.

List of Incumbents.[a]

RECTORS.

		Patron.
1235—1257	{ William Triket	Gilbert Passelewe.
	{ Alexander de Elnestowe	,,
1258—1293	{ Richard Hexon, subdeacon. By death of last.	Ralph Paselewe.
	{ John de Osingle	,,
1293, 3 Id. Mar.	Gilbert de Fulmer	Sir William de Kyrkeby, knight.
1301, 16 Kal Dec. -	Gilbert de Fulmer	,,
1330, 16 Kal. Jan. -	James de Bodkesham	Convent of Waterbech, co. Cambs.
1349, 3 Id. April -	William de Wykersane	,,
1384, Feb. 13 - -	John Tape, Pbr. By death of last.	Monastery of Denney in Cambridgeshire.
1385, May 15 - -	John Buddeby, in exchange with last rector.	,,
1398, July 19 -	Richard Kymeston de Couesgrave. By res. of last.	,,
1412, May 25 - -	John Clench	,,
	Thomas Moysell. By res. of last.	,,
1435, Sept. 16 -	Robert Aycogh	,,
	John Spechslive (Sperhawke)	,,
1454, May 7 - -	John Aylyffe. (Buried in the chancel here.)	,,

CHAPLAINS and VICARS.

		Patron.
1527, May 7 - -	John Lee, M.A. Vicar	Monastery of Denney
1537, June 3 - -	William Stoddard. By res. of last.	Isabella Dyve, widow
1538, May 18 -	Richard Holden alias Wright. By res. of last.	,,

---

[a] Lib. Instit. apud Lincoln. MS. Tattam. Regist. Paroch.

BIDDENHAM.

	Vicars.	Patron
1545	Henry Francklyn, Vicar.[a]	
1547	Richard Howden, Vicar.[b]	
1550	Richard Wright, Vicar.[c]	
1571	Thomas Negus, "Vicar of Bignam"	
1708	Andrew Moore	
1717	John Teap (*Curate* in Par. Regr.)	
1730	Thomas Tipping[d] (*Curate* Par. Regr.), a relative of Dr. Ichabod Tipping,[e] Vicar of Camberwell, who died 17 March, 1727-8, aged 70, as to whom see Lysons, *Envir. Lond.*, vol. i. p. 80, and vol. ii. p. 373; also Manning, *Surrey*, vol. iii. p. 430.	
1758, Jan. 14	William Fleming	Lord Trevor.
1761, May 11	Thomas Richards, M.A., Emmanuel Coll., Camb. 1769, "licensed to the Chapel of Bidenham."	,,
1799, April	John Jones, M.A. By death of last	Thomas Viscount Hampden.
1808, Aug. 22	Thomas S. Grimshawe,[d] M.A. By cession of last. Mr. Grimshawe was also Rector of Burton Latimer, Northants; he wrote some small tracts on religious subjects, and is the supposed author of "Episcopal Innovations." His other works are "A Memoir of the Rev. Legh Richmond," 1828, 8vo., 11th edition, 1846, 12mo. "Cowper's Works and Life," 1835, 8 vols. 12mo. Last edition 1847. "On the Future Restoration and Conversion of the Jews," 1843, 12mo. "Moravian Missions," a Sermon preached at Saint Saviour's, Southwark, by T. S. G. 24 March, 1819; "The Wrongs of the Clergy of the Diocese of Peterborough," 1822 [f]	,,
1850	Henry Rice, B.A., Ch. Ch., Oxon. brother to the present Lord Dynevor	Trustees.
1856	Boteler Chernocke Smith, B.A., Trin. Coll., Oxon. resigned, on taking the family living of Hulcote with Salford, Beds	
1865	Henry Wood, M.A., Trinity College, Cambridge	

[a] Witness to a will
[b] Witness to John Halsey's will
[c] Witness to Bart. Allen's will
} Northampton District Registry.
[d] Bur. at Biddenham.   [e] MS. Marsh.
[f] Rev. T. O. Marsh's notes. Add. MS. 21,067, fo. 85b.

Church.

There was a church at Biddenham as early as the reign of Henry III., and probably at a much earlier period. The present church, which is situated at the western extremity of the village, is dedicated to St. James, and the village feast in commemoration of the dedication is kept on the Sunday after the 25th of July.

The church is built of stone, having a nave and aisles, or, more properly speaking, a north aisle and south chapel, and is 41 feet long and 39 wide; the south chapel being 9 feet wide and the north aisle 15. At the west end of the church is a stone tower about 14 feet square, which has a wooden spire covered with lead, and surmounted by a weather-cock; from the effects of a fire which took place adjoining the church, the lead is partially melted and the spire slightly damaged.

The chancel, also of stone, 29 feet long and 16 wide, its roof being high-pitched and tiled, is mixed Decorated and Perpendicular. On the south side are two late third-pointed windows, and a similar one on the north—each of two lights. The east window is Decorated, of three lights, with flowing tracery. About the middle of the north wall a chimney rises nearly to the height of the ridge of the roof.

The principal entrance to the church is by a Perpendicular porch[a] on the south side, which projects about 11 feet from the body of the church, and 2 feet beyond the south chapel, the west end of which forms nearly one side of the porch; and by a circular-headed doorway of early type. Over the porch is a small room, lighted by a south window, and formerly having an entrance from the chapel.[b] There is also a door on the north side of the church. The roof of the nave is gabled, and covered with tiles like the chancel, but the aisles and the porch are covered with lead. The parapets of the aisles in a great measure hide the leads, the one on the south side being surmounted with coped battlements; but that on the north is plain, with a small square ornamented pinnacle at each corner. There is a small cross at the east end of the nave. A string-course is carried round the church, charged with gurgoyles at the angles, and one in the centre, on the north side; but on the south they appear to have been broken off. On the south side of the church there is one window of three lights and one of two lights, cinquefoiled-headed, and one at the east end of the south chapel of two lights, like the side windows in the chancel. There are two windows on the

---

[a] Porches of churches were anciently devoted to parish business, settling law suits, paying rents, and celebrating marriages.—Fosbrooke's Tourist's Grammar, p. 203.

[b] The room over a porch was either a school or place where records were kept.—Ibid. p. 202.

BIDDENHAM.

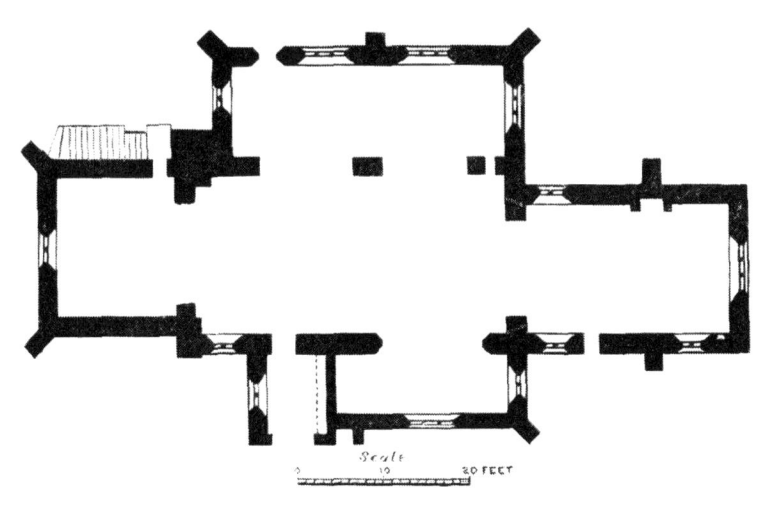

BIDDENHAM CHURCH.

GROUND PLAN OF CHURCH.

north side of three lights each, and a similar one at the east end of the north aisle; and one of two lights at the west end of this aisle, of the same character. The tower, the upper part of which is Perpendicular, has an embattled parapet, with a string-course below it charged with a gurgoyle at each corner, corresponding with those on the church. On its north side a flight of stone steps leads to a small door which conducts to the belfry. In the lower stage, on the west side, is a window of two lights, with a quatrefoil in the head, and a quatrefoil light above; in the south wall is a door-way closed up.

There are two arches on the north side of the nave; but the south chapel is entered from the nave by a single arch. There is a piscina in this chapel, occupying the usual position. When the church was repaired some years ago a round-headed recessed arch or closed-up window in the south wall was brought to light. The north aisle was founded by William Boteler, Esq., who died 17th February, 1601, and lies buried in the church. There is a sculptured figure above each of the end pillars supporting the arches which divide this aisle from the nave, one a dove carrying a roll, and the other a wyvern;[a] and above the capital of the centre pier is a shield with the arms of Boteler,—a fesse company, charged with three annulets, between six crosses crosslet. Lysons mentions a chantry in this church dedicated to St. William. Under the arch nearest the west end, on the north side of the church, formerly stood the Font, on a basement raised above the floor, supported by an octagon pedestal, on each side of which is a plain raised shield, in a square compartment, with an oval moulding round it. The font itself is octagonal, each face being ornamented with carving, some with trefoil leaves and a rose in the middle, and others with different tracery, well executed; it is now placed near the south door. The pulpit is at the south-east corner of the nave. The nave of the church had open oaken seats, carved at the ends, but the aisles were pewed.[b] The chancel is entered from the nave, under a plain Norman arch, and was formerly separated by a screen, now placed at the east end of the north aisle to form a vestry, the entrance to which is by a square trefoiled-

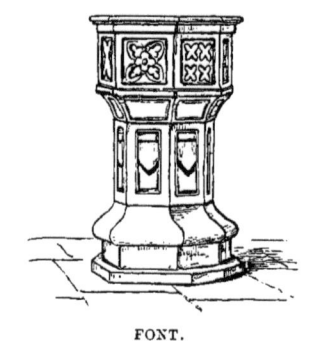

FONT.

---

[a] The crest of the Dyves of Bromham, to whom this advowson and rectory belonged before 1537; from which it would appear that they assisted in the building of the north aisle.

[b] The church is now fitted throughout with open seats.

headed doorway that is pierced through the wall between the eastern arch of the north aisle and the east end of the nave. On either side of the chancel-arch is a hagioscope or squint. In the south wall of the chancel is a piscina, into which the officiating priest used to empty the cleansings of the chalice, and the water in which he washed his hands, &c. About the middle of the south wall is a priest's doorway. On the north side is a modern fire-place.

The clock in the tower was presented to the parish by John Brooks, Esq. in 1787. In the bell-chamber are six bells.

The first has round it, a little below the crown, BE LIGHT AND GLAD, IN GOD REJOICE—EMMERTON FECIT—1787.

The second has round the crown—EMMERTON CAST THIS PEAL 1787.

The third has on it, EMMERTON FECIT. 1787.

The fourth, WILLIAM EMMERTON OF WOOTON FECIT[a] 1787.

The fifth has the following—EMMERTON FECIT, and, in a smaller character, FIVE OLD BELLS CAST INTO SIX AT THE EXPENCE OF MR. JOHN BROOKS.

The sixth has BLESSED IS THE NAME OF THE LORD. EMMERTON FECIT. 1787.

Belonging to the church is a very ancient and curiously embroidered altar-cloth, having the date 1542 or 1549 upon it, and the name ROLOFVOS wrought at two corners.

There is a silver flagon and chalice for the Communion Service, the flagon having engraven on it "The Gift of Francis Reeve, Gent., who died July ye 30th, 1689." The cover of the chalice has a boar's head engraved on the outside between the letters "W. B."

In the church are two oaken chests belonging to the parish, the larger one, which is iron-bound, containing an old quarto Book of Common Prayer, black letter, of 1638, and another small folio, with the date 1662.

---

[a] A bell-foundry at Wootton, near Bedford, was carried on from 1719 to 1743 by Russell, whose name appears on church bells in Wootton and Houghton Conquest. Rev. W. Lukis, in his "Account of Church Bells" (Parker, 1857), does not give Emmerton's name.

1521. Will of Isabella Low. Testatrix desired to be buried in the churchyard of St. James, Bydenham, left a small sum for her mortuary, also "to the church of Lincoln ij d., to the high aulter of Bydenham iiij d., to the bellys iiij d.," and bequeathed four acres of land "for to maynteyn and kepe a lamp before the Rood of the sayd Church." Names, Richard Low of Pusey, Thomas Chapman and Johanna his wife; John Chapman and John Harper, overseers. Witnesses, Faldo, Richard Camsey, Thomas Malot, John Pestell.

BIDDENHAM.

Monumental Inscriptions—Chancel.

On the north wall is a rich marble monument, with the sculptured effigies of a man kneeling on a cushion at a marble altar, which is supported by two angels, and covered with finely sculptured drapery, and his wife in the same attitude in a long cloak on the opposite side of the altar, and books opened before them; above the head of each is a shield, and over them a canopy studded with roses, supported by two columns of variegated marble with Corinthian capitals—above the canopy is another shield. Below the altar just mentioned is a smaller one, at which are the effigies of a man and his wife kneeling, in the same costume as above, a son is kneeling behind the man, with his hands closed together, and two daughters behind the mother, who holds a skull in her hands. The inscription is as follows—

Memoriæ Sacrum.—In Memory of WILLIĀ BOTELER, Esq. sonne and heire of Williā Boteler, Esq. sonne and heire of Sr Williā Boteler, Knight, whoe amongst many other his charitable deeds to this town did found ye north Ile of this Church, and in Memory of Ursula wife of ye said Williā, one of ye daughters of Thom^{as} Smith, Esq. durenge his life time sole farmor to ye great custome of England, is this monument erected through ye pious care and dutiful respect of Richard Taylor of ye town of Bedford, Esq., their sonne in law, and Oliver Boteler, their second son, Executo^{rs} (and in performance) of ye last will and testam^t of ye said Ursula. The said William Boteler and Ursula, havinge virtuously, bountifully, and religiously lived many years, dep^{r}ted this life, the said Williā ye 17 day of Febr^{ry} in ye year of our Lord 1601, and ye said Ursula ye 3 of June in ye year of grace 1621, and both lye buried here. They had between them 2 sonnes and 3 daughters: Sir Thomas Boteler, Knight, their eldest sonne and heire ; ye said Oliver Boteler; Alice deceas'd; Katharine, married to John Kinnersley of Wardend, in ye County of Warwicke, Esq.; and Elizabeth, now wife of ye said Rich Taylor.

Epitaphium sive Memoraculum Memoratissimorum :

GULIELMI BOTELER Armiger' haud procul sepult'.   URSULÆ BOTELER uxoris eiusd' subjacentis.

As he to Kinge and native soyle did owe	What bounty, pity, charity, and love
The service of his corps laide here belowe,	To poore, to ritch freinds, neighb^{rs} was requir'd,
As to Jehovah better part was due,	What piety, what zeal true faith might prove
Who soule and body doth make, save, renewe,	In this grave matron worthly was admyred ;
As he to needy neighb^{rs} owed his store,	Her lampe so wisely oyled for comon good
So he to these and all clear'd all his score.	Is to be wished for of all womanhood.
In martial trade as civityzed affayres	Here lyeth that mantle which from her did fall
In office each he well employed his cares ;	When she to heaven assumed bidd world adewe,
Implored his God, to poore applyed his good,	Here may it rest in peace till trumpets calle
Virtue ensude, each vice eschewed withstood.	In glorious sorte to clothe her soule anewe.
Thus walked he here uprightly ; his days ended,	Here liv'd beloved—here lyeth beloved though dead,
His soule ould Jacob's ladder is ascended.	That hand dispensing still her daily bread.

Arms—Boteler, with three quarterings, impaling Smith, with eight quarterings—Dexter—1. Gu. a fesse compony ar. and sa. between six cross-crosslets (or patonce) or. *Boteler.* 2. Gu. an inescutcheon vair between eight cross-crosslets or. *Mullesworth.* 3. Ar. a fesse and chev. in chief gu. *Kyrton.* 4. Gu. a chev. between three peacocks in their pride ar. *Pecock.* (*Harl.* 1531, *fo.* 94). Sinister —1. Azure, a chev. engr. between three lions pass. or. *Smith.* 2. Gu a fess raguly between three boar's heads erased ar. *Judde.* 3. Azure, three lions ramp. within a bordure ar. *Chich.* 4. Or, a chev. between three cinquefoils gu. *Chichele.* 5. Sa. a cross voided or. 6. Or, two chev. and a canton gu. *Crioll.* 7. Or, a cross voided gu. *Crevecœur.* (*Harl. MS.* 1428, *fo.* 14.) 8. Ar. a cross gu. within a bordure azure. 9. Or, a chev. sa. (? charged with a mullet or). *Mirfine.*

The arms of Boteler with his quarterings, and Smith with quarterings, are each repeated on a separate shield. It is to be regretted that the arms on this monument have at some period been recoloured by an unskilful hand, so that the tinctures as they appear thereon are not all correct.

On the same wall, nearer the chancel-arch, is a black marble mural tablet with a border of white marble, and death's head, cross-bones and hour-glass, sculptured on the sides. Above the tablet is a Lozenge, with the arms of Boteler, surmounted by helmet and crest; and beneath the inscription are the armorial bearings of Osborne,—the shield is quarterly of four.[a]

1. Quarterly erm. and azure, a cross or. *Osborne.* 2. Ar. two bars gu. on a canton or a cross of the second. *Broughton.* 3. Ar. a chev. vert between three annulets gu. 4. Sa. a fesse flory counter-flory or (charged with three lapwings ppr.) between three lions passant ar. *Hewit.*

ALICE, the wife of Edward OSBORNE,[b] of the Inner Temple, London, Esquire, eldest daughter of William Boteler, of Biddenham, in ye county of Bedford, Esq., having lived a short but a vertuouse life, at her age of 29 years triumphed over death and all human miseries, deceasing ye 12 day of June, 1615, and now rests with ye Lord in blisse for evermore, leavinge behind her two sonnes, Edward and William, and two daughtrs, Ursula and Anne. In pious memory of her, her justly grieved husband hath fixed up this monument, with this but half-expressing epitaph:—

> Among the best, above the most admired,
> Lovely to all, loving to whom she ought,
> In zeale to God and goodness holy-fired,
> Charie and chaste in word, and deed, and thought,
> Exact in all that in that sexe is dearest,
> Of vertue fullest, and of vices cleerest.

---

[a] This shield with the crest for Osborne, tricked at fo. 47*b*, Harl. MS. 1097. Crest, an heraldic tiger or, maned and charged on the shoulder with a pellet sa.

[b] Brother of Sir Hewett Osborne, son of Sir Edward, Lord Mayor of London 1583, and grandson of Richard Osborne, of Ashford, Kent. From Sir Hewett descends the present Duke of Leeds.—Notts. Visitation, an. 1614; Harl. 1400.

> Sweet young resemblance of old Sacred Mothers
>   Blessed example (present and to come)
> Of pious pity to her owne and others;
>   Rare help; rich hap to her deer Pheer at home;
> None such as she thinks hee who, still her debtor,
> Erects her this, but in his heart a better.

Formerly, on the floor opposite this monument was a blue slab, removed to the churchyard when the church was repaired a few years ago, with the following notice:—

Here lies interred ye body of ALICE, sometime wife of Edward OSBORNE, of ye Inner Temple, London, Esq., eldest daughter of William Boteler, of Bydenham, Esquire, departed this life on ye 12th day of June, 1615. Her life might have binn an example to all women. Her death is a spectacle of what remains for all mankind.

In the south wall is a small brass for John Ayliffe, the last rector on record; he died at the end of the fifteenth or the beginning of the sixteenth century.

On the floor opposite the priest's door Mr. Tattam noticed a blue slab, in which was inserted a brass, with the following memento:—

> Hic jacet dns JOHES AYLYFF quondam Rector
> Ecclesie parochialis de Bydenham juxta Bedfford,
> Cujus anime propicietur Deus. Amen.

On a mural tablet. Arms: A griffin segreant. *Grimshawe.* Impaling on a chev. another chev. between three leaves. *Livius.*

In memory of the Rev. THOMAS SHUTTLEWORTH GRIMSHAWE, M A., late Rector of Burton Latimer, Northamptonshire, and upwards of 40 years Vicar of this parish. He was eminently distinguished for his zeal and eloquence in advocating those christian institutions of his country which promote among Jews and Gentiles the unsearchable riches of Christ. He walked in faith, adorning his high and holy calling by a blameless life and a liberal mind, and closed in peace an extensive career of usefulness on the 17th Feb. 1850, aged 73 years.

Also in memory of JOHN BARHAM GRIMSHAWE, Esq., son of the above, who died at Trin. Coll. Cambridge, May 25th, 1835, aged 23 years. And of CHARLOTTE ANNE, the beloved wife of the above Rev. T. S. Grimshawe, who died June 28th, 1851, aged 58 years.

Underneath this tablet are deposited the remains of three infants, the lamented children of Rev. T. S. Grimshawe, Vicar of this parish, and of Charlotte his wife—viz., EMILY, died July 4th, 1813, aged 19 months. Likewise a still-born child. And FREDERICK, who departed June 11th, 1818, aged three months.

> Bold Infidelity, turn pale and die,
> Beneath this stone three infants' ashes lie;
> Say—are they lost or sav'd?

If death's by sin, they sinned because they're here;
If Heaven's by works, in heaven they can't appear.
Reason—ah! how depraved.
Revere the Bible's sacred page, the knot's untied;
They died, for Adam sinned; they
Live, for Jesus died.

A mural tablet, on the south wall, is inscribed:

In memory of JEMIMA LUCY BOUGHTON, the beloved wife of CHARLES LIVIUS GRIMSHAWE, Esq., of Fenlake, in the county of Bedford, and daughter of J. W. Boughton-Leigh, Esq., of Brownsover Hall, in the county of Warwick, who departed this life after only a few days' illness, on the 5th day of Dec. 1852, in the 31st year of her age, believing in the promise of the resurrection to eternal life, through her Lord and Saviour Jesus Christ.

Arms (not tinctured)—*Grimshawe* and four quarterings; impaling *Leigh*, quartering 2. 3, *Boughton*, 4, *Ward*. Dexter—1. A griffin segreant. *Grimshawe*. 2. A cross engr. couped between four bezants. 3. A fret. 4. Erm. on a fesse three annulets. 5. A fesse between two horses pass. 6. *Grimshawe*, as before. Sinister—1. A lion ramp. and a canton. *Leigh*. 2. A chev. charged with three buck's heads, between three cross-crosslets fitchée, on a chief a goat pass., a canton in the dexter corner. 3. Three crescents and a canton. *Boughton*. 4. A cross flory. *Ward*. Crest—A griffin, as in the arms.

On the same wall there is a tablet to Rev. Mr. Missing.

NORTH AISLE.

A stone with brasses of William Faldo and Agnes his wife and John Faldo is now in that portion of the north aisle which is used as a vestry. Mr. Marsh mentions this stone as being in the south chapel. It was engraved by Fisher in 1813. The Faldos were seated at Oakley, and very anciently at Faldo and Maulden, Beds.[a]

Near the north door of the church, inscriptions for

ANN, daur. of Thomas and Ann RICHARDS, who died 24 Apr. 1764, æt. 9 months.
ROBERT SAVILLE, 21 Nov. 1791, æt. 55, and MARY his wife, 23 Mar. 1817, æt. 75.

In this aisle is a large brown slab in which is inserted a brass plate with

---

[a] 23 May, 1536. Will of Nicholas Faldo, of Biddenham. Testator devised to Mawde, his wife, his house in Bromham Bridge End, for life, remainder to his sons William and John. Mentions his daughter Joane and his servant Thomas Bere.

1537. Robert Faldough of Bidenham. Bequeathed to his wife his "houses and lands as a dede made by the steward of Bedford doth express."

two persons in long cloaks with hoods engraven on it, and their hands closed together upon their breasts, but the inscription is broken off.

On the north wall is a brass plate in a stone frame (removed from a pillar at the east end) with a half-length engraving of a female, and an inscription underneath for Helena (Nodes), wife of William Boteler, Esq., who died 1639.

Tablet in the south chapel:

Sacred to the memory of ELIZABETH wife of John LAVENDER, who departed this life April 29th, 1819, aged 60 years. Also of JOHN LAVENDER, who died the 2nd day of October, 1821, aged 67 years.

In the churchyard, near the south gate, is the base of a cross. There are inscriptions for Rev. Robert Moore, D.D., 33 years Vicar of Thurleigh, who died at St. Alban's, 18th Oct. 1834, aged 77. Anne his widow died in London, 5th Oct. 1850, aged 88. Jas. Willasey, Esq., son of Jas. Willasey, Esq. of Allerton Hall, Lancashire, 1841. For the children of Rev. Boteler Chernocke Smith, Vicar of this parish, — Brooks, Esq., Grimshawe, Lavender, Felts, Johnson, Tipping, Wells, Savill, Adkins, Killingworth, West, Davis, Staines, Robinson, Manning, Maxey, Boarder, Ramm, Golding, Clifton, Goodman, Partridge, Burton, Bond, Hutchings, Bichenor, Bunbury, Missing, Nicholls, Landon, &c.

PARISH REGISTERS.

Parish registers were first established by Lord Cromwell in the year 1538. The first register book of the parish of Biddenham is a thin folio volume of vellum. The first entry it contains is in the year 1663, and the last 1731. The following are the most remarkable entries contained in the registers:—

1663 July 2.		Maria Filia Gulielmi Boteler Armig. et Eliz. ux. ejus Baptiz. fuit.
1667 Sep. 26.		Anna Filia Gulielmi Boteler Armig. et Alic. ux. ejus Baptiz.
1668 Feb. 28.		Dom. Sybyll Boteler vid. Sepult. fuit.
—— Dec. 10.		Richard Orlibar de Harrold Armig. et Jana Hatton filia dom. Mariæ Hatton de Long- (? *Stanton*) in com. Cantab. matrimonium contrax.
1669 Sept. 18.		Hatton Boteler fil. Guli. Boteler et Eliz. uxor ejus Baptizat.; et sepult. decim. nono.
—— Jan.		Gulielmus filius Gul. Boteler Armig. Bapt. vicesimo 6° die.
1671 May 1.		Gulielmus filius Gul. Boteler Armig. sep.
1674.		The entries commence in English and in a different hand.
1675 Dec. 14.		Elizabeth the daur. of Wm. Boteler, Esq., and Elizabeth his wife bap.
1676 Aug. 18.		Elizabeth the daur. of Wm. Boteler, Esq., bur.
1678 Feb. 24.		John Boteler, gent. bur.
1679 Mar. 2.		William Farrar, Esq. and Mary Boteler, marr.

1680 Apr. 8.		David Faldo, clerk, bur.
1682.		The signatures are in another hand.
1688.		The writing is in a different hand.
1691 June 9.		Pynsenet Charnock, Esq., and Mrs. Helen Boteler, daur. of William Boteler, Esq., marr.
1702 April 9.		Robert Chester of Barkway in ye county of Hertford, Esq., and Mary ye daughter of W^m. Farrer of Biddenham, Esq. mar.
—— Feb. 1.		W^m. Boteler, Esq., bur.
1707 Apr. 25.		Mrs. Elizabeth Boteler, widow, bur.
1716 Oct. 20-1.		Mr. Thos. Ffaldoe, clerk, bur.
1718 Mar. 8.		Mr. John Adkins, coachman to my Lady Russell, bur.
1718.		John Teape signs as curate till 1723.
1728.		Thos. Tipping signs as curate till 1757, when his burial is recorded.
1732.		The last entry in the register is February 6th.

The next register book is a thin folio volume which continues the entries regularly from 1732 to 1806:

1783.		Memorandum. Licence for entries of burials and baptisms commenced Oct. 7, 1783.
1801.		Jones first signs as Vicar, and continues till December, 1807.

The third register book is a folio volume, and commences April, 1806:

1808.		Thomas Shuttleworth Grimshawe first signs as Vicar.

About a quarter of a mile to the east of the church is an ancient mansion, the residence of Mr. Charles Howard. The farm-houses and cottages in this parish, as indeed generally on the Bromham estate, are substantially built, and many of them ornamental in design. The Parochial School, in the centre of the village, has been recently enlarged; annexed to it is a master's residence.

In the year 1801 the number of inhabited houses in Biddenham parish was returned as 57, uninhabited 1; there were 61 families, and a total of 252 persons. In 1851 the population was 373; in 1861, 350; and in 1871, 325.

BROMHAM.

Bruneham.—This village is situated on the banks of the Ouse,ᵃ three miles west-north-west from Bedford, near the road to Newport Pagnell. The scene from the bridge before-mentioned under Biddenham is very pleasing, and induced the eminent artist Mr. Pyne to delineate it, with some embellishments of his own. This landscape was in the Exhibition of the Royal Academy 1793.

The River Ouse flows round three sides of the parish, which is bounded on the north by Oakley and Clapham, in the hundred of Stodden; east by Clapham; south by Biddenham, Kempston, and Stagsden; north-west by Stevington; its extreme west point touching Turvey, at a place where four parishes meet. From Clapham-ford east to Stagsden west, is about two and a-half miles; from Oakley Mill north to Bromham Mill south, one mile and a-half. Area, as rated, 1798 A. 0 R. 15 P.

The soil is fertile but various, red sandy earth on the west, some woodland and clay toward Stagsden, the centre and southern part good grazing land; at one time, during the last century, woad is said to have been cultivated to some extent here—a close of forty acres is called the "cabbin-ground," where the huts of the labourers employed in its cultivation formerly stood. The woods are not very considerable—Solemn Thrift is above 20 acres, Bowels 10 or 12, Molliver Wood 7; the paddock or park, upwards of 70 acres, inclosed by Thomas second Lord Trevor, in 1733, is ornamented with some well-grown timber, and was formerly stocked with deer; the deer, it is stated, were sold off on account of a Lady Trevor having been frightened by one.ᵇ

A brook enters the parish on the west from Stagsden, and, running obliquely towards the south, empties itself into the river not far above the bridge. A spring rises near the Grange, another close to the bridge, a third is called "roaring spring," but for what reason is unknown, a fourth near the Hall was cleared and improved by Lord Hampden; the water of this spring is very pure,

---

ᵃ It is recorded that in 1399 and 1648 the waters of the river had so far deserted their channel that persons walked in its bed for nearly three miles in this part of its course.—Lewis's Topographical Dictionary of England, 7th ed. Lond. 1848.

ᵇ MS. Cooper.

and was in much repute with the country people, for its quality in healing fresh wounds.

Manor.—The land of Hugh de Belcamp in the half-hundred of Bochelai. In Bruneham Serlo de Ros holds six hides of Hugh. There is land for six ploughteams. In the demesne are two plough-teams and sixteen villans; they have four ploughs. There are five bordars, and six servi, and one mill worth twenty shillings and a hundred and twenty-five eels. There is pasture for six ploughteams. Wood for forty hogs. The whole worth seven pounds—when he received it a hundred shillings; in the time of King Edward four pounds. Alsi a man of Queen Eddith held and could sell this land.—Domesday, p. 213.

The paramouncy of this manor as parcel of the barony of Bedford[a] descended conformably with Beauchamp's pedigree.[b] Upon the death of John Beauchamp, last feudal lord of Bedford, who, having joined the rebellious Barons, was slain at the battle of Evesham, his estates were confiscated and given to Prince Edward, to whose great exertions the success of the day was attributed,[c] and who thereupon held the office of Sheriff of Beds and Bucks for five years,[d] but were afterwards divided among the heirs female. This manor was allotted to Amicia, wife (*sic*) of William de Beauchamp of Bedford.[e] William de Monte Caniso or Monchensi, who had married Beatrice, one of the coheirs, had livery of her purparty of the lands of Beauchamp's inheritance, and died seised of the manor of Bromham, leaving William his son and heir then twenty years of age.[f] Upon the death of this latter William, in the 30th King Edward I., Walter de Gloucester the King's escheator was ordered to seize all the lands and tenements of which William de Monchensi had been possessed, as the inheritance of Beatrice de Beauchamp, formerly his wife.[g]

John, second Baron Mowbray, grandson of Maud de Beauchamp, another coheiress of that family, was summoned to Parliament from 26th August, 1307, to 5th August, 1320, having been born on the 2nd November, 1286. This nobleman, whilst under age, was actively engaged in the Scottish wars of King Edward I., and had livery of all his lands before he attained majority, in consideration of those services. In the ninth Edward II. (1315-16), he paid one hundred pounds for the King's license to alienate his manors of Hammes, Wotton, Wylinton, Scotfald, Bromham, Lincelade, and Riassh,[h] which William de Brewos had;[i]

[a] The barony of Bedford is called "a capital honor."—Testa de Nevill, p. 248b.
[b] Vide Biddenham.   [c] Beauties of Eng. and Wales, vol. i. p. 13.   [d] Lipscomb.
[e] Cal. inq. p. m. 6 Edw. I. vol. i. p. 63, nu. 30.   [f] Ib. 14 Edw. I. nu. 27.
[g] Abbrev. Rot. Orig. 30 Edw. I. nu. 8.   [h] ? Kiassho (Keysoe).
[i] Abbrev. Rot. Orig. 9 Edw. II. vol. i. p. 230, nu. 21. Cal. inq. ad q. damnum. William de Braose

this might have been a precaution to save the estate, for we find that he afterwards took part in the insurrection of Thomas Earl of Lancaster, and, being made prisoner with that nobleman and others at the battle of Boroughbridge, was immediately hanged at York (15th Edward II.,) when the lands in his possession were seized by the Crown, and Aliva his widow, with her son, imprisoned in the Tower of London. This lady, who was daughter and coheir of William Lord Braose of Gower, was compelled to confer several manors of her own inheritance upon Hugh le Despenser, Earl of Winchester.

Lady Mowbray married a second husband, and died in the fifth King Edward III. Her son, John Lord Mowbray, died 4th October, 1361, seised of this manor,[a] and was buried in the Grey Friars at Bedford. His son John, summoned to Parliament from 14th August, 1362, to 20th January, 1366, as "John de Mowbray of Axholme," married Elizabeth, daughter and heiress of John Lord Segrave, by whom he had issue. Elizabeth, wife of John de Mowbray of Axholme, was possessed of land, &c., in Bromham, Biddenham, and elsewhere, as of the barony of Bedford.[b] At a later period, on a partition of the Mowbray property, their interest in Bromham was allotted, among other estates, to William Earl of

---

of Gower was Lord Mowbray's father-in-law. At the same time Adam Pigott had license to alienate lands in Bromham. Cal. inq. ad qd. damnum. 9 Edw. II. nu. 189 (p. 248).—Vide Biddenham, Beauchamp's Pedigree. In the Parliamentary Writs, vol. ii. div. 3, p. 367, John Botetourte, John de Mowbray, John de Pateshulle, Walter Teyes, John Picot, William Passelewe of Wawydone, and the Prior of Newenham, are said to be lords of Bromham and Biddenham. It is noticeable that some of the names are different to those, of the same date, given in the Nomina Villarum before quoted in a note at p. 3.

[a] Esc. 35 Edw. III. nu. 10.[1]   [b] Ib. 50 Edw. III. nu. 44.

---

[1] After this date, and until the partition of their estates, the *manor* of Bromham does not occur among the possessions of the Mowbrays, though they retained certain rights. Thomas Mowbray, Duke of Norfolk, was seised of Bedford Castle, &c. and of rents and services in Bromham, and in other places in Bedfordshire not in this hundred.—Esc. 22 Rich. II. nu. 101, and 1 Hen. IV. nu. 71A. Patron of Newenham Priory, founded by the Beauchamps.—Dugd. Mon. Ang. (ed. 1830 by Caley, Ellis, and Bandinel, vol. vi. pp. 376, 377). Previous to the coronation of King Henry IV., by his attorney Sir Thos. Grey, Knt. he claimed and had the office of almoner.—Beauties of England and Wales, i. p. 13.

Thomas Mowbray, Earl Marshal, had the like privileges in Bromham.—Esc. 8 Hen. IV. nu. 76.

John de Mowbray, Duke of Norfolk, was possessed of Bedford Castle with its members; also of six fees situated in this parish and in nine other places in Bedfordshire held by the Abbot of Wardon; of three parts of one knight's fee by the Prior of Caldwell, who also held other premises by the same service in Bromham and Skelton. This nobleman also had the advowson of the Priories of Newenham and Chicksand.—Ib. 11 Hen. VI. nu. 43.

John de Mowbray Duke of Norfolk was seised of divers fees and parts of fees in Bromham, Bletsoe, Radwell, Thurle, Sharnebrook, Turveye, and elsewhere in co. Beds.—Ib. 1 Edw. IV. nu. 46.

Nottingham, afterwards Marquis of Berkeley, grandson of Thomas Mowbray Earl of Nottingham, created Duke of Norfolk in the twenty-first Richard II.[a]

In the meantime, the lordship of Bromham passed into the family of Latimer. In the seventh Richard II. we find this manor enumerated amongst the possessions of Elizabeth, wife of William de Latimer, chevalier.[b] Elizabeth, only daughter and heir of William Baron Latimer of Danby, was the second wife of John Lord Neville of Raby; they had five manors in this county besides this lordship, with twenty knight's fees pertaining to the same in Sharnebroke, Pabenham, Hynewike, Carlton, Turveye, Stachesdon, Bromham, Bidenham, Bolnehurste, and in twenty-nine other parishes or places in Bedfordshire,—parcel of the barony of Bedford.[c] The Lady (Elizabeth) Neville is stated to have married a second husband, Sir Robert de Willoughby, knight.[d] A Robert de Wylughby, chevalier, and Elizabeth his wife, were possessed of rent in Bromham, and of manors and lands in this county.[e]

John de Neville, or Latimer, succeeded to this estate,[f] and was summoned to

[a] Lysons. See Pedigree of Mowbray and Berkeley.—Nichols, Leic. vol. ii. pt. i. p. 263. Act 19 Henry VII. c. 30 (reciting part of the 7th Henry VII. c. 16, whereby John late Duke of Norfolk and Thomas Earl of Surrey, with others, were attainted of High Treason). Petition by Maurice Berkeley, brother and heir of William late Marquis Berkeley and Earl of Nottingham, reciting agreement of partition made between John late Duke of Norfolk, father to Thomas Earl of Surrey, and the said William late Marquis then Earl Marshall and of Nottingham, whereby the said Marquis had (*int. al.*) the " Castell of Bedford and the Lordshippes and Maners of Scotfeld, Haunce, and Bromeham, in the Counte of Bedford, which were of the seid John sometime Duke and of other persones, to his use." To have, hold, &c. to the same Earl Marshall and of Notyngham according to the seid partition.

" Provided always, that this present Act in eny ways extend not to the castell of Bedford, nor to the manors of Bedford, Haunce, Bromeham, nor Scotfold, with the appurtenaunce, in the counte of Bedford, nor to any manors, &c. of w^h Sir Reignold Bray, knyght, or any other person or persons to the use of the same Sir Reignold and of his heirs or otherwise, to perform his last will, were or be seised in fee simple fee tayle for term of life or otherwise in demeane, remaynder, reversion, or s'vice; nor that the same Act in anywise extend or be prejudicial to William Sondys, knt. and Margerie his wife, cosyn and heir to the s^d Sir Reignold, nor to the heirs of the s^d Margerie of, for or to the said castle, &c.

" Provided always, that this Act in nowise extend or be prejudicial unto John Vynter of Cardington, nor to his heirs, for all tenements, &c. and lete in Cardington, p'cell of the manor of Hawnes named in the same Act, w^h the s^d John Vynter purchased of Sir Regnold Bray, kt."

[b] Esc. 7 Rich. II. nu. 52.   [c] Ib. 12 Rich. II. nu. 40.
[d] Dugd. Bar. vol. ii. p. 33. Collins, Peerage, vol. vi. pp. 599, 600.   [e] Esc. 20 Rich. II. nu. 54.
[f] Esc. 9 Hen. VI. nu. 24.

By Indenture dated 12 June, 21 Hen. VIII. the manor of Willington, co. Beds, with its appurtenances (except the patronage and foundation of Newnham and Chicksand), was conveyed to John Gostwyke by Thos. Duke of Norfolk and Lady Elizabeth Duchess of Norfolk.—*Act concerning the assurance of said sale*, 28 *Hen. VIII.* c. 47.

Parliament, in right of his mother the said Lady Elizabeth, as Baron Latimer, from 25th August, 1404, to 27th November, 1430, in which year he died without issue, whereupon his estates, being entailed, came, for the most part, to Ralph Earl of Westmerland, his elder half-brother,[a] the inheritance whereof, by a special feoffament, was given by that Earl to Sir George Neville, his younger son by a second wife. This manor, however, must have been excepted, at least for a time, for it was next in the possession of Matilda Countess of Cambridge,[b] who seems to have been followed in the seigniory by Thomas Wake, armiger, who died 10th December, 1458.[c] The above-named Sir George Neville was summoned to Parliament as Baron Latimer the 25th February, 1432;[d] he married the Lady Elizabeth, third daughter of Richard Earl of Warwick (coheir to her mother, Elizabeth Berkeley),[e] and died 30th December, 1469, seised of Bromham manor,[f] leaving his grandson Richard (son of Sir Henry Neville, who died before succeeding to the honours,) his next heir, aged about two years.[g] This lordship, together with those of Wotton, Dylwyke, Cardington, and Ronhale, "held by the service of performing the office of Almoner at the King's coronation," was next in possession of Johanna, wife (or widow) of the said Sir Henry Neville."[h]

[a] John Lord Latimer is said to have sold the barony of Latimer to his brother Ralph, Earl of Westmerland. Elizabeth, sister and heir of this John Neville Lord Latimer, married Sir Thomas Willoughby, and their great-grandson Sir Robert Willoughby Lord Brooke, steward to King Henry VII. "tried to be Lord Latimer but went without it."—Harl. 1233, f. 130, 162.—See account of the dispute touching the barony of Latimer.—Banks' Peerage.

[b] Esc. 25 Hen. VI. nu. 21. Widow of John Lord Latimer.—Burke.

[c] Ib. 37 Hen. VI. nu. 19.—John Wake, Esq. of Stoughton, living 1480, was an executor of the will of Elizabeth Lady Latimer.—See her Testament, N. T. V. p. 360.—Vide Biddenham, Beauchamp's Pedigree.[1]

[d] Created Lord Latimer by a new title.—Banks.

[e] In reference to a future note respecting the families of Boeles, Pippard, Fermband, and Wydeville, see this lady's descent from Wedon, Pipard, and de Insula or L'Isle (as partly conjectured) in Lipscomb's Hist. Bucks, under Wingrave.

[f] Esc. 9 and 10 Edw. IV. nu. 28.　　[g] Dugd. Bar.　　[h] Esc. 9 and 10 Edw. IV. nu. 52.

Besides the manor there were three other fees in Bromham at the general survey:—

Count Eustace Fee. Boulogne Honor. In the half-hundred of Bochelai, Count Eustace possessed in Bruneham one hide and a half of land, which Ernulf de Arde held of him. There was land for one plough-team and a half, and the like proportion of pasture. It was then worth ten shillings, when he received it twenty shillings. In the time of King Edward, Aluuold and Leuric, men of the King, held this land and

---

[1] Thomas Wake of Blisworth, chevalier, and Alice his wife, enfeoffed William Marschal, parson of M'shton, and John de Tudenham parson of the church of Blisworth, with lands in Cardington and Bromham.—Rot. Orig. 46 Edw. III. nu. 36. (John Mareschal of Wotton held certain premises in Bromham for John Mareschal and Johanna his wife.—Esc. 27 Edw. III.) Matilda, wife of Thomas Wake, chevalier, had premises at Bromham.—Esc. 3 Henry VI. nu. 20.

The Domesday possessor of the mesne lordship was Serlo de Ros, and in following its history many of the same names recur as in the preceding parish. In the thirteenth century certain lands with appurtenances pertaining to Beauchamp's fee here were in three distinct estates. Walter de Swinesheved[a] and could dispose of it at pleasure. (Domesday, p. 211.) Baldwin de Ghines, Earl of Ghines, living 1 King John, had the honor of Boulogne; he is said to have married a daughter of Ernulph de Ardres, with whom he had Tolleshunt, co. Essex. Robert de Ghines, uncle of Ernulph Earl of Ghines, purchased the honor of Chokes or Cioches and Gayton, which he sold in the 33rd King Henry III. (Baker's Northamptonshire, vol. ii. p. 273.) In the 7th King Edward I, William Passelewe held of this land one hide, under Baldwin Wake, as of the honor of Boulogne; in demesne were three virgates. Ralph Passelewe was one of the four free tenants. (Hundred Rolls.)

Judith Fee. In the half-hundred of Buchelai, Hugh held in Bruneham of the Countess Judith two hides; there was land for two plough-teams, and they were there, and there were five villans and two bordars, and one mill worth forty shillings, and a hundred eels. It was worth twenty shillings; in the time of King Edward ten shillings. Goduin the herald had this land, and was able to sell it. (Domesday, p. 217).

The King's bailiffs and almoners had one virgate and two parts of a virgate, held by Osiet; this was acquired by encroachment. There was land for one plough-team, which was there. Pasture for half a plough-team. Then worth 10s.; in the time of King Edward, when Istemet held it, absolutely, 5s. (Domesday, p. 219.)

Bartholomew le Blound[1] held half a hide by petit serjeanty, paying annually eighteen pence, yielded to the sheriff of Beds at the will of the King. He had sixteen acres in demesne. Free tenants, William le Ros, William le Freman, Ralph Leecke, and several others of whom four are named. (Rot. Hund. 7 Ed. I). 15 Ed. I., Bertram le Wyle held half a hide in Bromham, by the serjeanty of providing yearly one pair of saddle bows. (Blount's Tenures, 37.)

[a] In the time of King Ed. I. Robert Swynsheved had seven acres in Bromham.—Esc. 22 Ed. I. nu. 92.

John de la March held seventeen acres in this parish as of the barony of Bedford (Rot. Orig. 12 Ed. III. nu. 15. Esc. 12 Ed. III. nu. 9), sixteen of which were next in the possession of Galfridus atte Marche (Esc. 28 Ed. III. nu. 7), whose son and heir John seems to have died under age (Ib. 35 Ed. III. nu. 3); in the 28th King Edward III. John Parentyn, at a Crown rent of xx s. had the custody of one messuage, sixteen acres of arable, one acre of pasture, and viii s. rent in Bromham, which had belonged to the said Galfridus. (Rot. Orig. 28 Ed. III. nu. 6.) Alicia, daughter and heir of Stephen atte Marche, was possessed of a messuage, twenty-nine and a-half acres, one rood of arable land, and one acre of pasture here. (Ib. 35 Ed. III. nu. 18.)

Robert Parentyne of Bromham had a son William, who, in the 7th or 8th King Henry IV., purchased a tenement in Burcester, co. Oxon, opposite the priory gate; in which parish he had afterwards a considerable property, and his family became of note there. William Parentyn of Bromham, and Henry Bowells of Curtlington, made a grant of premises in Oxfordshire to William Pryns, sen. and Ralph ————, by deed dated 27th November, 7 and 8 King Henry IV. Richard Parentyn was prior of Burcester, 4th

---

[1] Blound, Blount, or Blunt, afterwards quartered Bygott, Marshall, Strongbow, Clare, FitzHamon, Peshall (Arg., a cross flory sa., a canton az.), Chetwyne, Carswell, Knightley, Pantolph, Swinerton, Beck, Hastings, Trussell, &c. Harl. 1982, fo. 77.

William Malherbe held one knight's fee in Bromham of the barony of William de Beauchamp of Bedford, and Gilbert Passelewe held half a fee of the said honor; Gilbert Passelewe and William Malherbe also appear to have been coparceners in a tenth part of one knight's fee.[a] The latter inherited the whole or part of his estate from his ancestors, one of whom, in the time of King Richard, had given thirty acres of land and the church of Bromham to Cauldwell Priory.[b] On the extinction of the male line of the Beauchamps, his land

August, 6 King Henry IV. and Nicholas Parentyn, 4 King Henry VI. Reginald Parentyn, witness to a deed dated at Chakynden, 19 King Henry VI.—Kennet, Par. Antiq. pp. 346, 545, 546, 558, 626, 629.

[a] Testa de Nevill (temp. Hen. III.—Edw. I.) p. 248 b. Harl. 313, f. 46.[1]

[b] Rot. Hund. Nigel and David Malerbe; also John Malerbe de Houton and his ancestors were benefactors to Newenham Priory, and John Malerbe was a witness to the Earl of Nottingham's charter to the same.—Dugd. Mon. Ang. vol. vi. p. 374, &c.

Simon Barescot (corrupted to Baskett) of Bedford, was a great patron, and is sometimes called founder of Caldwell Priory. The church of Oakley also belonged to the last-named house.—Ib. p. 391-393.

Adam, Vicar of Ocle and others, for the Priory of Caldwell, held one toft in Bromham.—Esc. 11 Rich. II. nu. 98.

27 King Henry VIII. the value of the estate pertaining to the said priory in Bromham was returned at £12 6s. 11d., issuing out of:—the rectory (£11), temporalities (15s. 11d.), out of the vicarage, or paid by the vicar (11s.) The yearly value of (or out of) Oakley rectory was £12.—Valor Eccl.

In the next year we have an account of the free rents in Bromham belonging to Caldwell Priory, being probably for the whole or part of the thirty acres given by William Malherbe's ancestor.—Ministers' Accounts, co. Bedford, 28 & 29 King Henry VIII. nu. 75:—

By whom payable.	Name of Lands.	Amount. s. d.
Sir John Dyve, Knt.	Pertnolls	0 4½
,,	(1 acre)	0 1
John Fitzjeffereye	(1 acre)	0 1
Vicar of Bromham	(½ acre)	0 1
Churchwardens of Bromham	(1 acre)	0 3
Thomas Russell	-	0 6
,,	-	0 1
Robert Stuckleye	Stuckleys al's Paynters	1 6
Lord Vauxe[1]	(1 messuage)	1 9
John Golestone	Morleys	1 8
Henry Cowp	-	10 0
	Total	16 4½

Temp. Eliz. Rent &c. in Okeley, Bromeham, and elsewhere, parcel of Caldewell, £16 6s.—Lansd. 5, fo. 31.

---

[1] By 27 Hen. VIII. c. 30, "An Acte conc'nyng the assur^{a}unce of c'ten Londs to the Lady Elizabeth

which he or another William held of the heirs[a] of the said barony of Bedford consisted of four hides; in his demesne were twenty-eight acres, he had eighteen acres of pasture, fourteen of wood inclosed, in common with Ralph Passelewe, a right of fishery in the Ouse from "Holme to Brochiseved," and his land was occupied by several customary and free tenants; among the latter by Richard Malherbe and William de Bosco.[b]

To Ralph Passelewe's portion, in the time of King Edward I., which he held immediately of William de Monchensi, belonged a several fishery from Holewell to his court, and a fishery in common from his court to Bidenham bridge. He had ten acres of wood inclosed;[c] Galfridus le Ros, Nicholas Freman, the above-named William de Bosco, and Nicholas Passelewe were among his free tenants. The Prior of Caldwell also held upwards of one virgate of this land of the said Ralph.[d]

William Passelewe was tenant of the third, or de Steyngreve's,[e] portion in this parish, which he held under Alexander Bosoun[f] of John de Steyngreve the chief lord, and it was occupied by two villans, and by William le Ros and eight other free tenants. The said William Passelewe's demesne comprised one hide four

[a] Vide Biddenham—Beauchamp's pedigree.
[b] Rot. Hund. 7 Ed. I.   [c] Inq. p. m. temp. Ed. I.   [d] Rot. Hund. 7 Ed. I.
[e] De Steingreve's interest descended to the de Pateshulls:[1] Sir John, son of Isabella de Steingreve by Simon de Patteshull her first husband, was, on the death of Walter de Tey[2] that lady's second husband, found to be heir to certain rents and premises in Bromham, Wotton, Lincelade, Hoghton Conquest, and to the manor of Knisso, parcel of Bedford barony. Sir William, the son and heir (sometimes called Baron Pateshull) was seised of rent in Bromham,[3] and a William de Pateshull had part of a knight's fee in Stacheden, certain lands in Bromham and Carlton, the manors of Salford and Keysoe, the advowsons of Houghton Conquest and Bletsoe in this county, and the advowsons of Midelton and Colintrowe, co. Northampton.[4]
[f] For the families of Bosoun and Goldington, see Nichols' Leicestershire, vol. ii. pt. 1, p. 132.

Vaulx in recompence of her Joynture":—the manors or lordships of "Clopham, Okely, Carleton, Chillyngton, and Bromeham, with all their members and appurtenances, in the county of Bedford, late belonging to Sir Nicholas Vaux, late Lord Harrowden," were settled on Thomas Lord Harrowden and the said Lady Elizabeth his wife, with saving rights to Sir William Parre, Knt. This, in so far as it regards Bromham, if not the original manor, may have reference to a part thereof, or to the seigniory in one or more of the other fees in this parish, noted at page 33. Anne Vaux, daughter of Thomas Lord Harrowden and the said Lady Elizabeth, married Reginald Bray of Stene.

[1] Vide Biddenham, Beauchamp's pedigree. Abbrev. Rot. Orig. vol. i. p. 87, nu. 6.
[2] Abbrev. Rot. Orig. 18 Ed. II., p. 282. Rot. Chart. 25 Ed. I. Walter de Tey and Isabella his wife are stated to have had part of Bromham manor, they also possessed 518 acres at Waterbeltham. Cal. Rot. Chart. 25 Ed. I., n. xi. p. 128.
[3] Esc. 33 Ed. III., nu. 40.   [4] Ib. 40 Ed. III., nu. 30.

virgates of land.[a] As these Passelewes were seated at Drayton in Buckinghamshire, or were cadets of that family, the following pedigree may not be altogether out of place here. In the time of King Henry III. Robert Passelewe held estates in this county by serjeanty,[b] and Lipscomb says :—"the lands of the Peverells being forfeited in the beginning of the reign of King Henry II. one of their manors in Bucks was afterwards held by grand serjeanty by the Norman family of Passelewe :"[c]—

PASSELEWE or PASLOWE. (Harl. 1982, fol. 61 ; 1396; 1241.)

Arms: Arg. a fesse between three mullets pierced az.

"Note, that Hugh Bigott, son of Roger Earl of Norf. gave to Hamon Paslow certayn landes in Drayton Paslow."

Hamon de Paslowe, 3 Rich. I. (Harl. 1241); of Drayton Paslew (Harl. 1396.)=

Sir Raphe Paslowe son of Hamon, had lands given him in Ireland=Lucy. as appeareth by his charter by Kinge John.

Sir John Pashlow, 12 Ed. I.; 2 Ed. I. (Harl. 1396.)=Margarett.

John Pashlow of Drayton Pashlow, 23 Ed. I. (Harl. 1241), 20 Ed. II. (Harl. 1396), 22 Ed. II.=

Nicholas Pashlow de Draiton, 50 Ed. III. (Harl. 1396.)=Margarett, dau. to Thomas Burghe of Watlesborough, co. Salop (Harl. 1396).

Nicholas Paslowe de Drayton (Harl. 1241).=

Richard Paslowe.=Isabella.   John Passlowe.

Raphe Paslowe, ar. (Harl. 1396.)=Amye (Amicia. Harl. 1396) dau. to Rich. Kynaston of Shropshire.   John Grendon of Grendon, co. Warwick.

Margaret Paslowe, dau. and h. of Raphe.=William Lacon of Cotton, 20 Rich. II.   *Arms:* Or, two chev. gu.

Sir Richard Lacon of Drayton, Brompton=Eliz. dau. and h. of Sir=John Grendon (1st hus.)...... and Buckton (2nd hus.) Hamon Peshall, Knt.   a dau.
William Lacon.=Madelyn Wisham. of co. Staffs. by Alice, John Grendon, wife to
dau. and heir to Robt. ob. s. p. an idiot. Gamell.
Lord of Harley.
Arms: Ar. a cross engr. couped flory sa.

Another branch of the Botelers of Wemme possessed the manor. Sir Philip

---

[a] Rot. Hund. 7 Ed. I. William Pinkeneye and William Passelewe, junr., lords of Hidenham (? Bidenham), co. Bedford.—Parliamentary Writs, vol. ii. div. 3, p. 367.

[b] Harl. 313, fol. 49, 51b.   [c] East Claydon.—Lipscomb, Bucks, vol. i. p. 165.

Boteler, knight, of Woodhall, was lord thereof,ᵃ as was Edward, son and heir of John Boetler,ᵇ to whom succeeded Philip Boteler, armiger.ᶜ

Thomas Wilde, esq., of Bursham, co. Denbigh, was possessed of Bromham in the fifteenth century, his wife Agnes being the daughter and heir of Sir John Ragon of Bromham. The whole or part of the Ragons' estate here came to them through the Widevilles. Sir Reginald Ragon of Baconhoeᵈ in this county, father of Sir John, was sheriff of Beds and Bucks in 1396 and 1402, and was living in 1417; he married Elizabeth, sister and heir of Thomas Wideville, she being also heir to her mother, Alice Mortymer of Grendon, co. Northampton; a John Wideville (probably grandfather to Elizabeth Ragon) had free warren in Bromham, Biddenham, and Hulcote in this county, and in Bollebrickhull and Caldecote, Buckinghamshire, before the year 1367;ᵉ he is, by Willis, conjectured to have obtained his estate at Bow Brickhill by the marriage of Fermband, that family being feudatories of the honor of Gloucester, to which the chief lordship was attached, as was also the case at Biddenham and Hulcote.ᶠ This conjecture seems to be confirmed from the circumstance of Fermband's arms immediately following those of Wideville in Dyve's shield;ᵍ and it is curious to observe how that at Bow Brickhill the Fermbands followed the family of Bocles or Bolle, whilst in this parish a wood and a small close retain the name of "Bowels."ʰ

ᵃ Esc. 8 Hen. V. nu. 78. He also had the manor of Heigham Gobion, through the heiress of Gobion,[1] and an estate at Wrest, and was descended from Raufe Boteler of Pulrebache, Salop (misprinted "Pulesburye" in Boteler's pedigree, under Biddenham), and of Northbury, co. Stafford. Arms: Gu. a fesse counter-compony ar. and sa. between six cross-crosslets of the second. Crest: On a wreath, an arm embowed in armour holding a sword proper.—Clutterbuck's Hist. Herts. vol. ii. p. 475.

ᵇ Esc. 6 Hen. VI. nu. 30.   ᶜ Ib. 31 Hen. VI. nu. 27.

ᵈ Backnoe, now a farm in Bolnhurst and Thurleigh: the house is in the former, but most of the land in the latter parish.

ᵉ 39 and 40 Ed. III Cal. Rot. Chart. p. 185, nu. 16.

ᶠ Vide Biddenham.   ᵍ See pedigree of Dyve.

ʰ Among the benefactors to Newenham Priory, Adam, Robt, and Walter Pippard; Nicholas, son of Simon de Bocles.—Dugd. Mon. Ang. vol. vi. p. 374, &c.

Simon de Borles paid 10s. a-year rent to the Prior of Stafford for two virgates and sixteen acres of land (no place named), the said prior holding by serjeanty.—Harl. 313.

Temp. King John.—John de Boels, disseised of a free tenement in Brechull, Bucks, which Annora, wife of Maubane (? *Bardolf*) was desirous of conveying to her brother John, the son of Henry Boels, their father.—Harl. 301, fol. 155.

---

[1] Henry Wideville of Grafton is said to have married the daughter of Gobion, alias Morena de Yarler. Arms: Ar. three fishes and a bordure engr. sa.—Bridges's Northants, i. p. 300.

Elizabeth, daughter and heir of Agnes Wilde (coheir to her father) by her marriage with Henry eldest son of John Dyve, esq., of Quinton, conveyed Bromham to that family, who made this their principal residence; and, as Baker says, deserted Northamptonshire, where they were formerly seated at Wyke, Brampton, Hollwell, Harleston, and Quinton. Gosceline de Dyve is mentioned among those Normans who had surnames at or before the Conquest,[a] and Dr. Holland, observing on the origin of the family, remarks that in Normandy is a river, a market town, and a Benedictine Abbey of this name.[b]

Temp. King John.—Henry de Bouels, seneschal or steward to Simon de Beauchamp.—Placit. Joh. p. 76.

„ Hen. III.—Thomas Fremond, 30 acres in Temesford, Beds.—Esc. 29, Hen. III. nu. 35.

„ „ William Pipard, 19 Hen. III. descended from .... Wedon.—Lipscomb.

„ Hen. III.-Ed. I.—Hugh de Boeles held half a fee in St'nshale (co. Salop or Stafford) of the barony of Roger de Som'y.—Testa de Nevill, p. 46 b.

„ „ John de Boeles had in demesne, two virgates of land in Stacheden, as of the barony of William de Beauchamp of Bedford.—Ib. p. 248 b.

„ „ Henry de Boeles gave all his lands in Stagsden which he held of Mowbray to Newenham Priory.—Mon. Angl. vol. vi. p. 374.

„ Ed. I.—Richard Fermbond held land of the honor of Wallingford 1292.—Lipscomb.

„ „ John de Wyvill—land south of Trent, of the heirs of Roger de Moubray.—Abbrev. Rot. Orig. 29 Ed. I. Ro. 11.

„ „ John de Boweles summoned from Beds and Bucks to perform Military Service in person against the Scots.—Muster at Berwick-upon-Tweed on the Nativity of St. John the Baptist, 24 June, 29 Ed. I.—Parliamentary Writs, vol. i. p. 489.

„ „ Nicholas Fermbaud, a Justice appointed to hear and determine offences, &c. in Beds and other counties, 33 Ed. I.—Ib. p. 594.

„ Ed. II.—John Pippard and Nicholas Fermbrand held Wingrave cum membris, Bucks, before temp. Ed. III.— Lipscomb.

„ „ John de Boweles, one of the lords of Grunhurst cum Ey; Nicholas ffermbaud and Nigel de Saleford, lords of Saleford cum Holecot; Nicholas ffirmbaud, lord of Badelesdone; all in co. Bedford, 9 Edward II.—Parliamentary Writs, vol. ii. div. 3, p. 369.

„ „ (1317), Nicholas Fremband held one knight's fee in Bow Brickhill, Bucks. (Partition of the Honor of Gloucester.—Cardigan MSS.) His son Thomas succeeded him in his Bedfordshire estate.—Placit. 4 Ed. III. p. 43.

„ Ed. III.—John de Boweles, lands, &c., in Wardon (no county named).—Esc. 1 Ed. III. nu. 24.

„ „ Cecilia, daughter of William Bolle de Swynesheved, co. Lincoln. Ib. 6 Ed. III. nu. 62, and 7 Ed. III. nu. 33. Sir John Fermband, patron of the church of Bow Brickhill between 1336 and 1349. (Willis's MSS.)—Lipscomb's Hist. Bucks, vol. iv. p. 51-52.

---

[a] Camden's Remains, p. 3; Guillim, p. 245.
[b] Insertions in the text of Camden. Ducarel's Account of Alien Priories.

The son and heir, Sir John, was sheriff of Beds and Bucks in 1510; he married Isabel, third daughter and coheir of Sir Ralph Hastings, knight, by whom he had two sons and a daughter,—William, heir to his father, John of Quinton, who died without issue in 1545, and Dorothy wife of Richard Wake of Hartwell, from whom the Wakes of Clevedon (baronets) descend. William Dyve, esq. married Anne daughter and heir of Lewis Aprice, of Hanslape, Bucks, and was father of a numerous family; his seven sons were Lewis, Christopher, John, George died 1589, William, Henry died young, and Thomas, the third son, of Bedford, died 1599 and was buried at Bromham; he had married Elizabeth Borne, of Bedford, widow of John West the elder, by whom he had a daughter Honor, who died without issue. Of the daughters, Isabell married Anthony Wood of Collingtree, co. Northampton; Eleanor was wife to George Clopton, of Sudbury in Suffolk; Elizabeth to Francis Downes of Ramplingham, Norfolk; Katherine to George Downes of Bromham; Mary to Thomas Boulles, gent., living 1572; and two others named Anne appear to have died unmarried.

Lewis Dyve, esquire, of Bromham and Quinton, sheriff of Beds and Bucks 37th King Henry VIII., was lieutenant of the town and county of Guynes under his cousin William Lord Grey de Wilton, K.G., 1558, and immediately after the winning of Calais by Francis Duke of Guynes, the town and castle of Guynes

Temp. King Ed. III.—Sir Thomas Fermbrand, knight, sheriff of Beds and Bucks, 1348.—Lipscomb.
,, ,, John Wydevile had free warren in Bromham, Bydenham, and Holcote, Beds, and in Bollebrickhull and Caldecote, Bucks.—Rot. Chart. 39 and 40 Ed. III.
,, ,, John, son of Richard Wydeville, presented to the church of Bow Brickhill, 1372.—Lipscomb, vol. iv. p. 53.
,, Rich. II.—John Wodeville of Grafton Regis, Northants, sheriff of Beds and Bucks, 1383.
,, ,, Thomas Frambald, lord of the manor of Batelesden, Beds.—Esc. 12 R. II. nu. 20.
,, ,, Henry Boeles, witness to a charter of Thomas Mowbray, Earl of Nottingham, &c., to Newenham Priory.—Dugd. Mon. Ang. vol. vi. 374.
,, ,, Thomas de Frambaud of Badlesdon, for John Bygon and Thomas Exton, seised of a certain rent of 10 li.—Esc. 14 R II. nu. 76.
,, ,, Thomas Frambaud, seised of one fee in Batelesdon, held of William, brother and heir of Thomas Earl of Stafford.
,, ,, Thomas Wodevyll, one fee in Bolbirkhull and Caldecote, Bucks, of the same.—Ib. 22 Rich. II. nu. 46.
,, ,, John Wydeville of Bow Brickhill, between 1372 and 1395.—Lipscomb, vol. iv. p. 52.
,, Hen. IV.—Thomas Frambald, co. Beds.—Esc. 5 Hen. IV. nu. 48.

The family of Fermband of Battlesden, co. Beds, represented that county in several Parliaments.—See Lipscomb's Bucks, vol. iii. p. 535, and iv. p. 52.

Freeman and Frenband bore the same arms, viz.:—Gu. a cross between twelve cross-crosslets or.—Burke. This is very similar to the coat for Fermband quartered by Dyve.—See Dyve's pedigree.

were violently besieged by the said duke; the garrison were driven to yield by composition, and all suffered to depart saving the Lord Grey, his lieutenant Sir Lewis Dyve, and other head officers; whereas the said L. Dyve was prisoner to M. de Sacres, who cruelly imprisoned him one whole year and three-quarters, and in the end he was driven to pay for his ransom 600 marks.[a] He appears to have been knighted in the reign of Philip and Mary. In 1566 there issued a writ from the Exchequer to Sir Lewis Dyve to show cause why the manor of Bromham should not be seized into the Queen's hands by reason of an alienation.[b] By his wife Mary, daughter of Sir Walter Strickland, knight, of Yorkshire, he had,—Lewis, one of the thirteen recommended by King Edward VI., 1552, to be elected a knight to serve in Parliament;[c] sheriff of Beds and Bucks 14th Elizabeth, and again of Bedfordshire in the 25th of the same reign, he was in the commission of the peace, and received the honour of knighthood in 1587,[d] but died in the lifetime of his father without leaving issue; John, afterwards knighted, succeeded to Bromham, &c.; and Humfrey, Henry, Mary, Elizabeth, Anne, and Katherine, who are all said to have died without issue. Sir Lewis the elder died in 1592, and was succeeded by his eldest surviving son,—

John, sheriff of Beds the 36th Queen Elizabeth, received the honour of knighthood on the occasion of the visit of King James I. to Salden House, Bucks,[e] in which year he again served the office of sheriff. His first wife was Douglas daughter of Sir Anthony Denny of Hertfordshire, Groom of the Stole to King Henry VIII., by which lady, who died 30th Nov. 1598, he had a daughter, Honour, who died young. Sir John married secondly Beatrice, daughter of

---

[a] Harl. MS. 1500, p. 57.

[b] Jones' Index to the Records in the Exchequer. "Albanye of Bromham," in a list of gentry about this time.—Lansd. 854.

[c] 1552, 7 Edw. VI. The King directed letters to be sent to the sheriffs, recommending therein persons to be elected knights to serve in Parliament. The one directed to the Sheriff of Beds was in commendation of Sir John St. John, Knt. and Lewis Dyve, Esquire. There were no more than thirteen recommendations by the King's letters, and these were for such as belonged to the Court, or were in places of trust about the King.—Strype, Eccl. Memls. vol. ii. p. 295.

1581. Will of John Gostwicke of Willington, esquire. Testator commits all his goods "unto the discretion and bestowing of my wellbeloved wife Elizabeth Gostwicke, and my wellbeloved freinde Mr. Lewis Dive, esquire, whom I make and appoint my full executors." Bequeaths: "to every of my pore tenants that have attended on me in my sickness vi. s. viii. d." Overseers, Mr. Richard Stonley and Mr. Robert Hattley, esquires; witnesses, Robert Hattley, Robert Gostwicke, John Johnsonne Minister.

[d] Morgan's Sphere of Gentry, b. 3.—Lansd. 53, nu. 89, fol. 191.

[e] 28th June, 1603. Salden House was then the seat of Sir John Fortescue.—Nichols's Progresses, &c. of King James the First, 191.

Charles Walcot, of Walcot in Shropshire, by whom he had two sons—Lewis, and John; the latter died young, and was buried at Bromham in 1601. Dame (Beatrice) Dyve was left a widow in 1607, and afterwards married Sir John Digby, knight, who in 1610 is called "lord of the manor of Bromham,"[a] no doubt in right of his wife, and who was created Earl of Bristol 15th September, 1622. From this match descended the Earls of Bristol of that name.[b] His lordship died at Paris in 1652; the Countess in six years after, and was buried at Sherborne in Dorsetshire.[c]

Sir Lewis, knighted at Whitehall, 19th April, 1620, the elder son of Sir John and Lady (Beatrice) Dyve, eventually came into the possession of this estate, and made it his residence when the Earl of Bristol went to live abroad. He was renowned for his loyalty and inviolable attachment to the royal cause, during the great rebellion, and was Colonel of the 11th Regiment of the King's army. Frequent mention is made of his exploits by Whitelock, Rushworth, Seward, Lord Clarendon, and other writers.[d] In the rencounter with the rebels near Worcester he was wounded in the shoulder;[e] in 1642 we hear of him at Hull. The following extract from a letter dated the 25th July of the same year, from Sir Thomas Tyrell of Castle Thorp, near Newport Pagnell, to Alfred Grenville, esq., High Sheriff of Bucks, would make it appear that His Majesty Charles I. rested at Bromham House: "The King hath been at Leicester, but we cannot learn what was done there yett. On Saturday night he came to Huntingdon, where he now is; and we heare that he intends to be at Sir Lewis Dive's house by Bedford, on Wednesday, and so come into the country then for Woodstocke."[f] In October 1643, Colonel Urrey, who revolted from the Parliament, and Sir Lewis Dyve, with a great party of horse, entered Bedford, took Sir John Norris and others prisoners there, and routed 300 of their horse, and sufficiently plundered the town and other parts of that country.[g] Sir Lewis was made Governor of Sherborne Castle

---

[a] Terrier. Articles of covenants and agreements made between Sir John Digby, Knt. then Lord of the Manor of Bromham, and John Stokes, vicar of the same, dated 1610.

[b] See Burke's Dormant and Extinct Peerages.   [c] Baker's Northamptonshire, vol. i. p. 83.

[d] Rushworth, vol. iv. pp. 348, 555; vol. v. pp. 307, 798, 758; vol. vi. pp. 59, 314; Hist. Independency, p. 173; New Monthly Magazine, vol. ii. p. 427; Whitelock, ed. 1742, pp. 109, 165; James Howell's Familiar Letters, edit. 1754, pp. 133, 347, 507; Athen. Oxon. vol. ii. p. 339; Harwood's Hist. Lichfield, 343: Memoirs of Col. Hutchinson, 1808, p. 102; Clarke's Life of James II.; Peerage of Ireland, edit. 1754, vol. i. p. 370.

[e] Clarendon's Hist. part 2, lib. 8.   [f] Seward's Anecdotes, vol. i. p. 320, and vol. ii. p. 510.

[g] Whitelock's Memorials, ed. 1742, pp. 76, 166, 288; Rushworth, vol. vi. p. 61.

in Dorsetshire, and commander-in-chief of that county; being left there with 150 veteran soldiers and some horse, in hopes of recovering Weymouth, then occupied for the Parliament, he surprised and took the middle fort and town, 11th February, 1644;[a] in December of the same year, being at Dorchester with about 300 horse and dragoons, he sent a party to face Lyme Regis, and at their return, Major Sydenham of Poole, with about 60 horse, fell upon them near Dorchester, wounded Sir Lewis, and took some prisoners. On the 15th August in the next year Sherborne Castle was taken by Sir Thomas Fairfax.

A minute account of the various attacks on Sherborne, and subsequent taking of the castle, has been given by Mr. Hutchins in the History of Dorsetshire, and, as another great Bedfordshire name figured there somewhat conspicuously, a few further particulars, gathered from that work, may perhaps interest the reader. "In 1642, the Earl of Bedford and a body of 7,000 foot came to Sherborne, where was the Marquis of Hertford, who had been attempting to raise forces for the King at Wells, whence he was obliged to retire to Sherborne. The Earl of Bedford sat down before the castle 2nd Sept. 1642: while he besieged the castle, tradition reports that the Countess of Bristol, his sister, was then at the lodge. He sent a message to desire her to quit it, as he had orders from the Parliament to demolish it. She immediately went on horseback to his tent, and told him 'if he persisted in his intention, he should find his sister's bones buried in the ruins,' and instantly left him; which spirited behaviour in all probability preserved it."—Hutchins's Dorsetshire, vol. ii. p. 387. Sir Lewis Dyve was half-brother to George Digby, afterwards Earl of Bristol, who married Anne, daughter of Francis Russell, Earl of Bedford; but it must be observed that tradition errs in styling the lady "Countess," because her father-in-law John Earl of Bristol was alive ten years after this date, and her mother-in-law Beatrice Countess of Bristol (widow of Sir John Dyve) did not die till 1658. A portrait of George second Earl of Bristol, by Van Dyck, was in the collection of the Hon. John Spencer. He was born in 1612, and died 1676; his Countess died in 1696, and was buried at Cheneys.[b]

In July 1645 Sir Lewis Dyve was in Sherborne Castle, at the end of which month it was beleaguered by Sir Thomas Fairfax, and, after three ineffectual summons to surrender, Sir Lewis at length, on the 15th August, at two in the morning, sent out a drummer with this letter to Fairfax:[c]

[a] Clarendon's Hist. part 2, lib. 8.
[b] Hutchins, vol. ii. p. 290.
[c] Ayscough's Catalogue of MSS. p. 192, nu 60.

Sir,—I must acknowledge the advantage you have of me, by being master of my walls; and that you may not think me obstinate without reason, I have sent this drum unto you, to let you know, that if I may have such conditions from you as are fit for a soldier and a gentleman with honour to accept, I shall surrender this castle into your hands; otherwise I shall esteem it a far greater happiness to bury my bones in it, and the same resolution have all those that are with me. And give me leave to add this, that your victory will be crowned with more honour by granting it, than you will gain glory by the winning it with the loss of as much blood as it will cost.

I am,
Your servant,
L. Dives.

Sherborn Castle, August 15, 1645.

The answer returned was, "No terms but quarter, and he was not to expect that, except he surrendered immediately." After a siege of sixteen days the castle was taken. Sir L. Dyve's secretary was killed by a shot, Lady Dyve and many other persons being made prisoners. Sir Lewis Dyve and Sir John Strangeways were brought to the bar of the House of Commons, where Sir Lewis refused to kneel till compelled, and with Sir John was committed to the Tower for high treason.[a] On the 14th January, 1647, the House issued orders for " Sir L. Dyve to be kept in safe custody, and for Mr. Solicitor to prosecute him, and Sir John Stowel and Judge Jenkins to Tryal the next Term." On the evening of the 15th our knight attempted to get clear from the custody of Sir John Lenthall, the Speaker's brother, but was retaken; he made a successful escape, however, on the night of the 30th January next year, in company with a Mr. Holben or Holden, the prince's agent, through the house of office in Whitehall, standing over the Thames,[b] "making," says Lloyd, "a cleanly conveyance away from thence, though through a common shore, and so beyond sea, where he continued with his Majesty during his banishment." Sir Lewis published a letter, printed in quarto, 1648, giving an account of his escape out of the Court of King's Bench.[c] He had rendered the King admirable assistance in the counties of Bedford, Bucks, and Dorset; he did also good service in Ireland, and suffered greatly, to the loss of a hundred and sixty-four thousand pounds, which obliged him to sell Quinton and other Northamptonshire estates.[d] On the total ruin of the royal cause in Ireland, Sir Lewis retired to Holland, when he published a long letter on the state of Ireland, addressed to the Lord Marquis of Newcastle, printed at the Hague (1650, quarto).[e] He married in 1624, at Abbotsbury in Dorsetshire, Howarda, daughter of Sir John Strangeways, of Melbury Sanford, widow of Edward Rogers, esq., of Bryanston in the same county, by whom, who died in

---

[a] Hutchins's Dorset, vol. ii. pp. 387—389. [b] Whitelock, 376, 1.
[c] Allibone's Dictionary of Authors, 1859.—Add. MS. 21,067, fol. 93b.
[d] Add. MS. 5490, 1, 2. Lloyd, Mem.

RAGON AN[D DYVE]

(Harl. MSS. 1531, 2109, &c.)   (Lansd. MS. 864)

Arms: Dyve, with fourteen [quarterings]

1 and 16. Gu. a fesse dancetté or between three escallops ar. (Dyve.)
2. Erm. on a chief indented az. three fleurs de lis ar.
3. Ar. three chev. gu. within a bordure sa. bezantée.
4. Vaire ar. and az. three bendlets gu. (Bray.)
  Note.—These are the arms for Longvale, but borne long time for Bray. (Harl. 1095, fo. 147.)
5. Gu. on a bend ar. three martlets sa. (Quinton.)
6. Sa. a chev. betw. three bees ro[...]
7. Gu. a fesse dancettée betw. six [...]
8. Gu. three roaches naiant in pa[...]
9. Ar. a chev. sa. on a chief of th[...]
10. Ar. a chev. betw. three hart's h[eads]
  (Another coat for Ragon,
  heads couped gu.—sixth q[uartering])

Crest: A wyvern with wings endorsed gu. (Harl. 1095, fo. 110.) Another crest for D[yve]

John Wodeville or Wydevile had free warren in Bromham, Bydenham, and Holcote, Beds, and in B[...]

Alice, da. and h. of John Mortymer, of Grendon, Northants.=Richard Wyd[e]
Arms: Erm. on a fesse az. three crosses moline or. | Northants.
(Harl. 2109, fo. 26.) | 33 b.)

Sir Reginald Ragon, of Baconhoe. Sheriff of Beds and Bucks 1396 and=Elizabeth, sist. and h. of Thomas Widvile, of Grafton (Regis), Northants,
1402. Living 1417. (Son of Sir John Ragon, of co. Beds, and of | "neptis" Rich. Widvile com. Rivers, K.G." Living 1441-2. (Heir to her
East Haddon, Northants. Sheriff of Beds and Bucks 1372. Died | mother. Harl. 1531, fo. 33 b.)
1377. Seised of the manor of East Haddon aforesaid, also of the | Baker, in his pedigree of the Widevilles (Hist. Northants, ii. 166)
following in Bedfordshire :—30 acres in Ravensden, Backeno Manor, | gives two sisters besides Elizabeth Ragon, viz., Cath. wife of John Pashley,
6 acres in Bolnhurst, 40 acres in Maldon, and one cottage at Forthe, | and Agnes, wife of William Holt. Bridges also mentions these two, placing
near St. Neot's. Esc. 51 E. III. nu. 24.) | Agnes first, but not the husbands.

Thomas, of Bromham, living 1441, ob. s.p.
Thomas Ragon and John Malyns held lands at Ravensden under John de Moubray, Duke of Norfolk. (Esc. 11 H. VI. nu.
John and Thomas Ragon, of Bromham, among those gentlemen of Bedfordshire who, in the 12th [...]

Agnes, d. and h. of Sir John Ragon. 1st wife.=Thomas Wilde or Wylde, of Bursham, co. Den
 (In Harl. 1241, fo. 129,—Katherine, da. of [...]
 named. The said Katherine m. Willia[m]

William Salisbury, of Horton, Northants, 2nd h. ob. 1498.=Elizabeth, d. and coh. of Thom[as]

Elizabeth.=John Enderby of Stratton, Beds.   Margerett.=Will[...]

Eleanor, d. and h.=Francis Pigott, of Stratton, ar., sheriff of Bed-   Sir John [...]
  fordshire 14 H. VIII. (Harl. 1097, fo. 37 b.)

Thomas Pigott, of Stratton. (Harl. 1531, fo. 33b.) Sheriff of Bedfordshire 5 and 6 P. and M. (Harl. 1097, fo. 37b.)   (Note.—

William Dyve, Esq., of Bromham.=Anne, da. and h. of Lewis ap Rice,   John of Quinton,
  of Hanslope, Bucks.   ob. s. p. 1545.

Sir Lewis Dyve, of Bromham=Mary, da. of Sir Walter Strickland, of Cyser, | Christopher. | Henry, d. young. | Thomas,
and Quinton. Sheriff of | co. York. | John. (? m. Audrey, da. of Thomas | George. Bur. 4 Dec. | of
Beds and Bucks 1544. | Arms: Three escallops, 2 and 1. (On monu- | Wanton, of Gt. Staughton, but ob. | 1589. | Bur.
Bur. 3 Aug. 1592. | ment, north aisle, Bromham church.) | s.p. Harl. 1531.) | William. | 1599.

Douglas, da. of Sir Anth. Denny, of co. Herts,=Sir John Dyve, Knt., of Bromham. 2nd son. Knighted after 1600.=Beatrice, da. of Charl[es]
Groom of the Stole to K. Hen. VIII. 1st wife. | Sheriff of Beds 1593 and 1603. Ob. 1607, bur. 29 Dec. | 1st Earl of Bristol,
Ob. 30 Nov. 1598. Bur. 7 Dec. | "His funeral observed with greater solemnity upon the 19th Jan. 1608." | The Earl of Bristol
"Her funerals were observed with greater | Sir John erected the alabaster tomb at the east end of the aisle in | (Hutchins's Dorset,
solemnity upon the 29th Dec." | Bromham church to commemorate his father, mother, and first wife. | Arms of Walcot:

Honour, d. young.   Sir Lewis Dyve, of Bromham. b. 3 Nov. 1599; bap. 25 Nov. same year. Sponsors, Mr. Franci[s]
  Goodwin, the Lord St. John of Bletsoe, in his own person, and Mrs. Boteler, of Byddenham
  deputy for the Countess of Warwick. m. 1624 at Abbotsbury, Dorset. M.P. for Bridport
  1 Car. I. Sold Quinton temp. Car. I. d. 17 April, 1669 ; bur. at Comb Hay, Somerset.
  (Collinson's Hist. Somerset. vol. iii. p. 336. Baker's Northants, vol. i. p. 83.)

Captain Lewis Dyve, of=Mary, da. | John, b. the last day of April, 1628, and was bap. in a private house in the parish of | Grace, da. of Giles=Fran[...]
Bromham, b. 1633, ob. | of | St. Clement Danes without Temple Bar, London, 13 May. Sponsors: The Lord of | Strangeways, bur. | Do[...]
at Bromham 7 Jan. | Arms: A | Bristol, and Sir John Strangeways, and the Lady Pagett. He d. and was bur. in the | 13 Jan. 1663. 1st | the
1686, bur. 30th Jan. | bend betw. | parish church of St. Clements within a week after. | wife. | est[...]
 | six birds; | | | Br[...]
 | on grave stone at Bromham.

Mary, b. at New Ross, | Anna Maria, b. at | Christiana . . .=Lewis Dyve, Esq., of Bromham 1708—about which time the=Catherine . . .
co. Wexford, 17 Mar. | New Ross, 4 | 1st wife. | estate was sold to the Trevors—b. at New Ross 2 Jan. 1677. | 2nd wife
1674. | May, 1676. | | Other (supposed) members of this family. See note 12 below.

 | Christiana, b. 1700. | Charlotte, b. 1703, | Frances, b. 1704, | Temperance, b. 1705, | James, bap. 1[...]
 | | bap. 14 Aug. | bap. 23 Oct. | bap. 27 Nov. | bur. 2 July, 1[...]

[For notes to the above Pedigree, see back.]

)IVE OR DYVE.

(See also Baker's Hist. Northants, vol. i. p. 82, 163, &c.)

rterings. (Harl. 1531, fo. 48.)

ar. (Sewell.)	11. Ar. a fesse and canton gu. (Woodvile or Wideville.)
ss-crosslets ar. (Longvile.)	12. Gu. a cross betw. twelve crosses fitchée or. (Fermband or Fremband.)
r. (Roche.)	13. Ar. a maunch sa. (Hastings.)
cond three martlets of the first. (Wilde.)	14. Party per pale indented gu. and . . . . a chev. or.
s couped sa. (Ragon.)	15. Ar. on a fesse az. three boar's heads couped or, in chief a lion passant gu.
r. a chev. sa. fretty or betw. three stag's	(Ap Rice.)
er in Dyve's shield. (Harl. 1095, fo. 110.)	

: A horse's leg embowed or (the foot shod az.) betw. two wings gu. (Harl. 1531, fo. 48.)

brickhull and Caldecot, Bucks, 39 and 40 Edw. III. (1366-7.) (Calend. Rot. Chart. nu. 16, p. 185.)

, of Grafton,=Elizabeth, da. of Thomas Beauchamp, of co. Somerset.¹ 2nd
arl. 1531, fo. | wiffe. (Harl. 2109, fo. 26.)
 | Arms: Vaire. (Harl. 1559.)

............, 1st wife. =Thomas Widvile, twice=............, 2nd wife.   Richard, Earl Rivers. (Harl. 1531 and 1559, fo.
Arms: A chev. between married, but ob. s. p. Arms: On a chief a fleur de   196.)
three (?squirrels) sejant, the For whom the brass in lis.³ (Rogers or Fitz Rogers,   Note.—Baker, Bridges, and Hasted each differ
two in chief respecting each the chancel of Brom- of co. Dorset. Ar. on a chief as to the ancestry of Richard Wideville, first Earl
other.³ (Holt bore, Ar. a chev. ham church, circ. 1435. or a fleur de lis gu. Berry. Rivers. Compare Baker's Northants, vol. ii. p.
gu. between three squirrels   See also Hutchins's Dorset, 166 ; Bridges' Northants, vol. i. p. 300 ; Hasted's
sejant or. Berry.)   vol. i. p. 87.)   Kent, vol. ii. pp. 97, 98.

John, of Bromham. (Sir John Ragon, Knt. Harl. 1531.)=

ry VI., could dispend £10 by the year. (Fuller's Worthies, Beds.)

gh. m. 2ndly Ancharet, d. and h. of H. ap Jevan, by whom he had two daughters.
omas Wilde, is placed in the pedigree as sister to Elizabeth Dyve, but neither of Thomas Wilde's wives are
Brereton, of Bursham, and their descendants quartered Corbet, Peshall, Wilde, &c.)

Wilde, heir to her mother,=Henry Dyve, Esq. of Bromham, jur. ux., eldest son of John Dyve, of Harleston, North-
 | ants, by Eliz. his wife, da. of George Longvile, of Lit. Billing, in that county, by Eliz.
 Cowper, of Horton. | his wife, the da. and h. of John Baron Roche, in Wales.

e, Knt., of Bromham. Knighted after 1510, in which year he was Sheriff=Isabel, second dau. and coh. of Sir Rafe Hastings, Knt.,
 of Beds and Bucks. Bur. 3 Nov., 1535.⁶ captain of the castle and town of Guynes, 3rd brother
omas Widvile's brass in the chancel of Bromham church was re-appropriated to William Lord Hastings, Chamberlain to King
to commemorate this knight, his mother, and his wife.) Edw. IV.

Dorothy, m. Richard Wake, of Hartwell, bur. at Roade, Northants.
A quo the Wakes of Clevedon Baronets.

son,=Eliz. da. of . . . . Isabell, m. Anthony Wood, of Collingtree, Northants. Anne.
dford. | Borne, of Bedford. Eleanor, m. George Clopton, of Sudbury, Suffolk. Mary, m. 28 Aug. 1572,³ Thomas Boulles, gent., whose
Nov. | wdw. of John West, Eliz. m. Fran. Downes, of Ramplingham, Norfolk, gent. da. Dorothy was bur. at Bromham, 3 Aug. 1578.⁸
 | the elder. Katherine, m. George Downes, of Bromham. Anne.

alcot, of Walcot, Salop. 2nd wife. m. 2ndly, Sir John Digby, Lewis,⁷ Sir (Knt.) Mary.
whom she left issue, and died 1658. Bur. at Sherborne, Dorset. ob. v. p. Eliz.   Honor, ob. s. p.
Paris 16 Jan. 1652-3. (Baker's Northamptonshire, vol. i. p. 83.) Humfrey. }ob. s. p. Anne. }ob. s. p.
ii. p. 290.)   Henry. Kath.
a chev. erm. betw. three chessrooks sa. (Harl. 1241, fo. 98.)

Iowarda, da. of Sir John Strangeways, of   John, b. 25 July, bap. on Sunday, 9 Aug.
Melbury Sanford, Dorset, wdw. of Edward   1601. Sponsors : Lewis Henry Lord Mor-
Rogers, Esq. (ob. 1623, æt. 21, s. p.) ; bur.   daunt, William Lord Compton, and Lady
24 Feb. 1645.⁸ ᵃ   Ratcliff, of Elstow. Bur. 12 Feb. 1602.⁸

. 4 Jan. 1632, at Melbury,=Theophila, da. of Dr. John John, ob.=Frances, da. of Sir Robert Jane, bur. 20 Aug. 1639.⁸ Beatrix, bap.
bap. 26 June. Sponsors :   Hacket. (MS. Cooper.) 1692.¹¹ Wolseley, of Wolseley, Grace, second wife to George Hussey, of at Melbury
of Bedford, Arthur Chich- M. 14 Dec. 1665.⁸ ¹⁰ Clerk of co. Staff. m. 29 April, Marnhull, co. Dorset, Esq. (Collinson), by Sampford,
nd Beatrice Countess of   Lichfield Cath. bur. 24 the Privy 1673, at St. Chad's, Lich- whom she had issue. (See Hutchins's Hist. 1625, ob.
Bur. 6 Mar. 1685.¹⁰   July, 1688.⁸ Council. field, ob. 1702.¹¹ Dorset, vol. ii. p. 397.) v. p.

, b. 4 May, Grace, b. 8 June, Lewis, b. 19 Sept. Frances (dau.), John, d. 25=Dorothy, d. and b. of Lewis. Charlotte, m. William
,bur. 2 Jan. bur. 25 Oct. 1666, bur. 28 b. 24 Aug. Jan. 1769. Walter Aston, of Mill-   Clayton, Lord Sundon,
).⁸   1661.⁸ June 1667.⁹ 1667.⁸   wich, co. Stafford.   and d. s p. 1741-2.

John of Ranton Hall, Staffs.,=Anne Dorothy, da. of Hugh   Charlotte, Maid of Honour to the Princess of Wales ;
Capt. in the Guards.   Montgomery, esq., m. Aug. 2nd wife to Samuel last Lord Masham, ob. s. p. 21 May
     1737.   1773, at 61 ; bur. at Laver, near Ongar, Essex.

Two sons, d. s. p.   Charlotte. m. 1759.=John Edmondes, esq.

Charlotte Edmondes. m. Llewellin Traherne, and had a son, the late
Rev. John Montgomery Traherne, F.R.S. and F.S.A., d. 1860.

NOTES TO THE PEDIGREE OF DIVE.

[1] A cadet of the Beauchamps of Hache. Thomas Beauchamp, by Elizabeth Carmion his wife, father of the above-named Elizabeth Wydville, was ... of Thomas, and Elizabeth, dau. of Randall Pettit, and grandson of John Beauchamp, Baron of Hache, temp. K. Edw. I., by Johanna Chenduit, ... ose elder son John, 2nd Lord Beauchamp, of Hache, was summoned to parliament from 24 Aug. 1336 to 24 Feb. 1343. (Harl. 1559, fo. 196.)

[2] Baker, the Northamptonshire historian, took this word, which is contracted to "nep." in some MSS., to signify "nephew," and, consequently, ...ught he had been misled by a pedigree of Vincent's.

[3] Arms on Thomas Wideville's brass in the chancel at Bromham; engraved for Lysons' Bedfordshire.

[4] For the family of Wilde or Wylde, see Nash's History of Worcestershire. From Richard, 3rd son to Wyld of Warwickshire, descended (5th in ...cent) Edmund Wylde, of Houghton Conquest, Beds. Kemsey, co. Worc. and Glasley, Salop. Ob. unm. 15 Dec. 1695, æt. 77. (Nash, vol. ii. p. 330.)

[5] From this match also descended Mary, wife of William Baron Parr of Horton, to whom she brought that estate. (Nash, Burke, &c.)

[6] Bur. at Bromham.

[7] Lewis Dyve, of Bromham, Sheriff of Beds and Bucks 16 Eliz. (Harl. 1097, fo. 37 b) and 26 Eliz.

[8] Bromham Register.

[9] Over one of the Vicars' stalls (not assigned to Prebends) in Lichfield Cathedral. (Francis Dive Armig. F.F.) (Kennett's Chron. p. 865.)

[10] 1670, Nov. 16. John Hacket, Lord Bishop of Lichfield and Coventry, bur. (Register of the Close, Lichfield.)

[11] Bur. in St. James, Westminster. Stowe's Lond. B. 6, p. 83, edit. 1720.

[12] 1733, February. Miss Sarah Dives, dau. of Col. Dives, now beyond sea, appointed dresser to the Princesses Mary and Louisa.
—— March 26. Death of Miss Dives, 2nd dau. of John Dives, Esq., one of the Under Tellers of the Exchequer.
—— Major Mardour, to be Lt.-Col. of the 2nd Troop of Horse Guards in room of Lewis Dives, Esq., resigned.
—— Miss Dives appointed one of the Dressers to the Princess of Orange.
—— Ensign Dives promoted to Lieut. in the Coldstream Regiment.
1737, July. William Dive, Esq., married to Miss Holden, of Surrey.
—— August. Captain Dives, 2nd Regiment Guards, married to Miss Montgomery, of Yorkshire.
1740, Sept. 9. The Lady of Colonel Dives, of a son and heir.
—— Naval promotion, Lieutenant Henry Dives, of the Rupert's Prize.
1745, June 17. The Rev. Dr. Tomard, married to Miss Dives, Maid of Honour to the Princesses Amelia and Caroline.
1758 Promotion of Lewis Dive, Esq., Ensign 2nd Regiment Guards.
1769, Jan. 25. Died, John Dive, Esq., of Queen's Square.
1772, Oct. 29. —— John Dive, Esq., of Hertford Street, May Fair.
1812, July 12. —— Mrs. Dive, at the residence of her son. Lewis G. Dive, 3, Tavistock Street, Bedford Square. Aged 70.
(Gent's Mag. vols. iii. iv. vii. x. xi. xv. xxviii. xxxix. xlii. lxxxii.) (Court Guide 1819, &c.)

February 1645, and was buried here, he had issue, John, died young; Francis, next heir, born 1632, at Melbury, Dorset, married first, Grace, daughter of Giles Strangeways, who died 13th January, 1663, having had issue a son and daughter, who both died in infancy. Francis married secondly, 14th December, 1665, at Lichfield Cathedral, Theophila, daughter of Bishop Hacket,[a] by whom, who died in 1688, he had a son Lewis, born in 1666, and died the next year, and a daughter, Frances, born 24th August, 1667. In 1661 he joined his father in conveying Ragons Manor in East Haddon, co. Northampton, to Sir Justinian Isham, Bart.,[b] and, dying in March 1685, was buried in the chancel here. Lewis (Captain), born 1640, succeeded his brother Francis at Bromham. Another John, married, 29th April, 1673, Frances, daughter of Sir Robert Wolseley, of Wolseley, co. Stafford, and had issue. One daughter, Jane, was buried here, 20th August, 1639, and another, Grace, was second wife to George Hussey of Marnhull, co. Dorset, esq.,[c] and left issue. Beatrix, the eldest child, died in her father's life-time.

A good portrait[d] of this gallant soldier was in the possession of the late Lewis George Dive, esq. Sir Lewis died 17th April, 1669, and was buried at Combe Hay, co. Somerset, leaving three sons and one daughter surviving.[c] Francis, the eldest son, died as above stated in March 1685, without leaving male issue, when this estate devolved to his brother,—

Captain Lewis Dyve, born 1640, who was either quartered or settled at New Ross, in the county of Wexford, and only survived his brother Francis ten months, being buried here 30 h January, 1686. By Mary his wife he had issue, with two daughters, Mary a Anna Maria, both born at New Ross, a son, Lewis Dyve, esquire, of Bromha ., so styled in a terrier dated 1708;[e] who by Christiana, his first wife, had a daughter born 1700, named after her mother; by Catherine, his second wife, he was father of three other daughters, viz., Charlotte, born 1703, Frances, 1704, and Temperance, born in 1705; and one son James, baptized and buried in July 1708.

About the year 1708-9 Bromham was purchased by Sir Thomas Trevor, a member of the Inner Temple, of an ancient and knightly family, descended from

[a] MS. Cooper. John Hacket, D D., Archdeacon of Bedford, afterwards Bishop of Lichfield and Coventry. Walker's Sufferings of the Clergy (Lond. 1714) p. 44, 45.

[b] Baker's Northamptonshire, vol. i. p. 163.

[c] Inscription on Sir ewis Dyve's monument.—Collinson's Hist. Somerset, vol. iii. p. 336.

[d] There is a private plate of this picture engraved by Philip Audinet at the expense of the late Rev. John Montgomery Traherne.

[e] "Lewis Dyve, the present Lord of the Manor."—Terrier, 1708.

John Trevor of Brynkinalte in Denbighshire, who died in 1495. He was knighted by King William III. in October 1692. After filling the offices of Solicitor and Attorney General, Sir Thomas was called to be a Serjeant-at-Law, 29th June in the last year of King William's reign, and on the accession of Queen Anne appointed Lord Chief Justice of the Common Pleas. On the 1st January 1712, Her Majesty called him up to the House of Peers by the title of Baron Trevor of Bromham; in the 12th King George I. he was appointed Lord Privy Seal, and one of the Lords Justices of Great Britain; in 1730 he became Lord President of the Council. He was also F.R.S., and a Governor of the Charter House. By his first wife Elizabeth, daughter and coheir of John Searle, esq. of Finchley, he had two sons, Thomas second, and John third, Baron. By his second wife Anne, daughter of Robert Weldon, esq., of London, widow of Sir Robert Bernard, bart., of Brampton, Hunts, he had issue Robert, who eventually succeeded to the title and estate; Richard, Bishop of Durham, died 9th June 1771, aged 64; and Edward; the two younger sons dying without issue. This eminent person died in the 72nd year of his age, 19th June, 1730, being buried here on the 1st July,[a] and was succeeded by his eldest son, Thomas, second Lord Trevor, who departed this life without leaving male issue[b] 22nd March, 1753, when his only brother of the whole blood,

John became third Baron; he was also bred to the law. Admitted a pensioner of Corpus Christi or Benet College, Cambridge, 1st May, 1711. He became King's Counsel, and on 5th November, 1724, was appointed one of the Judges for the Principality of Wales; in 1741 and 1747 he was M.P. for Woodstock. He died at his house in Berkeley Square[c] in 1764. His wife was Elizabeth, daughter of the celebrated Sir Richard Steele, a lady who inherited much of her father's abilities,[d] by whom he had an only child Diana, born 10th June, 1744. His lordship thus dying without male issue, 27th September, the year above-mentioned, the title and estate of Bromham devolved on his half-brother,

---

[a] The funeral took place about eight o'clock in the evening, all his sons attending; the pall-bearers were Sir John Chester, Sir Rowland Alston, Mr. Orlebar, Mr. Cater, Mr. Lounds, and Mr. Beacher. Add. MS. 21,067, fol. 15, from the Diary of the Reverend Benjamin Rogers, which contains the following entry: "1733, Oct. 2. Told of my good Lady Dow. Trevor's misfortune, who, as she was walking in son Sir John Barnard's park at Brampton, she fell down and put her shoulder out, and broke a bone her wrist; happened Sept. 25."

[b] His only daughter was married to the Earl of Sunderland, who became Duke of Marlborough. Lady Grace's birthday used to be observed at Bromham with great festivity and rejoicing.—Rogers' Diary.

[c] Add. MS. 21,067, fol. 57, 194. Collins says "at Bath."

[d] Master's Hist. of C. C. Coll. Camb. p. 407, and British Chronologist. i. 93.

TREVOR

Edmondson's Baronagium; Burke's Extinct and Dormant Peerages, &c.; Lipscomb's Hist.

Arms[a] of Trevor, Baron of Bromham: Per bend si

Crest: Upon a chapeau gules turned up ermine, a

Supporters: Two wyverns reguardant sable.

Motto: Stat Lege Corona.

(Monumen

Sir John Trevor, son and heir of Sir John o Trevallyn, one of the principal Secretarie of State, and a P. C. temp. Car. II., ol v. p. 28 May, 1672.

Elizabeth, da. and coh. of John Searle, Esq. of Finchley, 1st wife. *Arms:* Ar. on a fesse betw. three crescents gu. as many fleurs-de-lis or. = **Sir Thomas, 2nd son, cr. Baron Trevor of Bromham, 31 Dec. 1711, ob. 19 June, 1730, bur. 1 July.[b]** (Bromham regist.) = **Anne, da. of Robert Weldon,** Esq. of London, widow of Sir Robert Bernard, Bart., 2nd wife.[b] bur. 13 Dec. 1746. (Bromham regist.) | John co. husl.

...omas, 2nd Bar. Trevor, ob. 22 ... bur. 29 March, 1753.[b] (Bromham regist.) = **Elizabeth, da. of Timothy Burrell,** Esquire, of Cuckfield, a coh. *Arms:* Vert, three escutcheons ar., each with a bordure engr. or. | **John, 3rd B. Trevor, formerly K.C. and M.P., and a Welsh Judge, m. 31 May, 1731,[c] ob. 27 Sept. 1764, æt. 69.** (Add. MS. 21,067, fo. 15.)[b] = **Elizabeth, da. of Sir Richard Steele, a coh., d. in Dec. 1796.[e]** *Arms:* Ar. a bend counter-compony az. and erm. betw. two lion's heads erased gu., on a chief az. three billets arg. | **Anne. Lætitia, m. Peter Cock, Esq. of Camberwell. Elizabeth.** | **Robert, 4th B. Trevor, b. 1718,[c] assumed the name of Hampden in addition to and after that of Trevor. Cr. Visct. Hampden of Hampden, Bucks, 14 June, 1776, m. in 1743, ob. 22 Aug. 1783. This nobleman and his descendants bore the arms of Hampden in the 1st and 4th quarters, and those of Trevor in the 2nd and 3rd.** = **Constantia de ..bert, da. of Baron Von ..ningen, in ..land.**

..izabeth Trevor, only child, m. 23rd May, 1732,[d] Charles Earl of Sunderland, afterwards Duke of Marlborough. | **Diana Trevor, only child, b. 10 June, 1744.**

..omas Trevor Hampden, 5th Baron and 2nd Viscount, m. 1st, in 1768, Catharine, d. of General David Græme; and 2ndly, 12th June, 1805, Jane Maria Brown, sister to Lady Wedderburn, but ob. s p. 1824. Will proved the same year. | **John Trevor Hampden, 6th Baron and 3rd Viscount, b. 24 Feb. 1748-9, m. 1773 Harriet, only da. of Rev. Daniel Burton, D.D., Canon of Christ Church, Oxford, ob. s.p. 1824.** | **Maria Constantia Trevor Hamp Henry Howard, 12th Earl of S..shire, d. in childbed 1767. Anne Trevor Hampden, d. unm. 1**

George Talbot, 3rd Baron Dynevor, b. 8 Oct. 1765, resumed his paternal name of Rice 1817, m. 20 Oct. 1794, ob. = **Frances To.. 3rd da. of 1st Visct.**
Arms: 1 and 4. Ar. a chev. sa. between three ravens ppr. (*Rice.*) 2. Gu., a lion ramp. within a bordure engr. or, a crescent for difference. (*Talbot.*) 3. Ar., two chev. sa. between three trefoils slipped vert. (*De Cardonnel.*)
Motto: Nihil alienum. (Collins' Peerage.)
Supporters: Dexter, a griffin per fesse or and az. wings addorsed and inverted, the tail between the legs; Sinister, a talbot arg. ears erm. collared flory counter-flory gu. and charged on the shoulder with a trefoil slipped vert.

George Rice Rice-Trevor, 4th Baron Dynevor, D C.L., b. 5 Aug. 1795, m. 27 Nov. 1824, d. at Malvern, Oct. 1869, bur. at Barrington, co. Gloucester. *Arms:* Quarterly, 1st and 4th, Trevor; 2nd and 3rd, Rice. *Crests:* 1 Trevor; 2 Rice; supporters as 3rd Baron. Motto: Secret et hardi. Or, Secret and hardy. (Burke.) = **Frances, eldest da. of Lord Charles Fitzroy.** | **Frances. Cecil. Harriet Lucy. Caroline Mary. Katharine Sarah. Maria Elizabeth.** | **Harriet Ives, da. of D. Raymond Barker, Esq., m. 1830, ob. 1854, 1st wife.** = **Rev. Francis William Rice, Vicar of Gloucester, b. 1804; succeeded to 5th Baron Dynevor at the death o the 4th Lord.** *Arms:* 1 and 4, Rice; 2, Talbot; 3, d *Mottoes:* Humani nihil alienum. hardi. N.B. The trefoil on the porter. (Lodge.)

..ances Emily Rice-Trevor, m. 1 May, 1848, ob. 26 Nov. 1863. = **Edward Ffolliott Wingfield, Esq. (Captain 2nd Life Guards) of Maids Moreton, Bucks, b. 8 Aug. 1823, ob. 26 Sept. 1865.** | **Caroline Elizabeth Anne Rice-Trevor.** = **Sir Thomas Bateson, Bart.** | **Selina Rice-Trevor, m. 12 Nov. 1862.** = **William, Earl of Longford.** | **Eva Gwenlian Rice-T d. 28 July, 1842, æt. Elianore Mary Rice-Tr**

---

[a] Trevor quarters: Madoc, Lord of Mawddwy, Ap Elider, Cambré, Ap Griffith, Ap Rhys, &c. Some members of
[b] Buried at Bromham. (Parish Register.) [c] Diary of Rev. Benjamin Rogers,
[e] The Queen granted to this gentleman, 1870, the style, rank, and precedence of a younger son of a Baron.

ND RICE.

ks, vol. ii. p. 296 ; Horsfield's Hist. Lewes, vol. ii. p. 117 ; Collins's Peerage, vol. vi. p. 291.

ter ermine and ermines, a lion rampant or.

vern, wings elevated, sable.

at Bromham.)

=Ruth, da. of John Hampden, Esq. of Great Hampden, Bucks.
Arms: Ar. a saltire gu. betw. four eagles displ. az.

vor, Esq. of Trevallyn, nbigh, eldest son, 2nd	=Elizabeth (Clark), widow of William, eldest son of Col. Herbert Morley of Glynde, Sussex.		Richard.	Edward.	Susannah, 1st wife to William Morley of Glynde.

lu- he ei- ol-	Richard Trevor, Bp. of Durham, s.p. rebuilt the church at Glynde. Edward Trevor, ob. s p. (Collins' Peerage.)	John Morley Trevor, Esq. of Trevallyn, Plasteg, and Glynde, b. 1681, ob. 12 April, 1719. John Trevor, Esq. of Trevallyn, &c., eldest surviving son, Commissioner of the Admiralty, 1742, m. Elizabeth, d. of Sir Thomas Frankland, of Thirkleby, co. York, who d. 1742. He d. s.p. 1743.	=Lucy, d. of Edward Montague, Esq. of Horton, Northants. John Morley Trevor, ob. s.p. 1706. Thomas Trevor, ob. s.p. 1707.	Thomas, b. 1684, ob. 1707. William. Grace Trevor. Mary Trevor. Margaret Trevor. Ruth Trevor, ob. 1764. Arabella Trevor, b. 1714. Lucy Trevor, d. in infancy. Ann Trevor, m. 17 July, 1743, Hon. General George Boscawen, who d. 3 May, 1775, leaving issue. Gertrude Trevor, m. Hon. Charles Roper, 3rd son of Henry, 8th Baron Teynham, and had issue.	all died without leaving issue.	Elizabeth m. David Polhill, Esq. of Otford, Kent. Arabella m. 1st, Robert Heath, Esq. of Lewes and 2ndly, Colonel Edward Montague, brother o George Earl of Halifax. Lucy Trevor, eldest da. b. 1706 =Edward Rice, Esq. of Newton, or Newtown M.P. for Caermarthenshire. *Arms:* Ar. a chev. between three ravens sa. *Crest:* A raven sa. George Rice, Esq. of Newton, M.P., and Lieutenant of co. Caermarthen, m. 16 Aug. 1756, ob. 3 Aug. 1779. =Cecil (Talbot) de Cardonnel, b. 1733 Baroness Dynevor, only surviving child of William, 2nd Baron and 1s Earl Talbot, created Baron Dynevor with remainder to his daughter and her issue male. Lady Dynevor d 14 March, 1793. (Burke.) *Arms:* De Cardonnel of Barrington Gloucestershire. A chev. voided az. betw. three trefoils slipped vert (another, sa.)

n, m. 25 May, 1764, olk, and 5th of Berk- o.	William Rice, ob. s.p.	Edward Rice, D.D., Dean of Gloucester, b. 19 Nov. 1776, m. 9 July, 1800, ob. 15 Aug. 1862.	=Charlotte, 2nd da. of General Lascelles, ob. 1832.	Henrietta Cecilia, m. 1788 Magens Dorrien Magens, Esq., who d. 1849, and she 17 Dec. same year. Maria, m. 1796 Admiral John Markham, and d. 1810.

airford, co. he title as his cousin Cardonnel. Secret et xter sup-	=Eliza Amelia, da. of Rev. H. Carnegie Knox, Vicar of Lechlade, m. 18 Nov. 1856, 2nd wife.	Henry Rice, in Holy Orders; formerly Vicar of Biddenham, m. 12 Dec. 1837, Emma, da. of W. Lowndes-Stone, Esq. of Brightwell, and has issue. John Talbot Rice, m. 1st, 13 Oct. 1846, Clara Louisa Reade, who d. 1853 ; and 2ndly, 24th Oct. 1855, Elizabeth Lucy Boyd.	Charlotte Rice, m. 1st Sept. 1835, Rev. A. Cameron, and has issue. Cecil Rice, m. 4 Jan. 1837, Col. C. A. Arney, and d. 2 June, 1852. Maria Rice, 2nd wife to Rev. E. Bankes, D.D., whom she m. 3 Sept. 1839 Lucy Horatia Rice, m. 7 June, 1832, Rev. W. S. Escott, M.A., afterwards Rector of Carlton with Chellington, Rural Dean of Clapham Beds. and has issue. Frances Emma Rice, m. 20 March, 1842, Rev. William Wiggin, and had issue.

ror, b or.	Arthur de Cardonnel Rice, b. 1836.	=Selina, da. of Hon. Arthur Lascelles.	Ellen Rice, m. 1855, Rev. J. G. Joyce.	Francis Carnegie Rice, b. 13 July, 1858, d. 24 July, 1868.	William Talbot Rice, b. 24 Mar. 1861.	Cecil Mina Rice, b. 16 Nov. 1859. Alice Sophia Rice, b. 16 July, 1862. Mary Charlotte Rice, b. 13 Sept. 1863.

is family, between 1589-1624, were buried at St. Bride's Church, Fleet Street. (Stow's Lond. vol. i. p. 740.)
ctor of Carlton.   d East Barnet Register.
f The style, rank, and precedence of a Baron's daughter granted to this lady 1870. (London Gazette.)

Robert (born in 1701), fourth Baron Trevor of Bromham, who had previously, in compliance with the last will and testament of John Hampden of Great Hampden, in Buckinghamshire, esq., assumed the name and arms of Hampden,[a] and had been Minister at the Court of Vienna, to which he was appointed in November 1737, and two years after Envoy at the Hague; he was also a Commissioner of the Customs in Ireland, and Joint Postmaster-General. In June, 1776, he was advanced to the dignity of Viscount Hampden.[b] His lordship was F.S.A. and F.R.S., and is described as a person of polite accomplishments, an excellent classic, and a good poet. Of both these kinds of literature he has left some specimens, privately printed at Basle. His son John, afterwards third Viscount, has given a testimony of filial veneration, by a splendid edition of some of his father's Latin poems, printed in folio (with the beautiful types of Bodoni) at Parma, 1792; of the work entitled *Villa Bromhamensis*, in hexameter verse, 115 copies were printed on ordinary paper, and 15 on vellum paper.[c] These poems are praised by Lords Hardwicke and Lyttelton. Robert, Lord Hampden also wrote notes on Milton and Martial, and a commentary on Horace, a long and valuable work, amounting to five thin folio volumes, which he called his "Gleanings."[d] In 1743, during his residence in Holland, he married Constantia, daughter of Peter Anthony de Hubert, Baron von Creiningen, by which lady (who died of the small-pox, 15th June, 1761, and was buried on the 17th at Hampden, Bucks)[e] he had two sons and two daughters; his own death took place at Bromham House, 22nd August, 1783, from a dead palsy, which struck him on Wednesday in the preceding week, when he was in the entire enjoyment of all his faculties, after spending that day in his favourite diversion—fishing.[f] He was of the age of sixty-five, having been born in the year 1718, and was succeeded by his elder son,

Thomas Trevor Hampden, second Viscount Hampden, and fifth Baron Trevor, who was born in Holland, married first, Catherine, only daughter of Major-General David Græme of Braco Castle, N.B., and secondly, Miss Brown, daughter of George Brown, Esq., of Edinburgh,[g] but died childless in 1824, whereupon

---

[a] Collins's Peer. vol. vi. p 291.

[b] Relative to this event Collins relates an anecdote:—Some years before, in an audience, the King said to him, "My Lord, why do you suffer the great name of Hampden to drop?" "Peers," replied Lord Trevor, "do not change their names without the permission of the Sovereign."

[c] One copy of "Villa Bromhamensis," on vellum paper, sold at Junot's sale for £15 15s.; ordinary copies have sold at £1 16s. to £6 6s.—Allibone.

[d] MS. Cooper.   [e] Lipscomb, vol. ii. p. 296.   [f] Add. MS. 21,067, fol. 14 b.

[g] Collins. Debrett, 1812.

the honours devolved to his brother, John Trevor Hampden, third Viscount, sixth and last Baron, born 24th February, 1748-49, educated at Westminster School, and Ch. Ch. Oxford, M.A. Mr. Trevor Hampden was Minister Plenipotentiary to the Elector Palatine, and Minister at the Diet of Ratisbon in 1780,[a] and in February 1783 appointed Envoy at the Court of Turin. He married in 1773 Harriet, only daughter of Rev. Daniel Burton, D.D., Canon of Christ Church, but had no issue. Lord Hampden died in 1824,[b] when his honours became extinct; while this, and other Bedfordshire estates, passed under his will to his kinsman the Hon. George Rice Rice, (only son and heir of George, third Baron Dynevor,) who assumed the name and arms of Trevor, and frequently resided here. Mr. Rice-Trevor succeeded to the title as fourth Lord Dynevor, 9th April, 1852, when, in accordance with the terms of the said will, this estate, together with others at Biddenham, Stagsden, Carlton, and Chellington, now usually known as the "Bromham estate," became the property of the daughters (or their representatives) of the last named nobleman. He died at Malvern, 7th October, 1869, without leaving male issue, being succeeded in the Barony of Dynevor by his first cousin, Rev. Francis William Rice.

The manor-house, about a quarter of a mile from the church, in beautifully timbered grounds, lies in a valley immediately adjacent to the river, so close that in former years it was liable to floods. It presents a diversity of architectural styles, having received additions at various times. The pointed doorway at the entrance (judiciously restored in 1868 by direction of the late Lord Dynevor) appears to have belonged to a much more ancient edifice; it is not shown in the woodcut, being concealed by the porch with its Tudor archway. The rooms are small, but numerous; the staircase is very ancient, and of rude workmanship, being constructed of rough blocks of oak. The pictures in this mansion consist principally of family portraits, most of them in a good state of preservation: in the dining room are the following:—

1. Elizabeth (Searle) 1st wife of Sir Thomas Trevor (1st Baron).
2. Thomas Trevor, Baron of the Exchequer.
3. Robert Viscount Hampden, æt. 78.
4. Sir Richard Trevor, a distinguished naval and military officer, knighted in the field in the reign of Queen Elizabeth. On the canvass is the following:—" So then—Omnipotent Father, I

---

[a] Gent's Mag., v. 53, p. 204.
[b] Buried at Glynde, by the side of his brother.—Add. MS. 21,067, fo. 31 b. As to the works of this nobleman, see Coxe's Life of Lord Walpole, p. 305.

BROMHAM HALL (ENTRANCE FRONT).

BROMHAM HALL (GARDEN FRONT).

humbly render thanks for thy manifold blessings here on earth to me, my children's children's children and familie, beseeching that by thy Grace and mercy we may be to glorify thy holy name in Heaven for thy Sonne Jesus Christ sake.—An. Dm. 1626. Ætat. 67."

5. Sir John Trevor of Endfield and Kew, K.B.
6. Unknown.
7. (? John Locke.)
8. Lord Chief Justice Dyer.
9. Sir John Trevor of Trevallyn.
10. Sir Thomas Trevor, Attorney-General (1st Baron).
11. Thomas Viscount Hampden in his Parliamentary robes, a three-quarter piece.—Hoppner.
12. Sir John Trevor of Trevallyn, Plasteg, &c.
13. (? Prince Rupert).
14. Thomas, 2nd Lord Trevor.
15. John Viscount Hampden.
16 Queen Anne.

On the staircase is a curious old portrait, bearing date 14—, and an inscription in which the words "Madoc" and "Denbighshire" can be deciphered.

In a paper, giving a catalogue of pictures in this house, made by the late Mr. Cooper, there are said to be portraits of some of the Princes of Orange, "the celebrated Grotius," Sir Richard Trevor of Plasteyn. He likewise mentions a coloured drawing of Glynde in Sussex, and a sketch in Indian ink of Bromham House, by Henry Humphrey Goodhall,[a] whom he speaks of as "an ingenious young man, a native of the village." In the drawing-room is a picture with portraits of Mrs. Rice, (daughter of John Morley Trevor,) her son George,[b] afterwards M.P. for Carmarthenshire, and her daughter Lucy.[c]

A table on a gilt frame, with the initials "A. R." in cypher, surmounted by the crown, was presented by Queen Anne to the first Lord Trevor; it is of unpolished light-blue composition with a polished white border. Another very curious and beautiful table, which formerly stood in this mansion, was removed many years ago to Hampden House, Buckinghamshire.[d]

[a] The geologist and antiquary. See an obituary memoir of him in "The Gentleman's Magazine for March 1836."

[b] Father of the third Baron Dynevor.

[c] At Brynkinalt, in Wales, was a portrait, by J. Allen, of Sir John Trevor, Master of the Rolls and Speaker of the House of Commons ; this was engraved by W. Bond, and published in 1798. R. Hutchinson took the picture of Richard Trevor, Lord Bishop of Durham, who died 9th June, 1771, aged 64. J. Collyer engraved it. Of these engravings the former was one of the plates in "Yorke's Royal Tribes of Wales," 1799; the latter is published in "Hutchinson's History of Durham," 1785, p. 580.

[d] MS. Cooper. Rev. Mr. Smith, formerly rector of St. Mary's, Bedford, has described this table in his "History of Nevis" (p 173).

Some fossils and curiosities of that nature were discovered in a well which was opened at Biddenham; for interesting and full particulars of which the reader is referred to the Bedfordshire Archæological Society's publications 1858. Some of these relics are now at Bromham Hall. Here too must not pass unnoticed a pair of boots and spurs, also a blunderbuss (without date) assigned by tradition to the hero of the house of Dyve.

The chapel or chantry, situated in what was formerly known as the hamlet of Biddenham Bridge-end in this parish, has been before alluded to;[a] remains of it are still traceable in the south portion of the miller's house;[b] in the south wall

MILLER'S HOUSE.

of a room up-stairs may be seen a small part, about three and a-half feet, of the moulding or hood of a pointed window, the width of which seems to have been eight or nine feet; in the east wall of the passage or landing a projecting stone, probably a bracket; and lying about the premises two or three loose stones, one of which appears to have been the drain of a *piscina*. The following account of its revenues, &c. is from Chantry Certificates (co. Bedford), in the Augmentation Office, Book I. p. 9, made in the time of King Henry VIII.

[a] Vide Biddenham.
[b] It was in a room in this house that Mr. Fisher is said to have partly executed his engraving of the bridge; judging from his drawing (dated 1812), the bridge must have been considerably altered since that day. Mr. Cooper, who died 3rd May, 1801, says there were twenty-one arches—four over the river, and seventeen over the Biddenham meadow.

The Chantry of Biddenham Bridge in the parish of Bromham.

Lands, tenements, and rents to the said chantry belonging.
Valued in :—

    The free rent of one messuage in the tenure of William Butler, paid yearly at the feast of St. Michael the Archangel only . . . . 6d.

    The free rent of a tenement there in the tenure of Thomas Malcot, by year as abovesaid . . 3s.

    The farm of one cottage with a garden and two acres of land in the tenure of William Payton, and payeth by the year at the Annunciation of Our Lady and St. Michael the Archangel equally . . . . 5s.

    The farm of one messuage with a garden and two acres of land in the tenure of Robert Weyver, by year as is abovesaid . . . . 8s.

    The farm of an other messuage with a garden and a close in the tenure of William Nell, by year as is abovesaid . . . . 10s.

    The farm of two acres of meadow in the tenure of Peter Weyver, clerke, by year as is abovesaid . . . . 8s.

    The farm of a cottage with a garden and one close in the tenure of Thomas Malcot, by year as is abovesaid . . . . 6s.

    The farm of one messuage with a close lying in the parish of Bromham, three acres of meadow lying in the parish of Bydenham, two acres of land in Kempston, one piece of land in the quarry pits in Bromham, with other appurtenances, in the tenure of Robert Dawson, and payeth by year as is abovesaid . . . . 50s.

    The farm of certain lands, meadows, lesnes, pastures, and headlands in the tenure of Thomas Warnet, by year as is abovesaid . . . . 53s. 4d.

    The farm of the quarry pits there in the tenure of Peter Wever, clerk, by year as is abovesaid 6s. 8d.

    The farm of a certain grovett there in the tenure of the said Peter, by year as is abovesaid . 5s.

                                               £7 15s. 6d.

Reprizes :—

    In reserved rents to our sov'eign lord the King for the certainty in Bydenham, by year 9d.; to our sov'eign lord the King for the lands called the Dewplate, by year 3d.; to the hospital of St. John in Bedford, by year 7d.; to William Buttler, by year 3s. 4d.;[a] to the parson of St. Mary in Bedford, by year 9d.; to Lewes Dyve, by year 10d.;[b] to the Lord Mordaunt, by year. 4d.; to John Butler, knight, by year, 1¾d.;[c] to our sovereign lord the King for the certainty in Bromham, by year, 1d.; to the prebend of Lincoln, 2s. 6d.;[d] 9s. 6¼d.

And so remaineth clear by the year £7 5s. 6¼d. (According to the return made, 27th King Henry VIII. £5 17s. 2d. gross, out of which was payable to the Prior of Newenham 3s. 4d.; to Sir John Dyve, Knt. 11d.; to the Prebendary of Bedford 2s. 6d.; to the

---

[a] For ten acres of land in Bromeham. Particulars for Grants, Edw. VI. Augmentation Office.
[b] For quit rent. Ib.
[c] Afterwards payable to the heirs of Philip Butler. Ib.
[d] For one cottage and two acres of land in the tenure of Thomas Malcute. Ib.

Master of St. John's in Bedford 7*d*.;^a to the Rector of St. Mary's 9*d*.; to the Sheriff of Beds, for the certainty, 1*s*. 6*d*. . . . . Total 9*s*. 7*d*.

(Valor Eccl)

Goods and ornaments belonging to the said chantry, as appeareth by inventory, remaining with two bells, valued at . . . . £3 10*s*. 4*d*.

Plate belonging to the said chantry, that is to say, parcel gilt, 10 oz. 3 quarters.

M^d. that it doth appear by a licence, dated the 2nd day of June, in the 12th year of the reign of King Edward the Fourth, that Simon Wulston, priest, might give and grant certain messuages, lands, and tenements for the foundation and establishment of a chauntry at Bydenham Bridge, in the parish of Bromham,^b the same to be called the Chauntry of Our Lady and St. Katherine, which chauntry is founded and established accordingly to the intent a priest should in the chapel there sing mass and say other divine service daily, and pray for the souls of the said founder and Jeffrey Smith and all Christian souls. Also the said chapel is distant from the parish a quarter of a mile and more. Also Peter Weyver is incumbent there, a Frenchman, and made denizen, and hath no other promotion but only the chantry. And there hath been kept no grammar school nor preacher since Michaelmas last, neither any money or other profit been paid at any time within this five years to any poor person intended to have continuance for ever.

In a later certificate, in the same reign, the chapel is said to be "of no necessity." Its yearly value £7 3*s*. 10*d*.

Whereof:—   £   *s*.   *d*.
Paid to the King's Matie for rents 13*d*., and for tenths 10*s*. 9¾*d*.
Paid to divers other persons 8*s*. 5¾*d*. 1   0   4½
And so remaineth for the priest's salary or stipend £6 3*s*. 5½*d*.

The ornaments appertaining to the said chapel or chantry be esteemed to be worth, as by the inventory thereof, as appeareth, £4 13*s*.

There is a chalice appertaining to the said chantry or chapel which is esteemed to be worthe, as appeareth by the said inventory, 20*s*., remaining in the hands of Peter Wiver, incumbent.

There hath been no dissolution, purchase, or obtaining of any part of the said possessions or goods of the said chantry or chapel since the 4th day of February, in the 27th year of the Kings Ma^{tys} reign aforesaid.

---

^a (Property held by the Rector and Master of the hospital of St. John Bedford.) Ancient rent payable from land of the Hon. G. R. Trevor in Biddenham: Reserved rent 7*s*.

Report of the Commissioners for inquiring concerning Charities. 32nd Report, part ii. vol. xxvi. (1837-38) p. 593.

^b Cal. Inq. ad qd. damnum, 18 Ed. II. nu. 152 (p. 279.)

Chaplains of the Chantry of Biddenham Bridge.[a]

1324—1339	Simon Wolston or Wulstan.
1340—1347	John Becke.[b]
1347—1361	{ Ric. de Wombewell. { John Wrabet de Naresby, Pbr. By res. of last.
1363—1397	{ John Wryghte, Pbr. Also Vicar of Bromham. { Robert Burgh.
1398—1450	{ John Cook. { Robert Baldock.
1450—1456.	John T———. By res. of last.
1471—1479.	Nicholas Skypwith.
1480—1494.	Robert Halytreholm. By death of last.
Circa 1530.	Henry Atkynson, Pbr.
1536.	Henry Boswell.
	Peter Weyver.

At the end of the certificate: "Peter Wayver is Incumbent there, of the age of 50 years, but meanly learned, and hath no other living but the revenues of the said Chantry;" pension 100s.

A paper by John Woode, in the Augmentation Office, of Particulars for Grants, temp. King Edward VI. to William Place and Nicholas Spakeman, describes the rents and premises pertaining to the chantry.

In Bromham: the farm or rent of three messuages, one cottage, three gardens, three pightles, ten acres of land, and one piece lying in the quarry pytte in Bromham and Bydenham.

In Bydenham: the farm or rent of three acres and one rood of pasture, one acre called Bridge acre, pasture land and premises in the open fields, late in the tenure of John Wright, free rent issuing out of one messuage and one close in the tenure of Thomas Malcute, and out of certain land in the tenure of William Butler.

In Kempston: the farm or rent of two acres of land.

Also the farm of one cottage with garden, and other closes containing two acres. (No parish named.)

The whole amounting to £7 3s. 10d.

Of the reprizes, the rents formerly payable to the King and to the Rector of

---

[a] Lib. Instit. apud Lincoln.

[b] William son of William son of Peter le Smyth and John Becke the Chaplain had a dispute respecting certain premises in Bromham.—Abbrev. Rot. Orig. vol. i. p. 143.

St. Mary's Bedford were extinguished, so that the outgoings were reduced to 7s. 8¾d., leaving a clear annual value of £6 16s. 1¼d.

The houses of the said chantry are described as being "verye ruinouse and in sore decaye."

Advowson.

This church in the time of King Richard I. was given by an ancestor of William Malherbe to the Priory of Cauldwell or Caldwell, near Bedford, a foundation of the Beauchamps of whom the Malherbes held their estate. Not being a very wealthy establishment, the great tithes of this parish were soon appropriated to the use of the priory, viz., before the year 1257,[a] and so continued with the patronage of the vicarage[b] until the time of King Henry VIII. The Crown, after presenting, granted (1st June, 1 King Edward VI.) the advowsons of the vicarages of Bromham and Oakley, together with the rectories of the said parishes, to Eton College,[c] which foundation seems to have leased this rectory and the right of patronage, or from time to time to have sold presentations, to the Dyves. Lewis Dyve made the appointment next on record after that by the Crown; in 1560 the Bishop of Lincoln presented, *by lapse;* in 1564, Eton College; in 1588 no patron is named; one of the Dyves again presented in 1597; Sir Richard Dyer, knight, of Staughton, in 1605; Beatrice Dyve, widow of Sir John, in 1608, which Beatrice married secondly John Digby, created Earl of Bristol, who, in 1633, appointed to this living in right of his wife; since which time, with one exception, by lapse, in 1671-2, the Royal College of Eton has enjoyed an uninterrupted right of patronage.

	£	s.	d.
Rental 1817, paid to Eton College:[d]—			
Brumham Rectory, Ld. Visct. Hampden, tenant (Lady day)	2	6	8
Wheat, 128 gal. 1 qr.	13	4	6¼
Malt, 168 gal. 3 qr.	10	7	5
For 20 wether sheep at Midsummer	12	0	0

[a] Harwolde Priory had a small portion amounting to 5s. in the 27th King Henry VIII.—Valor Eccl. (In the time of Eliz. "Rente in bromeham parcell of Herold l. xxii. i s." Lansd. 5, fo. 31.)

[b] About the year 1345, the church of the parish of Bromham was found to be taxed at six marks and a half; on the oaths of Galfridus de la Marc, John Parentyn, William le Roos, John le Chapman, John Paton, and Thomas Hardy. Nonar. inquis. p. 19.

[c] Deeds in the Augmentation Office.

[d] Third report, minutes of evidence before Select Committee (House of Commons) on Education of Lower Orders, p. 80.

		£	s.	d.
Rent money at Michaelmas		2	6	8
Wheat, 128 gal. 1 qr.		10	0	4¾
Malt, 168 gal. 3 qr.		10	7	5
Entertainment		2	0	0
		62	13	1

This living is a vicarage,¹ with that of Oakley annexed; the vicarage-house, built in 1831,² is of red brick, with a slated roof.

VICARAGE.

CHURCH LANDS &C. AS PER TERRIER 1724.

	A.	R.	P.		A.	R.	P.
Houses, Barn, Pightle, and Close of	10	0	0	Close call'd Coblers	0	3	6
Meadow, Close, Cottages (? let) to				Meadow belonging to the Grange	0	1	4
William Groves	8	0	0	Bowels Close	0	0	8
3 little Houses by the Pound	1	1	0	A little Pasture called the Stripe	0	1	0
Co. (? cottage)	0	10	0	2 Closes call'd Hinney's, price of			
Miller's Burrow	0	0	6	2 Bush. Malt.ᶜ			

¹ Valued in the King's Book at £8; on the authority of the late Rev. O. St. J. Cooper, its certified value was £57 10s. 1d.; and the sum of 3s. was payable to the Archdeacon. On 26th March 1818 the College of Eton petitioned the Bishop of Lincoln to unite and consolidate the Vicarages and Parish Churches of Bromham and Oakley that they might immediately from thenceforth remain and continue knit together as one benefice. This was followed by the presentation of Robert Mesham (or Measham) to the united benefices. Evidences of Rev. W. A. Carter, Vicar of Bromham, Bucks.

² Lewis's Topographical Dictionary, 7th edit. Lond. 1848

ᶜ "There is paid from two closes, the price of 4 Bushels of Malt, to be usually spent by the Parishioners when they make customary parochial perambulations."—MS. Cooper.

BROMHAM.

VICARAGE LAND.[a]

Pightle (adjoining the garden) 2 acres
Close and Pightle - 10 or 11 „
Meadow (near Clapham) - 5 or 6 „

LIST OF INCUMBENTS.[b]

WILLIAM SACERDOS DE BRUMHAM.[c]

	Vicars.	Patron.
1235—1257	Radulph de Bedeford / F	Cauldwell Priory.
1258—1279	Ralphe de Bedeford	,,
1280—1299	Roger de Graveby. By death of last.	,,
1363—1397	John Hayle	,,
	William Wandesford, Pbr. By res. of last.	,,
	Elias Witenford, Pbr. By res. of last.	,,
	Robert Boregh	,,
	John Wryghte, Pbr. By res. of last. Chaplain of Bydenham Bridge Chantry	,,
1456—1470	Thomas Aythrope	,,
	Thomas George. By res. of last.	,,
	Richard Lounde. By res. of last.	,,
1471—1479	John Faune	,,
1480—1494	William Alen	,,
1495—1513	John Wryght. By death of last.	,,
	William Aby. By death of last.	,,
1521—1546	Thomas Mendar	,,
	John Patynson[d]	
	Alexander Clerke	Crown.
circa 1556	Henry King[e]	Lewis Dive.
1560, March 10	Thomas Symons[e]	Bishop of Lincoln, by lapse.
1564, Nov. 9	David Vaughan[e]	Eton College (Wm. Day).

---

[a] Mr. Goodhall thus describes the church property (? glebe) : The Vicarage-house with garden and field adjoining ; two small closes of pasture adjoining the Vicarage green ; a small house and garden adjoining the park ; a small piece of pasture adjoining the river, opposite Clapham, called the " Parson's meadow."

[b] Lib. Instit. apud Lincoln. Reg. Paroch.

[c] Witness to a Charter of Henry de Alno of Turvey, living temp. King Stephen or Henry II.

[d] Witness to the Will of Richard Maud of Bromham, 1533. Northampton District Registry. John Patenson, Vicar, temp. Henry VIII. Valor Eccl.

[e] MS. Cooper.

BROMHAM.

	Vicars.	Patron.
1588, Oct. 31	Richard Maddocks [a]	
1597, July 19	Nicholas Barton [a]	John Dyve of Bromham, Armr.
1605, March 8	George Daniel, M.A. [a]	Sir Richard Dyer, knight, of Gt. Staughton, Hunts.
1608, Jan. 26	John Stokes, M.A. [a]	Dame Beatrice Dyve, widow.
1633, Nov. 20	Antony Waters, M.A. [a]	John (Digby) Earl of Bristol.
	Nicholas East [a] [b]	
1661, Aug. 15	Andrew Cater	Eton College.
1671-2, April 15	Robert Whitehead, M.A., Emman. Coll. Camb., 1668	William, Bishop of Lincoln, by lapse.
1684, July 2	William Tucker, M.A., Clare Coll. Camb., 1680. By cession of last. Inducted by Richard Gotobed, curate of St. John's, Bedford. [b]	Eton College.
1688, May 13	Simon Gale, M.A., Queens' Coll. Camb., 1679. By resignation of last. Inducted by Edm. Bourn, curate of St. Cuthbert's, Bedford. [b] Also Vicar of Oakley, Beds. [c]	,,
1712, Dec. 10	Robert Richards, M.A , Emman. Coll. Camb., 1720. By death of last. Buried at Bromham, 27 Feb. 1758. (Parish Regr.)	,,
1758, March 4	Wyat Francis, M.A., Fell. of Magd. Coll. Oxon. By death of last. Also P.C. of Little Brickhill, Bucks.	,,
1769, Feb. 9	Thomas Richards, B.A., Sidney College, Camb. By death of last.	,,
1799, July -	Robert Measham, M.A. By death of last.	,,

	Vicars of Bromham with Oakley.	Patron.
1818, May -	Robert Measham, M.A.	Eton College.
1823 - -	Robert Measham, M.A.	,,
1827, Sept	James Joseph Goodall, M.A., Pembroke Coll. Oxon. By death of last.	,,
1866 - -	Alfred James Coleridge, B.A. Magd. Coll. Oxon. By resignation of last.	,,

The church is said to be dedicated to St. Owen, which may be a re-dedication,

---

[a] MS. Cooper. [b] Parish Register.
[c] Died 1st August, 1712, aged 57, buried in the chancel of Oakley Church.

CHURCH (1866).

for Thomas Brownfeld, by his will, anno 1511, and Richard Maud, by his will, dated 2nd May, 1533, desired to be buried in the churchyard of St. Andrew of Bromham;[a] and it is to be observed that the clergyman of the parish was generally a witness or overseer of the early wills, otherwise a mistake on the part of the testator might be suspected.

It is remarkable for its picturesque aspect, and is prettily situated in the paddock or park. It consists of a chancel and nave, with a tower at the west end, a north aisle, and north and south porches of wood and stone respectively, having a room over each approached by steps from the outside: that over the north porch, having a lofty brick chimney, was for some time used as a school, the other is a library.[b] The gabled roofs of these rooms are tiled; the flat roofs of the nave, aisle,

[a] In the copy of John Warnet's will, dated 7th Oct., 1532, it is called "Sanct Andwyne at Bromham," but this may be a clerical error on the part of the transcriber.—Bedfordshire Wills, Court of Probate, Northampton District Registry.

[b] On a stone let into the wall near the entrance:—

"This small Library was founded and freely given for the use of the minister and parishioners of Bromham by Thos. Lord Trevor, in the year 1740; no book to be taken out without leave of the minister or lord of the manor."

It has been stated that it consists of about 600 volumes, among which Walton's Polyglot Bible and Pool's Synopsis are especially mentioned; also "a curious little print of the bust of King Charles I., the outlines of which are strong and some of them gilt; the interstices contain (in the smallest characters) the Lord's Prayer, Ten Commandments, the King's speech on the scaffold, his private meditations during his troubles, the service appointed for the commemoration at his death, with his speeches to the Lady Elizabeth and the Duke of Gloucester."

and tower being covered with lead, the latter much hidden by embattled parapets." The north elevation has been improved by the addition of a mortuary chapel and vestry, erected by the late Lord Dynevor, adjoining the chancel. The former dilapidated chancel has been replaced, with the exception of a small portion, by a new one, raised upon the old foundations, at the expense of the Hon. Miss Rice-Trevor, both the chancel roof and that of the chapel being high-pitched and covered with tiles. This work, with a general restoration of the church, was carried out under the direction of Mr. Butterfield, the cost being defrayed by the subscriptions of the parishioners and landowners, headed by £150 from the authorities of Eton College. The contract for the whole work, amounting to about £1,400, was taken by Mr. Osborn of St. Neot's, the masonry being entrusted to Mr. Whitehead of Royston. The service of re-dedication was performed on the 4th May, 1869. The east window of three lights is an exact reproduction of its predecessor; the other windows in the chancel, comprising two, having a door between them, and a lower one, square-headed, on the south side, are of two lights. In the former chancel were three windows on the south, besides the lower westernmost one (which has been retained *in situ*), and two on the north, of which, one of three lights remains as a screen between the chancel and the new organ-chamber.

On each side of the south porch is a large window of three lights (Perpendicular); the aisle is lighted by a window of three, and one of two, lights at the east and west end.

The tower is 70 feet high, and has a sexagonal turret staircase at the south-east angle, carried up about 4 feet above the parapet; it is of four stages, the upper having on all sides a window of two lights, divided by a transom and capped with a square hood; the next has a smaller west double-light window and an opening to the east; in the stage below is a west window of three lights (Perpendicular), beneath which is a doorway. Below the parapet is a string-course, and there are gurgoyles at three angles, that at the south-east being broken.

The body of the church, particularly the north side, is much overgrown with ivy. There is a cross at the apex of the embattled parapet of the nave, another on the gable of the chancel, and one on the chapel. The gable end of this chapel faces north, and is filled with a window of four lights, on either side of which is a shield, one bearing the figures 18 and the other 68. The organ-chamber to the west recedes, and is lighted by three small square-headed windows;

" In 1825 the tower was struck by lightning, which forced out two (?) of the south windows; in 1844 £100 was expended on repairing the church.—Lewis.

CHURCH (NORTH-WEST VIEW).

the vestry to the east, erected in the angle of the chapel and the chancel walls, is entered by a pointed doorway and lighted by a square-headed window on the north and by a small round-headed double light on the east.

In the interior, between the nave and aisle, are three early Decorated arches; the western arch was thrown open during the recent restoration; at the same time the oak seats were refitted, the floor paved with red and black tiles, and the windows re-glazed. A handsome oak pulpit, by Rattee and Kett (the iron stand for the hour-glass, which was fixed to its predecessor, being retained),[a] and an oak lectern were also presented to the church. The font, octagonal Perpendicular, formerly stood on the same plinth with the first pillar from the west end,[b] but is now moved more into the nave, set upon a new base, and furnished with a raised oak cover, the gift of Lady Dynevor. On the south side of the chancel arch is

FONT.

[a] The former pulpit was on the opposite (north) side of the chancel arch: on the support to the sounding-board of the old pulpit was rudely carved—

1630
Prædica Ȩ Ș evangelivm
vic   vic

[b] The ancient alms-chest is now placed against this pillar.

the staircase, which led up to the rood-loft, entered by a door in the south wall. The rood-screen, with gates, was removed when the church was undergoing repairs.

The chancel, opening from the church by a lofty arch, designed after those which separate the aisle from the nave, has an open timber roof, the spaces between the rafters being plastered, as also are the panels (coloured light-blue) into which the two bays above the sanctuary are divided. The stalls are of oak, their desk-ends surmounted by poppy-heads, designed after two which remain from the old work, and are employed to form the ends of the prayer-desk on the south side. The head of the original window on the south side has been filled with fragments of early glass, collected from other windows of the church, and the lights with quarries, by Messrs. Lavers and Barraud, in imitation of a few old examples found in the course of the restoration. The reredos is of white stone inlaid with red, from the celebrated Babicomb quarry, the raised space above the holy table being occupied with the characters I. N. R. I., and the compartments on either side with the monograms I H S. and C H R., within a diamond, upon a S. Andrew's cross. The original piscina, formed by the angle of the wall and the jamb of the south-east window, with an opening to the two sides and a shaft between them, was laid open in the alterations; below the same window is the sedile. Within a small recess in the opposite wall, formed for a credence, is the following inscription: "This Chancel was rebuilt by the Hon'ble Elianore Mary Rice-Trevor, in the year of our Lord 1868." This recess is surmounted by a large cross of white and red stone inlaid in the wall. The floor is laid with Minton's tiles. The old altar-rails had been given by Thomas second Lord Trevor.

Opening transept-wise from the chancel by a bold arch is a large mortuary chapel over the family vault. The head of the window is filled with heraldry, and the lights with stained glass,[a] beneath which is the following inscription upon

---

[a] The subjects illustrated are the six Corporal and the six Spiritual works of Mercy. The monogram I H S., and the date 1870, occupy two small compartments of this window, at the foot of which is the following:—

To the Glory of God and in Memory of George Rice Rice-Trevor 4th Baron Dynevor, Born August 5th 1795, and Departed this life October 7th in the year of Our Lord 1869.

The heraldry displayed in the rose light is the standard of Lord Dynevor surrounded by six shields:—

1. Trevor, surmounted by his crest. 2. Rice, impaling Talbot de Cardonnel, surmounted by Rice's crest. 3. Rice, bearing in pretence de Cardonnel in a lozenge surmounted by a baronial coronet. 4. Talbot, bearing in pretence de Cardonnel; an Earl's coronet. 5. Rice quartering Talbot de Cardonnel, impaling Townshend-Vere; a Baron's coronet. 6. Rice-Trevor, quartering Talbot and de Cardonnel, impaling Fitzroy; a Baron's coronet. Motto: Secret et Hardi.

gray marble: "This Chapel is built by Lord Dynevor, A.D. M.DCCC.LXVIII. in memorial of his eldest daughter Frances Emily, who departed this life Nov. xxvi. A.D. M DCCC.LXIII aged xxxvii., and of her husband Edward Ffolliott Wingfield, who departed this life Sept. xxvi., A.D. M.DCCC.LXV. aged xlii. years. William Ffolliott, 5th son of the above, who departed this life Dec. viii. A.D. M.DCCC.LXI. aged viii. months, is also buried here." A doorway has been pierced through the east wall of the aisle into a small organ-chamber communicating with this chapel. The entrance to the vestry is on the east side of the chapel.

The quarto Bible and Prayer Book were an offering from the women, and the alms bason and bags were given by the poor men, of the parish.

There are six bells in the key of E; the tenor weighs about 24 cwt.; the inscriptions are as follows:—

1. "This given by Thos. Lord Trevor in the year 1739."
   "Thomas Rvssell of Biddenham and William Rvssell of Wootton They made me."
   Three coins stamped with "Anna Dei Gratia" and reversed.
2. "Thomas Rvssell of Biddenham and William Rvssell of Wootton made me in 1739." Marks of two coins with heads of Anna Dei Gratia, and one reverse.
3. "R. Taylor and Sons Founders. MDCCCXXVI."
4. "Chandler made me 1686."
   "Gulielmus Tucker VIC:"
5. "C and G Mears Founders. 1852"
6. "Chandler made me 1686."
   "Lodovicus Dyve, Armig:"
       "M D."

The chalice is of silver, on the edge is graven: "Bibite ex hoc omnes. Ex dono Domini Lodovici Dive Militis." On the cover is a wyvern between the initials L. D. The paten, also of silver, bears the following: "Ex dono Thomæ Domini Trevor Baronis de Bromham A.D. 1737."

The benefactions to the church amount to about £10, arising from some dwelling-houses, several little closes, and a rent-charge.[a]

The village feast is kept on the Sunday after S. Michael.

[a] Lamp and light in the parish of Bromham. Valued in:—
The farm of one acre of land divided, lying in the fields of Bromham, in the tenure of James Harper, given to the sustentation of a lamp, by year at the feast of St. Michael only	4d.
The farm of three roods of arable land divided, lying in the fields of Bromham aforesaid, in the hands of the Churchwardens there, given to the use aforesaid and payeth by the year	3d.
The farm of one rood of meadow, lying in Northmede, in the tenure of William Bardall, given to the use aforesaid, by year	6d.

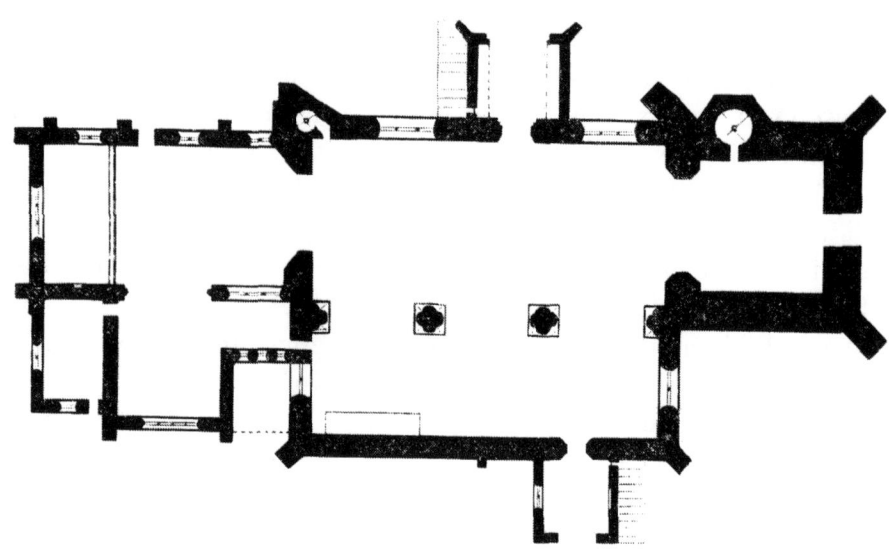

GROUND PLAN OF CHURCH.

Monuments.

Several monuments have been removed from the positions which they occupied prior to the restoration of the church.

Chancel.

The great object of interest is the very beautiful brass, figured in Lysons,[a] originally laid down to the memory of Thomas Wideville and his two wives, about 1435, and re-appropiated, to commemorate the great-great-grandson of Thomas Wideville's sister, viz. Sir John Dyve, who died in 1535, his mother, and his wife. It represents a knight and two ladies, in the style of the fifteenth century, under a triple canopy, the centre surmounted by the arms of Dyve, on either side of which a shield is wanting. On the dexter side of the knight, a

---

The farm of two acres of arable land divided, lying in the fields of Bromham aforesaid, in the tenure of Alexander Clerke, given to the support of a lamp, by year . . . . 8d.

The farm of five roods of land divided, lying in the fields of Bromham aforesaid, in the hands of Robert Poole, given to the use aforesaid, by year . . . . . . 5d.

2s. 2d. (*Certificate, Augmentation Office.*)

According to the Bedfordshire Post Office Directory (1869), there are thirteen acres of land left to the Church for repairs of chancel by an unknown donor.

[a] Magna Britannia, Beds, p. 33.

fesse and canton for Wideville impaling a chev. between three (? squirrels), the two in chief respecting each other; on the sinister side Wideville, impaling on a chief a fleur-de-lis, which latter were the arms borne by Rogers of Bryanston till the year 1419, and perhaps a little later.[a] An account of it is given by Mr. Albert Way in the Archæologia, vol. xxx. page 124, and by Mr. John Gough Nichols in the "Topographer," 1845, vol. i. p. 159. A conjecture has been hazarded to the effect that this brass may have been brought by the Dyves from Northamptonshire, as Thomas Wideville's father was of Grafton in that county, but the fact that the Widevilles possessed an estate in this parish and in Biddenham seventy years before the earlier date assigned to this brass, and served the office of sheriff for Beds and Bucks, seems to contradict that supposition. Before 1866 this brass was close to part of the north wall (recently taken down) immediately west of the communion rails. The stone measures 7 feet 3 inches by 4 feet.

Against the same (demolished) wall, next west of the brass, was the monument of John 3rd Lord Trevor, by Prince Hoare of Bath. Arms: Per bend sinister erm. and ermines, a lion rampant or.—*Trevor*. On an escutcheon of pretence, Ar. a bend counter-compony az. and erm. between two lion's heads erased gu. on a chief az. three billets of the first.—*Steele*. Surmounted by a Baron's coronet, above which the crest, viz., a wyvern, wings elevated, sa. fixed on a chapeau gu. turned up erm. Supporters: Two wyverns reguard. sa. Motto: Stat lege corona.

> Near this place[b] lie the Remains of
> The Right Honorable John Lord Trevor,
> Who died 27th of September, 1764, aged 69.
> In Gratitude, Respect, and Affection
> to whose Memory
> Elizabeth Lady Trevor (his Widow)
> caused this Monument to be Erected.

This is a mural monument, having on a table of syenite an emblematical figure of Eternity, sitting on a tomb, embracing in her left arm an urn, in fine alto relievo.

On a flat stone (removed to the east end of the aisle)—

Arms: Dyve, impaling a bend between six birds (? martlets).

Over Dyve's coat, his crest on a helmet, and over the wife's another helmet and crest.

---

[a] Hutchins's Dorsetshire, vol. i. p. 160. See patronage of the Church of Bryanston.

[b] Altered to—" In this Church," on account of this monument being now placed at the north-west of the aisle.

Here lyeth interred yᵉ Body of Captain
Lewis Dyve yᵉ son of Sir Lewis Dyve
who departed this life yᵉ 7ᵗʰ Janʸ
1686
at his house at Brumham in yᵉ
County of Bedford
in the 46ᵗʰ year of his age.

Here lies the Body of Ann Lady Dowager Trevor, widow of Thos. Lord Trevor, who died on the 4th Decr. in the year of our Lord 1746, aged 76.[a]

Also the mortal remains of Eva Gwenlian Rice Trevor, 3rd daughter of the Hon. George Rice Trevor, who died on 28 July, 1842, in her 13th year.

William Ffolliott Wingfield, born April 10, died Dec. 8, 1861.

There was, according to Mr. Cooper, an escutcheon of Dyve, impaling, Sa. three piles in point ar. on a chief gu. a lion pass. ar.—*Hacket*. This was for Francis Dyve, esq., who married Theophila, daughter of Bishop Hacket.

Three achievements have disappeared from the chancel since 1866:—

I. Arms. *Trevor*, and, on an escutcheon of pretence Vert, three escutcheons ar. each within a bordure engr. or. *Burrell*. A baron's coronet, and Trevor's crest and supporters as before.

(Thomas, 2nd Baron, married Elizabeth daughter of Timothy Burrell, Esq., barrister-at-law, and was buried here 1753.)

II. Arms, quarterly: 1 and 4, Arg., a saltire gu. between four eagles displayed az. *Hampden*. 2 and 3, *Trevor*. A viscount's coronet. Crest, on a wreath, a talbot statant erm., plain collared and chained gu. *Hampden*. Motto: Vestigia nulla retrorsum. Trevor's supporters as before.

(Robert, 4th Baron, created Viscount Hampden, when a widower, in 1776, died 1783.)

III. Arms, *knight and lady* (the lady survived her husband). Dexter, quarterly: 1 and 4 *Hampden*; 2 and 3 *Trevor*. Sinister, ar. a cross engr. between four lions pass. az. Hampden's crest and motto, and Trevor's supporters, as in number II.

Suspended from the south wall is a helmet, with a sword, and a Baron's coronet.

Manorial Chapel.

Against the east wall stands the monument of the first Lord Trevor, which was formerly in the chancel against the north wall, erected at a cost of £250, Mr. John Trevor, the judge (eventually third Baron), bearing the expense. The Rev. Benj. Rogers has left it on record in his Diary that it was finished on the

---

[a] Inscribed on one of the panels of the first Lord Trevor's monument.

25th October, 1732. Some of the marble cost Mr. Spangor, the statuary, in the block in Italy, 18s. per foot, which stood him in 26s. per foot when brought to London; this was black with yellow veins.

At the top of the monument is a shield of arms with helmet, crest, and supporters. The arms of the husband being impaled with those of the first and second wife on either side. Sculptured in white marble is a cushion on which rests a Baron's coronet.

Arms.—*Trevor.* Per bend sinister erm. and ermines, a lion ramp. or.

Impaling { dexter, *Searle.* Arg. on a fesse between three crescents gu. as many fleurs-de-lis or.
sinister, *Weldon.* Arg. a cinquefoil gu. on a chief of the second a demi-lion ramp. or.

Crest.—On a cap of maintenance a wyvern rising sa.

Supporters.—Two wyverns reguard. sa.

M.S.
Thomæ Domini Trevor Baronis de Bromham
Johannis Trevor Eq: Aur. Regi Carolo II.
Primarii Status Secretarij
Filij Secundi.
Olim Juventus, et Ingenij Ver
Eloquentiâ facili effloruit:
Maturior Ætas protulit Virum,
In Foro, in Senatu, planè admirabilem.
Sollicitatoris, dein Attornati Generalis Partibus,
Difficillimis temporibus,
Summâ cum laude functum
Præfecit Gulielmus III.
Curiæ Communium Placitorum
Capitalem Justitiarium.
Hunc antiquâ Stirpe nobilem,
Raris animi Dotibus, Virtutibusq' conspicuum,
Ac plurimis in Rempublicam meritis præfulgentem,
Ad Patriciam Dignitatem
Evexit Regina Anna.

Publicis Negotiis cum diu operam dedisset,
Rure Suburbano respiravit paululum,[a]
Ut Sibi, Suisq' viveret;
Potitus literato cum dignitate otio.
At Tali carere Viro
Non Rex voluit, non Respublica;
Itaq' ad nova Regni obeunda munera
Evocavit Philosophum è dulci Secessu
Georgius Primus.
A Secundo pari, aut majori habitus in gratiâ,
Utriq' Regi Custos Privati Sigilli,
Atq' a Sanctioribus Consilijs;
Deinde Secreti Concilii Præses creatus
(Tot inter favores Principum
Nunquam non Patriæ memor),
Restitit hic, Honorum satur,
Et jam majus aliquid meditans
Subitâ valetudine decessit
XIX Die Mensis Junij A.D. MDCCXXX.
Ætatis suæ LXXII.[b]

[a] Lord Trevor had a villa residence at East Barnet, Herts, called Trevor Park. In 1739 it belonged to W. P. Ashurst, esq., who bequeathed it to Dr. Hugh Smith; in 1796 it was the property and residence of the widow of the last-named gentleman.—Lysons' Env. Lond. vol. iv. p. 11.

[b] The epitaph is said to have been composed by his son, Right Hon. Thomas, second Lord Trevor. The following translation is from the pen of Rev. Benj. Rogers, a former Rector of Carlton:—

On the west wall is now placed the much admired sculpture commemorating the third daughter of the Hon. George Rice Trevor:—

Sacred to the Memory of Eva Gwenlian, 3rd daughter of the Honble. George Rice Trevor, who died July 28th, 1842, in her thirteenth year. She had received largely of every good gift and was remarkable for her great docility and for her kind and affectionate spirit towards all. But her bereaved Parents and her dear Sisters desire that she should be remembered chiefly for her love towards them, her meekness, and her cheerful patience under suffering, for her Christian Charity, and above all for her early and fervent piety and for her entire but humble trust in God her Saviour.

Aisle.

At the north-east angle of the aisle is an Elizabethan tomb of alabaster 7 feet 5 inches long, and 3 feet deep, on which lies the figure of a knight in armour, with a long flowing pointed beard falling on his breast, under a canopy, the ceiling of which has twenty-one compartments, supported by Ionic columns; the height to the top of the ornaments is 11 feet 1 inch. It bears no inscription, and the arms and helmet of Dyve over it, between the initials " 𝕴 𝕭 𝕯 " on the wall-plate on one side, and "1603" on the other, have induced a general belief that it is the monument of Sir John Dyve. On the western half of the south face of the tomb is a shield with Dyve's coat and ten quarterings,[a] impaling, three escallops

Sacred to the Memory of
Thomas Trevor, Baron of Bromham,
Second son of John Trevor Knt.
Principal Secretary of State to King Charles II.
His Youth and the Spring of his Genius
was early graced with an easy eloquence;
A riper Age presented the Man,
at the Bar, and in the Senate exceeding famous.
After he had discharged the offices
of Solicitor, then of Attorney, General,
in difficult times,
with the greatest applause,
William III. advanced him
to the Court of Common Pleas
Chief Justice.
By an ancient Line ennobled,
for rare endowments and virtues of the mind eminent,
and by deserving very much of the Public illustrious,
Queen Anne raised him
to the Dignity of Peerage.

After a long application to Public Business,
he retired awhile to a country seat near the City
that he might live to Himself and his Friends,
enjoying a learned and honourable leisure.
But the want of such a Man
nor King nor Commonwealth would suffer,
Therefore George the First
called forth the Philosopher from his sweet Retirement
to undertake new employments of the State.
By the Second he was had in equal or greater esteem.
To both Kings Keeper of the Privy Seal,
and of the Privy Council;
Afterwards being created President of the Council
(Amidst the favors of so many Princes
Never regardless of his Country,)
He rested here, replete with Honours;
And now fixing his thoughts on something greater
He died of a sudden illness
the 19th day of the Month of June 1730,
In the 72nd year of his Age.

[a] These quarterings are blazoned on a paper appended to the pedigree by William Harvy Clarenceux,

(2 and 1) for Strickland, on the other half Dyve only, impaling Strickland; at the west end, Dyve, impaling a saltire between twelve crosses patée, for Denny, and at the top of the monument, Dyve facing south, and Strickland west. The heraldry on this tomb, therefore, shows it to be in memory of Sir Lewis Dyve, who died 1592, and of his wife Mary, daughter of Sir Walter Strickland of the county of York, the father and mother of Sir John, whose first wife Douglas, daughter of Sir Anthony Denny, died 1598, and is also intended to be honoured by this handsome monument. The date and initials above probably indicate the year when the monument was erected and by whom. Sir John seems partly to have followed the example of his ancestor who re-appropriated Wideville's brass to commemorate three persons (in that instance a husband, wife, and husband's mother). He died in December, 1607. The puzzle has arisen from the circumstance of three escallops being borne by a family of the name of *Walcot*, but the arms of Sir John's second wife, who was a Walcot of Walcot, co. Salop, were Argent, a chevron between three chess-rooks ermine, as appears by her monument in Sherborne church, Dorset.[a]

The small stone cross inserted in the wall over the north door was found under the old pulpit, at the north side of the chancel arch.

On a small marble tablet (now on the south wall of the nave)—

S. M. Rosamond, the wife of Robert Mesham, M.A., Vicar of this parish, died Oct. 10th, 1819, aged 52 years.

Nave.

Tablet on south wall—

Near this place Lies the Body of Robert Richards, A.M., Vicar of this parish upwards of 46 years. He died Feb. ye 23rd, 1758, in the 78th year of his age. In the same grave lies Alice, Relict of the above Robert Richards; she died Apr. 19, 1764, aged 80.

Flat stones (now in the tower)—

Robert Richards (whose remains are deposited under this stone) was born at Souldrop, 1704; and died at Bromham July 28th, 1785. Vitæ summa brevis. Thomas Richards, A.M., Vicar of this parish, son of the above, and nephew of the late Robert Richards, Vicar, was buried here March 23rd, 1799, in the 64th year of his age.

This Stone is Sacred to the Memory of Ann Richards, widow of the above Rev. Thos. Richards, who died Jan. 2nd, 1803, aged 59 years.

1566. (Harl. 1,500, fol. 57). They are:—1. Dyve. 2. Longvale or Bray. 3. Quinton. 4. Sewell. 5. Longvile. 6. Roche. 7. Wilde. 8. Ragon. 9. Wideville. 10. Hastings. 11. Ap Rice. For the blazon, see Dyve's pedigree.

[a] MS. Cooper.

In Memory of Ann Richards, daughter of the above Thos. and Ann Richards, who died at St. Peter's parish, Bedford, where she was buried Dec. 16th, 1850, æt. 82.

Tablet, with a short sword and scabbard above it, on south wall—

This Tablet is erected to perpetuate the memory of William Richards (son of the late Thos. Richards, Vicar of this parish), who was for upwards of 20 years a Surgeon in his Majesty's 15th Regt. of Foot. He died suddenly on his arrival in England from the Bermudas, and was buried in London in the parish church of St. Sepulchre, Dec. 23, 1820, aged 46 years. A Tribute of affection to the best of brothers by his sorrowing family.

Flat stone (now near west door)—

T. W. D., gentleman, ob. 24 Nov., A.D. 1831. Æt. 21.

Inscriptions in the Churchyard :—

Near this place lies—the Body of M. Jos. Phillips—who died Oct. ye 23rd 1720—aged 49 years.—Alice Woodward wife of—the above Mr. Joseph Phillips—who died Nov. 17th 1751—aged 70 years.—Also Wm. Phillips—son of the above Joseph—Phillips died Sept. ye 18th—1770 aged 66 years.

Here—lies the body of—Elizabeth widow of the late—Thomas Goodhall, gent.—who departed this life —Nov. 2nd. 1792—aged 57 years.

In Memory of—Thomas Goodhall, son of—Thomas and Elizabeth Goodhall—who died Oct. 20th 1794 —aged 35 years.

One of the gravestones affords a singular instance of longevity, to perpetuate which (the woman being poor) it was erected by the direction of Lord Trevor—

In Memory of—Joan Birt widow—who was born at Biddenham—in this county in the year—1665, died in this parish—Augt 2^d 1770—Wisdom is the grey hair unto Man and an unspotted Life is old age— Ecclesiastes.^{a}

Other Names :—

Waller, Crump, Branch, Gurney, Bundy, Pheazey, Gibbons, King, Biggs, Reynolds, Lett, Burr, Maxey, Hallifax, Staines, Goodman, Harris, Odell, Macock, Hart, Sanders, Wood, Hoddle, Swepson, Osborne, Islip, Garner, Harrison, Allcock, Rogers, Hebbs, Ward, Gibbins, Millard, Church, Henman, Swannell, Preden, Cambers, Mayhew, Chambers, Bates.

The register begins in the year 1570. In addition to extracts already inserted in the pedigrees, the following have been selected :—

1572 Sept. 30.   Baptized, John Dygbey, son of Thomas + 22 Jan.
1577 July 21.   ——— Ann Dygbey, daughter of Thomas.

---

^{a} It sh^d be " Wisdom," iv. 9. (MS. Cooper.)

BROMHAM.

1579 Mar. 6.	Baptized,	Douglas Dygbey, daughter of Thomas.	
1581 June 4.	———	Thomas, son of Thomas Dygbey.	
—— Sept. 29.	Buried,	Alice Eaton, daughter of Thomas (drowned).	
—— Sept. 30.	———	Joan Dygbey.	
1582 June 8.	———	John Smith (drowned).	
1586 Oct. 25.	Married,	Thomas Gardiner and Jhoan Dygbey.	
1587 Feb. 4.	Buried,	Matt. Midd, steward to Sir Lewis Dyve, Knt.	
1589 Apr. 7.	Married,	John Colebeck, gent. and Elizabeth Downes.	
1595 Mar. 17.	Buried,	Margaret Dygbey.	
1599 Dec. 15.	———	Thomas Dygbey.	
1601 May 14.	———	Leonard Fitzgeffrey, gent.	
1603 Dec. 3.	———	Mrs. Margaret Fitzgeffrey, widow.	
1605 Nov. 25.	Baptized,	Beatrice Walcott, daughter of Mr. Ellis W., and Mrs. Dorothy his wife.	
1608 May 6.	———	Elizth. daughter of Mr. Ellis Walcott, and Mrs. Dorothy.	
—— Sept. 18.	George Daniel ———, the end of George Danyel, ye beginning of Jno Stokes, vicr.		
1609 Aug. 10.	Baptized,	Jno., posthumous son of Mr. Ellis Walcott, and Mrs. Dorothy.	
1610 May 4.	———	Maria, daughter of Sir John Digby, Knt., and Lady Beatrice his wife, in the church of St. Martin-in-the-Fields, London.	
1612 July 21.	Buried,	Cornelius Coleman (suspensus apud Bedford).	
1613 Mar. 3.	Married,	Thos. Whitbread, and Dorotha Rochel.	
1615 Mar. 12.	Buried,	Antonina, daughter of John Smith and Antonina his wife.	
1618	Baptized,	Dorothea, daughter of John Smith and Antonina.	
1622 Oct. 20.	———	John, son of John Smith and Antonina.	
1628 May 29.	Married,	Oliver Cobb, gent, and Mary daughter of John Smith and Antonina.	
1629 Apr. 13.	Baptized,	Antonina, daughter of Olr. Cobb, gent. and Mary. Bur. 16 Novr.	
1630 Aug. 14.	Buried,	John Smith.	
1640 Mar. 19.	———	Francis Holne, servant to Sir Lewis Dyve, Knt.	
—— Oct. 21.	———	John Pilkington, servant to Sir Lewis Dyve.	
1646 May 13.	———	Lucy, wife of Nicholas East, minister of this church, and daughter of Lewis Conquest of Houghton Conq. Armig. Buried in the church of Houghton Conq. the 15th.	
1647 Second Book begins.			
1653 Third Book.			
1654	Marriages during the usurpation, before John Eason, gent., one of the Justices of Peace for the Town of Bedford, also before John Spencer and Dr. Banaster, Justices for the county.		
1655 Feb. 5.	"The Contracht of Mairedge betwene John Godfrey of Brumham Register, and Joane Younge, was published on three severel daies in thre severall wekes in bedd (Bedford), and thay did express ther consent to maridge before Mr. Simont Becket the Mair and wane of ye Justices of the Peace for the cowinty of Bedd, on the fift day of Febweary in the year ouer Lord 1655."		
1657 June 13.	Buried,	Archibald Simner, Clark.	
1672 Second Register of Marriages.			
—— Aug. 1.	Married,	Gerrard Franklin and Margareta Giddings.	

1672 Oct. 17.	Baptized,	Eliza, daughter of Lewis and Anne Rachell.
1673 May 9.	Buried,	Keterine, wife of Robert Whitehead, Clerk.
1676 Nov. 15.	Baptized,	Arbella, daughter of Arbella and Robert Whitehead, vic.
1677	Married,	John Dodson, clerk, of Stukeley in co. Hunts, and Sara.
1679 June 1.	Buried,	Arbella, wife of Robert Whitehead, vic.
—— Oct. 26.	——	Robert, son of Robert Whitehead, vic.
—— Feb. 19.	——	John Herbert, falconer and servant to Francis Dyve, Armr.
1680 Aug. 18.	——	John Hutchinson, A.B., son of John H. of Astbury, Cheshire.
—— Jan. 16.	Married,	Thos. Nottingham, and Francisca Radwell.
1705 May 29.	Buried,	Priscilla, daughter of Lewis Dyves.
1743 June 7.	Married,	Revd. Wm. King of Pertenhall, and Mrs. Jane Newcomb, by banns.
1749 Aug. 26.	——	Benjn. Joy, and Susannah Roberas, by banns.

The following table shows the state of the register for ten years, at three different periods[a]:—

From the year.	Baptisms.			Burials.			Marriages.
	Males.	Females.	Total.	Males.	Females.	Total.	
1573	34	43	77	20	18	38	19
1672	27	26	53	20	21	41	29
1784	47	39	86	28	35	63	22

Bromham Wills.[b]

| 1504 | John P'tnoll of Bromham, his will attested by Wm Aby "capell's." |

1504 — John P'tnoll of Bromham, his will attested by Wm Aby "capell's."

1507 — John Derling. To be buried in the church yard of Bromham: "to the hy autur xx d., to the bellys xii d., to the hy autr of Steventon xvi d., also to the hy autr of Stacheden viii d." Names Joane his wife and Richard his son.

1511 — Thomas Brownfeld. "To be buried in the church yard of St Andrew of Bromham. To the high Altar for tithes forgotⁿ vi d., to the church of Lincoln ii d., to the Rode lyght in Bromham ii d.; some loose ston to mende the way from my house towards the p'sonnage; to my wife my house with the appurtenances, and one acre and a half of land with half an acre of mede." Names his son William, and his daughters Marye and Helen.

1530 May 26. Will of Gregory Compton of Bromham, of this date.

1532 Oct. 7. John Warnet. To be buried in the church or church yard of Sanct Andwyne at Bromham; to the high Altar of Bromham church vj d for forgotten Tithes; to the church at Lincoln ii d.; to the bells (Bromham) iij s. iiij d.; to Jone his wife indenture of lease (22 years) from the prior and canons of the house of Caudewell. Witnesses, John P—— vicar of Bromham, Th. More, Thos. Keyworth.

1533 May 2. Richard Maud. To be buried in the church yard of St. Andrewes. To the high

---

[a] MS. Cooper.
[b] Northampton District Registry.

BROMHAM.

Altar of the same church xx d. for Tithes forgotten, to the church of Lincoln ij d. "John Harper to have my ferme If John Harper will help Jane my wife." Overseers, John Patynson vicar of the same towne and John Harper; witnesses, Sir Thos Pye, W^m clarke, — Cowper & others.

1539. S^r W^m barsenton preste, witness to a will.

1557 Nov 10. Will of John Dyve of Houghton Regis of this date. Testator mentions Joane his wife, Alys & Joane his daughters, and his brothers Richard & Thomas.

1561 Dec 21. William ffaldo of Bromham husbandman.

1563 David Vaughan, witness to a will.

1599 March 20. William Dixe of Bromham yeoman. To be buried in the Parish Church of Bromham; to the poor of Bromham xxs. to be distributed by the Minister and Churchwardens; to the church of Lincoln iiij d.; to Robert Careles (son-in-law) and to Jane (daughter) his wife xx li.; to John Barton (son-in-law) and unto Dowglase (daughter) his wife xx li.; also a like sum to their children; with gifts to seven servants; to repairs of the Parish Church of Bromham ij s. vi d.; "Item to ffranc's S^{nt} John Gent. my good ffreend one silu^r spoone, to my ffrend John Davies Gent one spoone, the rest of my plate to Jane Careles & Dowglase Barton, the residue to my wife Dorothie executrix, hoping & desiring her to be good to my daughters and their children."

Witnessed by Nich. Barton clk.

Proved (Archd. Bedf.) 5 June 1600.

1600 May 13. Dorothie Dixe of Bromham widow, To be buried in the Parish Church; to the poor people of Bromham xiij s. iiij d. Names her daughters Joane Barret & Marye Savage; her Kinsman William ffranklyn of Bromham, and leaves the residue of her estate to her son Ralphe Coop al's Smyth her executor. Witness, Nic. Barton clk.

Proved (Archd. Bedf.) 5 June 1600.

1600. Will of Ralfe Smyth al' Coop of Bromham yeoman, witnessed by Nich. Barton clk.

1603 Dec 22. Margaret ffitzgefferye of Bromham widow. To be buried in Bromham church. Names a son Francis, and four daughters, viz. Ursula Hampton, Eliz, Mary White and Anne Pixeley wife of William P. her son-in-law. Witness Nich. Barton.

About the year 1786, this parish was occupied as follows:—[a]

Mansion—Robert Ld. Visct. Hampden.
Robert Richards, Vicar.

Thomas Negus, Farmer ⎫
John Negus,   ,, ⎬ Brothers and sister.
Mary Osborn,   ,, ⎭
William Maxey,   ,,
John Saunders,   ,,
John Negus,   ,,   the Grange.

---

[a] MS. Cooper.

BROMHAM.

Water Mill, ——— Willshire, Miller.
Small farm, ——— Burr.
Swan Inn,[a] Thomas Jeffries (half of this house in the parish of Kempston).

In 1641. when the Land Tax was 4s. 6d. in the pound, the whole parish was estimated at £850. The Poor Rates in 1837 amounted to £190.[b]

Very handsome School-rooms, with house for the mistress, and all other buildings complete, forming a great ornament to the village, have been erected by the Countess of Longford and the Hon. Miss Rice-Trevor. The building is of stone, and is surmounted by a clock-turret, the projecting roofs of the gable-ends being decorated with barge-boards. On those near the entrance is carved in large letters: "Those that seek Me early shall find Me."

POPULATION.

Year.	Inhabited houses.	Number of separate occupiers.	Uninhabited houses.	Building.	Males.	Females.	Total of persons.
1801	43[c]	—	—	—	—	—	297
1831	61	—	—	—	—	—	334
1841	—	—	—	—	—	—	314
1851	—	—	—	—	—	—	343
1861	67	82	1	1	169	192	361
1871	77	83	—	—	180	193	373

[a] It is said that the sheriff in former days met the judges on the Norfolk circuit at this place.
[b] Parliamentary Gazetteer.
[c] 58 families.

APPENDIX TO THE HISTORY OF BROMHAM.

MORE ABOUT SIR LEWIS DYVE.

An elaborate memoir of Sir Lewis Dyve—from the pen of Mr. John Gough Nichols, F.S.A.—appeared in the Gentleman's Magazine 1829;[a] this, in a slightly altered and revised form, is now transferred to these pages by the kind permission of its distinguished compiler.

The family of Dyve was early established at Brampton, in Northamptonshire, and a pedigree under that parish in Baker's History of the county, vol. i. p. 82, traces the descent from Henry Dyve, who was living in the reign of Henry the Third, through thirteen generations to Sir Lewis, the subject of this memoir. The family acquired the estate of Bromham in Bedfordshire from a co-heiress of Wilde in the reign of Henry the Seventh; and, having changed their residence to that mansion, are supposed to have finally sold Brampton in the reign of Elizabeth.

Sir John Dyve, of Bromham, the father of Sir Lewis, was twice married. By his first wife, a daughter of the celebrated Sir Anthony Denny, groom of the stole to Henry the Eighth, he had an only child, a daughter, who died young. His second lady was Beatrice, daughter of Charles Walcot, of Walcot in Shropshire, esquire, by whom he had only one surviving child, Sir Lewis; another, named John, having died an infant.

The following letter relative to Sir John Dyve is perhaps worthy of insertion,[b] both as illustrative of his history, and of female patronage during the reign of our great female sovereign:—

My verie good Lo. I doubt not but Mr. John Dive is knowen to your Lo^p. to be as ancient a gentleman as any in his contrie, who, notwithstandinge he was in the laste comission for the

---

[a] Biographical Memoirs of Sir Lewis Dyve, signed with the initials J. G. N.—Gent. Mag. 1829, vol. xcix. part 2, pp. 20, 124, 202, 321.

[b] The original is preserved in the Harleian MSS. 6996, art. 101.

peace, yet in this that is nowe goinge out is left out; wherefore I doe earnestlye entreat your Lo^p. that he maye be put in againe, soe shall the gentleman have his desired dispache, and will rest beholdinge to you for the same, and myself will as many other as well as for this favorable pleasure still remaine thanckfull; and soe, comendinge me verie hartilie to you, I comitt your Lo^p. nowe and ever to the tuic'on of Th'almightie. From the Court the xxth August, 1594.

Your lo^s. moste Assured frynde,

ANNE WARWYCK.

I pray your Lo^p. geve hym hering and favurabell Aunsare for my Sacke [sake].

The signature and postscript only are in the Countess's handwriting.^a

Sir John Dyve died in 1607; he had four years previously erected a monument in the church of Bromham, a mural altar-tomb, having, under a canopy supported by three columns, the recumbent effigies of a knight in armour; his head bare, and with a long beard; resting on a mat, and his hands raised in the attitude of prayer. On the wall-plate above are the arms of Dyve and the initials I.B.D. 1603 (John and Beatrice Dyve). On the basement the arms of Strickland, three escallop shells, are impaled by eleven quarterings, viz.:—1. Gules, a fess dauncetté or, between three escallop shells ermine, Dyve; 2. Vaire, three bends gules, Bray; 3. Gules, on a bend argent three martlets sable, Quynton; 4. Sable, a chevron between three gadflies argent, Seywell; 5. Gules, a fess indented between six cross-crosslets fitchée argent, Longvile; 6. Azure, three roaches naiant in pale, barways, Roche; 7. Argent, a chevron sable, on a chief of the second three martlets argent, Wylde; 8. A chevron sable, fretty or, between three stag's heads couped gules, Ragon; 9. Argent, a fess and canton gules, Widvile; 10. Argent, a maunch sable, with a mullet for difference, Hastings; 11. Argent, on a fess azure three boar's heads couped or, in chief a lion passant guardant gules, Aprice. At the end of the monument are also the arms of Dyve; impaling, Sable, a saltire argent between twelve crosses patée or, Denny.^b

Beatrice, widow of Sir John, and mother of Sir Lewis Dyve, was married

---

^a Anne Countess of Warwick was the eldest of the three daughters of Francis, second Earl of Bedford, K.G., and her two sisters were the Countesses of Bath and Cumberland. She became the third wife of Ambrose Dudley, Earl of Warwick, K.G., and was left his widow, without children, in 1589. She was "a lady of excellent character, and of most refined parts and education, and one of Elizabeth's few female favourites." She died Feb. 9, 1603-4. There is a monumental effigy of her at Cheneys; and her bold Elizabethan signature is engraved in the recently published volume of "Autographs," folio, 1829. There is also an article on her biography in the Gent. Mag. N.S. vol. xxxv. p. 350.

^b Arms of Denny: Sa. a saltire arg. between twelve crosses patée, fitchy at the foot, or.—Clutterbuck, Herts, vol. ii. p. 107.

secondly to John Digby, afterwards Earl of Bristol, and gave birth, at Madrid, in October 1612, to George, the second Earl. She had also another son, John, born in 1618; and two daughters, Lady Mary, who was married to Arthur Earl of Donegal; and Lady Abigail, married to George Freke, esquire. Having survived the Earl about six years, she died in 1658, and was buried at Sherborne, where a flat marble within the altar-rails was thus inscribed:—

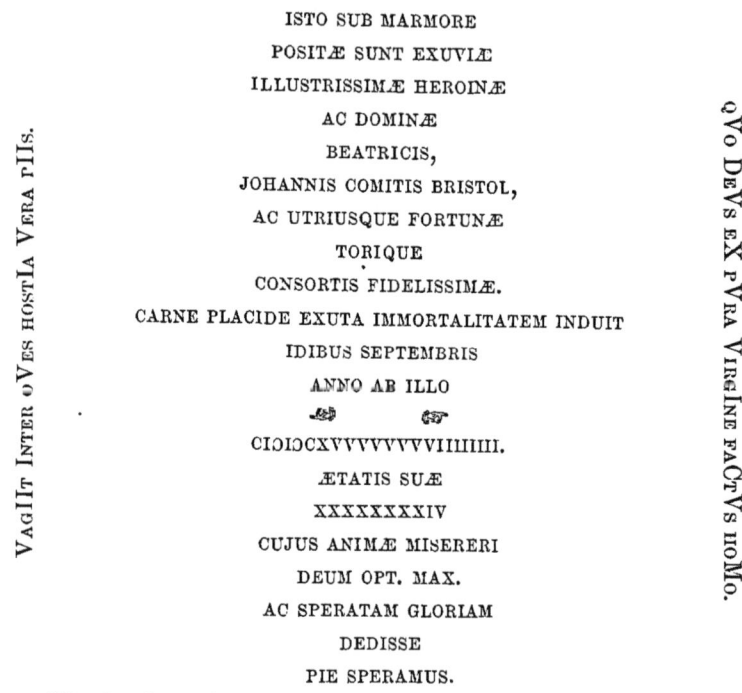

<pre>
                    ISTO SUB MARMORE
                    POSITÆ SUNT EXUVIÆ
                    ILLUSTRISSIMÆ HEROINÆ
                       AC DOMINÆ
                        BEATRICIS,
                JOHANNIS COMITIS BRISTOL,
                   AC UTRIUSQUE FORTUNÆ
                         TORIQUE
                  CONSORTIS FIDELISSIMÆ.
         CARNE PLACIDE EXUTA IMMORTALITATEM INDUIT
                    IDIBUS SEPTEMBRIS
                      ANNO AB ILLO
                  CIƆIƆCXVVVVVVVVIIIIIIII.
                       ÆTATIS SUÆ
                       XXXXXXXXIV
                  CUJUS ANIMÆ MISERERI
                      DEUM OPT. MAX.
                   AC SPERATAM GLORIAM
                         DEDISSE
                      PIE SPERAMUS.
</pre>

with side inscriptions: "VagIIt Inter oVes hostIa Vera pIIs." and "qVo DeVs eX pVra VIrgIne faCtVs hoMo."

[*The hands are intended to point to the two lines on each side, the larger letters of which give the date 1658.*]

The name of Lewis was introduced into the Dyve family by the marriage of William Dyve esquire, great-grandfather of the subject of this memoir, with Anne, daughter and heiress of Lewis Aprice, of Hanslope in Buckinghamshire, esquire. William had a son Lewis, the father of Sir John Dyve, and of an elder son, Sir Lewis, who died in the lifetime of his father without leaving issue.

Sir Lewis (son of Sir John, as before mentioned) was born and christened at Bromham in 1599.[a] The next notice we have of him is that he was knighted at

---

[a] Lewis, the son of the R^t Worshipful Jno Dyve and Mrs. Beatrice his wife,[1] born 3d Nov. being

[1] Among the family portraits at Sherborne Lodge, is one by Vandyck, in which the Earl, as in Hou-

Whitehall, April 19, 1620. The probability is, that he accompanied his mother to Spain, when his stepfather went ambassador to that country; and spent his youth chiefly in the Court of Madrid, as we find him quite at home there in 1623. It was then the incident occurred which is narrated in the Private Memoirs of Sir Kenelm Digby.[a] On the evening after Sir Kenelm's first visit to his cousin the Earl of Bristol, the latter

sent his son Leodivius,[b] with many of his servants and torches, to accompany him to his lodgings, which was not far off. But the night had slided so insensibly away while they were in their pleasing conversation (it being the nature of long absence of dear friends to cause at their first encounter much greediness of enjoying each other,) that when they came out of the house they found the streets quiet, and no living creature stirring in them; and the moon, which was then near the full, shining out a clear light upon them, so that the coolness and solitude was the greatest sign that it was not noon-day. Wherefore they caused the lights and other servants to stay there (who then could serve but for vain magnificence), and Theagenes[c] sent his servants to his lodging before, while he, and Leodivius, and another gentleman that Leodivius took with him to accompany him, that he might not return all alone to his father's house, came softly after, sucking in the fresh air, and pleasing themselves in the coolness of the night which succeeded a hot day, it being then in the beginning of the summer. But, as they were entertaining themselves in some gentle discourse, a rare voice, accompanied with a sweet instrument, called their ears to silent attention, while with their eyes they sought to inform themselves where the person was that sung; when they saw a gentlewoman in a loose and night habit, that stood in an open window supported like a gallery with bars of iron, with a lute in her hand, which with excellent skill she made to keep time with her divine voice, and that issued out of as fair a body, by what they could judge at that light, only there seemed to sit so much sadness upon her beautiful face, that one might judge she herself took little pleasure in her own soul-ravishing harmony. The three spectators remained attentive to this fair sight and sweet music, Leodivius only knowing who she was, who coming a little nearer towards the window, fifteen men all armed, as the moon shining upon their bucklers and coats of mail did make evident, rushed out upon him with much

---

Saturday bet. 11 and 12 at night. Bapt. 25th. Godfathers Mr. Francis Goodwin, the Lord St. John of Bletsoe in his own person, and Mrs. Boteler of Bydenham, deputy for the Countess of Warwick. (Bromham Register.)

[a] Edited by Sir Harris Nicolas, 1829. 8vo.
[b] Sir Lewis Dyve, the Leodivius of Sir Kenelm Digby's Private Memoirs.
[c] Sir Kenelm Digby himself.

---

braken's print, is accompanied by "his wife, a pretty woman, looking at him, in blue, with a red feather on her head, and a red knot on her laced handkerchief, her left hand on the shoulder of a boy with a gold chain and red coat, and by him another with a slashed striped coat and red gown:" probably the Earl's two sons, and the eldest not Sir Lewis Dyve.

violence, and with their drawn swords made sundry blows and thrusts at him, that, if his better genius had not defended him, it had been impossible that he could have outlived that minute; but he, nothing at all dismayed, drew his sword, and struck the foremost of them such a blow upon the head, that if it had not been armed with a good cap of steel, certainly he should have received no more cumber from that man; yet the weight of it was such that it made the Egyptian [which name Sir Kenelm gives the Spaniards] run reeling backwards two or three steps, and the blade, not able to sustain such a force, broke in many places, so that nothing but the hilts remained in Leodivius's hand; who seeing himself thus disarmed, suddenly recollected his spirits, and using short discourse within himself, resolved, as being his best, to run to his father's house to call for assistance, to bring off in safety his kinsman and his other friend, whose false sword served him in the same manner as Leodivius's had done, as though they had conspired to betray their masters in their greatest need.

It would extend the extract to a great length to allow Sir Kenelm to relate in this place the whole of his account of this hazardous adventure, particularly as he enlarges very copiously on his own chivalrous defence when left as the sole combatant. After slaying the head of the opposite party, he was enabled to follow Leodivius back.

By this means, he continues, Theagenes, who received but little hurt, had time to walk leisurely to the ambassador's house, from whence, upon the alarm that Leodivius gave, many were coming to his rescue with such arms as hastily they could recover; the cause of whose coming so late (for he met them half-way) was, that it was long before Leodivius, though he knocked and called aloud, could get the gates open, for all in the house were gone to take their rest.

The next day the cause of this quarrel was known; which was, that a nobleman of that country, having interest in a gentlewoman that lived not far from Aristobulus's [the Earl of Bristol's] house, was jealous of Leodivius, who had carried his reflections too publicly; so that this night he had forced her to sing in the window where Leodivius saw her, hoping by that means to entice him to come near to her, while he lay in ambush, as you have heard, to take his life from him.

It is a matter of some surprise that after the fatal catastrophe in which this affray terminated, no bad consequences are said to have accrued to the victorious party; for, though the Spaniard was the aggressor, yet it might have been expected that his death would have been in some way resented. It is true that the retinues of ambassadors were extraordinarily protected by the customs of the age; but it is probable that the arrival of the Prince of Wales at Madrid, which we are told occurred the very next day, induced the Spaniards to treat the English with more than customary indulgence, it being their object to conciliate them as much as possible at this crisis. As for the slayer of the Spanish nobleman, the only consequence to himself which he mentions, is, that "this action made the name of Theagenes known not only in Egypt, but in Morea [England];" and, for Sir Lewis Dyve, we find a passage in Howell's Letters, which shows that he was riding in the streets of Madrid within two days of Prince Charles's arrival. "Now," says that amusing letter-writer, "it was publicly known among the vulgar that it was the Prince of Wales that was come; and the confluence of people before my Lord of Bristol's house was so great and greedy to see the Prince, that, to clear the way, Sir Lewis Dyve went out and took coach, and all the crowd of people went after him; so the Prince himself a little after took coach," &c., &c.

The Earl of Bristol returned to England in the beginning of 1624, and his stepson about the same time. It was in this year that Sir Lewis entered into the state of matrimony. His bride was a young Dorsetshire widow, whom he met when with his stepfather at Sherborne Castle. She was Howarda, the eldest daughter of Sir John Strangeways, of Melbury Sampford, knight (ancestor to the Earls of Ilchester), by Grace, daughter of Sir John Trenchard of Woolveton. This young lady had been first married in 1622 to Edward Rogers, of Brianston, in Dorsetshire, esquire; but he had died without issue in the following year. Sir Lewis's first child, a daughter, was christened at Melbury Sampford in 1625, and named Beatrix, after her grandmother, the Countess of Bristol. She died before her father; his sons Francis[a] and Lewis, who survived him, were baptized at the same place in 1632 and 1633. They will be further noticed in the sequel. Lady Dyve died February 24, 1645-6, as appears by the parish register of Bromham, where she was buried.

On the recall of his stepfather, the Earl of Bristol, from his Spanish embassy, the court life of Sir Lewis Dyve was probably interrupted. As he married soon after, it would also be natural that he should settle at his seat of Bromham, and become the country gentleman. We have seen, however, that his lady gave

---

[a] The following entry of the baptism of Sir Lewis's son Francis was transferred to the register of Bromham from that of Melbury Sampford:—

1632. Franciscus Dyve, Ar. fil. Dom. Lodovici Dyve, Militis, et D'næ Howardæ uxoris ejus, natus erat apud Melbury in com. Dorset, 4° die ejusd. mens. susceptores erant prænobilis et honorandus Dom. Dom^s. Franciscus Comes Bedfordiæ, Arthurus Chichester, et prænobilis et honoranda Dom' D'na Beatricia Comitissa de Bristol.

The Earl of Bedford was nephew to the Countess o Warwick, who had been Sir Lewis's own sponsor. (Sir Lewis's half-brother, Lord Digby, married Lady Anne Russell, daughter of the same Earl.) The other godfather was the child's uncle by marriage, who was afterwards created Earl of Donegal.

birth to three of her children at her father's house in Dorsetshire: and, as Sir Lewis did not serve sheriff for Bedfordshire, it is probable that he resided but little at his paternal seat. He may have preferred the neighbourhood of his mother's and wife's connections; or, from the expensive habits acquired in courts, he may have been in the condition of one of those "poor knights" which the dramatists of the age describe as so numerous.

Howsoever his intervening years were spent, we find him early conspicuous in the more stirring times which succeeded. So active, indeed, was he as a military commander, when his loyal services were required, that by no less an authority than the notorious Hugh Peters, he is designated (in a letter hereafter quoted) as "the great Royalist."

In 1634 we find Sir Lewis Dyve performing an active part in a quarrel between his half-brother, Lord Digby, and Mr. (afterwards Lord) Crofts. The circumstances are thus related in a news-letter from the Rev. George Garrard to the Earl of Strafford, dated June 3, that year:—

The Lord Digby and young William Crofts of the Queen's side have had a quarrel. It was for three or four months whispered that Mr. Crofts should say he had kicked the Lord Digby. At length it comes to Digby's ear, being told him by his brother Sir Lewis Dyve, who then watched an occasion to speak with Mr. Crofts. They met both upon the bowling-place in the Spring Gardens[a] by chance, both swords at their sides, Mr. Crofts a walking stick in his hand, who walked off into the upper garden with the Lord Newport; Digby followed apace, joined himself with them, having gotten a cane from some friend he met, and walked along. Then the Lord Digby taking him aside into an alley, asked him whether he had spoken those disgraceful words of him; his answer, as Digby reports it, was—"Well, what then?" Wherewith with his cane he struck him cross the face a home blow. But Mr. Crofts saith, he gave him that blow before he made any answer. They drew their swords; but by some that came in, my Lord Newport, Lewis Dyve, and Herbert Price, they were parted. Thus sundered, Will. Crofts steps to Dyve and tells him, that, if his brother had any care of his honour, he should presently meet him at a place near Paddington, with his sword in his hand. Dyve replied, he should attend him there. There they met, and fought long enough to have killed each other; then were parted, no hurt done.

The King hearing of it, commanded the Earl Marshal and the two Lord Chamberlains[b] to examine this business; which being reported to his Majesty, and so much contrariety found in their relations, he caused them to be re-examined, with purpose to call them into the Star-cham-

[a] The spot contiguous to St. James's Park, which was the Vauxhall of the time.—See Evelyn and Pepys, *passim*.

[b] The Lord Chamberlain of the King, and the Lord Chamberlain to the Queen, Crofts belonging to the household of her Majesty.

ber. They were required to set their hands to their examinations, which Mr. Crofts did, and was presently set at liberty. The Lord Digby refused, so was committed to the custody of Laurence Whitaker; after three or four days was called before the Board, where he still refused to underwrite his examination, so then he was sent to the Fleet. 'Tis conceived he doth it to avoid an *ore tenus*, not but that by his oath he will confirm whatever he hath confessed.[a]

In a letter, dated Strand, Jan. 11 following, Mr. Garrard says:—

My Lord Digby, for William Crofts' business in the Spring Garden, is called into the Starchamber, and not only he, but Sir Lewis Dyve is charged to be a provoker and setter-on of his brother the Lord Digby in this business.[b]

In the two parliaments summoned in the first year of Charles the First, Sir Lewis Dyve was one of the members for Bridport in Dorsetshire. On the assembling of the Long Parliament in 1640, he was again returned;[c] but was afterwards "disabled," probably in 1643, when several members were under that term expelled, for their then holding commands in the King's army.

Although Sir Lewis does not appear as a speaker in parliament himself, yet we find he was active in 1641 in publishing the speech which his half-brother Lord Digby had made against the condemnation of the Earl of Strafford, and which was afterwards publicly burnt by the common hangman. It was delivered on the 21st of April that year, and on the 15th of July the House resolved, "That Sir Lewis Dyve and John Moor, as also Thomas Parslow, printer of the said speech, are delinquents, in printing and publishing thereof." Lord Digby, in his "Apology," issued in Jan. 1641-2, states, that he "did not only find that it was unfaithfully reported and uncharitably represented, but was informed that copies went abroad of it, so falsely and maliciously collected, as made the whole speech a justification of my Lord of Strafford's innocence; and Sir Lewis Dyve, having heard of such a copy in the house of a citizen of good quality, where he heard me

[a] Lord Strafford's Letters and Dispatches, vol. i. p. 261.

[b] Ibid. p. 358.—Soon after this, the parties appear to have been bound to peace; but the quarrel again burst forth, as appears by a third letter of the same party, dated May 19, 1635:—"The quarrel that lately broke out betwixt my Lord Digby and Will. Crofts in the Black-Fryars at a play, stands s it did when your brother went hence. Crofts stands confined to his father's house, because by striking he broke his bonds of £5,000, but there was a great difference in the parties that stood bound; my Lord Bedford [his father-in-law] and Sir John Strangwick [Strangways,—his brother-in-law,] stipulated for my Lord Digby; Tom Eliot and Jack Crofts, men of small fortunes, for the other; that they should keep the peace during the suit depending in the Star-chamber; the Lords have heard it, and reported their opinions to the King, and there it rests."—Ibid. p. 426.

[c] List of that Parliament in Cobbett's Parliamentary History; the list of Burgesses in Hutchins's Dorsetshire, in which the two former elections of Sir Lewis are found, gives other names under 15 Car. I.

mentioned as a person fit to have his name fixed upon posts that it might be torn to pieces by the people, upon that reason earnestly desired me to give him a true copy of what I had said in that argument, which I did; and he forthwith gave directions for the printing of it, without any privity of mine."

At the close of 1640, Sir Lewis preferred a petition to the House of Commons, apparently in reply to one of the county of Bedford; but the matter in dispute has not been ascertained. On the 26th of January, 1640-1, it was "Ordered, That the several petitions delivered this day from the knights, esquires, and gentlemen of the county of Bedford, and the petitions this day exhibited by Sir Lewis Dyve, be referred to the Committee formerly appointed for a former petition exhibited by Sir Lewis Dyve;" and, on the resumption of Committees on the 1st of April following, it was ordered "That Sir Lewis Dyve's Committee meet to-morrow at two of clock in the afternoon, in the Court of Requests."[a]

In February, 1641-2, the officers of the Parliament intercepted a packet from Lord Digby, who had then taken refuge at Middleburgh in Holland, addressed to Mr. Secretary Nicholas. It contained two letters from his lordship, one of them addressed to the Queen, and the other to Sir Lewis Dyve; which for a length of time became the butts of republican anathema. That to Sir Lewis was read forthwith; but the House manifested considerable hesitation before it could summon sufficient assurance to open that to the Queen. The first step taken, on the 14th of February, was to send their serjeant-at-arms for Sir Lewis, "as a delinquent." At a conference with the Lords the Earl of Holland proposed that the letter should be sent to the King, with a copy of that to Sir Lewis Dyve; but the House resolved directly counter to this, and on the following day the Queen's letter was opened. Sir Lewis Dyve was on this occasion examined at the bar, and afterwards referred for further examination to a committee, and again to a conference. For these purposes he was kept in the custody of the serjeant-at-arms till the 17th; and then discharged, the House taking his father-in-law Sir John Strangways' word for his re-appearance.[b] Rushworth has printed both Lord Digby's letters, as well as the Message of the House to the King on the subject. His lordship tells his brother, that, "If you knew how easie a passage it were, you would offer the King to come over for some few days your self;" a hint which, as will be found, Sir Lewis soon after followed.

In the Parliament's "Declaration" respecting the King's attempt to enter

---

[a] Journals of the House of Commons.
[b] Journals of the House of Commons; where these proceedings are detailed at a considerable length.

Hull, they connected it with Lord Digby's letters; affirming that the fears which had directed their first movements regarding Hull, were " the more confirmed by the sight of some intercepted letters of the Lord Digby (a principal person of that party) written to the Queen and Sir Lewis Dyve, whereby that party discovered an endeavour to persuade his Majesty to declare himself, and retire into some place of safety in this kingdom, in opposition to ways of accommodation with his people."[a]

Sir Lewis Dyve is mentioned by Lord Clarendon under 1641, on occasion of the vacancy which occurred that year in the Lieutenancy of the Tower. That office was then bestowed on Sir Thomas Lunsford;[b] and " was quickly understood to proceed from the single election of the Lord Digby, who had in truth designed that office to his brother Sir Lewis Dyve, against whom there could have been no exception, but his relation; but he being not at that time in town, and the other having some secret reason to fill that place in the instant with a man who could be trusted, suddenly resolved upon this gentleman."

In 1642 Sir Lewis occurs as an actor in that memorable scene which took place at Hull on St. George's Day that year. In the autobiography of James the Second, it is related that his royal highness, then eight years of age, had been sent into that town on the previous day, " as if it were only out of curiosity to see the place." " The next morning, the Duke being then on the platform, accompanied by the governour, Sir Lewis Dyve came in, and told his highness that the King was coming; then turning to the governour, he acquainted him from the King that his majesty would dine with him that day. At which news Hotham suddenly turn'd very pale, struck himself on the breast, and return'd no answer to him; but immediatly desir'd the Duke, with his company, to retire to his lodging," and caused the gates to be shut. " Had the King," it is afterwards remarked, " instead of sending Sir Lewis Dyve, surprised the governour by an unexpected visit, and without warning of his coming, in all probability he had been master of the place." " Another great errour in this conduct was that the King did not instruct some one bold and vigorous man of their number who were sent before with the Duke, with a commission to secure the person of Sir John Hotham, in case he should prove refractory, and with a positive order for the rest to obey the person so intrusted upon his producing the commission. This might

---

[a] Rushworth, vol. iv. p. 570.

[b] Very copious memoirs of Sir Thomas Lunsford, compiled by George Steinman Steinman, esq., F.S.A., are printed in the Gentleman's Magazine.

easily have been effected, either when Sir Lewis Dyve first brought the message from the King to the governour, or a little after, when Hotham came into the room, unattended by any of his officers, where he had confin'd the Duke and all his company. And many since have wondered at it, that amongst so many noblemen and gentlemen who attended the Duke, no one of them should think of making use of such an opportunity of doing the King so considerable a service." No want of spirit, however, can be attributed to Sir Lewis Dyve; for we now come to an anecdote most characteristic of him. "True it is," continues the narrative, "that Hotham was no sooner out of the room, than Sir Lewis Dyve and Mr. William Murray (one of the grooms of the Duke's bedchamber, and a much honester man than his namesake[a]), without imparting their design to any one, made a shift to get out after the governour, with a firm resolution either to throw him over the walls, or to kill him. But he, seeing them approach whilst he was speaking with the King, immediately ordered them to be seiz'd, and a guard to be sett on them, which was accordingly executed, and they detained prisoners, till such time as the Duke departed out of the town; and then they were dismiss'd, because he was not able to prove any thing against them."[b]

It appears from the Parliament's Remonstrance, May 26, 1642, that "Sir Lewis Dyve, a person that took not the least part in this late business of Hull, was presently despatched away into Holland;"[c] and there exists a letter of the Queen, in which she mentions having heard from the mouth of Sir Lewis, at the Hague, a detail of the recent proceedings.[d]

The departure of Sir Lewis was well timed; for on the 29th of April the House

---

[a] It was Mr. Murray of the King's Bedchamber who was supposed to have fanned Hotham's fears for his own safety.

[b] "Life of James the Second," edited by Dr. Clarke, vol. i. pp. 2, 4.—Clarendon, in the manuscript of his "Life," mentions Sir Lewis Dyve as occurring in this scene, but in a different manner. He says, the Duke was "attended only by a few gentlemen and servants, whereof Sir Lewis Dyve was one, who had much acquaintance with Hotham." This "acquaintance" is evidently inconsistent with the relation of Sir Lewis's conduct above quoted; and the statement that he attended the Duke at first, is doubtless equally incorrect with the subsequent relation that it was Mr. Murray whom the King sent in the morning. The testimony of the Duke of York, who was present, and on whom (though so young) the occurrence must have made great impression, and become with him a frequent subject of conversation in after years, is certainly to be preferred. Clarendon was probably himself uncertain, as, in transferring the occurrence to his "History," he gave no name to the messenger, but called him "a gentleman." See the Oxford edition of his great work.

[c] Rushworth, vol. iv. p. 585.

[d] Seward's Anecdotes, vol. i. p. 320.

of Commons "Ordered, That the Serjeant be required to bring in Sir Lewis Dyve, who is a delinquent by a former Order of the House;" and on the 9th of May, a letter was received "from Sir Christopher Wray and Mr. Hatcher, of the 6th of May, from Hull, concerning the pinnace that lay in the mouth of the river, which, since it conveyed Sir Lewis Dyve into Holland, is returned to the road of Scarborough. Resolved upon the question, That Sir John Strangewayes shall be injoined to bring in Sir Lewis Dyve within a month, according to his former engagement."[a]

Later in the same year Sir Lewis was engaged with Prince Rupert and Prince Maurice, and his brother Lord Digby, in an action near Worcester, in which they were victorious, but our hero received a wound in the shoulder.

It was in this campaign also that, says Mrs. Hutchinson, " a troope of cavilliers, under the command of Sir L. Dyve, came to Stanton, near Owthorpe, and searcht Mr. Needham's house, who was a noted Puritane in those dayes, and a Collonell in the Parliament's service, and Governor of Leicester. They found not him; for he hid himselfe in the gorse, and so escap'd them. This house being slightly plunder'd, they went to Hickling, and plunder'd another Puritaine house there; and were comming to Owthorpe (of which Mr. Hutchinson having notice, went away to Leicestershire), but they, though they had orders to seize Mr. Hutchinson, came not at that time because the night grew on."[b]

In the same summer (1642), we find an expectation of Sir Lewis becoming a host of royalty. Sir Thomas Tyrrell, of Thorp in Buckinghamshire, in a letter dated "Throp, 25 July, 1642," says, "On Saturday night the King came to Huntingdon, where he now is; and we heare that he intends to be at Sir Lewis Dive's house by Bedford on Wednesday, and soe to come into the country, then for Woodstocke."[c]

Bedfordshire, in which Sir Lewis's estate was situated, was one of the first counties which associated against the King, pursuant to a licence which passed the House, November 30, 1642. Lord Clarendon remarks that Charles had not in it any visible party, nor one fixed quarter. It was to remedy this failing that for some time the efforts of Sir Lewis Dyve were unremittingly devoted; and so troublesome did the Parliament find him, that they commissioned Sir Samuel Luke, the original of Butler's immortal Hudibras, to apprehend him at his house

[a] Journals of the House.   [b] Memoirs of Col. Hutchinson, p. 102.

[c] Seward's Anecdotes, vol. ii. p. 510; vol. iii. Appendix No. v. This letter is addressed to Richard Grenville, esq. (not *Alfred*, as before stated at p. 42,) and it goes on to say :—" What the meaning hereof is, and with what force he comes, I cannot yet learne; nor am I sure of the truth of his cominge."

at Bromham. "In this crusade" (says the author[a] of the elaborate memoirs of Sir Samuel Luke, in the Gentleman's Magazine for 1823,) "Sir Samuel was confessedly repulsed, whilst Sir Lewis saved his life by swimming the river Ouse; but the plunder of his house at Bromham rewarded the soldiers, and when the commissioners assessed it, they found nothing of any value."[b]

On the 12th of November, the House "Ordered, That Sir Samuel Luke be required, and hereby authorized, to seize the horses of Sir Lewis Dyve, Sir William Boteler, and the Lord Capell, and to employ them for the service of the Commonwealth."[c]

In April, 1643, Sir Lewis was engaged with Prince Rupert in endeavouring to assist the besieged garrison of Reading. On the 22nd of that month, he sent "into the towne from the Lord Craven's howse" at Caversham "a servant, one Flower; whoe swam the river both forwards and backwards, but was taken, comming out of the river, by a drummer of the blew coates." And on the 25th, in a skirmish on Caversham Hill, "Sir Lewis Dyve his regiment had the van, and he led them on."[d]

At the battle of Newark, March 21, 1643-4, Sir Lewis commanded one of the ten troops of Prince Rupert's regiment.[e]

Assisted by Colonel Urrey, who had deserted from the Parliament party, and by Sir John Digby, Sir Lewis Dyve had at one period attained considerable strength in the northern parts of Bedfordshire. The town of Bedford itself was taken by the Royalist forces; but so little has the history of Bedfordshire been investigated, and so almost entirely has that of its county town been neglected, that it has not been ascertained whether Sir Lewis Dyve was engaged in this service, or whether it was personally executed by Prince Rupert. Heath says Sir Lewis was the commander, and that, "being sent into Bedfordshire with 2000 or 3000 horse, he came first to Ampthill, then to Bedford, which town he entered, and took Sir John Norris and other Parliamentary officers prisoners." Whitlocke also names our hero, relating that "Colonel Urrey and Sir Lewis Dyve, with a great party of horse, entred Bedford, took Sir John Norris and others prisoners there, and routed 300 of their horse, and sufficiently plundered the town and other parts of that county." The account of Lord Clarendon, how-

[a] The Rev. J. T. Mansel, of Lathbury, in a series of papers entitled THE CENSOR.
[b] Perfect Diurnall, No. 8. Addit. MSS. Brit. Mus. 5494.
[c] Journals of the House.
[d] Sir Samuel Luke's Diary of the Siege of Reading, printed in Coates's History of that Town.
[e] Rushworth, vol. v. p. 307.

ever (and Mr. Lysons, in his *Magna Britannia* under Bedfordshire, has not ventured to pronounce which is correct), is, that "in October 1643 the King sent Prince Rupert with a strong party of horse and foot into Bedfordshire;" and that he "took the town of Bedford, which was occupied as a strong quarter by the enemy." His lordship adds, that "this expedition was principally designed to countenance Sir Lewis Dyve, whilst he fortified Newport Pagnel, at which place he hoped to fix a garrison." In the memoirs of Sir Samuel Luke, before quoted, it appears that this garrison was to have consisted of 1,500 men; and that Sir Lewis issued orders for bringing in provisions, and compelled the inhabitants to work at the fortifications; designing to establish a barrier between Bristol and Peterborough, and to cut off supplies from the metropolis.[a]

At the same time, Sir Lewis found an opportunity to retaliate upon Sir Samuel Luke, at his house at Hawnes, the plunder which he had suffered at Bromham.

The Parliament, however, had no sooner heard of the success of the King's party, than they adopted the most vigorous measures to repair their losses. Determined to recover a spot, in Needham's phrase, "geometrically situated for the defence of the associated counties," they committed this affair to the Earl of Essex, assisted by Skippon, Harvey, Wilson, and Luke. The troops halted at Dunstaple, on Monday, October 30, and on the Saturday proceeded by way of Brickhill to Newport, which they entered in the evening, not without resistance. The Governor does not appear to have neglected his trust; he fortified the town, and encouraged his soldiers by reports of a disaffection among the trained bands; till, finding his means unequal to the object, he quitted his post, and retired to the Court at Oxford.[b] Newport-Pagnel, of which Sir Samuel Luke was subsequently Governor, proved, as remarks Mr. Lysons, "a very useful garrison to the Parliament, during the remainder of the war."

Relinquishing, after this reverse, his hopes of present success in his own county, Sir Lewis Dyve next devoted his loyal efforts to the Royal cause in Dorsetshire; and it is an evident proof that his abilities were more than ordinary, that he is there again found in the chief command.

The two following letters[c] appear to have been written by Sir Lewis, in the

---

[a] See Gent. Mag. vol. xcIII. ii. p. 30, where two curious paragraphs from contemporary newspaper respecting the works at Newport-Pagnel are extracted.

[b] *Mercurius Civicus*, Nov. 2. "Clarendon's account is rather improbable, and inconsistent with the character of Sir Lewis Dyve." Gent. Mag. ubi supra.

[c] Among the papers of Secretary Walker, in the Harl. MSS. 6802, are two letters from Sir Lewis Dyve, dated Sherborne, Jan. 7 and 31, 1644-5, relative to an intended court martial on Colonel Ashburn-

crisis of the conflict, before Weymouth was quite lost; though their date is the 26th, and one from "Dorchester." They were intercepted, and published by the Parliament.[a]

To Sir John Berkeley at Tiverton.

Noble Sir,

You will, I presume, receive notice by Collonel Froad, before this will be with you, of the disaster that happened to us this day, by negligence of some of our Horse, which were beaten off their guards, and persued by the enemy to Weymouth; whereupon a hundred muskettiers were drawn out of Weymouth to relieve them, which the enemy in Melcombe taking all advantage of, made a sally over the draw-bridge, and have surprised Chappell Fort; but the two principall forts, where our provisions and ammunition lyes, wee still maintaine, and doubt not by God's assistance to keep them still, hoping that this misfortune will turne to our advantage, and bee a meanes that wee shall gaine both the towne and fort together. Whereupon my Lord Goring hath set up his rest to goe through with it, being confident of your speedy assistance in a worke of that infinite importance to his Majesties service; and in case Waller should draw this way, which is not probable, yet your strength, united with my Lord's, will be much superior to Waller's, so as doubtlesse wee may fight with him upon advantage; for Kell. Digby came this night to Sherborne from Oxford, who assured me that Essex and Manchester's forces have absolutely left him, and that he hath not a considerable party with him, his army being utterly broken; so that, this place being taken, which we are confident cannot be a work of many days, the West is not only secured thereby, but my Lord Goring will likewise have an opportunity of advancing into the Associated Counties, which are now left naked. And there is order likewise taken, that two thousand horse from Oxford and the Vize [Devizes] shall be ready to attend Waller's motion, so shall by God's blessing our game goe faire, if not mar'd in the playing.

LEWIS DYVE.

Feb. 26, 1644.

That to the Earl of Bristol:—

Dorchester, 26 Feb. 1644.

My Lord,

The Church Fort by a strange misfortune was surprised this night by the enemy in Melcombe, but the principall forts, where all our ammunition and provision lies, wee still maintaine. Sir John Berkley is sent for hither by my Lord Goring, to draw his forces hither to joyne with ours, he having set up his rest for the taking both that and the towne of Melcombe together, which by God's assistance we doubt not to effect, Waller's forces being so scattered by the withdrawing of

---

ham, the Royalist commander who had lost Weymouth. As they are only signed by Sir Lewis, and appear to have been the composition of his Secretary, they may for brevity's sake be here omitted.

[a] In "God Appearing for the Parliament, in sundry late Victories," 4to, pp. 24, printed pursuant to an order of the House, "4 Martii 1644."

Essex his horse and Manchester's foot from him, as he is not in a condition to advance towards us; and this newes was last night confirmed to us by Kell. Digby, who came from Oxford. I beseech your Lordship be pleased to employ all your interests with Sir Richard Greenvile, to hasten the sending of fifteene hundred foot, or two thousand horse, at the least, towards us, to make good Devonshire against the forces about Taunton, and that we may be at a nere distance to joine together, if there be occasion, and he shall want no horse from us that he shall have need of. *The businesse is of that importance, as little lesse then the Crowne depends upon it;* so as we are confident he will not be wanting to us in this extremity. So ceasing your Lordship's further trouble, I remaine

Your Lordship's most humble servant,
LEWIS DYUE.

To the Right Honourable the Earle of Bristoll at Exeter.

As soon as Colonel Sydenham had taken possession of his recovered garrison, he proceeded to take vengeance on those individuals who had assisted the Royalists in making entry. The examinations taken before his Council of War are printed in a tract entitled "The last Speeches and Confession of Captain John Cade and John Mils, constable, who were hanged at Weymouth," &c. (4to, pp. 16); and to which is prefixed "an insolent and bould letter sent by Sir Lewis Dyve to Colonell Sydenham," which is well worth quoting here, as it is indeed composed with a boldness of heart and firmness of purpose which seem to have naturally attended the writer on every occasion of difficulty:—

For Master Sydenham at Waymouth.

Sir,—In your last civill letter, which your trumpetter brought me, you charge me with treacherie, and Fabian Hodder and his wife for intelligencers and traitors. Look but upon your own heart, and there you shall finde that character cleerly written, wherewith you falsely and iniuriously accuse other men. The desire I had to preserve their innocencie from your barbarous inhumanity, was for that I knew their approved loyalty to their Sovereigne was a crime sufficient to make them expect the worst of ills, from a traytor's hand. But do your will, and heape vengeance on your owne head, by shedding more innocent blood. Paty shall die, deservedly by the law of armes; for having quitted the King's service, wherein he was entertained, and turning rebell. And whereas you threaten others of a higher orbe shall follow him, know this, That, were all my children under the power of your cruelty, I would not be diverted from justice to save their lives. And, for conclusion, be best assured that, if you put to death those innocent persons, I will vindicate their blood, to the utmost of that power wherewith God shall enable me, upon you and yours, without ever giving quarter to any one who hath relation to you, which shall faithfully be performed by him that professeth himselfe your enemie,

LEWIS DYUE.

Sherborne, the 12 *of March* 1644.

APPENDIX.

"To this malepart paper Colonell Sydenham returns" an answer, which is also printed. It is styled "the modest but souldier-like answer;" but, from the scraps of Latin, "parson-like" would, perhaps, have been a more appropriate epithet, and it is possible that the colonel was chiefly indebted to his chaplain for its composition. However that may have been, the modesty of its boasts, the moderation of its taunts and threats, and above all its delicate irony, are certainly too remarkable for its suppression:—

For Sir Lewis Dyve these, at Sherborne Lodge.

You call my last letter civill, and yet seem to be somewhat angry at it; which I should admire, had I not lately given you sufficient cause, for I must confesse ingenuously, had I livery and seizon of your castle, I should not be so soon dislodged without some indignation, especially if an army of mine own party[a] stood by and lookt upon it. You desire me to look upon my own heart; which I have done, and find written there, in the fairest characters, a true desire of advancing God's honour, maintaining the King's just power, and contending for the priviledges of the Parliament at Westminster, and the liberty of the subject; which when I finde you soe maliciously opposing and despightfully stiling treason and rebellion, I am induced to think this age hath produced unparaleld monsters, who are (without slander) *pestes humani generis*, for traytor I may not call you, who cannot be possibly guiltie of such a sin in the opinion of Aulicus,[b] the only author which (it seems by your language) you are verst in.

You are very tender of shedding innocent blood, and therefore Patie must die; but, good Sir Lewis, for what crime? He served, you say, on your side; I have heard 'twas (as you do) onely as a scribe; and hath since turned rebel, because he would not tamely stand still, whiles you were plundering him. *Heu nefas infandum!* for this, right or wrong, the poor man must suffer, and (setting honesty aside) you will be just for certain. May it please your Worship to be mercifull too, if not to him, yet to me and mine (when we fall into your hands); till when your last experience might remember you that I am as far from fearing, as my present condition is far from needing your quarter, which I hope I shall have an opportunitie to dispute further of with you; whom, or any man in England, I shall answer in this quarrell. In the mean, know that I intend to make a halter of your letter to hang Hodder with; whose crime is the first contrivance of that treachery, which you after (though, blessed be God! but simply) acted to the losse of what you lately valued worth a Crown.[c] Patie you may hang, but will not be able to bury; which may occasion a great mortality amongst you. And therefore be advised to forbear, by him, to whom proclaiming yourself a professed enemy, you have invited me as professedly to subscribe myself,

Yours,

W. SYDENHAM.

March 25, 1644.

[a] Alluding to that of Lord Goring.   [b] Mercurius Aulicus, the Court newspaper.
[c] This alludes to the passage in the intercepted letter of Sir Lewis to the Earl of Bristol (printed in italic).

The King, on his return from Cornwall, reached Sherborne in Dorsetshire (the seat of the Earl of Bristol, our hero's stepfather,) on the 30th of September, 1644, and there, says Lord Clarendon,[a] "Sir Lewis Dyve was left with his own regiment of one hundred and fifty old soldiers, and some horse, and made commander-in-chief of Dorsetshire, in hope that he would be able shortly by his activity, and the very good affection of the county, to raise men enough to recover Weymouth; and he did perform all that could reasonably be expected from him."

On the 21st of November, 1644, says the *Mercurius Aulicus*, "intelligence came that Sir Lewis Dyve went from Sherborne to dislodge a party from Poole, &c., who had posted themselves at Blandford; whither he returned, and after a week's stay there, marched to Dorchester; and, understanding that four troops of rebel horse lay near, he intended to beat up their quarters, but was betrayed by the townsmen, who sent for assistance two hours before. He charged them with a small party of horse, and they fled instantly. Next day Sir Lewis retired to Sherborne, having increased his strength by this march, besides those horse, arms, and prisoners taken from the rebels."

This is a Royalist report, the next a Parliamentarian:—About the 30th of November, "Sir Lewis Dyve, being at Dorchester, with about 300 horse and dragoons, sent a party to face Lyme, which they did accordingly, and went backe without attempting any thing; but Major Sydenham, impatient at such empty flourishes, drew out [from Poole] about 50 or 60 horse, that night, and went to Dorchester, fell on the enemy in the town, charged them through and through, wounded Sir Lewis Dyve, slew many, and tooke divers prisoners."[b]

At the commencement of the following year, the attack on Weymouth, to which Sir Lewis had been particularly commissioned, was pursued with vigour. "On the 9th of February, Sir Walter Hastings, Governor of Portland, took the great fort of Weymouth; and two days after Sir Lewis Dyve, then Colonel-General of Dorset, took the middle fort, surprised the town, and possessed himself of the forts and upper town, the rebels retiring into the lower town," as Melcombe was called. They were there "looked upon as prisoners at mercy;" but the event proved that the Royalists erroneously so regarded them, as on the 24th of the same month Colonel Sydenham, the Parliamentarian commander, recovered the greater part of the place, and "next morning Lord Goring and Sir Lewis Dyve drew out of Weymouth, and marched to Dorchester, leaving behind them the ordnance taken at Weymouth, and taking with them nothing but the

---

[a] Clarendon, vol. ii. p. 541.   [b] *Perfect Diurnall*, No. 71.

plunder." The blame of this "fatal loss" does not appear to have attached to Sir Lewis; but, says Lord Clarendon, was "with great plainness imputed to General Goring's want of vigilance," his lordship having been sent to the garrison "with 3,000 horse and 1,500 foot (besides what he found in those parts)."

"All Dorsetshire," says Clarendon, was now "entirely possessed by the rebels, save only what Sir Lewis Dyve could protect by his small garrison at Sherborne and the island of Portland, which could not provide for its own subsistence." Affairs remained thus until the summer; when Sir Thomas Fairfax, on returning from his victorious campaign in the West, arrived at Sherborne, and "laid close siege to it on the 2nd of August." On the 6th he received the following manly and defiant letter from our hero :—[a]

S^r,

I have received your second Sum'ones this daye for the surrenderinge this Castle of Sherborne unto your hands for the use of the Kingdome. I shall endeavour to purchase a better opinion wth you (before I leave it) then to deliver it upp uppon such easie termes; I keepe it for his Maiestie my Soveraigne, unto whom this Kingdome belonges, and by the blessinge of the Almightie am resolved to give him such an accompt thereof, as becomes a Man of Honor to doo; who is, S^r, your humble servaunt,

LEWIS DYVE.

Sherborne Castle, August 6to, 1645.

Sir Lewis sustained the siege for nine days after the date of the above; and the following anecdotes of his dauntless conduct are extracted from a circumstantial narrative of the siege, written by Sprigge, the contemporary historian of the triumphs of Fairfax. When perused with a caveat upon that detraction which was the writer's object, they will not otherwise than increase our esteem for the chivalrous Royalist.

On the 12th, "the Generall, according to his wonted nobleness, said to Sir Lewis Dyve, That, if he pleased to send out his Lady, or any other women, he would give way to it. Sir Lewis thankfully acknowledged the favour, seemed to incline to accept of it, but gave no positive answer, expressing withall his resolution (souldier-like) to hold out to the last; but, under favour, it was a madnesse

---

[a] From the original in the Sloane MSS. 1519, fol. 60. The signature only is Sir Lewis's writing The letter is written in a bold, correct hand; and it is interesting to remark, that on the last day of the siege, having a few hours before penned the letter hereafter inserted, "Sir Lewis Dyve his secretary was slain by a shot."—Sprigge's *Anglia Rediviva*, p. 85.

rather than valour, seeing he despaired of relief; and since that he hath felt the misery of it by a long imprisonment in the Tower."

On the 14th, "after the breach was made, such was the noble and mercifull disposition of the Generall, that he sent a third summons to surrender the castle, or to expect extremity; which drove the Governour into a great passion (which is not hard to doe), in so much as he said he would hang the drum; and when the drum, delivering his message stoutly, was as he thought sawcy, he told him he must have more manners in his presence,[a] and sent an answer to this purpose, That the language was so far differing from what he had formerly received, that he would not believe that it came from the same hand; but said, that he would not lose his honour to save his life (it may be, as one sayes of him, because his cause and carriage had already lost it); if the last were, he should think it well bestowed in the service."

At two in the next morning, "the Governour, having cooled his brain with a little sleep (without any other provocation), sent out a drum with"—this letter:[b]

Sir, I must acknowledge the advantage you have of me, by being master of my walls; and that you may not think me obstinate without reason, I have sent this drum unto you, to let you know that, if I may have such conditions from you as are fit for a souldier and a gentleman to accept, I shall surrender this Castle unto your hands; otherwise I shall esteem it a far greater happiness to bury my bones in it; and the same resolution have all those that are with me. And give me leave to add this, that your victory will be crowned with more honour by granting it, then you will gaine glory by the winning it, with the loss of so much blood as it will cost,

I am your servant,

Sherborn Castle, August 15, 1645.   L. DYVE.

"Answer was returned, 'No terms but quarter, seeing he had slipt and slighted the opportunity; and he was not to expect that, except he rendered speedily.'" The besiegers proceeded with the storm; and when they had made their way into the great court of the castle, the garrison was at length compelled to yield. "They pulled down their bloody colours, hung out a white flag, had no power to make opposition, and sent a drum for to crave quarter; but before he could get it and return, a great part of our foot were entred, they within had thrown down their arms, and cryed for quarter to our souldiers, which our souldiers (inclining rather to booty than revenge) gave them; but stript they were to the purpose, all except Sir Lewis Dyve, and his lady, and some few more. And

---

[a] "He told him," says Vicars, "he was in the presence of a better man than his Generall."
[b] Sprigge goes on to say, "a message:" but the letter is supplied by Vicars.

so we became master of the castle, and all within it, the souldiers finding plunder of great value, the taking of which in a disorderly manner could not then be prevented. There was taken about 400 prisoners in the castle, Col. Giles Strangewayes [Sir Lewis's brother-in-law], formerly a Member of Parliament,[a] Sir John Walcot [his cousin], Col. Thornhill, and others of quality, and 18 pieces of ordnance, and a mortar piece. The reducing of this place was of the greatest concernment, in regard of the influence it had upon the disaffected Clubmen in those parts, who, having the countenance of this garrison, were made so much the more bold in their attempts and meetings."[b]

"About the 24th," says Vicars, "the prime prisoners were brought to London by sea, and two of the chief of them were (as this day) brought to the House of Commons, viz. Sir Lewis Dyve, and Colonel [Giles[c]] Strangeways; who were by a strong guard attended, and at last caused to come into the House to the bar. Here, with spirit unbroken, Dyve, we are told, " demeaned himselfe very superciliously and proudly, seeming to refuse to kneel on both his knees till he was compelled unto it; and then the Speaker of the House of Commons [Lenthall] told him, that he was much to be lamented, who, notwithstanding that he had been a meanes to shed so much innocent blood, and had committed so much treason against his native Kingdome, endeavouring to destroy the same, and helping (as much as in him was) to draw the King from his Parliament; and yet his heart should no more (nay not at all) relent, but that he looked before that Honourable presence as one whom God had given over to hardnesse of heart, and impudency of carriage. He therefore for his Treasons pronounced the commitment of him, and of Colonel [Giles[c]] Strangeways, to the Tower of London, there to remaine prisoners till justice should further proceed against them."

About the same time the estates of Sir Lewis were sequestered.[d]

[a] Vicars and Whitelocke enumerate among the prisoners, " Colonel Sir John Strangeways," the father; but do not mention the son. Perhaps both were taken, as both were sent to the Tower about the same time. (See their memoirs in Hutchins's Dorset, edit. 1867, vol. ii. p. 664.) Another prisoner was "one of the Lord Powlet's sons."

[b] Sprigge's *Anglia Rediviva*, fol. 1647, pp. 83-86.

[c] Vicars, in error, names him "Sir George;" but see note [a] above.

[d] In Addit. MSS. (Brit. Mus.) 5494, is a list of the rents of Delinquents' Estates, co. Beds. The tenants of Sir Lewis Dyve, in the parishes of Bromham, Steventon, and Houghton, were in number twenty-one, and their total rents amount to 481*l*. 5*s*. 4*d* ; the demesnes of the manor of Bromham, not let, were valued at 139*l*.; and the parsonage at 30*l*.—The next article in the same volume is a list of the delinquents' goods, which is curious, as generally describing the furniture of the mansions. The goods of Sir Lewis Dyve, however, only consisted of barley, the residue having been " caryed away by soldiers before they were

In the "Familiar Letters" of James Howel,[a] there are three letters to Sir Lewis Dyve, two of which were addressed to him when a prisoner "in the Tower." The first is dated "23 Feb. 1645[-6], from the prison of the Fleet;" and, in a quaint style of chemical phraseology, turns on the subject so appropriate from one captive to another,—the benefits that may be derived from patience in confinement.[b] The second is as follows:—

> Sir, To help the passing away of your weary hours between them disconsolate walls, I have sent you a King of your own name,[c] to bear you company, Lewis the Thirteenth, who, though dead three years since, may peradventure afford you some entertainment; and I think that dead men of this nature are the fittest companions for such as are buried alive, as you and I are. I doubt not but you, who have a spirit to overcome all things, will overcome the sense of this hard condition, that you may survive these sad times, and see better days. I doubt not, as weak as I am, but I shall be able to do it myself; in which confidence I style myself
>
>   Your most obliged and ever faithful servitor,
>
>   J. H.
>
> *Fleet*, 14 *Feb.* 1646.
> My most humble service to Sir J. St.[d] and Sir H. V.[e]

Sir Lewis Dyve may now for a time be made his own biographer; as in 1647-8 he appeared as an author, with (to use a modern term) a "personal narrative" of the circumstances of the escape which he had then recently accomplished. His "Letter"[f] was evidently published in vindication of his word of honour, on account of his being accused of having broken his parole. "I shall not looke backe," he says, "upon those many miseries I suffered since my first imprison-

---

sequestred." In Dorsetshire were sequestered "the old rents of the manor of Sutton Walrond, value 11*l*. 13*s*. 2*d*., and the farm belonging to Sir Lewis Dyve, Knt. in right of his wife, then dead." Hutchins's Dorsetshire, vol. iii. p. 372.

[a] In a letter to Sir Edward Sackville, dated March 26, 1643, Howel also mentions Sir Lewis. Among some *badinage* respecting the legacies which he had intended in a late "shrewd disease," he says he thought to bequeath "my Spanish to Sir Lewis Dyve and Master Endymion Porter, for, though they are great masters of that language, yet it may stead them something when they read *la picara Justina*."

[b] Epistolæ Ho-elianæ, p. 334.

[c] This was Howel's "Lustra Ludovici; or, The Life of Lewis XIII. King of France; and of Cardinal de Richelieu. London, 1646," folio.

[d] Probably Sir John Strangeways, Sir Lewis's father-in-law, also a prisoner in the Tower.

[e] Sir Henry Vaughan; see the list of Prisoners hereafter.

[f] "A Letter from Sir Lewis Dyve, written out of France to a gentleman, a friend of his, in London; giving him an account of the manner of his escape out of the King's Bench, and the reasons that moved him thereunto. Printed in the yeare 1648," 4to, pp. 8. By a memorandum on the copy among the King's pamphlets in the British Museum, it appears to have been published Feb. 24, 1647-8.

ment in the Tower, nor upon those heavie oppressions wherewith I was there loaded, contrary to the law of armes, the law of nature and nations; for if I should begin my storie from thence it would fill a volume. It shall therefore suffice that I begin from the time of my being removed from the Tower, where I continued above two years, and the greatest part of that time close prisoner; from whence, towards the latter end of last Michaelmas terme, I was by pretence of a habeas corpus, procur'd by the subtiltie of my adversaries, by force and violence brought before the King's Bench barre, by Colonel Tichborne the Lieutenant of the Tower, upon an action of debt, whereas I stood charg'd and committed before for high treason by the House of Commons,—a strange president, and not to be paralel'd, as I beleeve, before these unhappy times. From the King's Bench barre I was immediately turned over to be a prisoner at the King's Bench, without any due processe or forme of law." He proceeds, however, to explain the circumstances; which arose, he says, from his having been engaged for the Earl of St. Alban's and Sir Edward Stradling, for certain great sums of money, the lands assigned for the liquidation of which had been sequestered.

On arriving at his new prison, Sir Lewis was conducted to the Marshall, Sir John Lenthall, who, he says, " treated me with much civilitie; and having (as it should seeme) understood by some who had long knowne me, that, if I would engage my word unto him of being a true prisoner, it would hold me faster then all the locks and guards he could devise to put upon me, he in a very generous and free manner proposes it unto me, telling me withall that he had ever heard me esteemed for a man of honour; so as, if I would engage my word, he would esteeme it as the best securitie that could be given him. The franknesse of his proceeding prevailed with me (I must confesse) even against the resolution I had taken not to bind my selfe up by my word upon any condition whatsoever; which I yeelded neverthelesse to doe, being overcome by his kindnesse, adding this protestation withall, that, were it to save my life, he might be confident I would not breake with him, *untill I should first give him faire warning, by revoking it.*" This "warning," it will be afterwards seen, forms the gist of the whole story.

Having taken lodgings within the Rules, "there was seldome any day past that I came not by way of gratitude to visit him or his lady." But it was also perceived that Sir Lewis did not confine his visits within such narrow bounds; and Mr. Speaker Lenthall "sent a strict charge to his brother Sir John to have a speciall care of me as of a most dangerous person." Sir John Lenthall having communicated these unpalatable directions in a friendly manner, Sir Lewis Dyve was for some days particularly careful not to stir out of the Rules; hoping that the attention of his enemies might in the mean time be diverted. "But, contrarie to my hopes, the next newes I heard was that it was resolved the fittest place to secure me was the common gaole; and I had further intelligence given me by two persons considerable with them, and no strangers to their counsells, that there were desperate intentions against me, and therefore wished me, as I tendred my life, to make my escape now I had an opportunitie to doe it, for the meanes might otherwayes be suddenly taken from me."

His word of honour given to Sir John Lenthall was the only obstacle to Sir Lewis in following this advice, and he proceeds to relate the artful manœuvre by which he contrived to remove, or rather evade, it. "The warrant for my close commitment,"[a] he says, "I knew precisely when it would be brought to Sir John Lenthall, and that very night, Friday the fourteenth of January, I went to visit Sir John at his own house; where, finding him sitting in conversation with his lady and some others of his family, I fell into discourse with him, and after a while I tooke occasion to tell him that, 'out of my respects to him, I had confined my selfe in the nature of a close prisoner for a good while; but that, having some speciall occasions to draw me into the towne the next day, I intended to goe in the evening, which should be done with that wariness that no notice should be taken thereof.' This stroake gave fire immediately, according to my expectation; whereupon he said, that 'it was in his thoughts to have spoken unto me the next morning by way of prevention, for that divers of the House [of Commons] were so much incensed at my going abroad, as he beleeved there would be an order for my close imprisonment.' I seemed much moved with the

---

[a] From the *Perfect Occurrences*, No. 55, it appears that this measure of the Parliament originated from a "libell dispersed amongst malignants about the City of London, pretending to be (as for the King, so) for the liberty of the Subject, promising a rising, and threatening to possesse the Tower, and to murder the Parliament men; and that (upon the rising) whosoever shall have any Member of Parliament in their house, and not discover it to the then Governour of the Tower (by them placed), shall be hanged at their own dores. In this designe it is said that there were about 100 officers, of which the lowest a Captain. Some suspition against the Lord Cleaveland, *Sir Lewis Dyve*, and others, *because many cavaliers resort to them*, and notice was taken of many that had been in armes against the Parliament that came lately to London. Above 100 in severall companies came in the evening before." Sir Lewis, as his letter was written for publication, of course does not himself enter into any of these proceedings; but among the immediate resolutions of the House of Commons on the 14th of January (the same day mentioned by Sir Lewis) were these: "that the Earl of Cleaveland be remanded by the Lieutenant of the Tower, and kept close; that Sir John Lenthall take care that Sir Lewis Dyve be kept close in the King's Bench; and that Mr. Soliciter do effectually prosecute Sir Lewis Dyve, Sir John Stowell, and Mr. David Jenkins, by indictment against them for their lives, at the King's Bench bar, the next terme."

newes, and told him 'I hoped he would not be the instrument to execute so unreasonable and unjust an order, having given him my word to be his true prisoner.' 'Alas!' said he, 'what would you have me doe, in case I am commanded? For, as I am their servant, if I disobey their orders, they will thrust me out of my place, and ruine me.' 'By the same reason,' said I somewhat tartly unto him, 'if they should bid you knock out my braines, or starve me, you must then doe it.' He desired me not to make such inferences, for that he knew they would command him no such thing; but for the keeping me a close prisoner, in that he was bound to obey them. When he had thus farre declared himselfe, I held it a fit time for me to revoke the engagement of my word; which, that he might suppose it to be done rather out of choler than designe, I fell into a strange passion (not misbecoming my usage,[a] though it might be thought it did by my condition,) and in great heat told him, *I would not longer be ingag'd upon my word,* with some other expressions of deepe resentment of the barbarous usage I had from time to time receiv'd, but that I valued not the uttermost extremitie that tyrannie could inflict upon me; and so, thrusting from me the chair whereon I sate, I made a short turne in the roome, taking in my hand a candlestick which stood upon a side table, and, striking it with violence upon the board, did much bruise the fashion thereof; and all this was done in a breath, so as it seemed but one motion.

"The women that were there, were somewhat amazed at this; but the Lady Lenthall herselfe, who holds it a high reputation to be thought a woman of spirit,[b] what with the bruising of the candlestick, and some words that fell from me, which she interpreted to the disparagement of her husband (though I professe they were spoken with no such intent), grew suddenly in such a fury as passionate women are wont to expresse when they are thoroughly angred. The words that kindled her choler was, as I remember, something that touched upon my 'being turned from jaylor to jaylor,' which she highly aggravated after her manner, entring upon comparisons of her husband's worth, which I meant not in the least to diminish; with whom being unwilling to have any dispute, the work for which I came being performed, I went towards the door with intention to retire to my lodging, there to bethinke my selfe of what more interrupted me; but, as it happened, her ladyship at that time fill'd up the passage with her

[a] A candid confession this! We have seen (in p. 96) the same characteristic of Sir Lewis mentioned by Sprigge.

[b] This high-spirited lady was Bridget, third daughter of Sir Thomas Temple, of Stowe, Bart. ancestor of his Grace the Duke of Buckingham.

person, so as, to passe by, I tooke her by the hand to remove her a little out of the way, which she took for so great an affront, that she presently cryed out that I had struck her; but the truth is, had not Sir John Lenthall himselfe, and some of his daughters in the roome, interposed betweene her and me, I verily beleeve it would have fallen to my share to have complained of a beating, which I should much better have borne from a lady's hand, than the reproach she layd on me of having struck her. I then became a stickler to perswade her to patience, and to desire her that she would not through passion doe her selfe so much wrong as to say that of me which, should she sweare, would never be believed by any body that knew me, and to intreat her pardon, 'if by transportation of the same passion which was now so prevalent in her self, I had either said or done anything that might give her the least offence.' With these and the like perswasions, we all grew after a while into a more sober temper; and then I took my leave of them both, and was from thence well guarded to my lodging.

"The next morning my kinsman Sir John Wake[a] came unto me, and told me for certaine, 'that Sir John Lenthall had received an Order from the House of Commons to remove me that night into the Common Gaole.' I desired Sir John Wake to goe to Sir John Lenthall from me, to request this favour in my behalfe, that my removall might be suspended for a day or two, untill I might be able to furnish my lodging with bedding and other necessaries fit for me; but the answer I received was, 'that he durst not doe it for feare of the displeasure of the House.' When I saw there was no remedie, I sent to have the chamber made clear, and aired with a good fire, as there was good cause, for I was told by some that saw it, that it was a most nastie and filthy roome, not fit for a dogge to lye in. Whil'st this preparation was making, and a heape of coales which lay in the chamber removing, the evening grew on, and my fatall houre of removing to a quick[b] buriall. In the meane time I bespake supper, and invited divers gentlemen of my acquaintance in the Rules to sup with me, to take a farewell of them, not knowing when I should have the happinesse to see them againe. Foure or five were pleased to come to me, to affoord me that favour, all of them much lamenting my condition; by this meanes there was a necessitie of passing to and fro out of my lodging, by reason my supper was dress'd abroad. I sent for wine, and disposed my selfe to be merry with my friends, not imparting my intentions to any creature, alwayes having a watchfull eye how those that were set to guard

---

[a] Sir John Wake, the second Bart. of Clevedon in Somersetshire, and ancestor of the present Sir Herewald Wake, was nephew to the Earl of Bristol, Sir Lewis Dyve's stepfather.

[b] In the old sense of "living."

me were placed, with a resolution to have forced my way through them if there had been no other remedie. But the darknesse of the night favoured my attempt so, as, taking the nick of time when supper was bringing in, I slipt from my companye, and got out of the gate unespyed, conveying my selfe suddenly into a place where I knew I should be welcome, leaving my friends to be merry without their host.

"For some few dayes I lay close, untill I found an opportunitie to convey myselfe, where by God's blessing I have now the leysure to satisfie both you and the rest of my friends with this true relation of the businesse; hoping there can nothing be objected against me, in the whole progresse thereof, misbecoming a man of honestie,[a] who desires and shall ever endeavour to approve himselfe so in all his actions to the world."

Not disheartened by his long imprisonment, Sir Lewis appears to have speedily returned to activity, and to have joined the King's forces in Scotland. But a very short time again found him a prisoner, as in May, 1648, his name occurs with those of five other English Royalists, for whose delivery to the government at home agents were then in treaty with the Scottish Parliament.[b] It was, however, only a twelvemonth after Sir Lewis's escape from the King's Bench, that he accomplished another, in a manner even more extraordinary than the former. It is stated by Whitlocke that it took place on the very day of King Charles's execution, the 30th of January, 1648-9;[c] and the circumstances are thus mentioned in Heath's Chronicle:—"Sir Lewis Dyve and Master Holden,[d] being brought to Whitehall upon examination, pretending to ease themselves, got down the common shore to the waterside, leaving their warders in the lurch, and to a vain research after them." We have, however, a more particular account of the

---

[a] Sir Lewis made his escape on a Saturday, and the next day the House of Commons sat, viz., on Monday the 17th, his flight was thus reported :—" That Sir Lewis Dyve, *engaging his honour* to be a true prisoner, was permitted to make a feast, and his guests being all ready, and the meat on the table, he made an excuse to fetch some thing wanting, but made his escape and is gone." It is to this public imputation on his honour, as before suggested, that we owe the animated and amusing narrative which has been so fully quoted.

[b] Calendar of Antient Charters, &c. in the Tower, 4to. 1772, p. 407.

[c] On the same day the Duke of Hamilton contrived to escape from Windsor, but was unfortunately retaken in Southwark. This attempt, and Sir Lewis's escape, made the Parliament hasten the trial of his Grace, of the Earl of Holland, and Lord Capel, who were soon after beheaded.

[d] Whitlocke describes this personage as " Mr. Holder the Prince's agent." Lloyd calls Sir Lewis's companion " Judge Jenkins,"—an error arising from the circumstance that that Judge was ordered to take his trial at the same time as Sir Lewis.

adventure, as Sir Lewis himself related it to the celebrated John Evelyn. It was effected "the very evening before he was to have been put to death,[a] by leaping down out of a jakes two stories high into the Thames, at high water, in the coldest of winter, and at night; so as by swimming he got into a boat that attended for him, though he was guarded by six musquetceres. After this he went about in women's habite, and then in a small-coaleman's, travelling 200 miles on foote; and embark'd for Scotland with some men he had raised, who coming on shore were all surpriz'd and imprison'd on yᵉ Marq. of Montrose's score, he not knowing any thing of their barbarous murder of that hero. This he told us was his fifth escape, and none less miraculous; with this note, that the chargeing thro' 1000 men arm'd, or whatever danger could befall a man, he believ'd could not more confound and distract a man's thoughts than the execution of premeditated escape, the passions of hope and feare being so strong."

Evelyn's account, however, must be regarded as giving but a very general view of Sir Lewis's adventures. Montrose's "barbarous murder" was not perpetrated until May, 1650; it is clear that Sir Lewis was at that time in Ireland, and therefore it must have been Sir Lewis's visit to Scotland, on his previous escape, of which Mr. Evelyn had been told.

Sir Lewis's actual movements in the first part of 1650 appear from his own pen; for in that year he again came forward as an author, and not as the memoir-writer of merely personal adventure, but as the historian of the political occurrences of a country, harassed by the diversified operations of a widely extended civil war. The publication is entitled—

A Letter from Sʳ Lewis Dyve to the Lord Marquis of New-Castle, giveing his Lordship an account of the whole conduct of the King's affaires in Irland, since the time of the Lord Marquis

---

[a] Here Evelyn must have misunderstood Sir Lewis; who had not yet been brought to trial, but would have had one, as well as the Royalists mentioned in a previous note.—Sir Lewis's escape is also alluded to in the first edition of Wood's *Athenæ Oxonienses*, in connection with the assassination of Dr. Dorislaus, the Parliament's Resident at the Hague. "This desperate attempt," he says, "coming to the knowledge of the Parliament, they became so enraged that they resolved to sacrifice the life of a certain Royalist of note, Sir Lewis Dyve, then in their custody, and certainly they had done it, had he not made a timely escape." As the death of Dorislaus did not occur until May 12, 1649, this account is of course to be rejected; and Wood appears himself to have discovered his error, as the name of Sir Lewis Dyve was omitted after the first edition. Such being the case, it may appear trifling to notice the circumstance; but, as the *variæ lectiones* are restored in the last magnificent edition, it is desirable to trace Wood's motive for his alterations, particularly if they are in correction of errors, which is probably the case with a large proportion of them.

ot Ormond his Excellencies arrivall there out of France in Septem. 1648, until S¹ Lewis his departure out of that Kingdome, in June 1650. Together with the annexed Coppies of sundry Letters mentioned by S¹ Lewis Dyve as relating to the businesse he treats of. From the Hague $\frac{18}{28}$ July 1650. Hague, printed by Samuell Broun, English bookeseller. 1650. 4to, pp. 80.

Sir Lewis's letter alone occupies fifty-four closely-printed pages; and, if it be his own unassisted composition (which there seems no reason to doubt), may support the opinion that this extraordinary man excelled with the pen as well as with the sword. It does not contain any other personal anecdotes, except that on his first arrival in Ireland he found the Lord Lieutenant at the house of Sir Luke Fitzgerald, Tecroghan, co. Kildare, and then first had the honour to kiss his Excellency's hand; and that he left the country (as the title mentions) in June, 1650. In the commencement of the letter he tells the Marquis of Newcastle, as an apology for writing it, that he did "not know whether the necessitie of my occasions (or indeed the usuall thwartnesse of my fortune in what I most covet) would allow me so great a hapiness as personally to waite upon you before I left this country." Whether he did again venture home before the Restoration has not been discovered.

When his visit to Ireland was first known, we find it thus mentioned in a letter of Hugh Peters, "Minister of God's Word," dated Milford, 7 Feb. 1649:—"Sir Lewis Dyve, the great royalist, that broke away to save his head when the Lords were to be tryed, is among the popish Irish: I believe his being there is to see what is probable to be done by them for their King there."[a]

Lloyd, in his *Memoirs of the Loyalists*, says of Sir Lewis, that "he was famous for his services in Bedfordshire and the Associated Counties, in the English war, and (after a cleanly escape from a house of office at Whitehall) *in the Irish*, and for his great sufferings with his Majesty beyond sea, to the loss of £164,000." To the last-named scene we must now follow him; but of his "great sufferings" we shall find little more than his cruel destiny to the consumption of two good dinners. On the 6th of September, 1651, Mr. Evelyn went from Paris with his wife "to St. Germain's, to condole with Mr. Waller's losse, and carried with him and treated at dinner that excellent and pious person the Deane of St. Paule's, Dr. Stewart, and Sir Lewis Dyve." Again, on the 3rd of December following, "Sir Lewis Dyve dined with us, who, relating some of his adventures, shew'd me divers pieces of broad gold, which, being in his pocket in a fight, preserv'd his life by receiving a musket bullet on them, which deaden'd its violence, so that it

---

[a] Several Proceedings in Parliament, Feb. 14 to 21.

went no further, but made such a stroake on the gold as fix'd the impressions upon one another, battering and bending severall of them; the bullet itselfe was flatted, and retain'd on it the colour of the gold. He assur'd us that, of an hundred of them, which it seems he then had in his pocket, not one escap'd without some blemish.

"He affirm'd that his being protected by a Neapolitan Prince, who conniv'd at his bringing some horses into France, contrary to order of ye Viceroy, by assistance of some banditti, was the occasion of a difference between those great men, and consequently of ye late civil war in that kingdom, the Viceroy having kill'd the Prince standing on his defence at his owne castle.

"He told me that the second time of the Scots coming into England, the King was six times their number, and might easily have beaten them, but was betraied, as were all other his designes and councils, by some even of his Bedchamber, meaning M. Hamilton,[a] who copied Montrose's letters from time to time when his Ma^{ty} was asleepe."

And here, at the close of Sir Lewis's stories, may well be appended the opinion which Mr. Evelyn formed of him after the previous dinner, that "this Knight was indeede a valiant gentleman, but not a little given to romance when he spake of himselfe!"[b]

The third of the before-mentioned letters in the Epistolæ Ho-elianæ was addressed to Sir Lewis when at Paris. It has no date; but was probably written about 1653. From its commencement we learn that the correspondence between

---

[a] This means the Marquis, or, more correctly, the Duke, of Hamilton, who suffered under great suspicion, though there is reason to believe very unjustly.

[b] It is remarkable that in this particular Sir Lewis had as illustrious an example as Sir Kenelm Digby, who was in some measure his kinsman, and to whom we are indebted for his introduction to our present notice. Sir Kenelm, like Sir Lewis, and "as was reason," took the lead in conversation; but his philosophical anecdotes were as much distrusted as Sir Lewis's military ones. Evelyn expresses such difficulty of credit; and the following is an extract from the recently published Memoirs of Lady Fanshawe:—"When we came to Calais, we met the Earl of Strafford and Sir Kenelm Digby, with some others of our countrymen. We were all feasted at the Governor's of the castle, and much excellent discourse passed; but, as was reason, most share was Sir Kenelm Digby's, who had enlarged somewhat more in extraordinary stories than might be averred, and all of them passed with great applause and wonder of the French then at table; but the concluding one was, that barnacles, a bird in Jersey, was first a shell-fish to appearance; and from that, sticking upon old wood, became in time a bird. After some consideration, they unanimously burst out into laughter, believing it altogether false; and, to say the truth, it was the only thing true he had discoursed with them; *that was his infirmity*, though otherwise a person of most excellent parts, and a very fine-bred gentleman."

Howel and our hero was more extensive than appears in print:—"Noble Knight, yours of the 22 current come to safe hand; but what you please to attribute therein to my letters, may be more properly applied to yours in point of intrinsic value; for, by this correspondence with you, I do as our East India merchants used to do: I venture beads and other baggatels, out of the proceeds whereof I have pearl and other oriental jewels return'd me in yours." It is to be lamented that none of these gems of Sir Lewis's pen have occurred for insertion here. Howel proceeds with some reflections on the fanaticism of the age, and introduces a poem on that subject. A subsequent paragraph gives at second hand the subject at least of Sir Lewis's last letter: "You write that you have 'The German Dyet,' which goes forth in my name, and you say, that 'you never had more matter for your money.' I have valued it the more ever since in regard that you please to set such a rate upon't, for I know your opinion is current and sterling. I shall shortly by T. B. send you a new History of Naples, which also did cost me a great deal of oyl and labor." Howel's "German Diet" was published in 1653, and his "Parthenopeia, or History of Naples," in 1654. These dates nearly fix that of this letter; in the conclusion of which Howel desires "to present the humblest of service to the noble Earl your brother," who had then recently succeeded to the title, on the death of the first and celebrated Earl, January 21, 1652-3.

My biographical collections regarding Sir Lewis now cease until the period of his death, which occurred nine years after the Restoration, in the seventieth year of his age. He was buried in the church of Combe Hay in Somersetshire, where, within the altar-rails, is the following inscription on a brass plate:—[a]

☦

Here lyeth ye body of Sr LEWIS DYVE of Bromham in the county of Bedford, kt. only son of Sr John Dyve of Bromham, kt. by Dame Beatrice his wife, daughter of Charles Walcot, of Walcot[b] in ye county of Salop, esq. who was afterwards married to ye R^t Honble John Earle of Bristol, by

---

[a] Collinson, in the *History of Somersetshire*, makes the strange blunder of placing this inscription in Dunkerton church; he also gives but an imperfect abstract, omitting all mention of the connection with the Bristol family. Combhay became the property of Sir Lewis in 1644; it afterwards went to the Husseys, the family into which his daughter was married.

[b] On the flat marble to the memory of this lady in Sherborne church, Dorsetshire, are the arms of *Digby*, impaling quarterly, 1 and 4, a chevron between three chess-rooks ermine, for *Walcot* of Walcot; which shows that the monument in Bromham church, erected by her first husband, Sir John Dyve, was intended, by him, for his father, Sir Lewis, whose lady was Mary, daughter of Sir Walter Strickland, and whose arms, viz., Three escallops, impaled with Dyve, occupy the chief place on that monument.

whom she had issue ye R^t Honble George now Earle of Bristol. The said Sr Lewis Dyve took to wife Howard daughter of Sir John Strangeways, of Melbury Sampford in the county of Dorset, and by her had issue at the time of his death three sons, Francis, Lewis, and John, and one daughter Grace, who married George Hussey, of Marnhull in the county of Dorset, esq.[a] He dyed April 17th, an'o Dom' 1669.

Of Sir Lewis's three surviving sons, the eldest, Francis, married, first, his cousin Grace, daughter of Giles Strangeways, esquire; and secondly, December 14, 1665, at the parish of the Close, Lichfield, Theophila, daughter of John Hacket, D.D., Bishop of Lichfield. He was a benefactor to the repairs of Lichfield Cathedral, where his name is inscribed on one of the stalls of the choir, FRANCISCUS DYVE, ARM. F. F. He appears also to have put up a new pulpit in Bromham church, which had on it the arms of Dyve impaling Hacket. He was appointed a gentleman of the King's privy chamber in 1669;[b] and died (without surviving male issue) in 1685, leaving his next brother Lewis his heir.

Lewis was a military man, as appears from his epitaph on a flat black stone in Bromham church:—

Here lyeth interred ye body of Capt Lewis Dyve, ye son of Sir Lewis Dyve, who departed this life the jst of Jan. 1686, at his house at Brumham in the county of Bedford, in ye 46th year of his age.[c]

Captain Dyve was married, as his arms, carved at the head of this epitaph, impale a bend between six martlets; and each coat being surmounted by its crest (a custom occasionally practised in the seventeenth century,[d] though discountenanced by most heralds), that of the lady's side is a (? cock's) head erased. He had three children, one son and two daughters. His son Lewis, born at New Ross, co. Wexford, January 2, 1677, was twice married, and had one son, who died an infant, and four daughters. This Lewis appears by the Bromham register to have been living there from 1700 to 1708, but it was about the latter year that he sold the old family estate to Sir Thomas Trevor.[e]

[a] Mr. Hussey's first wife had been a Walcot; a cousin of his second through the Countess of Bristol her mother. The daughter of Sir Lewis Dyve was grandmother of the excellent artist Giles Hussey, esq. of whom there is a portrait and memoir in the History of Dorsetshire.

[b] Carlisle's *Gentlemen of the Privy Chamber*, p. 183.

[c] The inscription is correctly copied from the stone in Bromham church; but the age is evidently incorrect. Capt. Lewis Dyve was born in 1633.

[d] See Sir Nicholas Bacon's entrance to the chapel of Corpus Christi College, engraved in the Gentleman's Magazine, vol. xcvi. i. 393.

[e] In reference to the early history of Bromham it may be noted here (having been previously overlooked)

APPENDIX.

John, the youngest son of Sir Lewis Dyve, was married April 29, 1673, at St. Chad's, Lichfield, to Frances, third daughter of Sir Robert Wolseley, the first Baronet of Wolseley in Staffordshire. He was appointed one of the Clerks of the Privy Council in 1691. (Jones's Index.) He died in 1692, and was buried in St. James's, Westminster, as was his widow Frances, who died in 1702. By that lady he had John his successor, another son named Lewis,[a] and a daughter Charlotte, who was married to William Lord Sundon, and died childless January 1, 1741-2. His lordship (when Mr. Clayton) was one of the executors to the will of the great Duke of Marlborough (see the will in the 6th vol. of Coxe's Marlborough). His wife was the friend and correspondent of Sarah Duchess of Marlborough, and enjoyed the confidence of Queen Caroline.[b] There are portraits after Kneller of Mr. and Mrs. Clayton, with an inscription in Latin, stating that they were presented in 1728 by Mrs. C. to Dr. Freind, the celebrated physician, who had attended Mr. Clayton in a dangerous illness. There is also a whole-length portrait of Lady Sundon on Lord Ilchester's staircase at Melbury.

The succeeding John Dive[c] married Dorothy, daughter and heiress of Walter Aston, of Millwich in Staffordshire, esquire, great-uncle of the sixth, seventh, and eighth Lords Aston of Forfar. This Mr. Dive[d] died at a very advanced age, January 25, 1769, at his house in Queen Square, Westminster. He left issue a son John, and a daughter Charlotte, who, having been a maid of honour to the Princess of Wales, became, February 4, 1762, the second wife of Samuel second and last Lord Masham; she died without issue May 21, 1773, aged 61; and is buried in the churchyard of Laver near Ongar in Essex.

The third John Dive (then a captain in the Guards) married in 1737 Anne Dorothy Montgomery; by whom he had two sons, who died without issue; and a daughter Charlotte, married in 1759 to John Edmondes, esquire, whose daughter Charlotte became the wife of Llewellin Traherne, esquire, and the mother of the

---

that in the will of one of the Lords Hampden there is mention of a manor called 'Bowels, Wakes and Brays'; the same nobleman's estate also extended into Stevington and Kempston. In 1787 Viscount Hampden had a farm and about 78 acres of wood in Odell.—Cooper.

[a] See the Account of Loans to the Lords and Commons in 1722, where Lewis Dive and John Dive are called brothers of Mr. Clayton. Index Rerum et Vocabulorum.—Tracts in London Institution, vol. 144, No. 7.

[b] The Life of Lady Sundon, by Mrs. Thomson, was published in 1847.

[c] The family latterly always wrote their name with an i; and this gentleman did so in a power of attorney dated March 7, 1719 (penes Henry Humphrey Goodhall). He was then resident in Queen Square, Westminster, where he died fifty years after.

[d] This is "Tommy Townshend's Mr. Dive," as Mr. Daniel Wray calls him in 1745; see Nichols's Literary Illustrations of the Eighteenth Century, vol. i. p. 58.

late Rev. John Montgomery Traherne, F.R.S. and F.S.A. (who died February 7, 1860), to whose contributions this memoir has been considerably indebted.

The foregoing exhaustive narrative may be appropriately supplemented by the following selections from a poem or ballad entitled:—

A Loyal Song of the Royal Feast, kept by the Prisoners in the Tower, in August, 1648, with the Names, Titles, and Characters of every Prisoner.

By Sir F. Wortley, Knight and Baronet, Prisoner.[a]

(1.) God save the best of Kings, King *Charles*,
The best of Queens, *Queen Mary*,
The Ladies all, Gloster and York,
Prince Charles so like old Harry:

---

[a] Printed in London, in the same year as is supposed. It consists of 25 verses, and the copy preserved in the British Museum has MS. notes, most of which are introduced (in brackets) in the subjoined—

LIST OF PRISONERS.

Marquis of Winton.
Bishop of Ely (14 years Prisoner in the Tower).
Judge Jenkins.
Sir F. Wortley, Knt. & Bart.
Sir Edward Hayles, Knt. & Bart.
Sir John Strangwayes, Knt. & Bart.
Sir Benj. Ayliffe, Knt. & Bart.
Sir — Benefield
Sir Walter Blunt
Frank Howard } (Romishly affected, but enemies to Jesuites).
— Slaughter
Sir James Hewet, Knt. & Bart.
Sir Thomas Lunsford, Knt. & Bart.
Sir Lewis Dives, Knt.
Giles Strangwayes, Esq., Col. in the K. Army.
Sir John Marlow, Knt. (the Valiant Mayor of Newcastle).
Sir William Morton, Knt.
Thos. Conisby, Sheriff of Hartford, Esq.
Sir Win Bodman, Knt. (Prisoner in the Tower 7 years).
Sir Henry Vaughan (a valiant Knight and the Earl of Carbarrow's uncle).
John Lilburn, Gent. (he had Squint Eyis and died a Quaker).
Tom Violet, goldsmith (who for bringing up to Lond. his Majesty's Letters from Oxford for peace 1647, had taken from him to the value of Eleven Thousand Pounds).
— Hudson, D.D. (that guided the King's Majestie from Oxford to Newark; he was murtherd by the rebels at Lincolnshire, and flung from the top of a house headlong into a mote, and pricked to Death wth Pikes).

God send the King his own again,
His Towre, and all his Coyners,
And bless all Kings who are to raign
From Traytors and Purloyners.
The King sent us poor Traytors here
(But you may guess the reason)
Two brace of Bucks to mend the cheere,
Is't not to eat them Treason?

       *   *   *

(9.) Old Sir *John Strangwayes* he came in,
Though he himself submitted,
Yet as a traytor he must be
Excepted and committed.
Yet they th' exception now take off,
But not the sequestration,
He must, forsooth, to Goldsmiths'-Hall,
The place of desolation.
      The King sent us, &c.

       *   *   *

(14.) Sir *Lewis*[a] hath an able pen,
Can cudgel a Committee,
He makes them do him reason though
They others do not pitty:
Brave *Cleaveland*[b] had a willing mind,
Frank Wortley was not able;
But *Lewis* got four pound per week,
For 's children and his table.
      The King sent us, &c.

(15.) *Giles Strangwayes* has a gallant soul,
A brain infatigable,
What study he ere undertakes,
To master it hee's able.
He studies on his Theoremes,
And *Logarithmes* for number,
He loves to speak of Lewis Dives,
And they are nere asunder.
      The King sent, &c.

       *   *   *

---

[a] " Dives Knight," under which, in MS., " a Gallant Soldier."
[b] " An Earl, a famous Souldier in the K. Army."

(25.) Wee'l then conclude with hearty healths,
To King Charles and Queen Mary,
To the black Lad in buff (the Prince),
So like his Grandsire Harry.
To York, to Gloster, may we not
Send Turk and Pope defiance;
Since we such gallant seconds have
To strengthen our alliance?
Wee'l drink them o're and o're again
Else we're unthankful creatures,
Since Charles the Wise, the valiant King,
Takes us for loyal Traytors.
This if you will rhime dogrel call
(That you please you may name it)
One of the loyal traytors here
Did for a ballad frame it;
Old Chevy Chase was in his mind,
If any sute it better
All these concerned in the song
Will kindly thank the setter.

[In justice to Mr. Collinson, it may here be stated that the portion of note (ª), page 107, which attributes to that gentleman an error with regard to the parish under which the inscription for Sir L. Dyve is placed in the History of Somersetshire, is incorrect.]

STAGSDEN.

Stachedene.—Adjoining Bromham on the south-west is this parish, which has Turvey for its northern boundary; Astwood, in Buckinghamshire, on the west; Kempston, in the hundred of Redbornestoke, on the south; and contains upwards of 3,300 acres. The village, situated on rising ground, is four and a-half miles west from Bedford. It possesses a chalybeate well, now in a neglected condition; during very dry summers water is rather scarce here. Besides the village there are a few scattered houses at West End, Hill Farm, Up End, Wick End, North End, and Bury End. The soil is mostly stiff clay, and there is plenty of stone. This parish was inclosed by Act of Parliament, 52 King George III.

The manor and most of the land, together with the advowson of the vicarage, are the property of the owners of the Bromham estate, one of whose predecessors conveyed about 70 acres to some members of the Independent persuasion, and they have a place of worship here. In the register of voters for the county of Bedford 1873, John Lay is entered as a 40 shilling freeholder in this village. In 1867-68 there were two 40-shilling freeholds. During the last century the Farrers had an estate or residence in the parish.

On account of the varied interests created, owing to the numerous small estates and holdings into which the lands of Stagsden were divided and subdivided, the general history of the descent of property in this parish, to be gathered from public records and the other available sources of information, is neither very clear nor well connected.

Manor. Beauchamp Fee. Bedford Honor.[a] (The land of Hugh de Belcamp in the half hundred of Buchelai.) Hugh himself holds Stachedene, taxed at five

---

[a] Vide Bromham.

Further records of this parish in Domesday Book:—

Baieux Fee. (The land of the Bishop of Baieux.) In the half-hundred of Bochelai, Herbert son of Ivo holds of the Bishop three hides and three virgates in Stach . . . e. There is land for four ploughs. There are now three plough-lands and a-half, and a-half can be made. There are twelve villans and six bordars. Pasture for one plough-team. Wood for forty hogs. The whole valued at seven pounds—when he received it nine pounds; in the time of King Edward twelve pounds. Twelve socmen, men of King Edward, held this land and were able to sell it. (Domesday, p. 210.) Odo, bishop of Baieux in Normandy,

hides. There is land for five plough-teams. In demesne—two hides, and there are two plough-teams; and twelve villans, they have three ploughs. There are eight bordars and two servi, pasture for one plough-team. Wood for a hundred hogs. Two men of King Edward held this manor, and a vassal of Earl Harold, and each one could give his land to whom he would.—Domesday, p. 213.

was uterine brother of William the Conqueror, who bestowed on him the earldom of Kent, and upwards of four hundred manors in different counties. The charge of Dover Castle was consigned to him after the battle of Hastings, and most, if not all, his lands were subjected to castle-guard of Dover. At length, after a restless course of disappointed ambition, he abjured England, forfeited his title and possessions, and became prime councillor to the duke in Normandy. (Baker, Northants, vol. ii., p. 183.)

Count Eustace Fee. Boulogne Honor. (The land of Count Eustace in the half-hundred of Bochelai.) In Stachedene, Godwin, an Englishman, holds one virgate of Count Eustace. The land is for half a plough-team, and there is one ox-gang. This land is worth two shillings—when he received it five shillings; in the time of King Edward ten shillings. (Domesday, p. 211.) The whole of Count Eustace's fee in Bedfordshire was situated within the limits of the modern hundred of Willey. The head of the division of the honor of Boulogne in this county seems to have been Stevington, under which a general account of the property of Count Eustace in Bedfordshire will be more appropriately placed.

Judith Fee. (The land of Countess Judith in the half-hundred of Buchelai.) In Stachedene Hugh holds of the Countess one hide. There is land for one plough-team, and there it is, and (there are) two villans and two bordars. Wood for forty hogs. It is worth and has been worth ten shillings; in the time of King Edward twenty shillings. Two socmen of King Edward held this land, and could sell it to whom they would. (Domesday, p. 217.) Most of the extensive possessions of the Countess Judith, niece of William the Conqueror, subsequently constituted the Honor of Huntingdon, of which an extended notice is reserved for Harrold, one of the principal manors of that portion of the honor, within this hundred.

Adam, Vicar of Ocle and others, for the Priory of Caldwell, held premises in Milton and Stachesdon.[1]

In this parish, Sir Gerard Braybrook, Knt. junr. and others, held the lands, &c. of the Prioress and convent of Harewold;[2] the sum of two shillings free rent belonging to Harewold, was payable by the heirs of Simon Cornwallys, 28-29 Henry VIII.[3] and a close of pasture with appurtenances in Stagsden, in the county of Bedford, situated between the park and the boundary of Astwood, late in the tenure of Robert Taylor or his assigns, and which had belonged to the said convent, was (int. al.) granted, 29th September 36th King Henry VIII., to Henry Audeley and John Cordall, gentlemen.[4]

St. Alban's Abbey possessed land in this parish.

The Prior of the Hospital of St. John of Jerusalem, on being summoned to show by what right he

---

[1] Esc. 11 Rich. II., nu. 98.

[2] Ib. 16 Rich. II., nu. 75.

[3] Ministers Accounts co. Bedford, 28, 29 Hen. VIII., nu. 75.

[4] Particulars for Grants. Henry Audley, 36 Hen. VIII. section 2, (2). Patent Roll, 36 Hen. VIII., part 23, (31). The sum paid by Henry Audley and John Cordall for the lands, &c., included in this grant was £1,194 10s. 2d. A close of pasture in Stagsden, called Nun's Close, contained 14 acres.

Being another member of Bedford barony,ᵃ the descent of the seigniory to the time immediately preceding the partition of the barony was the same as that of Bromham. From its first coming into their possession, however, the Beauchamps also retained a considerable portion of the lands of Stagsden in their own hands, possibly for sporting purposes. William de Beauchamp of Bedford held part in demesne.ᵇ The Beauchamps' interest in this parish was afterwards, in various proportions, in possession of de Monchensi, de Steyngreve (succeeded by de Pateshulle),ᶜ de Holebury or Hoobury, Paganell, and le Strangeᵃ—through the coheirs. William Latimer had free-warren temp. King Edward III.,ᵉ and Stagsden occurs among numerous other places in Bedfordshire, comprising in the whole twenty Knight's fees appendant to certain manors of John de Neville de Raby, chevalier, and Elizabeth his wife, living in King Richard the Second's time.ᵈ

Under William de Beauchamp, in the time of King Henry III. John de Boeles held two virgates of land here in demesne. Galfridus de Burdeleys one hide in demesne. Galfridus son of Robert one hide. Walter de Stached one hide. Mathew Blund one hide. Peter de Goldington and Galfridus Goliston one hide. William the son of Richard one hide. Also, subordinate to the honor of Bedford at the same time, Thomas Murdoc and Simon Arlewine possessed one hide, the Prior of Newenham and Galfridus Burdeleys a third part of one Knight's fee— holden of the Abbot of Wardon, Robert Golston one virgate, the Prior of Bushmead two virgates and a-half, Nicholas Pinceware one virgate, John Cocus one virgate, Goce (clericus) half a virgate, and William P'teshull half a virgate.ᵇ

The Prior of Newenham, William le Heyr, Hugh Goldston, and Robert Goldston as freeholders, and seventeen inferior tenants, held under William de Monchensi, the most considerable subdivision of Beauchamp's fee in this parish, which comprised three hides of land, a capital messuage, one ancient park, and a

---

claimed view of frank-pledge, &c. of his tenants in this county, proved that he had four tenants in Stagsden, and that they were bound to attend his court leet in his manor of Bedford twice a year.¹

ᵃ Rot. Hund.
ᵇ Testa de Nevill, p. 248ᵇ, 249.
ᶜ Vide Bromham, p. 36, note c.
ᵈ Ib. p. 32.
ᵉ Placita de quo warranto.

---

¹ Placita de quo warranto, Ed. I. Ed III.

wind-mill. The patronage of the church was formerly appendant to the manor, but at this time (7th Edward I.) it belonged to Newenham, having been given in the reign of King Henry II.

The Priory of Newenham in the parish of Goldington, dedicated to St. Paul, was founded by Simon de Beauchamp, who, according to the design of his mother, Rohese or Roisia, removed hither the priory of Black Canons from the collegiate church of St. Paul, Bedford, in the time of King Henry II.;[a] the said Roisia de Beauchamp gave Stagsden Church with land,[b] and the subfeudatories of the Beauchamps made considerable grants to this priory from time to time, mostly confirmed by a charter of Thomas Mowbray, Earl Marshall and of Nottingham, printed at great length in the Monasticon Anglicanum. A Register or Chartulary of Newenham is preserved among the Harleian MSS. number 3656: its contents relate to "Stacheden, Bydenham, Scharnebrok," and other places in this county. The following names of benefactors are taken from the folios headed "Stacheden" and "Bydenham," (143-159) :—[c]

> Robert de Broy de Dilewyc, with consent of his wife and heirs,—grant of a wood called Esthey, eleven acres in Dilewic, and eighteen selions in the same place.
> Robert de Broy de Blecheshou,—an annual rent of twelve pence in Craulei.
> Robert de Broy,—twenty-one selions of land in Dilewic.
> Anselm de Broy, son of Robert de Broy of Stacheden, confirms his father's grants.
> Matilda, relict of Robert Broy of Dilewyc.
> Thomas Boseghate of Astewode.
> In a grant or confirmation of a garden called "Broyes-orcheard," lying in the vill of Stacheden, and of the land of Margarett Bozoun, formerly wife of Alexander Bozon, the following are named: Baldwin Brygham, Thomas Gyllpyn, John Golde, John Clyfton de Baldok, John Galyon, John terry de Stacheden, Agnes formerly wife of Thomas de Bosegate.

[a] Mon. Ang. vol. vi. p. 372, &c. "Roisia, wife to Pagane de Beauchamp, made the priory of Chiksand, and there was she buried in the chapter house. One of the Lord Latymors wifes lyeth at Newnham. Simon de Beauchamp was buried before the high altar of St. Paul, Bedford. One Edward Clynton, Esq. that married a dutchess of Northfole, lyeth at Newenham, not far from the Lady Latimor. There lyeth one Hasilden and one Launselin that had a house and land by Mr. Gascoyn; and Pigot giving in armes the hammer. Gascoyn had part of Pygot's lands." Leland's Collections, vol. i. p. 69. The site of Newenham Priory passed from the Crown, 31 King Henry VIII. to Sir Urian Brereton. In the third Edward VI. the reversion, in case of defect of heirs on the part of Sir Urian, was granted to Sir George Brooke. It is said to have been the residence of Sir Robert Catlin who died 1574, formerly Chief Justice of the King's Bench. Afterwards the property of William Lord Cobham. In 1813 it belonged to Mrs. Mary Best.

[b] Rot. Hund.

[c] At folio 150 are several charters of the Passelewes.

Adam, the son of Dru,—seventy acres of arable land, and a wood called "le ffrith" containing seven acres, in the vill of Stacheden; also land in Dilewic.

Henry Bueles,—40 acres in Stacheden. Henry Buelde gives one acre to the Church of Stacheden, dedicated in honour of St. Leonard, which land was W. le Hode's, lying between the land which was William Bigge's and Robert Gernun's.

Symon de Bueles,—a croft and nine acres of land which were W—'s, the son of Robert de Gravenhurste.

Walter de Stacheden,—half an acre near the wood called "le hoo."

Walter, son of Walter de Stacheden.

Reginald, son of Ernald de Stacheden.

Henry Blund, and Mathew his son.

Mathew Blund de Stacheden,—grant of "Brocmade."

Hugh, son of Henry le Blond.

Thomas, son of Hugh and Nicholas his son.

The sons of Nicholas, son of Thomas de Stacheden.

Galfridus Burdeleye (Stacheden and Turvey),—grant towards sustentation of a lamp before the altar of St. Mary, in the church of St. Leonard at Stacheden.[a]

William Golestan.

John Golestan of Stacheden.

Nicholas, son of Roger Golestan,—land in Westfield, Stacheden.

Pagan, or Paganus.

Stephen, son of Pagan (campionis) de Stacheden.

William, son of R. de Stacheden,—land called "Chokeseth."

Robert Helewarde de Cameston.

Richard, son of Robert de Burnia.

Stephen le Bel.

Roger de Covinton and Alicia le Bel.

Robert, son and heir of Robert Gimices de Stacheden.

Sibilla de Gemis.

William, son of Robert Andrew of Kempston.

Nicholas, son of Roger Goldston.

Matilda daughter of Thomas de Bydenham.

Gilbert de Bydenham.

Hamon son of William de Bydenham.

Simon le zurgien de Bedford.

Robert Cristien of Bydenham.

Walter le ffraunceys of fforde in Bydenham.

---

[a] Patent Roll 17 Elizabeth, Part II. M. (5.) Grant, dated 22nd December, to Anthony Kynwelmersh gent. of a tenement and four acres of land in Stagsden. Quære, whether this was not parcel of Galfridus Burdeleye's gift.

Robert son of Astel de Bydenham.
W. ffrend of Bydenham.
William son of Clare de Boneton of Bedford.
Hugh son of Robert Lowe.
Hugh Grey of Bukyngham.
Robert Blancost of Bydenham.
Robert (? Correr) of Gravenhurst.
William son of Peter de Forde.
Hugh son of Nigel de Forde.
William son of Henry de Bydenham.
Robert Prat of Bedford.
Sara —— (widow).
Michael Coffin.
Nicholas son of Roger Goldston of Stacheden.
Roger son of Julian de Bydenham.
Richard de Ordeleye and Juliana his wife.
Symon Parys of Bromham. (John Cowpe named in this grant).
Adam son of William,—a croft, &c. in Bromham.

The Newenham priory lands of de Monchensi's fee were occupied by three tenants early in Edward the First's reign.[a] By an inquisition post mortem in the 20th King Edward III. it was found that a certain tenement in Stagsden called "Peretre" did not belong to the Prior of Newenham.[b] Baldwin Brygham and others held the lands and premises here for the said Prior and convent in the same reign.[c] In the 9th and 10th King Richard II. the Prior of Newenham had free-warren in this and several other parishes.[d]

Under John de Steyngreve Robert de Stachedene held one virgate of land; Peter de Goudintone, with his tenants, one half virgate (in right of his wife); and Alexander Bozon one hide, the latter having under himself two tenants.[e]

---

[a] Rot. Hund.
[b] Esc. 20 Ed. III. nu. 64.
[c] Ib. 50 Ed. III. nu. 54.
[d] Cal. Rot. Chart. pa. 191, nu. 22.
[e] Rot. Hund. 7 Edw. I.

Temp. John.—The King grants to Roger Gaugy land which was Peter de Goldinton's, in exchange for Caldecote returned to Ralph Martel.—18 King John, A.D. 1216. Rot. Lit. Claus. pp. 272, 351, 572. (Falkes de Breaut occurs as a party in the above transaction.)

„ Hen. III.—Peter de Goldington son of Peter de Goldington held land of the honor of Peverel in Northamptonshire and other counties, and died 37 Hen. III.; he married one of the

Hugh le Blund, in right of his wife, held of John de Holebury one virgate of land, occupied by his free tenants Berteram le Blund, Hugh de Hutt, Cecil de

> six daughters and coheirs of Sir R. de Salceto who held land of the honor of Peverel of Nottingham; another of the daughters of de Salceto married Simon de Thorpe of Harpole.—Baker, Norhamptonshire. The said Peter was lord of Worthington and had three daughters—Matilda who brought the manor of Worthington to her husband, Alan Rohaud, Knt. living 7 and 32 Edw. I.; Dionisia wife of Milo de Hastings; and Isabella, heir to her sister Dionisia, married first Sir Robert Bardolphe, and secondly to Ralph Bozon of Claxton co. Leicester, living 34 Edw. I., and had issue by the latter,—see Nichols's History of Leicestershire, vol. ii., pt. I., p. 132. Arms of Bozoun: Arg. three arrows (*boujons* or birdbolts) gu. feathered knobbed and headed or.—Ib. Also, Blomefield's History of Norfolk, vol. x. p. 81-84. Baker calls the husband of Matilda, Alan FitzRoald, and gives to Isabella only one husband—William de Nowers.—History of Northamptonshire, vol. i. p. 216.

Temp. Hen. III.—William de Goldinton held part of Goldinton, as of the barony of William de Beauchamp of Bedford.—Harl. 313, fo. 47. William Engayne, one of the eight tenants in Ravensden of the same honor.—Ib.

„ „ Peter de Goldinton seised of one Knight's fee in co. Bedford of the honor of Nottingham.—Harl. 313, ff. 48b, 58.

„ Ed. I.—Peter de Goudintone, in right of his wife, held premises in Stagsden, and Alexander Bozon in Stagsden and Bromham—all under John de Steyngreve.—Rot. Hund. 7 Ed. I.

„ Ed. II.—Oakley and Clapham were rated as one village (9 Edward II.), of which Henry Spig^rnel, John Conquest, Simon de Bayouse and John la Chamberleyn, were lords. At the same time, the Prior of Newenham, and William de Goldington, were lords of Goldington.—Parliamentary Writs, vol. ii. div. 3, pp. 367, 368.

„ „ John le Blund held Wildon manor and tenements at Blunesherst (Bolnhurst).—Inq. ad q. Damnum.

„ „ M P.'s for Bedfordshire (A D. 1307-1326)—Ralph Goldington, John de Pabenham, knt. John de Pabenham, junr. knt. John de Morteyn knt. Peter le Loring, John de Sudbury knt. Roger de Bray, Joh. and Thos Spigournel knts. Rich le Rous knt. Walter de Molesworth knt. Gerard de Braybroke knt. Nigel de Saleforde knt. John de Wolaston knt. Walter de Holewelle knt. David de Flitwyk knt. Robert Hotot knt. Hugh Bossord knt. John Morice knt. Robert Dakeny, Ralph Fitz Richard knt. Roger Peyvre knt. Henry de la Legh knt.—Ib. vol. ii. div. 1, p. i.

„ Ed. III.—Juliana the wife of Robert Houtot, seised of manors in Stachesden and Turvey.—Esc. 20 Ed. III. nu. 21.

„ „ John Blund or Blount died seised of lands in Wylden of the honor of Peverel.—Esc. 23 Ed. III. Richard son and heir of John le Blund enfeoffed Richard Chamberlayn with 20 acres in Wilden as of the honor of Peverel.—Esc. 33 Ed. III. See Croke's History of the Croke Family.

Newntone, John le Wyte, Nicholas le Rous, John de la Wykhend, Robert Cok, and the Prior of Bushmead; the Prior of Newenham possessed nine acres,

Temp. Ed. III.—Roger de Wolfreton the escheator in Essex, ordered to accept security for John Goldyngton son and heir of John de Goldyngton and Katharine his wife, of his manor of Spryngefeld holden of the honor of Peverel.—Abbrev. Rot. Orig. 32 Ed. III.

,, ,, John, son of Nicholas Engayne by Amicia daughter of Walter de Fauconberg, a knight banneret; he died at his seat in Huntingdonshire, 14th Feb. 1358, having had issue by Joane his wife, daughter of Sir Robert Peverell, a son, Sir Thomas Engayne (born 1336, died without issue), and three daughters, Joyce, married to William (John) de Goldington, Elizabeth, to Sir Laurence Pabenham, and Mary, to Sir William Barnak.—Wright's History of Essex.

,, ,, John Goldyngton and Jocosa seised of Eton Soken and Sondye.—Esc. 44 Ed. III. nu. 26. Held the manor of Eton for Laurence Pakenham (Pabenham) chevalier.—Ib. 47 Ed. III. nu. 5^b.

,, ,, Edmund Rose held land in the hamlet of Chateley of John son of Sir John Goldington, knt.—Abbrev. Rot. Orig. 49 Ed. III. Ro. 51.

,, Rich. II.—William Bosom, in conjunction with Johanna de Trayley and John de Goldington, presented to the Church of Carlton about the year 1398.—Lincoln Register.

,, ,, John Morice, who married Agnes daughter and heir of Richard Blound, paid a fine for license of entry upon one messuage and eighteen acres in Wilden.—Croke.

,, Hen. V.—John de Goldington of Litlington and others gave to the abbot and convent of Woburn the manor of Potesgrave, Beds.—Cal. Inq. ad q. Damnum, 3 Hen. V. p. 370, nu. 6.

,, Hen. VI.—William Bosoun seised of the manors of Rokesdon and Eton, and part of Wotton, co. Beds.—Esc. 2 Hen. VI. nu. 33.

,, Ed. IV.—William Goldyngton gent. and Margaret his wife,—brass in Lidlington church bearing date 1480, and a shield of arms: On a bend engr. three fleurs de lis or; impaling two coats on the sinister side, viz. 1: a saltire   ; 2: on a chief two buck's or stag's heads cabossed or. (? The last for Popham.—Nichols's Leicestershire, vol. ii. part 2, plate lxxvi. nu. 20, p. 445.) This brass was engraved by Fisher.

,, Hen. VIII.—Eliz.—William ffaldo of Malden and ffaldo married Margerett daughter of Richard de Okle and had issue William of Goldington, Thomas of Okley, and Richard the son and heir of Malden, first husband to Amphillis Chamberlayne, daughter and heir of John Chamberlayne alias Spicer of Normanton, by Jane Neville his wife; the said Amphillis married secondly Thomas Sheppard of co. Beds, and had issue by both husbands.

    Arms of ffaldo: Gu. three stag's heads cabossed or attired ar.
    ,, de Okle: Gu. a fesse between three escallops arg.
    ,, Chamberlayne: Gu. on a chev. between three escallops or a tower of the first.

The descendants of Richard and Amphillis ffaldo quartered Chamberlayne, Neville

given in pure alms by Hugh's ancestors in the time of King Henry son of King John.ᵃ

The purparty which came to Ralph Paganell or Paynell was in three distinct holdings, one of which was in the hands of Henry de Dylewik with his tenants; another, consisting of half a virgate, belonged to Richard Koc; and the third, also half a virgate, to Adam Harlew.ᵇ

The de Burdeleys occupied another parcel of Beauchamp's fee here. Part of John de Burdeleys' estate was in the portion allotted to Maud de Beauchamp, for we find that he held of Roger le Strange, that lady's second husband. John de Burdeleys was also free tenant of one hide of land in this parish, belonging to Wardon Abbey, which Abbey had received grants from Robert le Broy holding under the Beauchamps; and, besides John de Burdeleys, the Wardon Abbey estate here was occupied by five other freeholders; by a further subinfeudation, the prior and convent of Bushmead held two virgates of land, and Ralph Goldston, Thomas Downe, and Adam Goyz, one messuage each, under the said John;ᵃ he was possessed of estates in Norfolk and Cambridgeshire, and ultimately was found to have been seised of the manor of Stagsden.ᶜ John de Burdeleys,

of Roleston, Neville, Bulmer, Inglebert, Roleston, Palmer of Holte, Bishopton, and ffencotts.

Crest of ffaldo: Three arrows gu. headed and feathered ar. two in saltire, and one in pale enfiled with a ducal coronet or.—Harl. 1531, ff. 94—96.

Temp. Jas I.—Thomas Chamberlayne, Vicar of Okley 1604.—Beds. Wills, Northampton District Registry.

ᵃ Rot. Hund. 7 Ed. I.

ᵇ Ib.

ᶜ Esc. 11 Ed. I. nu. 21. From the following it will be seen that this family held part of their estates in Norfolk by a very similar tenure to that by which the Bedfordshire Mapertyshalls held their lands, as hereafter noticed in page 124; the armorial bearings of the two families also present some resemblance.

The manor of Burdeloss and Newlands in Scoulton, Norfolk, belonged to the Picots, and at the death of Eustace Picot fell to the share of his daughter Lauretta, who carried it to Hugh de Burdeleys her husband, who died about 30th Henry II. and she survived him some time, and at her death it went to William de Burdeleys, her son and heir; he bore for his arms, Ermine, on a chief gules a lion passant or, and held this manor by grand serjeanty, namely, of being the King's chief lardiner;[1] William, his son, succeeded, and after him Hugh de Burdeleys, in 1245; he had it of his brother William's gift in 1232; by a record in 1236, it appears that Jeffery de Burdeleys, an elder brother of the first William, had it some time, but he died without issue, and so it came to William. In 1251, Jeffery, brother of Hugh, paid his relief; and the year following had livery of this and a manor in Madingle in Cambridgeshire, &c. and

---

[1] The officer in the King's household who presided over the larder.—Kelham's Dict. of Norm. French.

chevalier, son and heir of John Burdeleys, had land and rent in Stagsden in the time of King Edward III.[a] In the same reign, Richard Gregory, junr. and others held (int. al.) "Stachedon" manor for the abbot and convent of Wardon,[b] and the abbot was impleaded to show upon what grounds he claimed view of frank-pledge and other privileges.[c]

An estate, *in capite*, belonged to a family bearing the surname of Gemys.[d] For arms they bore: Paly of six argent and azure, per fesse counterchanged;[e] and usually had the cognomen "de Stagsden." In the thirteenth century Mabill de Gemys was seised of two parts of a knight's fee in Bedfordshire of the honor of Peverel of Dover.[f] Robert de Gemys held land here in capite by the service of a third part of one knight's fee;[g] his demesne consisted of one carucate, his villans and nativi were thirteen in number, and their daughters could not marry without the license of their lord. Robert had also twelve free tenants, of whom Henry de Dylewic, Hugh Wake, and Robert and Hugh Goldston may be named

---

had free-warren allowed him in all his lands. In 1256, it was found upon a *quo warranto* that he held by the serjeanty of keeping the King's larder on the day of his coronation, and another record says, when he would; he died in 1263, and it was found that King Henry had granted him a charter of free-warren in his manors of Scoulton in Norfolk, Sachesden (Stagsden) and Bereford (Barford) in Bedfordshire, Cumberton and Madingle in Cambridgeshire, and that Sir John de Burdeleys, knt. was his heir, and had assize of bread and beer, weyf and trebuchet: he married Margaret daughter of John de Creke, who survived him, and at her death it went to Jeffery de Burdeleys their son and heir, whose son John and Maud his wife held the manor: in 1333 it was found that Margaret widow of John de Burdeleys held it by the service of coming to the King's larder on the coronation day, with a knife in her hand, to serve the larderer's office. John son and heir of this John de Burdeleys died a minor in the King's custody, Aug. 9, 1346; and in 1347 his estate was divided between Thomas Marshall, who married Elizabeth, and Gilbert de Camera or de la Chamber of Epping in Essex, who married Joan, the sisters and coheirs of the said John. Upon the death of Elizabeth without issue, it appears that Joan also inherited her sister's part of the estate, except what she had aliened since the partition, and that she was at that time married to John Fitz John, otherwise called John de Middleton, her first husband being dead.—Blomefield's History of Norfolk, vol. ii. p. 347, and vol. viii. p. 450.

[a] Esc. 21 Ed. III. nu. 46.
[b] Ib. 43 Ed. III. nu. 16.
[c] Placita de quo warranto, Ed. III. p. 31.
[d] With its variations, G'ninges, Gyminges, Jemys, Jemmes, Gimeges, Gemelles, Jemmer, Gimices, &c.
[e] Halstead's Succinct Genealogies.
[f] Harl. 313, f. 58.
[g] Testa de Nevill, p. 242[b], 249. Harl. 313, fo. 38[b]. Where the name is spelt "G'ninges" and "Gyminges." The Gemys' estate was afterwards called a manor, and was known as well by the name of "Gymces, Jemmes," &c. as by that of "Stacheden."

as persons of some consideration.[a] Robert Gemys was lord of a manor in Stagsden,[b] in which lordship he was followed by another Robert; they were both living in the time of King Edward II.[c] In the following reign a Robert Gemys was seised of eighty acres of land, &c., in this parish.[d] John Gemys[e] enfeoffed Roger de Milton and Robert Suthewyk with two parts of his manor of Stagsden, and paid five marks for the King's license so to do. John, son of Robert Gemys, was afterwards found to have been seised of Stagsden manor.[f] John, son and heir of John Gemys, by Cristiana his wife, was probably a minor at the time of his father's death, for in the 40th King Edward III.,[g] William de Otteford, the escheator in Bedfordshire and Huntingdonshire, was ordered to accept security for two parts of the manor of Stagsden, and for two parts of a knight's fee in Botelbrigge, to which John the son was entitled. A manor here belonged to Cristiana Gemys,[h] and after her, presumably, to William Gemys,[i] said to have had a son, Robert, who died without issue. Johanna, daughter and heir of William Gemys, who had been wife to Nicholas Ravenhull, deceased, was found to have been seised of a manor in Stagsden called "Jemmes Manor;"[k] and a few years later Agnes, who was the wife of James Fynaunce, had the manors of "Stachedon" and "Hussheborn Crawle."[l]

[a] Rot. Hun. 7 Edw. I.

[b] Esc. 4 Ed. II. nu. 12. By the name of "Robert Jemys de Staches-don." One of this family, living about this time, married Sibyl, daughter of Hugh de Lizures,[1] which Hugh is said to have aliened his estates in 1214, and it is stated that the said Hugh (or his father, Fulk, son of Vitalis Engaine, by Alice de Lizures, an heiress of that family) assumed the latter surname. Sibyl de Gemys (Baker spells the name Gemelles) had two daughters, Emma, married to Hugh de Bovi; and Idonea to Baldwin de Drayton, from which match the Mordaunts of Turvey had a female descent.—Mr. Roger Dodsworth's Collections (Family of Drayton); Halstead, p. 94; Nichols, Leicestershire; Baker, Northamptonshire, vol. i. p. 9.

[c] Esc. 43 Ed. II. nu. 12.

[d] Ib. 8 Ed. III. nu. 18.

[e] Ib. 23 Ed. III. nu. 34. By the name of "John Gemys de Stachedene." Abbrev. Rot. Orig. p. 203.

[f] Esc. 40 Ed. III. nu. 15. (? a moiety of the manor.)

[g] Abbrev. Rot. Orig. p. 287.

[h] Esc. 2 Hen. VI. nu. 25. In which her estate is called "*Stachedon manor, co. Bucks.*"

[i] By an inq. p.m. taken at "Stacheden" on Friday after Easter, 6th Henry VI., it was found that William Jemmes held a manor in Stacheden, with appurtenances, called Jemmes manor, of the King in capite. That said William died on Monday in the first week of Lent just past, leaving a daughter, Johanna, wife of Nicholas Ravenhill, his next heir, she being thirty years of age.

[k] Esc. 25 Hen. VI. nu. 3.

[l] Ib. 37 Hen. VI. nu. 10. Both Flitwick and Husborne Crawley were part of William Lovet's fee at

---

[1] Arms: Az. a chief urdée ar.—Halstead.

By an inquisition post mortem, in the 9th King Henry VII. (number 18), taken at Bedford 30th November, it was found, that John Boteler was seised of three parts of the manor of Mepertyshall, and of the manor of Pulhanger in Bedfordshire, among other hereditaments; and left issue, Florence wife of John Ashefeld, and Joan wife of John Stanford; that these lands, together with the manor of Stackden, belonging to the said John Stanford, by certain deeds referred to, stood limited to the said John Stanford and Joan his wife in tail; that John survived Joan, and held by the courtesy; that there was issue between them a son, John, who died without issue, and two daughters, Elizabeth wife of William Cornwallis, and Margaret wife of George Hervey. That the said John Stanford, the father, died 3rd September, in the ninth year of Henry VII.; and that the said Elizabeth Cornwallis and Margaret Hervey were heirs of the said John Stanford; and the said Elizabeth Cornwallis was of the age of twenty years and upward, and the said Margaret eighteen years and upward. And it was further found, that John Leventhorpe was the son and heir (by a former marriage) of the said Joan, and was of the age of thirty-three years.

How this lordship came to the Stanfords[a] does not appear. The Botelers[b] succeeded the Mapertyshalls[c] at that place (now Meppershall), who long held an estate in that parish, and in Felmersham,—the former[d] by the serjeanty of performing the office of lardiner[e] on certain days, and the latter as feudatories of part of the honor of Huntingdon in Felmersham, viz., of De Hastings' moiety of the fee.[d]

the general survey. Afterwards a family surnamed De Flitwick possessed an estate in each parish. De Flitwick's moiety of the former passed through St. Amand, Cornwall, and Grey, to the Crown. Husborne Crawley was subsequently in the family of Finaunce.—Domesday, p. 216. Lysons.

[a] Arms of Stanford or Staunford (Stamford, Harl. 1428, fo. 3) of Stagsden: Az. a chev. between three ostrichs arg. legged gu.—Harl. 1555.

[b] Through the marriage of Mapertyshall.—Inq. p.m. Arms of Boteler or Butler: Erm. a chev. between three covered cups.—Harl. 1428, fo. 3.

[c] Arms of Mepersall: Sa. fretty arg. on a chief of the second a lion pass gu. Quarterings of Cornwallis.—Ib.

[d] Harl. 313, fos. 38[b], 49, 51[b].

[e] Gilbert de Mapertshale held two hides in Writtel, Essex, by serjeanty of being lardiner. Blount's Fragmenta Antiquitatis (Beckwith), Lond. 1815, p. 194. Walter, son of Gilbert, held four parts of one carucate in Maperteshale of the honor of Walingford; and Ranulph de Mepteshal held premises in Kaldecote by serjeanty as pertaining to the manor of Mepdeshal in co. Bedford.—Harl. 313, fos. 49, 51[b], 59[b], 61. " Land in Maperdeshale, in the county of Bedford, is held in capite by the service of being in the King's war, with a horse, not appraised, an habergeon (or coat of mail), a sword, a lance, an iron head-piece (or helmet), and a whittle, at his own proper costs."—Blount, p. 92.

John Leventhorpe, son and heir of Joan Boteler (by her first husband, John, second son of John Leventhorpe, esq., of Shingey Hall, Herts), did not inherit any part of Stagsden. His descendants, or heirs of his name, continued at Meppershall, as the following extracts from two wills testify:—

1607, March 28th.—Will of George Leventhorpe of Meppshal Gent. To be buried in Meppshal church "in the yle of my ancestors called the lordes yle." Testator devised the residue of his estate to Elizabeth his wife. Names his daughters, Anne Stringer (the eldest), Elizabeth Whitbreade, and Judith (the youngest), John Stringer, son of his said daughter Anne, Henry Whitbreade, son of the said Elizabeth; and appoints his son, Thomas Leventhorpe, executor.

1609, ———— Elizabeth Leventhorpe, widow of George Leventhorpe. Names Richard Hill, Thomas Hill, and Mary Moreton, wife of Thomas Moreton, her children by her first husband, Edward Hill; Judith Rentam, wife of Robert Rentam; and her son, Thomas Leventhorpe. Appoints Luke Norton esq[r], William Norton gent., and Giles Blofeild gent., supervisors. Proved (Archd. Bedf.) 9 January, 1609.

In Southill, a parish in the neighbourhood of Meppershall, is a place called Stanford Bury.[a] The mesne lordship of a small part of Meppershall was annexed to the honor of Walingford,[b] and in the time of King Henry III. Roger de Staunford was one of those who held land in this county pertaining to that honor.[c]

The husband of Elizabeth, elder daughter and coheir of John Stanford, of Stagsden, was Sir William Cornwallis, K.B., of Broome, Suffolk, who died in November, 1519. Their eldest son, Sir John, steward of the household to Prince Edward, son of Henry VIII., was ancestor of the Barons, Earls, and Marquises Cornwallis.[d]

The younger co-heiress, Margaret Stanford, had the manor of Stagsden for her portion, which she brought to her husband, George Harvy,[e] esq., of Thurleigh, sheriff of Beds and Bucks in 1508, knighted for his valour at the siege of

---

[a] Part of the estate of John Lord St.John of Bletsoe, which he had license to aliene 2nd April, 28 Elizabeth.—Patent Roll, nu. 1281, Part ii. M. (11).

[b] Harl. 313, fos. 59[b], 61.

[c] Ib fos. 48[b], 58.

[d] Burke's Dormant and Extinct Peerages. Visitation of Nottinghamshire, Harl. 1400, 1555.

[e] So written in the copy of his will (see note [b] page 127) and over the drawing of his standard (book of Standards marked I 2, in the Library of the College of Arms); but this surname was also frequently (and, at times, indifferently for the same person) spelt Harve, Harvye, Hervy, Harvey, and Hervey, occasionally with the prefix "de."—Vide Heralds' Visitations, &c.

Tournay, again served the office of sheriff in the eighth Henry VIII.[f] In 1520 he was one of the knights who attended the King and Queen to the Field of the

[f] In the list of sheriffs appended to Lipscomb's History of Buckinghamshire, he is described of Chilton in that county in 1508 and 1516. The name, however, does not occur in connection with property at Chilton before the year 1682, and the arms of the Herveys of that place, between whom and the Bedfordshire family there was no immediate relationship, if any, were: Argent, three pack-saddles sable (or azure); whilst the Thurleigh family, represented by Sir George, bore: Gules, on a bend argent three trefoils slipped vert. Berry also gives a list of sheriffs of Beds and Bucks, and does not distinguish Sir George by any seat, or place of residence, or county. By an inquisition taken at Eylysbury (Aylesbury) 26th October, 15th King Henry VIII., it was found, That Sir George Harvy, before and at the time of his decease, was seised of certain manors, lands, or tenements in demesne, with appurtenances, in the county of Bucks. That Thomas Vaux Lord Vaux, Sir William Parre, knt., Sir John Dyve, knt., Sir William Paston, knt., Sir John Mordaunt, knt., Sir Robert Lee, knt., John Seynt John armig', Henry Isseley,[1] Walter Luke, Nicholas Luke, William Dyve, and Thomas ffitzhugh, were seised of a certain annual rent of ten pounds six shillings and eightpence arising out of the manor of fflete Marston and Blaigrove, with appurtenances, in fee (upon trust) to the use of Sir George Harvey, knt., to perform his last will, by virtue of a certain deed executed by the same George. That on the 8th day of April, the 12th of the same reign, the said George made his last testament, by which he willed and declared that one Margaret Smart, late wife of William Smart, should enjoy the said rent for the term of her life, with remainder to a certain Gerard Smart, the son of Margaret, and the heirs male of his (Gerard's) body lawfully begotten, and, in defect of such issue, remainder to a certain John Harvey, son and heir-apparent of William Harvey, and the heirs male of the said John lawfully begotten; and, in defect of such issue, remainder to Elizabeth Atclyff, wife of William Atclyff, and the sister of the same George, her heirs and assigns for ever. That on the 23rd day of March, the 13th of the said reign, the same George died, after whose death the said Thomas Vaux Lord Vaux and all the other trustees were seised as before recited to the use of the said Margaret for term of life, and after her death then to the other uses above-mentioned. That the said George was seised of 100 acres of land and six acres of wood, with appurtenances, in Ellesburgh; and of thirty acres, with appurtenances, in Drayton; and of forty acres in Pychethorn, in the aforesaid county, in demesne as of fee, and being so seised (int. al.) enfeoffed therewith the said Thomas Vaux Lord Vaux, by the name of Thomas Vaux, son and heir-apparent of Sir Nicholas Vaux, knt., Sir William Parre, knt., Sir John Dyve, knt. by the name of John Dyve armiger, Sir William Paston, knt. by the name of William Paston armiger, Sir John Mordaunt, knt. by the name of John Mordaunt armiger, John Seint John armiger, Sir Robert Lee, knt. by the name of Robert Lee armiger, Henry Isseley, Walter Luke, Nicholas Luke, William Dyve, and Thomas ffitzhugh, to the uses of his will. That the said George, by his last will, executed the day and year beforementioned, made the said Sir William Parre, knt., Robert Lee, and John Harvey his executors; and his will was, that from and immediately after the time of his decease his executors should take and receive all the outcomings and profits of the before-named land and wood, with appurtenances, during the space of fifteen years for the purpose of performing his said last will; that on the expiration of the said term of fifteen years the aforesaid land and wood should devolve to Gerard, and the heirs male of his body lawfully begotten, and in defect of such issue remainder as

[1] A John Isseley or Islee, of Sundrish, Kent, was second husband to Agnes, daughter of Nicholas Morley of Glynde, and Sir George's mother by her first husband, John Harvy the younger, Usher of the King's chamber to Edward IV.

Cloth of Gold.ᵃ Sir George died 23rd March, thirteenth Henry VIII. (1522), leaving by the said Margaret an only child, Elizabeth. His will, dated 8th April, 1520, proved 8th May, 1522,ᵇ passes over his daughter in silence, though mention is made of her husband. The said Elizabeth, at the time of Sir George's death, was stated to be of the age of twenty-four;ᶜ she married Edward Wauton, of Elstow.ᵈ It appearsᵉ a pension of two pounds was payable to her from the monastery of Elstow at its dissolution; and that she died prior to the thirty-fifth year of Henry VIII., when her husband Edward Wauton and her son and heir George Wautonᶠ joined in selling her manor of "Stackden" to

John, first Lord Mordaunt, from which time, till about the year 1712, it descended with Turvey. By an inquisition taken at Bedford 30th Sept. 6 Elizabeth, after the death of Sir John Mordaunt Lord Mordaunt, it was found, among other things, that there was a manor in Stacheden known as well by the name of Gymces as by that of Stacheden, and another manor in Stacheden known as well by the name of Bozones as by the name of the manor of Stacheden: and that, by certain instruments referred to, the said John Lord Mordaunt was seised of and in the manors of Turvey and Stacheden, among other hereditaments, for term of his life, with remainder to Lewis Mordaunt for term of life. Charles Mordaunt, the third, but better known as the great, Earl of Peterborough, who was created Earl of Monmouth, sold his estate here to

Thomas, first Lord Trevor, and it has since attended Bromham.

before recited. That after the death of George the said Lord Vaux and the other feoffees stood seised of the above-named land and wood to the use of the said executors, for the purpose of performing the said will. And the jurors found, moreover, that the said land and wood in Ellesburgh were held of Lord Montagu, but by what service they knew not; and that the said land, with appurtenances, in Drayton, was held of John Cheyney armʳ, but by what service they knew not, and was worth by year 18s.; and that the said land in Pychethorne was held of the Rector of Asterych (? Ashridge), but by what service they knew not, and its yearly value was forty shillings. That Elizabeth Wauton, wife of Edward Wauton, was his (Sir George's) daughter and heiress, aged thirty years and upwards.

ᵃ Rutland Papers, pp. 32, 33, 37.

ᵇ By John Harvy and Sir William Parr. The original will is not to be found. A copy is registered in the Prerogative Court of Canterbury, from which Mr. Gage, in his History of Thingoe Hundred, Suffolk, gives copious extracts under the account of Ickworth.

ᶜ Inq. p. m. 15 Hen. VIII. nu. 108, taken at Huntingdon 6 June. Compare note ᶠ, p. 126.

ᵈ One pedigree says, "of Eston." A family of Wauton or Wanton had their seat at Great Staughton in Huntingdonshire, and bore for arms: Arg. a chev. sa. in the dexter chief point an annulet of the second; quartering Marmyon, Cretinge, and Cheneurotte. Crest: A trefoil slipped sa, charged with another arg.—Harl. 1531, fo. 156-165.

ᵉ Coles MSS. xxix. pp. 145, 146.

ᶠ Licenc. Alien. Pat. 35 Hen. VIII. 3 Jan. p. 7.

From the Abstract of Returns of Charitable Donations for Benefit of Poor Persons (26th George III., 1786), ordered by the House of Commons to be printed, 26th June, 1816, it appears that the poor of Stagsden are entitled to an annual sum (then £4 9s.), arising from land and house vested in the overseers, the gift of some person or persons unknown.

Rectory and Advowson.

By the gift of Roisia de Beauchamp, as before stated, this church with its appurtenances became vested in the prior and canons of St. Paul, Bedford, who removed to Newenham in the time of King Henry II., in which reign the gift was made.[a] The living was reduced to a vicarage at a very early period, there being no rector on record. About the year 1291, the church of Stagsden was rated at £10;[b] fifty years afterwards it was found to be taxed at fifteen marks, on the oaths of Henry le Rous, Richard Sampson, Henry Armlee, John Macclyn, John Campyoun, and John Goldston.[c] Shortly before its dissolution, the priory leased this rectory and the advowson of the vicarage to John Lord Mordaunt for a term of ninety-nine years.

Exchequer—$\frac{8\ 9\ 5}{1\ 1\ 7}$

Conventual Lease from the Prior of Newenham, Beds.

This Indenture made the 20th day of May the 30th yere of the reigne of our Sov'aigne lord Henry the viijth by the grace of god of England and of ffrance defender of the ffeith lord of Ireland and Suprme hedde of the Churche of England, betwene John asshewell prior of the monastery or the howse of Chanons of seynt paule of Newenham in the Countie of Beds and the tenent of the same place on the one ptie. And John Mordaunt of Turbey in the Countye of Beds knyght lord Mordaunt on the other ptie Witnessith that it is covenntyd, grauntyd, concludyd, condiscended, accordyd, and agreyd, betwene the seid pties and ev̔y of them, ffor theym, their heirs, successors, executors, administrators, and assignes, covenntith and grauntyth to and with other in manner and forme folowyng, that is to say, The said prior and covent by one assent and consent for them and their successors have demysed, graunted, and to farme lettyn and by these p^rnts do demyse graunt and to farme lette to the said Lord Mordaunt their psonage of Stacheden, in the Countie of Beds, wth all manner of tythes of Corne, haye, woode, wolle, and lambs, and all other manner of tythes, comodities, pfitts, emoluments and all other things whatsoev̔ they be to the seid prior and Convent in any manner of wyse belongyng and pteyning in Stacheden aforesaid and also all others their man⁹s, marsh lands, teñts, medowes, woods, pasture, rents, reversions, s^rvices, with thapptennces what soever they be in

---

[a] Rot. Hund.   [b] Taxation of Pope Nicholas, p. 34^b.   [c] Nonar. Inquis. p. 19.

Stacheden aforesaid. And the Advowson of the vicarage of the Churche of Stacheden. To have and to hold the seid psonage, Tythes, Mannͮ͡͡s, Lands, Teñts, advowson and all other the premisses before specyfied with all and singly their Appurtenances to the same Lord Mordaunt, his Executors, Administrators and assignes from the feast of the annunciation of our lady last past before the date hereof unto the end and time of ffowre score and nynetene yeres then and now next following and fully to be complete, without empechement of any man^r of wast, yelding and paying therfor yerely to the seid prior and convent and their successors twentye one pounds six shillings and eight pence of lawfull money of England at iiij termes of the yere that is to say at the ffeastes of Seynt John Baptyst, Seynt Michell tharchangell, the Natyvyte of our lord god, and the annunciation of our lady by eũ porcions. And yf it happen the said rent of xxi^l vi^s viij^d or any pte or pcell therof to be behynd unpayd after any of the said feasts at wch it ought to be payd by the space of syx weeks that then it shall be lefull to the seid prior and convent and to their successors into all the said psonage and other the p^{r}misses with thappurtnances to entre and distreyn and the distres therein so taken lawfully to lede dryve and carye awaye and with them to retain unto such time as they of the seid yerely rent of xxi^l vi^s viij^d with therrerages thereof (if any be) fully be contented and payd; and the seid prior and convent covenant and graunt for them and their successors to and with the seid lord Mordaunt his heyres, executors, Administrators and asignes that they and their successors shall bere and paye all man^r of divers rents and charges to the king our sovereign lord his heires and successors. And otherwise to all other whatsoever they be going oute of the seid psonage lands teñts and all others the premises aforesaid during all the seid terme. And of all the same and of every part thereof at all tymes during the said terme shall discharge exonerat and save harmeles the seid lord Mordaunt his executors and administrators and every of them. And the said prior and convent do covenant and graunt for them and for their successors to and with the seid lord Mordaunt his executors administrators and assignes by these presents that they and their successors during all the said terme at their own proper costes and charges shall keep repayre mayntene and susteyne al man^r of howses and buildings belonging to the seid psonage lands teñts and other the p^{r}mysses before lettyn except thakkyng and dawbing only whiche shall be at the costes and charges of the seid lord Mordaunt his executors administrators and asignes at all seasons during the seid terme when and as often as nede shall require. And the seid Prior and Convent do covenant and graunt for them and their successors to the seid lord Mordaunt his executors administrators and assignes for the good councell that the seid lord Mordaunt hath geven at all tymes to the seid Prior and Convent Twentye six shillings and eight pence to have and . . . . during the terme of ffowre score and nynetene yeres yerely. The whiche xxvi^s viij^d the seid prior and convent covenant and graunt for them and for their successors by thes presents to the said lord Mordaunt that he the same lord Mordaunt his executors administrators and asignes shall yerely from tyme to tyme during all the seid terme of four score and nineteen years next comyng reteyne and receave of the seid yerely rent of xxi^l vi^s viij^d before specified and in his and their own hands kepe and of soemuch thereof yerely during the seid terme of four score and nineteen yeres to be exonͮ͡ated and discharged any resignation or any other thyng conteyned in these Indentures to the contrarye notwithstanding. In Witnes wherof, to the one parte of these Indentures remayning with the seid lord Mordaunt the seid prior and Convent have put their covent and comon seale and to the other parte of the same Indentures remaining with the seid prior and Convent the seid lord Mordaunt hath sett his seale and signe manuell. Geven the day and yere first above written.

The great tithes—commuted 1839 [a]—are now vested in the Master and Scholars of Trinity College, Cambridge.[b]

In 1605 Sir John Dyve is called patron of the living. Elizabeth Countess of Peterborough, and Henry Earl of Peterborough, conjointly, made the appointment in 1661, and the latter alone in 1676; in the following year the right of presentation was in the Countess of Peterborough. The advowson was purchased of Charles, third Earl, by Thomas Lord Trevor—probably at the time that he acquired the manor and estate with which it has continued.[c]

The Vicarage, valued in the King's Book at 8*l*., is discharged from first-fruits and tenths.[d] There are a few acres of glebe; the vicarial tithes were commuted in 1839.[e] The vicarage-house, of stone, erected in 1844, is pleasantly situated near the church.

	VICARS.[f]		Patron.
1220—1234	Reginald de Stacheden		Newenham Priory.
	William de Bedeford		,,
1258—1279	Henry de Byegrave.	By death of last.	,,
	Henry de Abodesle.	By death of last.	,,
	Chas. de Latheburye.	By res. of last.	,,
	Radulph de C. . .	By res. of last.	,,
	John de Elnestowe		,,
1300—1320	William de Lull . .	By death of last.	,,
	John Page.		,,
1363—1397	John Denton.	By res. of last.	,,
	Rich{d} Rolby		,,
	Richard Worthyng.	By res. of last.	,,
1405—1419	H. de Frampton.	By res. of last.	,,
	William Harepeny		,,
	John Normanton.	By res of last.	,,
	Thomas Ligger		,,
1435—1449	Thomas Spenser.	By res. of last.	,,
	Thos. Goodsone.	By res. of last.	,,

[a] Aggregate amount 404*l*. 11*s*. 9*d*. due to the Master, Fellows, and Scholars of Trinity College, Cambridge.—Parliamentary Gazetteer, 1843. Great tithes commuted for 558*l*.—Lewis.

[b] Lysons.   [c] Lincoln Register.   [d] Certificate Augmentation Office.

[e] Parliamentary Gazetteer (1843). "Aggregate amount 231*l*. 3*s*. 2*d*. due to the vicar." "The vicarial tithes were commuted for 350*l*."—Lewis.

[f] Lib. Instit. apud Lincoln.

VICARAGE.

STAGSDEN.

	Vicars.	Patron.
1471—1479	Thomas Warner	Newenham Priory.
1495—1513	Robert Crofton. By death of last. Thomas Willme. By res. of last.	,, ,,
1521—1546	Robert Skin Willm Saunderson. By death of last. Robert Slingesby. By death of last.	,, ,, John Lord Mordaunt.
Circa 1567	John Burwey, or Burroway.^a	
1661, July 17	John Todd, B.A. Pemb. Coll. Camb. 1660.	Eliz. Countess of Peterboro' and Henry Earl of Peterborough.
1676, Mar.	John Draper. Deprived 1712.	Henry Earl of Peterborough.
1712, Dec. 22	Benjamin Rogers. Sidney Coll. Cambridge. Resigned on being appointed to the Rectory of Carlton, June 1720.	Thomas Lord Trevor.
1720, Aug.	John Teape, B.A. Also Incumbent of Biddenham.	,,
1723, June	Thomas Tipping, M.A. Camb. Also (after 1730) Incumbent of Biddenham.^b	,,
1758, Apr.	Robert Stokes, B.A. By death of last.	John, Lord Trevor.
1759, Sept.	Thomas Richards. By res. of last.	,,
1769, June	Thomas Richards, M.A. By cession of last.	,,
1799, Apr.	Edward Stone, M.A. By death of last.	Visct. Hampden.
1811, May	William Stephen, M.A. St. Joh. Coll. Camb. 1805. By death of last. Also Vicar of Bledlow, Bucks.	,,
1867, Apr.	Hon. Alan Brodrick, M.A. Balliol Coll. Oxon. By death of last.	

The present Vicar is the first resident incumbent for many years past. An extended notice of Rev. Benjamin Rogers is reserved for Carlton.

This Church, dedicated to St. Leonard, is situated on an eminence nearly surrounded by the village, and comprises chancel, nave, south aisle with porch, north chapel, and western tower containing a clock and five bells. The chancel is Decorated; on the south side are two two-light windows, and a priest's door between them; on the north side, one square-headed window of two trefoiled lights and a walled-up pointed doorway. The east window, of three lights, is similar to that at Biddenham, and many other neighbouring churches. The aisle

^a Witness to a will.—Northampton District Registry.
^b Mr. Tipping was maternal ancestor of the Misses Trevor of Tingrith, owners of the principal estate at Chellington.

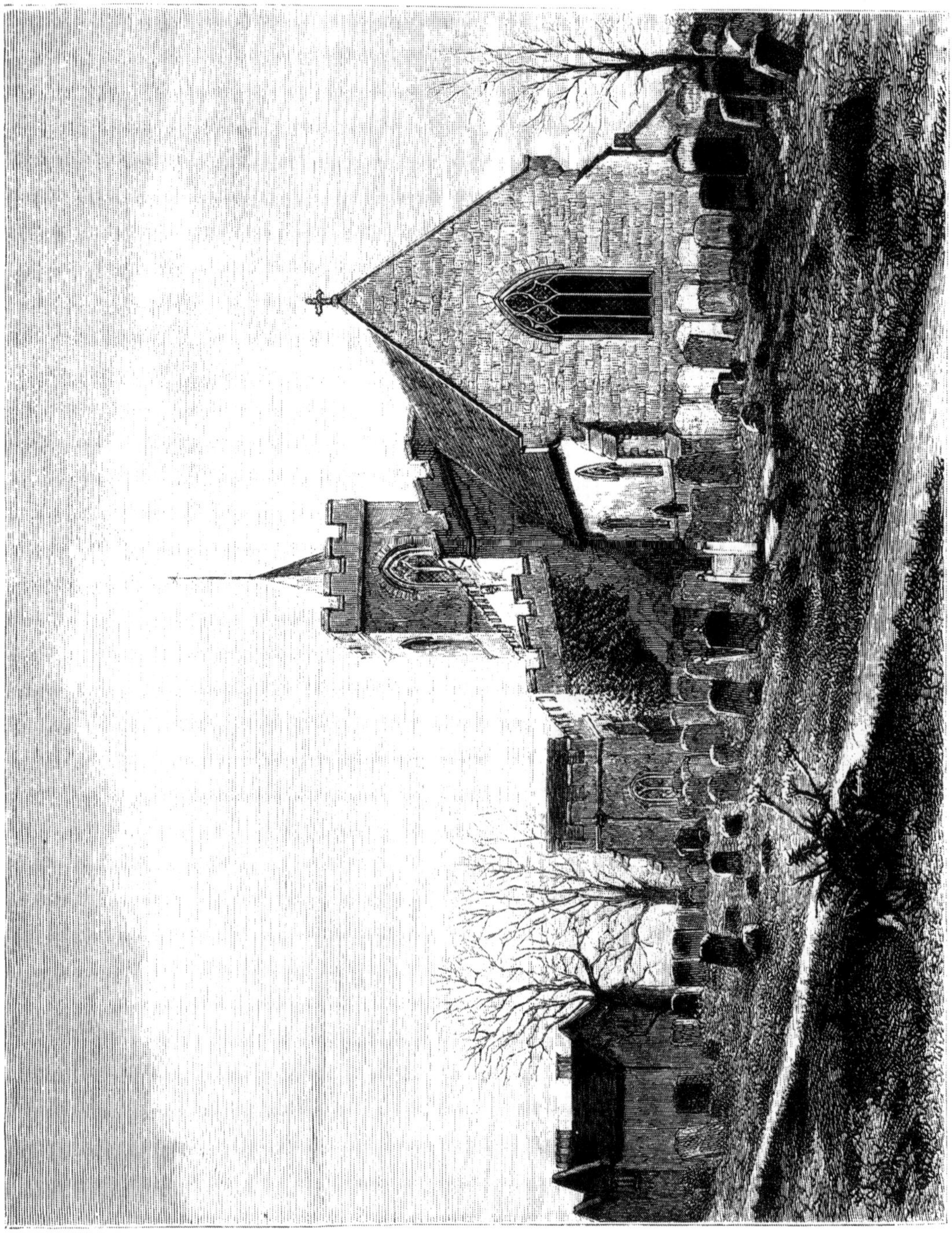

41

INTERIOR OF STAGSDEN CHURCH

is lighted by four uniform three-light windows on the south, of the same character as the three-light south window of Biddenham church, and by a good Decorated west window of two lights. The nave has two Decorated three-light windows with a closed-up north door between them; the north-west window contains fair tracery. Above the nave rises a Perpendicular clerestory of ten double lights (cinquefoiled) in square compartments under a string-course and embattled parapets, the latter hiding a leaden roof of low pitch. On the face of the south-east battlement is a sun-dial. The chapel, also covered with lead, has a plain coped parapet and string-course, and is lighted by four uniform three-light windows without tracery—two on the north side and one at each end; it is in the early Third-pointed or Perpendicular style. The belfry stage of the tower, of the same period, or perhaps a little later, has four quatrefoil-headed double-light windows, and is crowned with a low spire of lead, with vane, springing from within an embattled parapet,—another feature in which this church bears resemblance to that of Biddenham; this tower, however, is devoid of buttresses and gurgoyles. Access is given to the belfry by a newel staircase, which is contained in the semicircular projection at the north-east, terminating with the substructure of the tower. The shouldered west doorway and the lancet above it seem to be insertions. The string-course, and the battlements which conceal the leads of the aisle, extend along the side walls of the lofty porch, the tiled roof of which, having a gable end north and south, gives rather a singular appearance to its side elevations. The large plain double-light pointed windows on either side of the porch are blocked up.

The interior is fitted with open oak seats of recent construction, and paved with red and black tiles. Near the south door is a Decorated font, the bason octagonal, four sides large and four small; six of which are plain. On the other two are sunk panels, with small figures, the costume of which appears to be that of nuns. The lower part of the bason is ornamented with ball-flowers and heads; it is supported by a central octagonal pedestal with a square head and base, and by four octagonal shafts with plain moulded capitals and bases. Between the aisle and nave is an arcade of five Decorated arches, springing from elegant clustered pillars. The west arch is filled up with a wooden partition; the doorway to the tower staircase has a semicircular arch.

Under the north-west window of the nave is a broad pointed-arched recess, like an Easter sepulchre. John Lylyot, by his will dated 12th May, 1533, gave two bushels of barley to the sepulchre light. The most extraordinary thing in this church, from its singular position, is the small trefoiled light above the chancel arch on the

T

south side—for what purpose it was intended is unknown.ᵃ The clerestory has a good oak roof. In the east wall of the aisle are four niches (at the foot of one, a bracket on a head) and a plain bracket. Below the south-east window is a stone seat and piscina, and to the west of the same window another niche.

The chapel, which now contains the organ,ᵇ and is furnished with chairs for the choir, has two arches opening into it. At its south-east angle are remains of the rood staircase. All the windows in the church have recently been glazed with rolled cathedral glass, of a green tint, with a gray border—those in the clerestory being without a border.

The chancel arch springs from the side walls without any projecting jambs, capitals, or imposts of any kind; but its otherwise rather bare appearance is relieved by the Perpendicular screen separating the chancel from the nave, which, though somewhat mutilated, has fortunately been retained. The chancel roof is open, the spaces between the beams being plastered and coloured azure. Within the rails, on the south side, is a piscina under a trefoiled opening, to the east of which is a smaller pointed-arched recess, and in the opposite wall a shouldered recess, perhaps formed for a credence. Projecting from the east wall, on the north side of the holy table,ᶜ is a three-sided bracket.

A coating of plaster (tinted), which the walls have recently received, covers a fresco near the former north door of the nave; the position of this door is marked by a small brass commemorating that—

IN GRATEFUL REMEMBRANCE OF
GEORGE . RICE . RICE . TREVOR . 4TH . BARON . DYNEVOR
A CLOCK WAS PLACED IN THE TOWER OF THIS
CHURCH . BY . THE . PARISH . OF . STAGSDEN . A.D. 1872.
HON: ALAN . BRODRICK . VICAR.
LEWIS WALKER. } CHURCHWARDENS.
CHARLES BASS.

On the bells:—
1. 1634. William Marks and Francis Hoyt, Churchwardens.
   Henry Bailey made me.
2. 1844. C. and G. Mears, Founders, London.
3. 1652. Chandler made me.
4. 1652. Chandler made me.
5. 1769. Richard Cook, Thomas Bass, Churchwardens.

ᵃ In Kibworth church, Leicestershire, are two small lights (one square and the other diamond) filled with tracery, above the chancel arch, one on either side; but these also remain unexplained.

ᵇ This organ came from St. Mary's church, Bedford.

ᶜ The Communion table and chairs are new since the institution of the present vicar.

FONT.

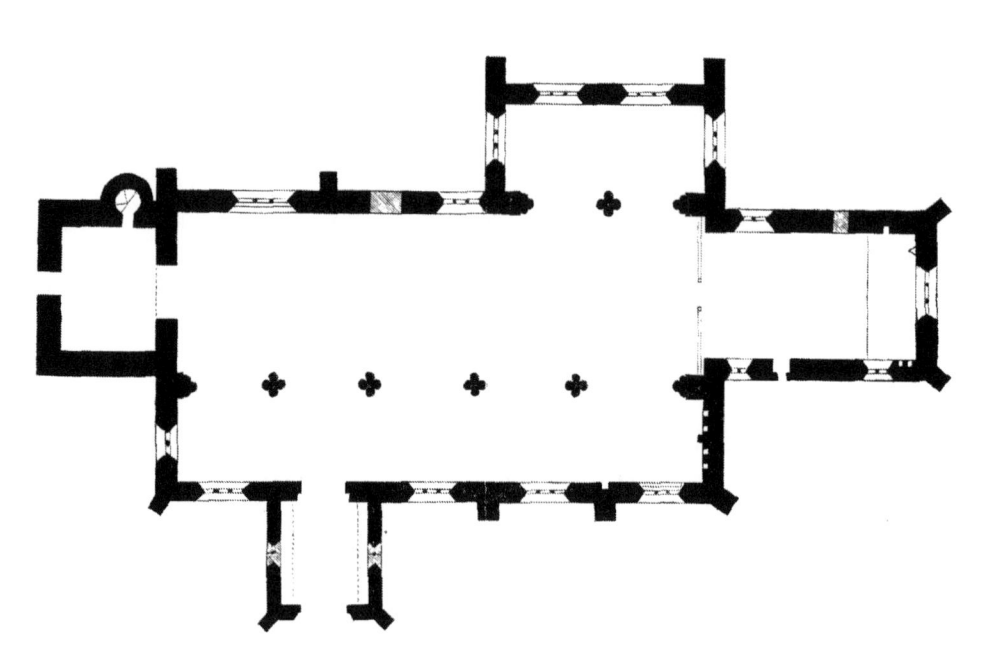

GROUND PLAN OF CHURCH.

T 2

STAGSDEN.

The chalice and flagon are of silver. On the former—"Thomas Gregory, Richard Sleath, Church Wardens of the Parish of Stagsden, Beds, 1825;" on the latter—"William M. Walker, Henry Gibbins, Church Wardens of the Parish of Stagsden, Beds, 1850."

The only monument remaining in the church is a brass (2 feet 6 inches by 2 feet) on the north wall of the chapel, an engraving of which, taken from a rubbing, is annexed.

REGISTER.

1670 Aug. 7.		Baptized,	Joh. sonn of William Steff and Margret his wife. (First entry.)
1671 Nov. 10.		———	Elizabeth, the daughter of John ffalldo and Eliz. his wife.
1672 Jan. 27.		———	John, son of John ffalldo and Eliz. his wife.
1674 Nov. 20.		———	Mary, daughter of John ffalldo and Eliz. his wife.
1682 Nov. 13.		Married,	Thomas ffisher and Mary Lambert.
—— June 29,		Buried,	Thomas Conquest.
1683		Baptized,	John, son of Thomas ffisher.
1695 Dec. 29.		Buried,	Francis Greathead.

The first register also contains entries of the names of Davers, ffrance, Skevington, Hardwick, Odell, Allen, &c.

1705	. . .	[Second Book commences.]
1719	. . .	Benjamin Rogers signs as Vicar.
1721	. . .	John Teape vicar, signs.
1723 June 5.	Buried,	The Revd. Mr. Jno. Teape, Vicar of ye Parish. (Francis Reade, curate.)
1733	. . .	Thomas Tipping signs as Vicar.[a] ⎱ Mr. Tipping, vicar of this parish and
1737	. . .	Thomas Tipping curate[a] (? vicar) ⎰ perpetual curate of Biddenham, died 1757.
1739 Feb. 17.	Baptized,	Elizabeth, daughter of Edward and Elizabeth Wagstaffe.
1743 Dec 25.	———	Anne, daughter of Edward and Catherine Wagstaffe.
1747 Nov. 5.	———	Alice, daughter of William and Elizabeth Lavender.
1761	. . .	Thomas Richards signs.

Other names in the second book:—Negus, Tindsly (yeoman) 1705, Ashbee, Newman, Grimditsh, Pickerin, Leach, Clarke.

---

[a] This gentleman resided principally, if not altogether, at Biddenham, which being but a chapelry at that time, the incumbent was accustomed to sign the register of that parish as "curate," and the habit having grown upon him, may account for Mr. Tipping styling himself in the same way in this register in 1737. He had no son, his wife was Mary, daughter of ——— Richards, gent., relict of Mr. Goodhall, of Bromham, by whom he had two daughters, co-heirs: Mary, married in 1760 to Rev. Edmond Williamson, Rector of Millbrook, co. Bedford; and Elizabeth, to Rev. William Aveling, Rector of Aspley Guise, in the same county, and both left issue.

HIC IACET IOHANNES COCKE GENEROSVS, NVPER VNVS QVATVOR GENEROSORVM
SERVIENTIVM SERENISSIMI PRINCIPIS DOMINI IACOBI NVNC ANGLIÆ SCOCIÆ
FRANCIÆ & HIBERNIÆ REGIS IN PRÆSENTIA EIVSDEM DOMINI REGIS QVI IN
VITA SVA DVXIT IN VXOREM ANNAM VNAM FILIARVM IOHANNIS MOYLE
NVPER DE ACTON IN COMITATV MIDDLESEXIÆ ARMIGERI: HABVITQ:
EXITVM PER EANDEM ANNAM TEMPORE MORTIS SVÆ VIVENTEM VIDE IC'
TRES FILIOS, & QVATVOR FILIAS, QVI POST LONGVM ÆGRITVDINIS TÆDIVM
SVMMA CVM PATIENTIA AC PIETATE (VT VIXIT) CIRCA SEXAGESIMVM ANNVM
ÆTATIS SVÆ IN ANNO DOMINI MILLESIMO SEXCENTESIMO & SEXTO DECIMO DIEM SVVM
CLAVSIT EXTREMVM, IN CVIVS MEMORIAM PRÆDIC TA ANNA VXOR SVA AMANTISSIMA
ET MÆSTISSIMA HOC MONVMENTVM VNA CVM INSIGNI SVPRAPENDENE AD IMPENSAS SVAS PRO
PRIAS SVMMA CVM PIETATE POSVIT ET EREXIT 20 DIE IVNIJ ANNO DOMINI 1617:
DEO VIVERE EST MVNDO MORI:

POST CONFECTIONEM HVIVS MONVMENTI, ET ANTE ERECTIONEM EIVSDEM, ELIZABETHA
VNA PRÆDIC TARV QVATVOR FILIARVM PRÆDICTI IOHANNIS COCKE DEFVNCTI, ET ANNÆ VXORIS
EIVS, TAM PIJS QVAM MORALIBVS VIRTVTIBVS DOTATA ANTE DIEM SVVM SECVNDO DIE IVLIJ,
ANNO DOMINI MILLESIMO SEXCENTESIMO ET DECIMO SEPTIMO, CIRCA ANNVM VNDECIMVM
ÆTATIS SVÆ, AD SVMMAM MATRIS SVÆ, ET AMICORVM SVORVM TRISTITIAM, IMMATVRE FATO
CECIDIT CVIVS QVIDEM ELIZABETHÆ CORPVS MATER SVA TRISTISSIMA IVXTA PATERNVM
TVMVLVM IN HAC ECCLESIA SEPELIRI, ET HANC EFFIGIEM SVAM VNA CVM HIS LITERIS IN
FIDÆ SVÆ PRÆDICTÆ MEMORIAM IN HOC SVO PATERNO TVMVLO EX AMORE SVO ERGA
FILIAM SVAM PRÆDICTAM INSCIDI ET INSCRIBI FECIT. 22 DIE IVLIJ ANNO DOMINI 1617:
MATVRATA MINVS SOLIDA:

1770 Sep. 28.	Buried,		Elizabeth, daughter of William Lavinder.
			Between 1761 and 1806 the names of Carrier, Jeffereys, Baskerville, and Wagstaff occur.
1813	.	. .	William Lambert Aspinwall, curate of Gt. Barford, signs.
——	.	. .	Charles Williams, curate.
1814	.	. .	Amos Westoby, curate. (Also served the cure of Emberton in Buckinghamshire, and that of another parish.)

Stagsden Wills.[a]

1503 May 2nd. John Cobbe, of Stagsden, directs his body to be buried at St. Leonard's, Stacheden. Mentions his sons Nicholas and Richard, to whom he leaves all his land and tenements in this parish.

—— . . John Suttyll. Leaves all his land to his son Thomas, and names Richard Suttyll. Witnesses, Thos. Wylme, vic., Joh. Coke, Nich. Coke, &c.

1507 . . Will of Judith Wodyll To be buried in the chancel of Stagsden. Bequests to the high aulter; to the Vicar to pray for her; for repairing the bridges of (?) Tymsyll and Bydenham.

1510 . . The will of Robert Sampsonn, contains small bequests to the high aulter (Stagsden) and to the mother chuch of Lincoln. Testator names Thos. Taller, Thos., John, and Elizabeth Lambert, Nicholas Cokke and Thomas Lowder. Witnesses, John Coventon, John Smythe, Stephen Cokke.

1516 . . Johanna Reed by her will desires to be buried in the churchyard of Stagsden; and leaves "To the high aulter for tithes forgotten iiij d. To the mother church of Lincoln ij d. To the Rode lyght xij d. To a preiste to syng for my sowl. Item to St James lyght xx d. To repairs of the Torchys xij d. To repairs of bells xij d. To Margery my dau^r ffyve sylu^r sponys. It. to Henr. Aslere my son in lawe my tenement with appurt^s in the parish of Bromham for his life, the residue to be disposed of by my faithful John Cowton." Witnesses, Robert Skynnar, John Lylyott, Regnold Kayle, Thomas lylyott, &c.

1533 May 12. John Lylyot of Stagsden, by his will so dated gave to the "Rode lofte there 3s. 4d, to the bellis 2 bushels of barley," to the torches the same, and to the sepulchre light the same. Names his son Robert. Witnesses, Sr Robert Sken, vicar of the said towne, William Churche, Richard Soull, Robert Hill, &c.

1537 Dec. 24. John Bolton, of Stachden, yeman.

1545 Apr. 29. Nicholas Cocks, of Stagsden. Names his wife Alles, and his sons Thomas and William.

1558 . . William Cocks, of Stagsden, yeman. Witnesses, William Bolton gent., Henry Cocks yeman, Sr Robt. Slyngesbe, Alexander Erle.

1592 . . Thomas Wheler of Stagsden.

The School is endowed with £6 per annum.[b]

---

[a] Northampton District Registry.   [b] Lewis.

In the beginning of Queen Elizabeth's reign Stagsden contained fifty-three families. In 1715 the families in the parish were distributed as follows:—At Bury End, nine; North End, eight; Church End, twenty-five; West End, nineteen; and at Wick End, nine; making in all seventy families. Assessed property in 1815, £3,376. Poor rates, 1838, £269 17s.[a]

Population.

Year.	Inhabited houses.	Number of separate occupiers.	Uninhabited houses.	Building.	Males.	Females.	Total of Persons.
1801	84[b]	—	—	—	—	—	492
1831	—	—	—	—	—	—	597
1841	115	—	—	—	—	—	632
1851	—	—	—	—	—	—	727
1861	140	174	1	—	348	360	708
1871	141	169	3	—	349	331	680

[a] Parliamentary Gazetteer.   [b] 114 families.

STEVINGTON.

Stiventone.—This village, which lies on the great oolitic stratum, a stiff clay covering the limestone, is situated on a slightly undulating slope forming one side of the valley of the Ouse, and though somewhat scattered consists mainly of two streets, intersecting each other at right angles at a point called the Cross. The land is almost wholly arable, and the population agricultural; but some of the women and girls employ themselves also in lace-making. The trade of mat-making was established here many years ago, and is still carried on. The majority of the cottages are built of limestone, with thatched roofs, and are almost without exception old.[a]

It is $4\frac{3}{4}$ miles west-north-west of Bedford.

An engraving of the village Cross will be found in Fisher's "Collections" (1836). The iron upright of the weather vane on the church tower was formerly on the cross. It was removed thence by Mr. Francis Green: at the same time the modern capital was imposed on the cross; the flight of steps has been built up with stone; the masonry contains a letter-box, and supports a low iron railing of recent construction.

The area of this parish is about 1,862 acres. It was inclosed under Act passed in 1805, and the Award is dated 1807. Stevington is bounded on the north by Pavenham and Oakley; south by Bromham, Stagsden, and Turvey; east by Oakley and Bromham; and west by Turvey and Carlton.

Crewe Alston, esq. is lord of the manor, and the Duke of Bedford is lay-rector and patron of the vicarage; Lieut.-Col. W. B. Higgins, Joseph Tucker, esq.,

---

[a] See the report of Dr. Thorne, who in 1870-1, pursuant to instructions, visited the sub-registration district of Turvey, in the county and union of Bedford, in order to inquire into the causes of a prevalence of fever, adverted to in a Report of the Registrar-General; the sub-district comprises three villages, namely, Stevington, Turvey, and Stagsden. It was published in the local newspapers early in January 1871.

and Messrs. J. C. Robinson, C. and H. Turney, J. Keech, A. Field, and R. Cox, are also landowners. At the east end of the village was formerly a park, long since turned into pasture, and at present the property of the Duke of Bedford.[a]

Here is a meeting-house of the Baptists, said to have been established during the time of the celebrated John Bunyan, and also one belonging to the Primitive Methodists, erected in 1863; the former of these is at West End. Rev. T. O. Marsh informs us that on 31 July, 1814, meeting was held for the first time in Great Tithe Barn—the meeting-house at West End being so much out of repair. The repairs came to £175, and Mr. Sutch was preacher at that time.

From the rock on which Stevington church is built issues a spring of water, called the Holy Well;[b] this spring is not known to have been frozen, nor dry in times of drought. The principal stream proceeds from an arched recess[c] under the north lateral chapel of the church; some smaller streams trickle out of the rock higher up, and run down the road, the whole falling into the Ouse at a very short distance, as does the water of an *incrustating* spring, at the distance of about two or three fields from the church towards Pavenham. It was customary to wash sheep from Carlton Hill Farm, and from Stagsden, as well as from Stevington, in Holywell.

Stevington village feast is on the first Sunday after September 19.

Manor. Count Eustace Fee. Boulogne Honor. (The land of Count Eustace in the half-hundred of Bochelai.) In Stiventone Ernulf (de Arde) holds of the Count three hides. There is land for twenty-four[d] plough-teams. In demesne is one plough-land and three can be made, and ten villans have five ploughs. There are eleven bordars and two servi; pasture for four plough-teams; pannage for twenty hogs. The whole worth fourteen pounds—when he received it twenty pounds; in the time of King Edward thirty pounds. Adeloldus, a thane of King Edward, held this manor and could sell it to whom he would.—Domesday, p. 211.

In addition to Stevington Count Eustace's fee in Bedfordshire comprised the manors of Pavenham and Little Odell, besides one hide and a half in Bromham,

[a] Gentleman's Magazine 1812, vol. 82, Part ii. p. 9.

[b] An acre of ground in the west meadow is said to abutt on *Holywater.*—Gent. Mag. vol. 82, Part ii. p. 9.

[c] See the engraving.—*Ib.*

[d] This number is so much in excess of that set down in the record of other and more extensive manors that there seems reason to doubt its accuracy.

one virgate in Stagsden, one hide in Turvey, and two hides in Sharnbrook; the Count also had possessions in Kent, Surrey, Hants., Somerset, Herts., Oxon, Cambr., Hunts., Essex, Norfolk, and Suffolk.[a]

Eustace Earl of Boulogne here mentioned has usually been considered as the second of the name, who was wounded at the battle of Hastings in 1066. The main points of his history are recorded in "L'Art de verifier les Dates," 8vo. edit. vol. xii. p. 350. The date of his death was probably 1080; "Gallia Christiana," expressly mentions his Countess (Ida) as a widow in 1082; if Ida was a widow in 1082, it follows that the Eustace of the Survey must have been her son and not her husband.

Eustace, the third of the name, married Mary daughter of Malcolm the Third, King of Scotland. Their daughter was Maud, the wife of Stephen, King of England.[b]

---

[a] Domesday, pp. 14, 34, 44[b], 91[b], 137, 157[b], 196, 205, 208; 26, 104, 106[b], 151, 303. Morant's History of Essex, vol. i. p. 400-1; vol. ii. pp. 106, 338, 341, 603. Clutterbuck, Herts, vol. i. p. 499-500; vol. iii. p. 423.

[b] Sir H. Ellis's Introduction and Indexes to Domesday, vol. i. p 416, note 5.

STEVINGTON.

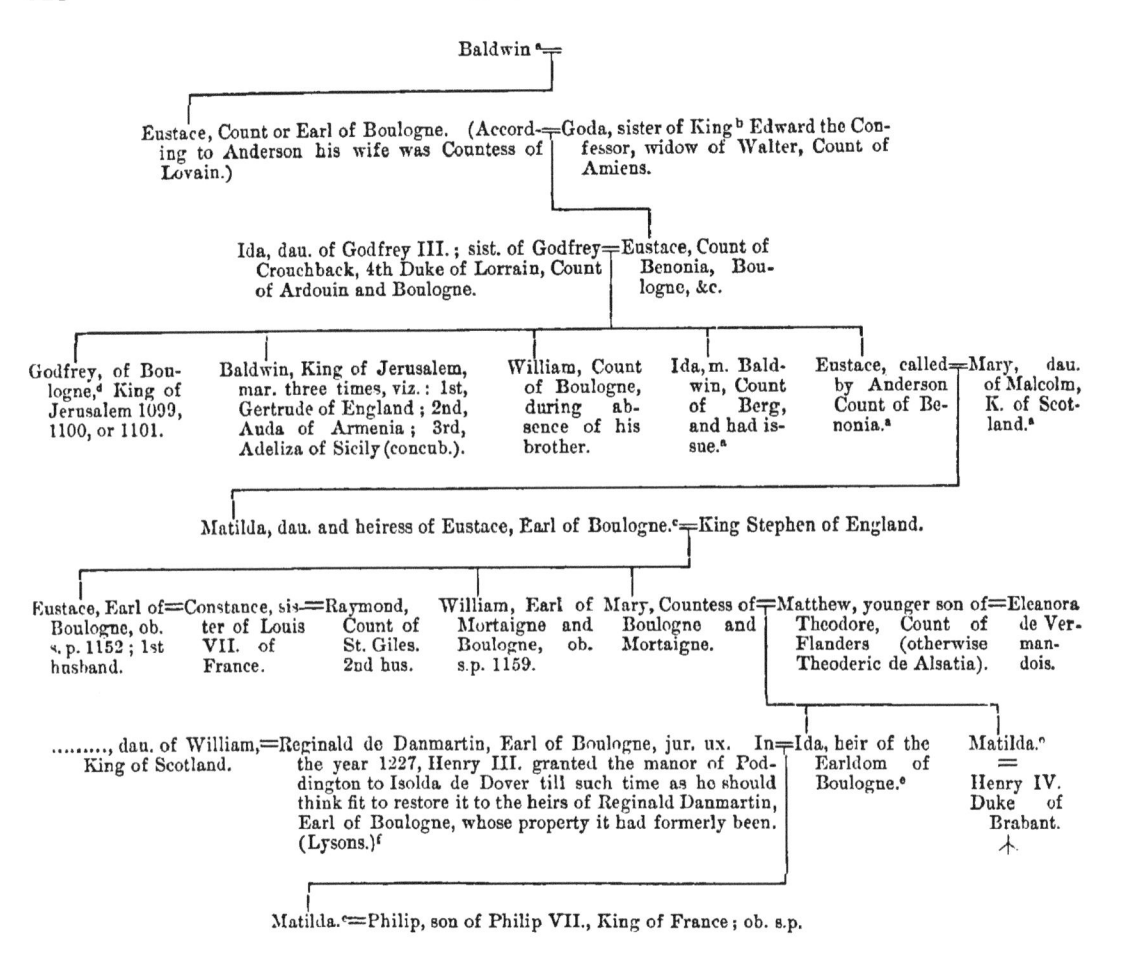

Baldwin [a]

- Eustace, Count or Earl of Boulogne. (According to Anderson his wife was Countess of Lovain.) = Goda, sister of King[b] Edward the Confessor, widow of Walter, Count of Amiens.

  - Ida, dau. of Godfrey III.; sist. of Godfrey Crouchback, 4th Duke of Lorrain, Count of Ardouin and Boulogne. = Eustace, Count of Benonia, Boulogne, &c.

    - Godfrey, of Boulogne,[d] King of Jerusalem 1099, 1100, or 1101.
    - Baldwin, King of Jerusalem, mar. three times, viz.: 1st, Gertrude of England; 2nd, Auda of Armenia; 3rd, Adeliza of Sicily (concub.).
    - William, Count of Boulogne, during absence of his brother.
    - Ida, m. Baldwin, Count of Berg, and had issue.[a]
    - Eustace, called by Anderson Count of Benonia.[a] = Mary, dau. of Malcolm, K. of Scotland.[a]

      - Matilda, dau. and heiress of Eustace, Earl of Boulogne.[c] = King Stephen of England.

        - Eustace, Earl of Boulogne, ob. s. p. 1152; 1st husband. = Constance, sister of Louis VII. of France. = Raymond, Count of St. Giles. 2nd hus.
        - William, Earl of Mortaigne and Boulogne, ob. s.p. 1159.
        - Mary, Countess of Boulogne and Mortaigne. = Matthew, younger son of Theodore, Count of Flanders (otherwise Theoderic de Alsatia). = Eleanora de Vermandois.

          - ...., dau. of William, King of Scotland. = Reginald de Danmartin, Earl of Boulogne, jur. ux. In the year 1227, Henry III. granted the manor of Poddington to Isolda de Dover till such time as he should think fit to restore it to the heirs of Reginald Danmartin, Earl of Boulogne, whose property it had formerly been. (Lysons.)[f] = Ida, heir of the Earldom of Boulogne.[e]
          - Matilda.[c] = Henry IV. Duke of Brabant.

            - Matilda.[c] = Philip, son of Philip VII., King of France; ob. s.p.

[a] Anderson's Royal Genealogies, p. 388.
[b] Old England, i. p. 363; also Pinnock's History of England.
[c] Burke's Royal Lineages.
[d] Wright's Hist. Essex, i. p. 63.
[e] Blore's Hist. Rutland, p. 31. Temp. Hen. III., Edw. I. Odo, and Thomas Danmartin, military tenants in Essex, as of the honor of Bononia.[1]—Testa de Nevill, p. 274-5.
[f] Isabel, sist. and coh. of William de Bruere (dead 17 Hen. III. *Rot. Fin. p.* 242.) mar. 1st, ... de Dover; 2nd, Baldwin Wake. See Wake's pedigree. William de Bruere enfeoffed Isolda de Cardun with the fee of Wymmington, for which a fine passed 41 Hen. III.; the said Isolda married William Inge.—MSS. in possession of Richard Orlebar, esq., of Hinwick. William le Mercer, of Wymmington, and Isolda his wife, temp. Hen. III.—Harl. MS. 313.

---

[1] Or Benonia, the ancient Honor out of which grew that of Boulogne.

Ernulf or Arnold de Ardres,[a] mesne lord of Stevington under the Domesday grantee, was a son of one Geoffrey, an officer of the Abbey of St. Bertin at St. Omer, who had the charge of its possessions in the county of Guisnes. Ernulf and his brother, Geoffrey, received an establishment of lands both in Essex and in the border shires of Mercia and East Anglia, under the superiority of their patron, Count Eustace.[b] In Bedfordshire, Ernulf was also mesne lord of Pavenham and Little Odell, and tenant in Bromham and Turvey.[c]

Baldwin de Guisnes, count of Guisnes (beforementioned in a note at page 34) is stated to have married a daughter of Ernulph de Ardres, and to have died before 1207. Robert de Guisnes held two knight's fees here *in capite*, and Adam Beneteleyg', citizen of London, farmed Stevington, under the said Robert, for xl[li]. The count of Guisnes had twelve Knights in Essex, Hertfordshire, Bedfordshire, and elsewhere, holding of him as of the honor of Benonia;[d] of these, three were in Stevington and Little Odell; and Reginald de Cornhull' had the custody of the count's lands.[e]

From the record of this parish in the Hundred Rolls, seventh Edward the First, we learn that Baldwin Wake, through Hawysia de Quincy his wife (the daughter of Robert de Quincy), held certain tenements in Stevington, by the service of two knight's fees, of the Earl of *Bowan* (Buchan), who held of the King as of the honor of Boulogne; and that at one time the mesne seigniory of Little Odell[f] attended Wake's estate. Baldwin was also subfeudatory of the said honor in Bromham, Carlton, and Pavenham; the member of Boulogne honor in the last named parish was likewise appendant to, or parcel of, Stevington manor, the customary tenants thereon rendering suit and service at their lord's court in Stevington. Here Baldwin held in demesne upwards of seven virgates of land, an ancient park of forty acres, a wood of five acres, a water-mill, and a fishery in common, from the fence (*a sepe*) of Radwell to the — (*ad maram*) between Stevington and Bromham. Besides seventy-five villans and twenty-five cotarii, there were

[a] Hardres, Arde, or Arda.

[b] Freeman's Norman Conquest, vol. iii. p. 313. Appendix Y, p. 713.

[c] Domesday.

[d] See note p. 144. Henry de Trublevill seems to have held the manor as the Count's Knight in Stevington, about the year 1221.—Rot. Litt. Claus. 5, Hen. III.

[e] Testa de Nevill (temp. Hen. III.—Edw. I.) pp. 242, 251, 257, 261, 274.

[f] In the time of Henry VI. Thomas Wodehull was seised (int. al.) of two parts of the manor of Little Odell *as of the manor of Stevington.*—Esc. 19 Hen. VI. nu. 6.

the following freeholders: Henry de Polescroft; Lucia de Burdeleys and John Alulf; Adam Alulf; Roger le Flemig and John de Gynes; Philip Barculf; Roger de Wylie; Ralph and Nicholas Passelewe; the Prioress of Harewold, who held ten acres in pure alms (by the gift of Roger de Quincy in the time of King Henry, son of King John); and Reginald le Clerk, who was possessed of one messuage. Baldwin Wake had also the advowson of the church of Stevington, the usufructuary interest of which belonged to the Prioress of Harewold, together with four acres of arable land and one acre and a-half of pasture (given to the said church in pure alms), which the said Prioress held in demesne. In 1281, Baldwin had the King's licence to build a Castle in Stevington marsh.[a] Edmund, Earl of Cornwall, obtained the custody of the lands which had belonged to Baldwin Wake;[b] and the latter's interest in Stevington, after passing through the families of La Zouche and Holand, as shown in the annexed pedigree, subsequently became vested in the Crown, and so united to the paramouncy.

By an inquisition taken at Leighton Bosard, 13th January, in the thirteenth Henry VIII. (number 4), it was found that

Henry VII. late King, was seised of the manor of Steynton als Stephynton als Steventon, with appurtenances, in the county of Bedford, and the said King, by letters patent bearing date 25th February, 4 Henry VII.[c] [granted to Thomas Stanley late Earl of[d]] Derby, sen. father of George Stanley, late Lord le Straunge, the aforesaid manor of Steventon, to have and to hold the said manor to the aforesaid late Earl and his heirs male. After whose death it came to Thomas, son of George, Lord le Straunge as next heir male, and the same entered and was seised in fee tail. Thus being seised, James, Bishop of Ely, Hugh Hesketh, Bishop of Mann, Henry Seynt John knt., George Holforth knt., John Irelond knt., Henry Sherman clerk, Edward Molyneux clerk, Richard Halsall clerk, Richard Heskethe, Thomas Hesketh, and Richard Snede, in the court of the lord the King at Westminster in Trinity Term, 5th year of the now King, claimed and recovered the said manor. James, Bishop of Ely, died, and the others survived. On the 18th May, 9th Henry VIII. a certain Indenture was made between Thomas, Cardinal Archbishop of York and Chancellor of England, and John Heron knight, by the name

---

[a] Lysons.

[b] Rot. Pat. 10 Edw. I. m. 3, 2; and 13 Edw. I. m. 21.

[c] Patent Roll, 4 Hen. VII. mem. 26.

[d] Illegible in the original. Thomas Stanley, first Earl of Derby, died in 1504; his will, dated 28 July that year, was proved Nov. 9 following. By Lady Eleanor Neville, his first wife, aunt to the Consort of Richard III., he had six sons and four daughters. George, the third but eldest surviving son, called Lord Strange, died 5th Dec. 1497. The Earl's second wife, Margaret, daughter and heir of John Beaufort, Duke of Somerset, the pious foundress of Christ's and St. John's colleges in the university of Cambridge, was the mother of King Henry VII., by her former husband, Edmund Tudor, Earl of Richmond.

TABLE OF CONSANGUINITY between the Families of DE QUINCI, WAKE, LA ZOUCHE, and HOLAND, lor

Saier or Saher de Quinci, made Earl of Winchester,=Margaret, younger sist. and coh. of Robert
Cart. 13 March, 1206-7. (Cott. MSS.) Fitz Parnell, Earl of Leicester.

Helen, eldest dau.=Roger de Quinci, Earl of Winton, Constable | Beatrice de Valle,=William de Bruere, a minor and | Robert de Quinci,
and coheir of | of Scotland *jur. ux.*; living 11 Hen. III. | concubine of | in ward to the King at his | before Roger, and
Alan, Lord of | (Rot. Lit. Claus. M. 21.) Lord of Ste- | Reg. de Corn- | father's death; m. Joan, da. | remainder, or had
Galloway. | vington, co. Bedf. (Esc. 48 Hen. III. | wall. | of Rad. de St. Sampson. Robt. de | vington after his
 | nu. 27.) | | B. (Wm's. father) had a grant | Rot. Pat. 48 Hen.
 | | | of Wymmington 14 Hen. III.

argaret de Quinci, eldest dau. and coheir, m. Wm. de Ferrars, Earl | Ela or Elene de Quinci, 3rd dau.=Sir Alan la Zouche | Græcia de Bruere.=Reg.
of Derby, to whom she brought estates in Leic., Cambr., Warw., | and coheir. Estates in Leic., | of Ashby, co. Leic.
Dorset, Berks., Northants., Wilts., Linc., Hunts., and Herts.ᵃ | Warw., Dorset, Berks., Camb., | | Eve, sister to Rich.=Will
izabeth de Quinci, 2nd dau. and coheir, m. Alexander Comyn, Earl | Hunts., Northants.,Wilts., Linc., | | Mareschal, Earl | B
of Buchan in Scotland. Estates in Leic., Warw., Dorset, Berks., | and Sussex.ᵃ | | of Pembroke.
Camb., Northants., Wilts., Linc., Hunts., Essex, and Sussex; also | | |
the advowsons of Eynesbury and B———, near St. Neot's.ᵃ | | | Eve de Braose, 3rd dau. and=Wi
 | | | coheir.

Ela, dau. and coheir of Stephen de Longespée.=Roger la Zouche. Eudo or Ivo la Zouche, lord paran
 as member of his honor

Lucia la Zouche, m. Sir Thos. Grene.   Roger la Zouche of Lubbesthorp.   Jo
 E

Eleanor, dau. of Nich. de=Alan, Baron Zouche of Ashby, lord of Stevington. (Esc. 7 Ed. II. nu. 36.)   Eudo la Zouche, ob.
Seagrave. | In the 5th Ed. II., he was constituted Governor of Rockingham Castle
 | in Northamptonshire, and steward of Rockingham Forest.   William Zouche, heir
 | N B.—The lands constituting the barony of Wahull were taxed to castle-   of Wymmington,
 | guard to Rockingham. (Rot. Hund.)   Haryngworth. (N

lizabeth la Zouche, 3rd dau. and coheir, a nun | Ellen la Zouche, eldest dau. and coheir, m.=Nich. St Maur, | Maud la Zouche, 2nd=Robert de Ho
at Brewood, co. Stafford. | 2ndly Alan de Charlton. | 1st husb. | dau. and coheir.

Nich. de St. Maur (3rd Baron St. Maur.)=Muriel, dau. and heiress of James Lovel. | Sir Thomas Holand, K.G.,=Joane, "the Fair Maid of Kent,
chard de St. Maur (5th Baron.)=Ela, dau. and coheir of Sir Job. St. Lo. | Earl of Kent, (2nd son,) | Earl of Salisbury; m. 3rdly
 Richard de St. Maur (6th Baron.)=Mary dau. and heiress of Thomas Peyver, | 2nd husb. | Seised of the lordship of Ste
 by Margaret his wife, dau. and coheir of | | nu. 54.)
 Sir Nigel Loring. | Thomas Holand, 2nd Earl of Kent, and=Alice,
 | | "Alesia" his wife seised of Steving- | Fitz
 Alice St. Maur, dau. and heir.=William, Lord Zouche of Haryngworth. | ton manor. (Esc. 20 Rich. II. nu. 30.) | Arno

 Joane Holand, whose 4th husb. was Sir Henry
 afterwards Lord Vesci, lord of Wymming

 Anne, dau. of John Montacute, Earl of Salisbury,=John de Holand, created Duke of
 2nd wife. | lord of Stevington. (Esc. 25 H
 | nu. 25.)

 a quo Neville,
 Earl of Westmerland.

 Henry de Holand, 2nd
 1st hu

ᵃ Partition of Knight's Fees of Rog. Quinci late Earl of Winton, made at St. Neot's on the V

Stevington, and DE BRUERE, DE CANTILUPE, LA ZOUCHE, and BROMFLETE, lords paramount of Wymmington.

.... de Dover.=Isabel, sist. and coh. of William de Bruere,=Baldwin Wake.
1st husb.   dead 17 Hen. III. (Rot. Fin. p. 242.)   2nd husb.

have died=Helen, da. of Llewelyn, the great Prince of N. Wales, wdw. of John Scot, Earl of Huntingdon.

Arabella de Quinci, m. Sir Richard de Harcourt, Kt., of Stanton-Harcourt, &c., and their s. and h., Sir William, m. 1stly Alice, sist. of Sir Alan la Zouche, and 2ndly Hillaria (or Eleanor) Hastings. Sir William's grandson, by the 2nd wife, viz., Sir John de Harcourt, m. 1st Eleanor, da. of Eudo la Zouche, and 2ndly Alice, da. of Peter Corbet.

Hugh Wake, ob.=Joane de 23 Hen. III. Stutevill, (Abbrev. Rot. sole heir. Orig.)

raose.   Ann de Quinci, dau. and coheir, a nun.
de   Joane de Quinci, dau. and coheir m. to Humphrey de Bohun, the younger.

Hawise or Hawysia de Quinci,=Baldwin Wake, had grant of=Ela de Beauchamp, sister and
dau. and coheir, brought the   free-warren in Stevington.   coheir of Joh. Beauchamp,
lordship of Stevington to her   (Rot. Chart. 8 Ed. I. nu. 17.) of Bedford.
husband. (Rot. Hund.)
                                (See Beauchamp's Pedigree, under Biddenham.)

de Cantilupe, (whose grandfather had grants of the forfeited estates of Richard and alis de Engain); lord of Eaton, co. Bedford, with its members, Wymmington, &c.

t of Wymmington, &c.,=Milicent de Cantilupe, (sister and heiress of Geo. de C.=John de Montalt, George de Cantilupe, lord of Eaton, ob. s. p.
Eaton, Beds.   lord of Eaton.)   1st husb.   Joan de Cantilupe, m. Henry de Hastings.

la Zouche, m. Sir Roger Corbet.   William la Zouche, of Haryngworth, lord of=Maud, dau. of Lord Lovel,
or la Zouche, 1st wife to Sir John de Harcourt.   Wymmington as before; ob. 26 Ed. III.   of Titchmarsh.

=Jane, dau. and heiress of William Inge.   John, Baron Wake.=Joan   Sir Hugh Wake, knt., of Blisworth, grandfather
his grandfather, æt. 30, 26 Ed. III. Lord   (Abbrev. Rot. Orig. of Sir Thomas Wake, who m. Alice sister and
efore—ancestor of the Barons Zouch of   3 Ed. II.)   coheir of William de Pateshull. (See Pedigree
's Leicestershire, vol. II., part 1. p. 372.)   of Beauchamp, under Biddenham.)

d.   Edmund of Woodstock, Earl=Margaret Wake, sister and   Thomas, Baron Wake (Thomas Wake=Blanche, dau. of Henry Plantagenet, Earl
      of Kent.   heir to Thomas.   de Lidell, seised of Stevington   of Lancaster. She had Stevington
                                                              manor, and Wodecroft wood, co.   lordship, fishery, &c., in co. Beds., and
1st William Montacute,   Bedf. Esc. 23 Ed. III. nu. 75.) estates in Westmerland, Yorks, Herts.
ward the Black Prince.   ob. s. p.   Essex, Middlesex, Linc., and Cumb
ton. (Esc. 9 Rich. II.   (Esc. 4 Rich. II. nu. 59.)

of Richard   John Holand, 3rd son, created Earl of=Elizabeth Plantagenet, dau. of John of
n, Earl of   Huntingdon and Duke of Exeter,   Gaunt. Had the manor and advowson
                  attainted. (John de Holand chevalier, of the ch. of Stevington for term of
iflete,   seised of Stevington manor.—Esc. 9   life. (Inq. ad qd. damn. 1 Hen. IV.
                  Rich. II. nu. 25.)   nu. 29. Esc. 4 Hen. VI. nu. 32.)

er,=Anne, dau. of Edmund, Earl of Stafford,
/I. widow of Edward Mortimer, Earl of
     March, 1st wife

e of Exeter,=Anne, dau. of Richard, Duke of York, sister to King=Thomas Selenger, arm.
            Edw. IV. Seised of the lordship of Stevington.   2nd husb.
            (Esc. 15 Edw. IV. nu. 36.)

f Holy Trinity, 1277, between the coheirs of his inheritance.—(Cott. MS. Nero, D.X. 196.)

of John Heron, esq., Treasurer of the King's Chamber, Commissioners of the said King by virtue of a commission to them directed to conclude with such persons as were indebted to the King on the one part, and the late Earl, the son,[a] on the other part: which Indenture witnesseth that the said Earl was bounden to the late King in fifteen several recognizances, every of them 400£, every of them for payment of five hundred marks, yet remaining in their force, over and above a thousand pounds by the said Earl paid, which debt was secured by certain covenants and agreements made between Sir Thomas Lovell knt., Edmunde Dudley esq., and Henry Wyot, on behalf of Henry VII. on the one part, and the same Earl on the other part, as by Indentures dated 26th July, 21 Henry VII. doth appear, wherein the same Earl is bounden by eight several recognizances   every of them in 200 marks for payment of 800£ over and above 200£ by the said Earl paid. The King on petition of the said Earl is pleased to remit 2,500 marks parcel of 5,000£, and is contented to receive [[d]] marks, and the said sum of 800£ thus—At the feast of St. Martyn in winter after the date hereof 200 marks and at Pentecost following 200 marks, and so yearly at St. Martin's and Pentecost 200 marks till said sum of 5,000 marks and said sum of 800£ to the said John Heron or other Treasurer of the King's chamber for the time being to the use of the said Sovereign be fully paid. And whereas James Bishop of Ely, now deceased, Hugh Bishop of Manne,[b] Henry Halsall,[b] John Seynt John, George Holforde and John Irelonde, knts., Henry Sherman,[b] Edward Molyneux,[b] Richard Halsall clerks,[b] Thomas Hesketh,[b] Richard Hesketh,[b] and Richard Snede,[b] recovered against him (the Earl) the manor of Steventon, with appurtenances, in co. Bedford, the manor of West Ludford and 20 " meases," with appurtenances in Blangden, co. Somerset, the manors of Bereforth St. Martyn, co. Wilts, Stegnow, co. Hertford, Kyng's Sutton, co. Northampton, Streyteley[c] and Ardyngton,[c] co. Berks, and Bassyngwarte, co. Cumberland, as shown by the King's Records of Common Pleas at Westminster, by force of which the said Bishop of Manne (and others as before) were seised in fee to the use of the said Earl and his heirs: which manors, lands, &c., were granted to be of the clear yearly value of 300£ over and above all charges and encumbrances; it was covenanted and agreed that the said Bishop, &c. and their heirs should stand so seised till the said King, his heirs and executors, had received of the profits of the said manors, lands, &c. [the remaining sum[d]] of 5,000 marks and 800£. And the said Earl agreed to appoint a receiver to be bound in 200£ to pay 400 marks yearly at said feasts, and, in case of his death, another receiver bound in like manner, said Earl having full liberty to " sett, lett, or demise to ferme," and to cut wood, &c. And the Jurors said that the manor of Steventon in the letters patent to Thomas late Earl of Derby senior specified, and the manor of Steynton in the

---

[a] The two Earls are distinguished as Thomas late Earl the *father*, and Thomas late Earl the *son*—of George, Lord Le Strange.

[b] One of the second Earl's executors, whose names are set out in his will at foot of the Inquisition. See extracts from his Will, pages 68—69, vol. iii of Collins's Peerage (edit. Lond. 1812.)

[c] Held of the honor of Wallingford.

[d] Illegible in original.

said Recovery and Indenture specified, are one and the same. And that Joan, late Lady Lestraunge, widow, long before her decease, was seised in fee of the manor of Wemyngton, co. Bedford, with the advowson of the church of Wemyngton, and, by the name of Johanna [a] Stanley widow Lady "de Straunge" and Lady "de Knokyn, Besset, Burnell, and Lacy," on the 8th February, 2 Henry VIII. demised the said manor and advowson with appurtenances and all lands, &c. in Wemyngton with the advowson of the churches of Wemyngton and Nowy. . . . . . to Margaret Stanley her daughter, to hold to the same Margaret and assigns for term of life, and the aforesaid Margaret entered into the said manor of Wemyngton and other premises and was and is still seised thereof as free tenant and still survives. And the aforesaid Johanna died seised of the reversion of the said manor of Wemyngton and other premises in Wemyngton with the advowson of the churches aforesaid as of fee, when the reversion descended to Thomas Earl of Derby (junr.) and son of Johanna; and the same Earl was so seised in reversion on the day of his death. And the same Earl, seised of the said manor of Steventon 21 Henry VII., took to wife Anne daughter to Edward Hastynges, Lord Hastynges and Hungerford, now living. And the same from the day of the recovery during his life received the rents and profits of the said manor of Steventon to his own use and up to the day of his death. And the same made and declared his testament and last will written on paper in divers sheets, the tenor of which is attached to the Inquisition, being shown to the Jurors. And the aforesaid manor of Steventon is worth 48£ per annum, and is held of the King *in capite* by the service of a knight's fee. And the said manor of Wemyngton is worth 60£ per annum and is held of the King by a knight's fee. And the same Earl held no other lands in co. Bedford, and died 24 May, 13 Henry VIII. and Edward is his son and heir, and next heir male of the late Earl, and also next heir of the said Joan; and Edward on the day of his father's death was aged 12 years and 14 days.

This concludes the part of the inquisition relating to the Earl of Derby, but it appears that the two Commissioners (Andrew Wyndesor and John Hales) with the Jurors sworn, had to inquire as well concerning two other matters: viz.—

1. The lands held by Edward Duke of Buckingham in Bedfordshire.

2. An encroachment by one Walter Curson, to whom Thomas Broke, Lord Cobham, had demised certain lands in Knottynge, which had been inclosed with hedges, &c.

The Jurors go on to say—

That Edward late Duke of Buckingham late of Thornebury, co. Gloucester, on the 22nd July, 4 Henry VIII. committed treasons and was attainted. At which time he was seised of the manors of Bakenho, Tylbroke, and Hardwyke, with appurtenances, in co. Bedford, and of the honor of Gloucester in the same county. And further that the manor of Bakenho was worth £8 19s. 6¾d. per annum, the manor of Tylbroke £10 10s., and the manor of Hardewyke 106s. 8d. And the

---

[a] The Earl in his Will calls her Jane.

MANOR-HOUSE (NORTH-EAST VIEW).

MANOR-HOUSE (SOUTH).

aforesaid honor of Gloucester was worth 39s. 4d. a-year. And that the same Duke received and had the profits of the said manors, &c. from the perpetration of the aforesaid treasons up to the Monday next after the morrow of the Ascension of our Lord, 13 Henry VIII. And they say that Thomas Broke, Lord Cobham, was and still is seised in fee of one messuage, 100 acres of arable land, and 40 acres of pasture, with appurtenances in Knottyng in the aforesaid county, &c.

The whole or principal part of the Stanleys' estate here passed subsequently to the Alstons,[a] who will be further noticed under Odell. In the month of July, 1873, was advertised for sale by auction, in lots, an extent of above 600 acres of freehold land, situated in the parishes of Carlton, Turvey, Pavenham, Stevington, and Felmersham, with fishing in the river Ouse, &c., part of the Alston family estates.

The lands and premises in this parish advertised for sale were comprised in three lots, viz., the "Manor Farm," 246A. 0R. 24P., and fishing in half the river, (Lot 11); "Burley Farm, situated at Pickshill," 46A. 0R. 25P. (Lot 12); and a freehold cottage and garden in the village of Stevington (Lot 13). The estates included in the two former were, on or about the 28th of the same month, sold by private contract, and are now the property of the Duke of Bedford and Lieut.-Col. Higgins, respectively.

Of the Castle, which Baldwin Wake had the King's licence to erect in 1281, but which probably never reached completion, the site may be traced in large earthworks near the Ouse, beside the footpath which leads to Pavenham.[a]

Mr. T. Fisher, writing in the Gentleman's Magazine, 1812, above quoted, says: "Very near to the church, on the south side, stands a long range of stone buildings, designed for separate inhabitation; each apartment opening under a small pointed arch to the area in front, and no internal communication existing between any two of them. A gate-house, or porter's lodge, and an unroofed chapel, were also standing here within the memory of man, of which the foundations may still be traced. These edifices Mr. Marsh supposes to have been occupied by some religious fraternity." The building here described has long been known as the manor-house; it was included in Lot 11 in the sale advertisement of 1873, and particularised as a "Farm Residence of considerable antiquity, said to have been the Hospital to Harrold Priory."[b] Manor-courts have at times been held here. An inhabitant of Stevington, named Fisher, by his will,

---

[a] Gent. Mag. 1812, vol. 82, part 2, p. 9.

[b] Fisher calls it an "Ancient Hospital;" see the engraving of the south-east view in his "Collections" (1812-36).

dated the 10th Feb. 1500, gave 20*l. to the repair of the chapel infra* (query *intra*) *cemeterium*. The old Chapel at Stevington, which contained piscinæ, stood across the yard, nearly opposite the porch of the manor-house. Mr. Alston's gamekeeper used to keep his dogs in it. It was about nine yards long, and six wide.[a] In a field to the south of the same house, and within twenty or thirty yards of it, numerous portions of foundations have been from time to time discovered.

Concerning lesser estates in this parish, and their owners or occupiers, the following particulars have been gleaned.

John de Stevyngton gave to the Prior of "Hautemprise" (Haltemprice in Yorkshire, founded by Thomas Wake de Lidell), a messuage and certain lands in "Stevyngton," Beds.[b]

A fine was levied, in Trinity Term, 4 and 5 Philip and Mary, between John, Lord Mordaunt, plaintiff, and Thomas Cokk, deforciant, of one messuage, two tofts, one garden, twenty-six acres of arable land, one acre of meadow, and three acres of pasture, with appurtenances, in "Stacheden, Bromeham, and Stevynton;" Lord Mordaunt paying £40 to the said Thomas. Sir John Mordaunt, Lord Mordaunt, was seised (int. al.) of certain small rents in Stevington and elsewhere.[c]

The estate of one of the Viscounts Hampden extended into this parish.[d]

In the time of Queen Elizabeth, Thomas Smythe, William Hatley,[e] Robert[e] and Peter Taylor, and Edward Wylkynson, were freeholders.[f]

A family surnamed Taylor, Taillor, &c. were tenants and resident in Stevington from very early times, and, if their pedigree is worthy of credit, "came into England with the lord of Guisnes," when they dropped their original name of Harthen, and assumed that of Taylor. In the 7th Edward I. John le Taylur occurs among Baldwin Wake's cotarii.[g] It is probable, that subsequently they may have occupied the manor-house, as some of them were buried close to the manorial chapel in Stevington church.

[a] MS. Marsh. Somes was the name of the tenant in Mr. Marsh's time.
[b] Inq. ad quod damnum. 13 Ed. III. nu. 33.
[c] Chancery Inq. 6 Eliz. nu. 6.
[d] Vide Bromham, Appendix, p. 108, note.[e]
[e] At Michaelmas, 2—3 Elizabeth, a fine was levied between Robert Taylor, plaintiff, and William Hatley and Elizabeth his wife, deforciants, of 40 acres of pasture called "Nuns close" with appurtenances in "Stagisden," and Robert gave to the said William and Elizabeth £40.
[f] Lansd. MS. 5, fo. 27.
[g] Rot. Hund.

TAYLOR.

(Harl. MSS. 1531, fo. 122 ; 4,600.)

Arms (granted Nov. 1610): Az. a saltire voided betw. four stag's heads cabossed or.
Crest: A buck's head cabossed ppr., pierced through with two arrows in saltire gu., headed and feathered or.

Richard Harthen came into England with the Lord of Guynes=
|— John surnamed Taillor or Taylor=
  |— John Taylor=
    |— John Taylor=
      |— Symond Taylor=
        |— Nicholas Taylor=
          |— John Taylor=
            |— Robert Taylor=
              |— John Taylor=

Isabell, dau. of John Wilkinson, of Stevington, m. 2ndly Oliver Bromhall, of Stevington, 1st wife. = Robert Taillor, of Stevington. = . . dau. of . . Kilby de com. Herts. 2nd wife.

Eliz., m. Willm. Harle de com. Bedford.
Margarett, m. Raffe Gostwick, of Marston, Beds. (Robert G., *Harl.* 1531, fo. 63), and had issue William, John, and Gertrude.

Eliz. Taillor, m. William Walker, de com. Beds.
Isabell Taillor, m. Chernocke, of . . Beds.

Robert Taylor, of Stevington (1613), d. 16th October, 1618, bur. in Stevington church. = Eliz., eldest dau. of John Broomhall, of Stevington, gent.

Judith, m. William Warde de com. Bedford.
Dorathe, m. Wm. A. de com. Northants.
Mary, m. . . B . . de com. Bedford.
Frances, m. Richard Sherman de com. Bedford.
Olive.
Martha.

Robert Taillor, æt. 9, 1613. (Harl. 1531.)

John. (Harl. 4,600.)

Elizabeth, m. John Bayly, of London.
Dorathie.
Ursula.
Margaret, m. John Anstey, gent. and d. a widow 20th Feb. 1668, buried in Stevington church.
Anne.

1559, Jan. 13. Will of Elizabeth Taylor of this date. To be buried in St. Paul's at Bedford. Testatrix bequeaths a messuage to her daughter Alyce H . . . for term of life, with remainder to Richard, son of Richard Weynman deceased. To the same Richard she leaves a silver goblet, a brass pot and pan, William Hatleye of Steventon to have the custody of the goblet (and spoons) till Richard be xx years of age. To Elizabeth Hatleye and Margaret Taylor a gold ring a-piece. To mending of the "grete bridge" in Bedford, xx s.

(Edward Tayler was Vicar of St. Paul's, Bedford, at this time.)

1567, Nov. John Tayler of Chellington, by his will, devised lands in Carlton, Chellington, Turvey, Pabenham, and Stevington with appurtenances to Margaret and Ione his sisters. To the poor of Carlton he gave vi s. viii d.

BROOMHALL.

Harl. MSS. 4600; 1531.

Arms: 1 & 4, Sa. a lion ramp. or.—*Bromhall*—quartering 2 & 3, Az. a chev. betw. three bundles of cotton yarn ar.—*Cotton*.

Crest: A demi-lion or, holding betw. the paws a cross-crosslet fitchée sa.

Motto: Calcar Virtutis Honor.

John Broomhall, of Stevington=Agnes, dau. of Thomas Answell, of Barforde.

| John Broomhall, of Stevington. | Robert Broomhall =Joane, dau. of Robt. Throgmorton, of Elmpton or Ellington, in com. Beds. | Lewis=Anne. | Oliver, of Sandy, in com. Bedford. | Isabell, dau. of Joh. Wilkinson, of Stevington, relict of Robt. Taylor, of the same place. | Katherine, m. Richd. Bass, of London, Attorney in the King's Bench. Ursula, m. Edward Charde, of London. Elizabeth, m. Robert Taylor, of Stevington, and had issue. |

Children of Robert and Joane: Oliver Broomhall, ob. at 18 yeres of age, 21 of November 1624. Sir John Bromhall. Robert. Elizabeth.

Child of Lewis and Anne: Anne Broomhall.

"On the 22nd April, 1601, being about 3 and 4 in the morning, John Bromhall, being of good memory, but sicke in bodye, concern^g the disp^s of his worldly goods, in the presence of these hereafter-named, spake to this effect: I geve all my goods unto my wife, shee paying my debts, and I doe not doubte but she will be good mother to her children and mine. And, good wench, geve unto my sonne Taylor my graye geldinge, with my best saddle and all ye furniture belonging; and geve unto my daughter Taylor the little silver boule, and to each of her foure children an ewe and a lambe. And unto this he desired his servants and such as were with him to beare witness."

Present—William Speringe, Oliver Bromhall, Edward Bromhall, Edward Grove, Thomas Forde, John Lovell, Martha Taylor, Elizabeth Whitwike.

Proved (Archd. Bedf.) 23 April, 1601.

CHARITIES.

The poor of Stevington are entitled to an annual rent-charge of 5s., the gift of Mrs. Anniseed, as is supposed.[a]

Barringer's Charity.

William Barringer, a native of this parish, who became a stationer in London, was founder of the Almshouses here.[b]

Present Trustees:—The Duke of Bedford, Lieut.-Col. W. B. Higgins, and Joseph Tucker, esq.; together with the Vicar and Churchwardens—*ex officio*.

The Commissioners' report concerning this charity in 1823 is as follows:—

William Barringer, by will dated 18th March, 1631, bequeathed the residue of his personal estate to his executors Thomas Barringer and Philip Alston, on trust, after payment of debts, legacies, and funeral expenses, to lay out the same in building as many almshouses for poor men, in the town of Stevington, as the said residue would perform and accomplish; and his will was, that if any of his own name should be in want, they should be preferred into the said almshouses before any others.

Thomas Barringer alone proved the will, and possessed himself of the personal estate of the testator, with part of which he erected five almshouses in the town of Stevington, and afterwards, under a Bill in Chancery, filed against him by the then vicar and churchwardens of Stevington, for an account, and to have the charity perfected, he paid the sum of £400 as the surplus of the residue of the said personal estate, which sum, by a decree of the Court dated 4th December, 1640, was invested in the purchase of the following premises, viz., a close or part of a close of pasture, called the Nether Cowlands, containing by estimation 20 acres, lying in Pavenham; a common field there, belonging to Badwell (Radwell), in the parish of Felmshaw (Felmersham), called the Upper Field, on one side of the said close, and a common field belonging to Pavenham, lying on the other side thereof; and part of a close called the Upper Cowlands, containing by estimation 5 acres in Pavenham, divided by a hedge and ditch from the other part of the said close called the Upper Cowlands, not intended to be conveyed; all which said premises were, by indentures of feoffment dated 28th March, 1651, executed under the direction of the Court, conveyed from John Alston, esquire, to Richard Barringer, William Dennys, John Barringer, John Mann, and Bernard Hopkins, their heirs and assigns, in trust, for the use and benefit of the poor people of the parish of Stevington, who should from time to time be placed in the said almshouses.

---

[a] Abstract of Returns of Charitable Donations for benefit of Poor Persons.
[b] Add. MS. 21,067, ff. 72, 73, 76, 205 b.

There does not appear to have been any subsequent or later conveyance of the estate to trustees. Thomas Barringer, the survivor of those mentioned in the deed, died in 1696, and from the great length of time that has since elapsed it is much doubted whether the heir at law, if there be one, can now be discovered. The Rev. — Barnard, of Riseley, and Mr. William Wootton (both now deceased), were the last persons who acted in the trusts of the charity, but it is not known under what authority they so acted; and since the death of Mr. Wootton, in December 1808, there has been no acting trustee of the charity whatever.

The five almshouses are small brick buildings, containing   rooms each; they are considerably out of repair at present; three of them, for a great many years past, have been inhabited by parish paupers, put in from time to time by the overseers; the other two are in the occupation of ———— Parker, who claims to live in one of them rent-free, on the ground of having married a Barringer, of kin to the founder; the other he has converted into a shop, and pays a small rent for the same.

The land, containing altogether 25A. 36P.[a] in four closes, called Cowlands East, Middle, West, and North Closes, is in the occupation of two persons named Lavender, whose ancestors are said to have occupied the same for nearly 150 years, for anything that appears to the contrary, as tenants, merely from year to year, paying rent to such persons as have from time to time acted as trustees of the charity. The present occupiers succeeded to the possession of the land in 1795, as tenants to Mr. Barnard and Mr. Wootton, the then acting trustees, at the rent of 15*l.* a-year, which was afterwards raised to 20*l.*; the rent was received by Mr. Wootton, until his decease in 1808, since which time there has been no person to receive it, and the arrears have accumulated in the hands of the tenants to the amount of 200*l.* or upwards. The tenants are stated to be responsible persons, and are willing, as we are informed, to pay the amount when called upon, to any person who may be duly authorized to receive it, and to give them a legal discharge for the same.

The rents, while they were received, after payment of £4 a-year to ———— Parker, the only person who could be considered as an almsman, appear to have been applied to the common benefit of the poor of Stevington, being sometimes distributed amongst them in bread and sometimes in money, according to the direction of Mr. Barnard and Mr. Wootton, and occasionally at the discretion of the tenants themselves. We could not ascertain how long this mode of applying the rent had existed, nor from what time the almshouses had been used, in part at least, as mentioned above, for the residence of parish paupers.

It appears from the above statement to have become indispensably requisite for the welfare of this charity that immediate means should be taken to vest the property in new trustees; and we are assured that a petition to that effect is, by advice of Counsel, about to be presented to the Court of Chancery, under the Act of the 51st Geo. III., on behalf of the present Vicar of Stevington, and other gentlemen of the neighbourhood, who are willing to undertake the office or trustees.

The Marquis of Tavistock, Francis Green, esq., W. B. Higgins, esq., Rev.

---

[a] According to a later estimate, 25a. 1r. 8p.

John Wing, M.A. Vicar, William Pratt, William Poole, and Isaac Keech, were the trustees of Barringer's Charity in 1836.

In 1841 the existing row of five almshouses was built from plans by Mr. James Tacy Wing, of Bedford. The past career of one of the inmates at the present time is worth recording. Samuel White, "bred and born" in this village, now in his 79th year, enlisted as a private in the Hon. East India Company's service about the year 1811, and was subsequently stationed at Tilbury, and the Isle of Wight. On the 21st June, 1813, he landed at St. Helena, where he remained seven years nine months; he used to groom Napoleon's horses, and remembers the names of two —*Oiseau* and *Mameluke*. About two or three months before Napoleon's death, White accepted his discharge in preference to the alternative of remaining beyond the Line for life, and returned to England and his native parish.

Rectory and Advowson.

The church of Stevington with its appurtenances was given to the priory of Harewold or Harrold by Baldwin de Ardres, in the time of King John,[a] and the living was reduced to a vicarage before 1220. In the reign of Queen Elizabeth, Thomas Adams obtained a lease of the rectory for twenty-one years; and in the nineteenth of the same reign Lewis Dyve of Bromham had a grant of the rectory, advowson, and tithes of Stevington.[b]

In the time of Queen Mary the advowson was granted to the Bishop of Lincoln. In 1561 the Crown presented to the living. Peter Floyer, esq. of Shenfield, Berkshire, was patron in 1712; he was also possessed of the rectory or parsonage, which afterwards came to Sarah, Duchess of Marlborough, who bequeathed it (*int. al.*) in trust for her grandson, John Spencer.[c] Lysons mentions Earl Spencer as the owner at the time he wrote.

---

[a] Rot. Chart. 7 John, mem. 1. Mon. Ang. vol. vi. p. 331. Rot. Hund.

[b] Patent Roll, 19 Eliz. part 2, mem. 10. Grant to Louis Dyve, dated at Gorhambury, 24th May.

[c] Sarah, Duchess of Marlborough, by her will dated 11 August, 1744, proved 2 Nov. in the same year, devised to her executors and trustees (Hugh, Earl of Marchmont, and Beversham Filmer, esquire, of Lincoln's Inn), divers estates in Bedfordshire, in trust (subject to certain annuities) for her grandson, John Spencer, and, after his decease, for his son, John Spencer, remainder in trust for his heirs male, remainder to the daughter or daughters of her grandson John Spencer in equal portions. Among other hereditaments, her

Francis 5th Duke of Bedford presented to the vicarage in 1776, and his Grace's grand-nephew the present Duke is now possessed of both the rectory and advowson. The estate in Stevington pertaining to the rectory is known as the Tithe Farm. Not many years ago there was standing a large barn of the fourteenth century, which probably was the Great Tithe Barn of the Priory; it was a long range of building, without any ornaments or mouldings, and was situated a few yards to the south-east of the vicarage-house.

VICARAGE.

The living is a discharged vicarage.' Upon the inclosure of the parish of Pavenham in 1769, the Vicar of Stevington, being entitled to the great and small tithes of copyhold tithing in that parish, had an allotment of land assigned him in lieu of them." In 1819, an estate was purchased at Felmersham, with Queen Anne's Bounty money, for Stevington vicarage.'

---

freehold and copyhold messuages, lands, &c., in the said county of Bedford which were late the estates of Sir John Meres knight, Bromsall Throckmorton esquire, Edward Snagg esquire, John Culliford and Mary his wife; and also her rectory and tythes of Stevenon, in the said county of Bedford, which were late the estate of Peter Floyer esquire. Also lands and tenements in Huntingdonshire and Berkshire; the former late the estate of Sir John Meres knight, and — Astell esquire, the latter of Thomas Bedford clerk, and Temperance his mother.

a Parliamentary Gazetteer.
b Lysons.
c Deeds executed at Bedford on the Visitation day, 7th April.—MS. Marsh.

STEVINGTON.

A stone, let into the wall of the north-east gable of the Vicarage-house, exhibits the letter "D" and "1678," under which a stone has been inserted bearing the coronet and arms of the Duke of Bedford. Another stone shows the date 1835. The house was much enlarged and improved by the present Vicar in the year 1863. It is situated near to the south side of the church.

List of Incumbents.

WILLIELMUS SACERDOS DE STEVINTON.[a]

	Vicars.[b]	Patron.
1220—1234	Nich. de Dicheford	Harwold Priory.
1280—1299	Joh. fil. Roger de Wotton	,,
1300—1320	Nich. de Harwold. By death of last.	,,
	Rob. de Harade.	,,
1347—1361	Simon	,,
	Nich. Hayward, Pbr. By death of last.	,,
1405—1419	Joh. Medydewelton, Pbr. By death of last.	,,
1456—1471	John Smart	,,
	Willm. Skypwith. By res. of last.	,,
	John Kyngden. By res. of last.	,,
	Thomas Boghton. By res. of last.	,,
1471—1479	Richard Crewe	,,
1561, May	Richard Harres[c]	Crown.
1570—1583	Robert G. . . .	
	Raphe Oullwhith.[d] By res. of last.	Lewis Dyve.
1595—1607	Nicholas Barton	
Circa 1699[e]	John Draper. Also Vicar of Stagsden. Deprived 1712.	
1712, Oct.	George Fern, B.A., St. John's Coll. Camb. 1706.	Peter Floyer, Ar., of Shenfield, Berkshire.
1716, Nov.	Peter Barker, B.A., Cai. Coll. Camb. 1696.	,,
1722, June	John Veneer, B.A.[f]	,,

---

[a] Witness to Charter of Henry de Alno of Turvey, living temp. K. Steph. or Henr. II.

[b] Lib. Instit. apud Lincoln.

[c] Rymer, Fœd. vol. vi. part 4, p. 114.

[d] Witness to the Will of John Cockes of Stevington, husbandman, 1580.

[e] Parish Register.

[f] Mr. Marsh mentions a tradition in the village to the effect that this Vicar was the Rev. John Veneer (Rector of St. Andrew's, Chichester), who wrote an "Exposition of the 39 Articles," published, Lond. 1725-1730. Also a "New Exposition of the Book of Common Prayer," 1727.—Add. MS 21,067, fo. 153 b. Allibone.

STEVINGTON.

	Vicars.	Patron.
1751, June	Willm. Sanderson, M.A. By death of last.	
1776, Mar.	Thos. Orlebar Marsh. By death of last.	Francis, Duke of Bedford.
1832, Jan.	John Wing, M.A. By death of last.	Duke of Bedford.
1849	William Henry Bond, B.A., Queens' Coll. Camb. Rector of Wymmington, 1834-39. Presented by the Duke of Bedford to the vicarage of Goldington, near Bedford, 1862. Author of *A Concise View of Ancient Geography*, 4th ed. 1852.	
1862	Edward Wilson Cook, M.A., St. John's Coll. Camb. By res. of last. Author of *Death and its Issues*, (Sermon on the Death of Francis, 7th Duke of Bedford, K.G.), 2 edits. 1861; and other Sermons.	

CHURCH (1866).

The Church of St. Mary is built in the form of a parallelogram, comprising chancel, nave, north and south aisles with porches, and a western tower, being (with the exception of the north porch) the portion of the fabric restored in 1872; on either side of the chancel is a lateral chapel in ruins, that on the north (which contains a piscina) being the property of Crewe Alston, esq., as lord of the manor; the one on the south belongs to the Duke of Bedford, but to what estate or messuage appendant is not known.

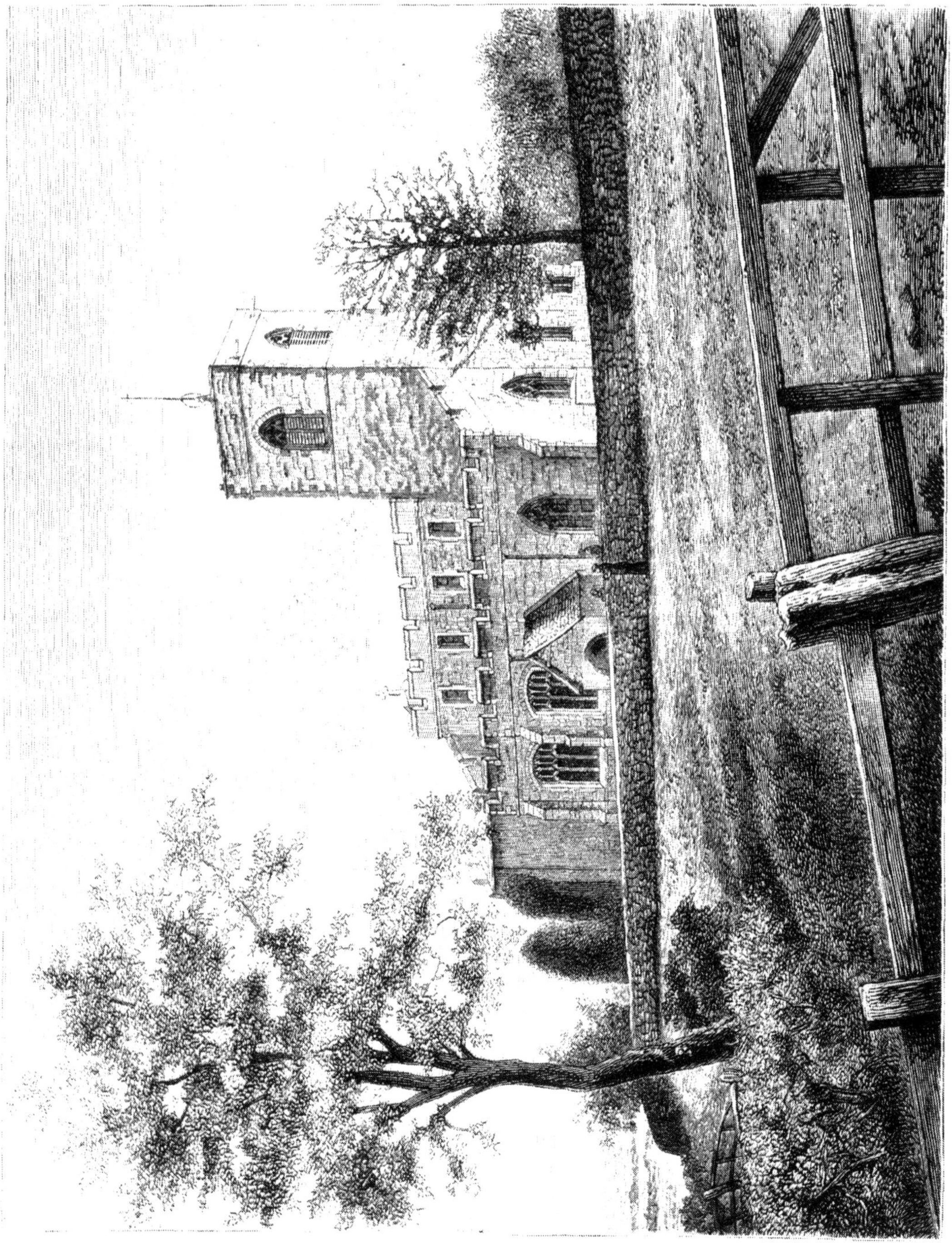

The walls of the aisles, south porch, and east end of the chancel have embattled parapets; prior to 1872 there were no battlements on the north side of the church. Both aisles extend westward as far as the tower.

The large Perpendicular east window, of five lights, is in part a copy of its predecessor, as may be seen on comparing with it an engraving of the east end of the church in the Gentleman's Magazine for 1812, from which we learn, also, that the south lateral chapel had a three-light east window with Perpendicular tracery.

The former square-headed south-east window of the south aisle, of four lights, has given place to two three-light Perpendicular windows, like the new ones on the opposite side of the church. The Decorated window to the west of the south porch retains the original characteristics of its style, but has a pointed arch in lieu of a square head. During the recent alterations the upper part of the south porch was taken down, when a weather line (on the aisle wall) was discovered, indicating that it formerly had a gabled roof—a more graceful and appropriate covering for a church porch than the flat roof, concealed by battlements, which was replaced.

The three small windows at the west end of the church, and the north-west window of the north aisle have been carefully restored, and are of the Second Pointed Period; with one exception, they are each of two lights, and appear to be original, the three-light west window being evidently an insertion, as the lower part of the tower exhibits very ancient workmanship in the interior, and what is known as "long and short work" on the outside. The north aisle shows traces of some early alteration; it is wider than the south aisle, and the string-course which runs at the foot of its west window suddenly falls at a point a little northward of the same window; its tiled porch is devoid of ornament, but protects a good doorway. The two new Perpendicular windows eastward of this porch have been substituted for two plainer ones of the same style, but without tracery. In the course of restoration two early Decorated windows of considerable beauty were brought to light, viz., a traceried one of two lights in the south wall of the chancel, which had probably been closed up when the south lateral chapel was erected, and a small trefoiled "low side window" in the wall below the westernmost light of the north-east window of the north aisle: the use of this interesting and perfect relic is a *vexata questio*. It is conjectured that "low side windows" were used for confessional purposes, as we read in a letter from Bedyll to Lord Cromwell at the visitation made at the suppression of religious houses and chantries:—"We think it best that the place wher thes freres have been wont to here outward confession of all commers at certen times of the yere be walled up, and that use to be fordoen for ever."

PISCINA, NORTH CHAPEL.

CLOSED-UP SOUTH WINDOW IN CHANCEL.

"LOW SIDE WINDOW," NORTH AISLE.

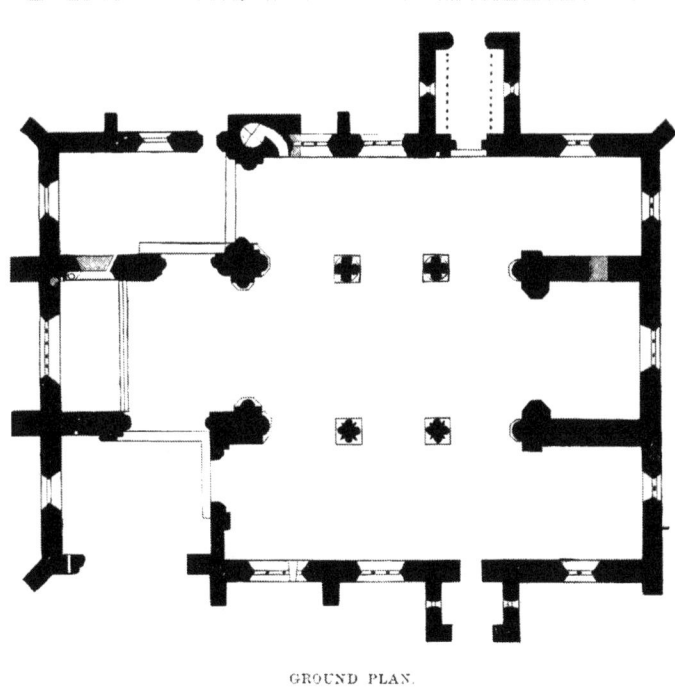

GROUND PLAN.

STEVINGTON CHURCH.

INTERIOR OF STEVINGTON CHURCH.

INTERIOR OF NORTH AISLE.

INTERIOR OF SOUTH AISLE.

The clerestory above the nave formerly had six small oblong glazed openings; it now contains eight trefoiled lights in square-headed compartments, and is surmounted by battlements.

The tower, containing five bells, is simple in design, even to plainness, but its appearance has been improved by the removal of a coating of plaster or rough-cast which disfigured its walls: it has four quatrefoil-headed two-light windows in the belfry stage, and is covered with a flat roof of lead, from the centre of which rises a vane. The leaden roofs of the nave and chancel and the slated roofs of the aisles are of low pitch.

The interior of this church bears a favourable contrast to its exterior. The nave has a stately appearance, and the arcades of three bays each dividing it from the aisles are very lofty in proportion to the length of the building, the pillars and mouldings on the north side being of a more elaborate description than those on the south; a dripstone is continued round both faces of the arches, on the north side springing from seven corbel heads.

In removing the plaster from the walls of the tower, two windows (north and south) and a semicircular archway, all apparently of the Saxon Period, were discovered; the situation of the latter is in the south wall, and its dimensions are remarkable, being nine feet high and only two feet nine inches wide. On the eastern side of the south-porch door an ancient stoup was brought to light, and over the door a fresco representing a distinguished person in a sitting posture and a procession passing before him, with an elaborately designed medallion, having the words "1633. James v. 9: Grudge not one against another, brethren, lest ye bee condemned: behold, the judge standeth before The door." This has been covered over again.

Near to the east end of the south aisle a lancet doorway was discovered; likewise a stone staircase, which apparently formed the approach to the rood-loft.[a]

The removal, or rather mutilation, of the chancel screen, with its curiously-painted panels, appears (with strange inconsistency) to have been countenanced by an enthusiastic antiquary, the Rev. T. O. Marsh, a former Vicar of this parish; he tell us, that "in August 1826, the screen which parted the chancel from the church was cut away to about as low as the pews, to give a fine view of the chancel." The remaining vestiges were removed during the recent alterations, and have been placed for preservation against the west wall of the north aisle, and also a pulpit cloth, bearing the words, "Ex dono Theodosiæ Charissimæ

---

[a] A somewhat similar position for the rood staircase is found in the church of St. John the Baptist at Halifax in Yorkshire.

Uxoris Henrici Chester de East Haddon in Comitatu Northamptoniæ Armigeri 1706." The ancient iron-bound parish chest, in this part of the church, likewise deserves attention.

The chancel is entered under a pointed arch, and the floor is now on a level with the nave, the whole being paved with red and black tiles. In the south-east angle of the chancel wall, and about equidistant from the floor with the sill of the east window, is the base of a slender shaft. The etching, representing (though very inadequately) the closed-up south window, shows the stone seat, piscina, and squint.

Each of the now ruinous chapels communicated, by means of arches, with the chancel and with the aisles respectively. These arches are now built up on the outside, forming recesses in the interior, which add considerably to the interesting appearance of the east end of the building. The pointed arch of the recess at the east end of the north aisle springs from foliated capitals—the only instance where such occur in the church; adjoining this recess on the north is another smaller one, with a very depressed arch, formed out of a beam of oak.

After having been closed a considerable time for an extensive and much-needed restoration, this interesting parish church was reopened with special services on Wednesday 22nd May, 1872. The works were carried out by Mr. Robert Tooley, of Bury St. Edmund's, under the superintendence of Mr. Clutton, and more immediately of Mr. Usher, of Bedford, the cost being defrayed by the landowners and parishioners, the Duke of Bedford bearing the principal part of the expense.

New roofs were placed over the aisles and chancel. The nave roof, of oak, was restored and strengthened where required; on the timbers of this roof are roses, stars, and figures holding shields. The chancel is fitted up with open benches in oak with solid ends and carved poppy-head terminals; the communion rail is of polished oak on ornamental iron standards, and the space within the rail, approached by three steps, paved with encaustic tiles from Messrs. Maw and Co.'s works. The seats in the nave and aisles are in yellow deal, varnished. The old pulpit has been placed on a stone base. The warming apparatus is by Gidney, of East Dereham. The bells, which have been re-hung, bear the following inscriptions:—

1. 'John Hodson made me—1654—
   I.L. H.N. C.WW—
2. 'John Hodson made me—1654—
   JOHN LATTON, HENRY NEGOUS, Churchwardens.'
3. 'John Hodson made me—IL HN. 1654—CWW—'
4. 'John Hodson made me—1654—
   JOHN LATTON, HENRY NEGOUS, Churchwardens.'
5. (Same as number 4, but without date.)

John Hodson's foundry is said by Lukis ("Account of Church Bells," Parker, 1857) to have been in London from 1653.

The chalice, with its cover formed for a paten, is of silver, and bears date 1570, and the initials " S. T."

In Plate II. accompanying Mr. Fisher's account of Stevington[a] are drawings of carvings in wood on the upright ends of the seats in the nave of this church. It appears very probable that they have a reference to the drinking, or church ale, for the maintenance of which seven acres of land were bequeathed before the Reformation. Of such drinkings or give-ales some very interesting notices may be seen in the 12th volume of the Archæologia, p. 10, communicated to the Society of Antiquaries by the late Rev. Samuel Denne, of Wilmington, Kent. As the ends of many of the old seats in Stevington church have been cut off, it is not improbable that there were originally more of these grotesque sculptures. The larger one of those illustrated by Fisher has been placed in the western portion of the south aisle, which is occupied as a vestry.

AUGMENTATION OFFICE.

Certificates of Chantries, Bodford.

2 Edward 6. i. page 14.

	s.	d.
Drinking in Steventon, valued in the Ferme of 7 acres of Land in Steventon in the tenure of Thomas Derling, given to a certain Drinking there by the yere	4	8
Reprizes. On Rent Reserved to our Sovereign Lord the King for certainty by yere 2d. Rent Reserved to the Lord Vaulx as to his Manor of Carleton by year 4d.	thereof 0	6
And so remaineth clear by the year	4	2

PATENT ROLL, 1 MARY, Pt. 3.

Grant to Thomas Reve and Henry Cotton, and their heirs, &c., in consideration of the sum of £1,951 14s. 1½d. (amongst others).

'And also all those our lands with the appurtenances, containing by estimation 7 acres, lying and being in Steventon, in the said county of Bedford, now or late in the tenure or occupation of Robert Derlynge, and being before the date of this grant assigned and appointed to the sustaining of an anniversary in the church of Steventon.'

'And moreover of 6d. issuing from the aforesaid lands in Steventon aforesaid and to the Lord Vaux, as to his manor in Carleton annually paying.'

Given at Westminster, May 29th, 1 Mary.

[a] Gent. Mag. 1812, vol. 82, Pt. 2, p. 9.

Drinking-Bush Hill is the name of a hill toward the western boundary of the parish. The parishioners, "beating the bounds," on arriving at this place, used to dig a hole, jump in it, and then drink to satiety. It is not known when this annual custom was discontinued, nor whether it had any connection with the church-ale; the situation of this hill, near the confines of Carlton, where Lord Vaux had a manor, as mentioned in the certificate and grant above quoted, seems to show that it had.

Monuments.

On the floor of the nave is a brass figure of a man in plate-armour, with the following inscription on a label at the foot:—

> Orate pro ai'a Thome Salle[a] armig'i
> q' obijt xxi die mens' Ap'lis
> Anno D'ni M.CCCCXXII.

The arms are two salamanders (or crocodiles) in saltire. There is an engraving of this brass in the Gentleman's Magazine for July 1812.

Black marble slab in the floor at the east end of the north aisle—

> Under this Stone lyeth y[e] body of Ro[t] Tayler
> of this parish Gen[t] he Exchanged this life for
> a better y[e] 16th of Octob[r] 1618, he Marryed
> Eleza: y[e] eldest Davghter of Robr[t] Bromhall
> of this parish Gen[t] & had issue by her 5
> Davghters & one Son: viz: Elez: Dorothy:
> Vrsley: Margarett: Ann: & Robr[t]:
> Here also lyeth y[e] body of Margarett
> Anstey y[e] 4th Daughter of y[e] abovesaid
> Robr[t] Tayler relict of John Anstey Gent,
> who departed this life in y[e] trve faith of y[e]
> Chvrch of England Died y[e] 20th of feb[ry] & was
> att y[e] sole Cost & Charge of this Stone, 1668.

Arms. Taylor, impaling Bromhall, surmounted by Taylor's crest on an helmet.

There are or were inscriptions on flat stones in the church in memory of—

Mrs. Susanna Ashton who departed this life April 2nd, 1749, in the 34th year of her age. Mr. Thomas Ashton, May 3rd, 1757, aged 87.[b] Susanna, Eliz. and Mary Wallis. Lucia Stonor, an infant. George

---

[a] This name is uncommon, in Bedfordshire; a John Salle was tenant of Wardon Abbey lands (Harl. 4765, fo. 6). John Salle occurs temp. Henry VI. seised of land in Wytham, Essex. (Esc. 6 H. VI. nu. 57).

[b] MS. Marsh.

Cox, 1724, aged 86.[a] Martha Stokes, 1756, aged 88.[a] George Cox, 1688. John Odell, 1773, aged 86.[a] Anne Cox, 1703. Ann Cox, 1723. Timothy Keach (stone near church door, defaced), aged 89.[a] Robert Gale, 1718, aged 89.[a]

A flat stone bears the date October xxii. 1680, but the rest of the inscription is illegible.

In the churchyard (east) may be seen some sepulchral crosses. A small one, found in the projection containing the rood-steps, is in the chancel.

There are inscriptions, in the churchyard, for—

(?John) Hyde 1787, aged 80.[a] William Henry, eldest son of Rev. John Wing, M.A., Vicar of St. Mary's, Leicester, and Anne his wife, 1857. Revd. John Wing, M.A., Vicar of this parish, and Anne wife of the above. Mary Eliz. their second daughter. Also Edwin, Charles John, and Theodora, their children, June 1857.

On a raised tomb near the south-east corner of the church—

> Here lyeth the Body of
> Joseph Barringer, Senior, who
> Departed this Life the 21st
> of May, 1714. In the 79th
> Year of his Age.[b]

Other names (1868)—

Pike, Hulett, Low, Pool, Field, Keech, Pratt, Sturges, Tysoe, Glidel, Battams.

REGISTER.

1653 Nov. 6.	Baptized, Jacob, son of Richard Cox. (Earliest entry.)	
1657 Oct. 10.	Buried, Robert Bromhall.	
1661	Collections to Briefs (in the cover of the register).	
1661 Sept. 10.	Buried, Elizabeth, the wife of Henry Frankling.	
1665 Nov. 2.	——— Margaret Bromhull, widow.	
1669 April 9.	——— Hellena, wife of William Palmer.	
1670 May 15.	Baptized, Katherine, daughter of William Taylor.	
1672	Buried, William, son of William Francklin.	
1675 Jan. 22.	Baptized, John, son of William Taylor.	
1678 April 14.	——— William, son of William Tailer.	
1679 May.	——— Thomas, son of John Draper.	
1680 Oct. 8.	——— John, son of John Draper.	
— Nov. 10.	——— Mathew, son of Mathew Draper.	
1682-3	——— Mary, daughter of William Taylour.	

---

[a] MS. Marsh.

[b] 1714 (May). Joseph Barringer, of Swineshead, in Hunts, was bury'd 25th.—Parish Register.

1686   Married, William Moody and Eliz. Morris.
1687 July 17. ——— Jeshua Taylour and Mary Wright.
1688 Jan. 28. ——— Thos. Taylour and Marg^t Ingersole.
1688 to 1692. Collections to Briefs (in cover of the book).
1688 Sept. 10. Married, Thomas Rolt and Mary Hays.
1689 May 16. ——— William Moody and Mary Crow.
1693 May 21. Baptized, Richard, son of William Taylour.
1694 Feb. 20. Buried, Priscilla Bray, widow.
1695 Jan.   Richard, son of Richard Lavender, born.
——— Apr.   Baptized, Edward, son of William Taylour.
1699. In a note, respecting certain houses in Pavenham, are named—

        Lewis Pooll, Baker.[a]
        Mr. John Alston.
        John Draper, Minister.
        George Casley, } Churchwardens.
        ——— Yarrow,   }

On the same page—

"All the males above 16 years of age doe pay head-pence, the King's Certainty money."

    (Signed)   Walter Hook, lawer.
                 Thomas Morris, farmer.

The following surnames also occur in the first register book:—

        Gurney, Bunny, Barringer, Dudley, Brabrook or Brabrix, and Cokin—with the variation Cockain.

1701   .   .   [The second Register book begins.]
1711 Aug.   Buried, Thomas Taylor, "A waddman."
1712 Oct. 8. ——— William Taylor, a butcher.
1713 .   .   . George Fern, vicar, signs.
——— Apr. 4. Baptized, Mary, daur. of Henry and Lucy Stonor.
1714 Aug. 10. Buried, Lucy, daur. of Henry and Lucy Stonor.
1715 May 21. Baptized, Henry, son of Mr. Henry and Lucy Stonor.
1718   Married, E. Goodman, and Mary Warner of "Pavingham in ye Parish of Stevington."
——— .   . . Fran. Reade, curate, signs.
1723 . .   . William Bedford, curate.
1729 . .   . J. Gamble, curate.
——— . .   . J. Gamble, LL.B., curate.
1730 May 31. Married, Mary Turner, daur. of Richard and Mary, of Olney, Bucks, and Rev. Henry Kilby, vicar of that parish.
1732–1779   Third Register. (The pages containing entries from 1762 to 1770 have been abstracted).

---

[a] The family of Pool, or Poole, have been bakers in this village for several generations.

1738 Mar. 5.   Buried,   Henery Stoner, gent.
—— Mar. 12.   ——   Elizabeth Stoner, a single woman—gent.
1754   .   .   .   Robert Stoakes, curate.
1768 Jan. 11.   Buried,   Thomas Ashton Wagstaf.
     Next follow two books containing registers (1) from 1763 to 1810; (2) from 1779 to 1812.
1772   .   .   .   Jos. Griffith, curate.
1775 Sept. 2.   Married,   James Baskervill, gent. of "Stagston," and Elenor Brains of Stevington. (By licence, Richard Jones, minister).
1780   .   .   .   Thos. Orlebar Marsh signs as vicar.
1780 to 1789, 59 baptisms, and 106 burials; 1790 to 1799, 71 baptisms, and 94 burials.
1831   .   .   .   E. H. Dawson, curate.

In March 1832, a fire broke out near the Cross (in the barn of Samuel Risely, a small farmer and butcher), spread across the West End Road, destroying a cottage, then across Silver Street, demolishing barns, stables, and a bakehouse, with two or three cottages on Park End Road.

There is a mixed elementary British School in the village. The building, a substantial stone structure, with master's residence, was erected by the Duke of Bedford in 1863.

Assessed property (1815) £1,786. Poor rates in 1838, £161 18s.

POPULATION.

Year.	Inhabited houses.	Number of separate occupiers.	Uninhabited houses.	Building.	Males.	Females.	Total of persons.
1801	78[a]	—	—	—	—	—	415
1831	103	—	—	—	—	—	500
1841	—	—	—	—	—	—	602
1851	—	—	—	—	—	—	586
1861	142	145	1	2	297	309	606
1871	150	177	1	—	394	343	737

[a] Ninety-nine families.

TURVEY.

Tornai, Torueie, Toruei, Torneia, Tornei,—for so the name is variously written in Domesday Book,—lies on the same stratum as Stevington, and is situated by the river Ouse, nearly seven miles, west-north-west, from Bedford. Within about fifteen years the village has been almost entirely rebuilt in native stone, the majority of the cottages being well and tastefully constructed. The streets and principal dwellings are lighted with gas. Turvey is a station on the Bedford and Northampton Railway.[a] The parish was inclosed by Act of Parliament 1782-3, and the Award is dated 7th April, 1785; the commonable lands contained 1760a. 3r. 15p., their annual value, £720 3s. 7d. Area of parish, according to Tithe Apportionment Map, 3,817 acres; the schedule attached to the map however gives the area, in detail, as amounting to 3,944a. 2r. 30p. It is bounded on the north by Carlton; south by Stagsden, and by Astwood, Hardmead, and Clifton Reynes, in the county of Buckingham; east by Stagsden and Stevington; west by Harrold, and by Lavendon, Cold Brayfield, and Newton Blossomville in Buckinghamshire. The soil is mixed gravel and strong clay.

Charles Longuet Higgins, esq., is lord of the manor, and William Francis Higgins, esq., is patron of the living.[b]

There are two meeting-houses in the village, one belonging to the Wesleyans, the other to the Independents; the latter congregation was formed in 1829.[c] In Stocker's End, very near the Wesleyan meeting, there is a close, now or lately containing some tomb-stones traditionally assigned to Quakers. There is a like burial-place at Elstow. In 1717 the Quakers' "yearly meeting" made an edict against "the vain custom of erecting monuments," and advised that all such monuments should be removed, which advice was repeated in 1766.

[a] Vide Introduction.

[b] The Higgins family are the principal landowners in the parish. The following are also freeholders, but most of them of very small holdings,—Messrs. Cox, Samuel and Frank Skevington, Finch, Noakes, Hinde, and Whitworth, and Miss Abraham. (July, 1873.)

[c] Parliamentary Gazetteer.

Turvey bridge connects this parish with Cold Brayfield, and there was formerly a causeway over a meadow on the Buckinghamshire side. The two arches on the Bucks side were much damaged by floods in the winter of 1872. In the water, between the mill and the bridge, is a statue, said to represent Jonah kneeling on a fish; it was placed here within the present century.

The Bedfordshire Reformatory, situated in this parish, was certified for the admission of Boys April 9, 1857.

In addition to the capital manor there were portions of seven other fees in Turvey at the general survey.^a

^a *Baieux Fee.*[1] (The land of the Bishop of Baieux[2] in the hundred of Wilga.) In Torueie, Wimundus holds one hide of Herbert and he of the Bishop. There is land for one plough-team. Pasture for half a plough-team. The whole worth twenty shillings; when he received it, and in the time of King Edward, forty shillings. One Aluuoldus of Stiuetone held this land and could sell it. (Domesday, p. 209 b.) The other lands in this hundred belonging to the Bishop of Baieux were in Stagsden and Carlton. He had also the manors of Eaton[3] (in Stanburge hundred) and Wilden, and lands in Eversholt, Milton (Bryant), and Bolnhurst. Herbert, the feudatory above-named, is elsewhere called Herbert the son of Ivo.[4]

Count Eustace Fee. Boulogne Honor.[5] (The land of Count Eustace.) In Wilge hundred, Ernulf de Arde holds one hide in Torueie of Count Eustace. There is land for two plough-teams. In demesne is one plough-land, and another can be made. There is one villan and one bordar; pasture for one plough-team. Its value ten shillings; when he received it, and in the time of King Edward, twenty shillings. Aluuoldus, a thane of King Edward, held and could give this land to whom he would. (Domesday, p. 211.)

Beauchamp Fee. Bedford Honor.[6] (The land of Hugh de Belcamp.) In the hundred of Wilga. In Toruei, Warnerius holds one hide of Hugh. There is land for two plough-teams. In demesne is one plough-land, and one villan has another plough-land. There are four bordars. Worth now, and when he received it, ten shillings; in the time of King Edward twenty shillings. Two socmen held this land and could give it to whom they would. (Domesday, p. 213 b.) The advowson of the church of Turvey (or part thereof) was originally appendant to the barony of Beauchamp of Bedford. This fee passed with Bromham and part of Stagsden to William de Monchensi.[7] Adam, the son of Robert, William Breres, and Ralph de Northo, held part of a knight's fee here of the honor of Beauchamp of Bedford.[8] Under de Monchensi, Ralph Perot, Henry de Leya, Roger de Wilie, William de Hotot or Houtot, and others were occupiers.[8]

Nigel de Albingi Fee. (The land of Nigel de Albingi in the hundred of Wilge.) In Torneia, Nigel de Wast holds of Nigel de Albingi one hide and half a virgate. There is land for a plough-team and a

---

[1] Vide Stagsden, *note*, pp. 113, 114.
[2] See Sir H. Ellis's Introduction and Indexes to Domesday, vol. i. p. 376 *n.*
[3] Eaton Bray.
[4] Domesday.
[5] Vide Stevington.
[6] Vide Biddenham, Bromham, and Stagsden. Liber Niger Scaccarii, ed. Hearne, vol. i. p. 198, &c.
[7] Rot. Hund. 7 Edw. I.
[8] Testa de Nevill, temp. Hen. III., Edw. I.

Manor. Coutance Fee. Honor of Gloucester.[a] (The land of the Bishop of Coutance,[b] in the hundred of Wilga.) The same bishop holds four hides in

[a] Vide Biddenham.

[b] Constantiens or Coutance, N.W. Normandy; Coustances (*French*). For the different spellings of this name, v. *Reductio Normanniæ*—Rob. Blondel. Edited from MSS. in the Imperial Library at Paris by Rev. Joseph Stevenson, M.A. (p. 279 more particularly). Lond. Longmans, 1863. See also a *History of the Diocese of Coutance*, Harl. MS. 4599.

---

half, which are there: and there are five bordars. Pasture for one plough-team. Pannage for twenty hogs. Worth thirteen shillings, and the same when he received it; in the time of King Edward thirty shillings. Aluuardus, a man of William, Bishop (of London), held and could give this land to whom he would. (Domesday, p. 214 b.) Nigel de Albingi, or Albini, died 3 Stephen. Roger, his eldest son, by command of King Henry the First, took the surname of Mowbray, from whom the Dukes of Norfolk are descended. Nigel's estates in Bedfordshire went to a younger son, who had a castle at Cainhoe,[1] and passed by a female heir to the St. Amands.[2] In this hundred his lands lay in Carlton, Radwell, and, as mentioned above, in this parish.

Todeni Fee. Belvoir Honor. (The land of Robert de Todeni.) In Wilge hundred. Two knights hold two hides and one virgate in Toruei of Robert. There is land for four plough-teams and a-half. In demesne are two plough-lands, and three villans have two plough-lands, and half a plough-land can be made. There are six bordars and two servi. Pasture for one plough-team. Pannage for ten hogs. Worth forty shillings; when he received it sixty shillings; in the time of King Edward seventy shillings. Osulf (son of Frane, a thane of King Edward) held this land. (Domesday, p. 215.) Todeni's fee in this county was of no great extent, consisting only, in addition to the above, of the manor of Stodham and four hides in Oakley. Robert de Todeni was the founder of Belvoir Castle, and of the cell of monks there, which he annexed to St. Alban's Abbey.[3] He died in 1088.[2][4] Isabel, daughter and heiress of William de Albini, feudal lord of Belvoir, who was the lineal descendant of Robert abovenamed, became the wife of Robert de Ros, whose father was then living. The barony and castle of Belvoir eventually passed from the family of Ros to that of Manners, by which they are now enjoyed in the person of the Duke of Rutland. Simon de Holewell and Philip (s'viens) had part of a knight's fee in Turvey; and Ralph the son of Reginald also had a part, all held of the honor of *Aubeny de Benner*.[5] William de Houtot was rated to the ward of Belvoir Castle for one hide and half a hide of this land as tenant of Richard de Bochard under Robert de Ros, and his demesne consisted of twenty acres. William again had tenants under himself, of whom were Roger son of Hugh de Wylie and Alexander Bozon, the

---

[1] As to the barony of Cainhoe or Kaynho, see Harl. 313, fo. 48.   [2] Ellis.

[3] Belvoir or Bever, *Lincolnshire*, a Benedictine cell to St. Alban's. Tanner. Beaulieu, or De Bello Loco, co. Beds, also a Benedictine cell to St. Alban's, to which abbey it was given by Robert de Albini and his mother, Cecily, about A.D. 1140.—*Mon. Ang.* Between the years 1363 and 1398, Thomas Tydy (? incumbent) of "Torvy" was presented to the living of "Camelton," co. Beds., by the monastery of De Bello Loco.—*Lincoln Register.*

[4] Dugd. Bar. tom. i. p. 111. See Nichols's Leicestershire, vol. i. pt. i. p. 23.

[5] Testa de Nevill, temp. Hen. III., Edw. I.

Tornai. There is land for six plough-teams. In demesne are two hides and three plough-lands. There are three villans having three plough-lands, and eight bordars, and one servus, and one mill of twenty shillings. Pasture for two plough-teams.

latter holding (in right of his wife) a wood of eight acres.[1] Juliana, the wife of Robert Houtot, was seised of a manor in Turvey.[2]

Walter Flandrensis' Fee. Wahul Honor.[3] (The land of Walter Flandrensis.[4]) In the hundred of Wilge. In Tornei Hugh holds one hide of Walter. There is land for two plough-teams: in demesne is one, and eight bordars and one servus have one. Pasture for one plough-team. Pannage for forty hogs. Worth thirty shillings; when he received it ten shillings; in the time of King Edward forty shillings. Leuenot, a thane of King Edward, held this land and could sell it to whom he would.— (Domesday, p. 215 b.) Sanson le Mansel held half a fee in Turvey of the barony of Wahul.[5] The De Greys[6] were feudatories of a considerable portion of the honors of Huntingdon and Wahul in Bedfordshire. Reginald de Grey was mesne lord of this fee under John de Woodhul or Wahul, and, by a subinfeudation, William Fitz Sampson le Maunsel held half a knight's fee under the said Reginald, and paid annually a reserved rent of three shillings, including a small sum to the ward of Rockingham Castle. Hubert Mauduit and Henry de Dylewyk were two of William's five tenants; and there were two virgates in demesne.[7] William, son of Sampson le Maunsel of Turvey, is said to have sold his lands to William Mordaunt in 1287.[8]

The land of the King's bailiffs and almoners. Aluuinus the presbyter holds of the King in Toruei, in the hundred of Wilge, a third part of half a hide. There is land for two ox-gangs and they are there. Worth, and hath been worth, three shillings. The same tenant held it in the time of King Edward, and was able to dispose of it as he would.

In the same hundred Osiet held half a hide of the King.—(Domesday, p. 218 b.)

Robert le Rowe or Reve held part of a knight's fee *in capite*, and of him the prior of St. Neot's held thirty acres, William de Houtot forty acres, and Ralph de Normanville two acres of wood (for a term of thirty years)—this was in 4 Edward I.; three years later the heirs of John le Reve were holding four virgates by serjeanty, of which William de Houtot held two virgates and a windmill and the prior of St. Neot's one virgate in pure alms.[9]

In the 21st Edward I. there was a lawsuit between Emma la Cheppere " de Turfeye," co. Beds., and

---

[1] Rot. Hund.
[2] Esc. 20 Edw. III. nu. 21.
[3] Vide Odell.
[4] Ellis, vol. i. p. 420 n.
[5] Testa de Nevill, p. 250 b.
[6] In the 45th Henry III. there was some litigation between Ralph Pirot and John de Grey respecting tenements in Carlton and Turvey.—Abbrev. Placit. ro. 15.
[7] Rot. Hund. In the 21st Edw. I. Beatrix Maunsel claimed against Reginald le Ken two shillings rent with appurtenances in Turvey.—Abbrev. Rot. Orig. ro. 27.
[8] Maunsel family of Turvey. Shirley, *Noble and Gentle Men of England*, 3rd edit. 1866, p. 163. *Memoirs* of the family, privately printed 1850.
[9] Rot. Hund.; also Testa de Nevill, p. 262 b.

Pannage for forty hogs. Its value six pounds—when he received it forty shillings; in the time of King Edward six pounds. Three socmen, men of King Edward, held, and were able to sell and give, this manor. The Bishop obtained this land in exchange for Bledone,[a] as the men testify.—Domesday, p. 210.

Geoffrey de Mowbray[b] became Bishop of Coutance in 1048. He was chief justiciary of England, and presided at the great trial in the county court held at Pinendene, in Kent, between Lanfranc Archbishop of Canterbury and Odo Bishop of Baieux. He was also one of the party who joined in Duke Robert's favour, in 1088, against William Rufus, and consequently all his lands in England were confiscated. He died Feb. 4th, 1093.[c]

The Bishop of Coutance had, in addition to Turvey, the manor of Chellington, and lands in Hinwick, Sharnbrook, and "Risedene," in this hundred; together with manors in Knotting, Melchbourne, Dene, Yielden, Shelton, and Riseley, and lands in "Estone," Bolnhurst, and "Neuuentone,"[d] in other parts of the county.

[a] An estate (Wake's manor) in Clifton Reynes, Bucks, was also acquired by the Bishop in exchange for *Bledone*; but it is difficult to determine where this place was situated.—Lipscomb, Bucks, vol. iv. p. 109.

[b] Montbray, Monbray, or Moubray.

[c] Sir H. Ellis, *Introduction and Indexes to Domesday*, vol. i. p. 400 *n*. Lipscomb, Bucks, vol. iv. p. 299. Harl. 4599; (in part 2, chap. iv. fo. 33*b*, of this manuscript, *Robert de Monbray*, the Bishop's nephew, is mentioned).

[d] Among the estates of this Bishop in Bedfordshire enumerated in Domesday Book, and immediately following lands in Stodden Hundred, is the notice of this place: In Neuuentone William dapifer holds of the Bishop one virgate. Worth, and hath been worth, twelve pence; in the time of King Edward sixteen

---

Hugh Malet and Agnes his wife, concerning some land and part of a messuage with appurtenances.[1] We find mention of a Thomas Chopper of Turvey as late as 1433.[2]

In the time of King John, Robert de Alneto was seised of half a hide of land with appurtenances in Staunford, &c., to the use of Robert de Broi of Dilewic; William, son of Bone, seised in fee of twelve acres with appurtenances in Turvey; and Ralph, the father of John Lutewin, was seised (on the day of his death) of land in the same.[3]

Robert le Velne had sixteen acres in the same.[4]

William Halybred and Agnes his wife, a messuage and land in Torneye.[5]

Johanna, the wife of Robert de Hilier, eight acres in *Turveye*,[6] which descended to John le Hilier;[7] John, the son of Robert le Hillier, sixteen acres in the same;[8] John le Huliere, the son of Robert, eight acres.[9]

---

[1] Abbrev. Rot. Orig. vol. i. p. 80. (Ro. 28.)
[2] Fuller's *Worthies*. (Beds. p. 119, ed. 1662.)
[3] Abbrev. Placit.
[4] Esc. 42 Hen. III. nu. 1.
[5] Cal. Inq. ad qd. Damnum, 14 Edw. II. nu. 96; Abbrev. Rot. Orig. temp. Edw. II.
[6] Esc. 14 Edw. III. nu. 1.
[7] Ib. nu. 9.
[8] Ib. 21 Edw. III. nu. 17.
[9] Ib. 36 Edw. III. nu. 87.

The whole or part of the Bishop's interest in Turvey, after confiscation, was added to the honor of Gloucester, and descended, like the paramouncy of Biddenham, to Edward Duke of Buckingham,[a] who, we find, had granted unto John Mordaunt, of Turvey, gent., and William Mordaunt his brother, *parcel of Gloucester fee*, before 17 King Henry VII.[b] In 9 King James I. the Crown granted to John Eldred and George Whitmore, armigers, certain rents of assize, courts-leet, and view of frank-pledge, together with other liberties, privileges, &c., in Yielden and Turvey, parcel of the honor of Gloucester, to hold to

[a] Rot. Hund. vol. i. p. 2. Esc. 8 Edw. II. nu. 68; 21 Edw. III. nu 59; 46 Edw. III. nu. 62; 10 Rich. II. nu. 38; 38 and 39 Hen. VI. nu. 59. Placita de quo warranto (Edw. III.) p. 79. Bishop Tanner in *Notitia Monastica* (Nasmith)[6] says of *St. Neot's, olim Eynulfesbury, or Henulvesbiri*, that it was a priory of black monks, subordinate to Ely, till, after the Conquest, Gilbert de Clare violently expelled those religious. But about A.D. 1113 Rohesia, wife of Richard, son to the said Earl Gilbert, gave this manor (St. Neot's or Eynesbury) to the abbey of Bec in Normandy, to which it became a cell.[7] It was seized during the wars with France among other alien priories, but made "prioratus indigena" by King Henry IV. being then in the patronage of the Earl of Stafford.

[b] Halstead, p. 509 See Appendix [A] to the account of this parish.

pence. Aluuin, a man of Borred, held this land, but was not able to give or sell it without licence.—(Domesday, p. 210.)

Newton (Blossomville) is supposed by Lipscomb to have been at the Domesday Survey included in Lavendon, and to have been part of the lands of the Countess Judith.[1]

The Bishop of Coutance had considerable grants in the latter place. In one of his manors there William was feudatory, and the Bishop's principal manor in Lavendon had been holden in the Saxon times by a man of Boret.[2]

A small estate in Turvey, parcel of the manor of Newton Blossomville, appears to have been annexed to the honor of Gloucester: at all events it descended therewith. Thomas Earl of Stafford had an interest in two parcels of lands in Turvey, below the park of Newton Blossomville, containing twenty acres and fifty acres respectively, parcel of the said manor. The interest in the twenty acres descended with the honor to Earl William and to Edward Earl of Stafford.[3]

Ralphe Basset of Drayton was seised (*inter alia*) of manors in Olney and Newton Blossomville, co. Bucks, and of twenty acres of land in Turvey, below the park of Newton Blossomville, in the county of Bedford.[4]

Nicholas Bradshagh was seised (*inter alia*) of pasture within the demesne of Stafford Castle; the manor of "Newnton Blosseville;" a messuage, &c., called Botelers and Wakes in Clifton; fifty acres, &c., in "Shirington," Bucks; and fifty acres in Turvey, parcel of the manor of "Newnton Blosmevyll," co. Beds.[5]

[1] Lipscomb, Bucks, vol. iv. p. 257.   [2] Ib. p. 208.
[3] Esc. 16 Ric. II. nu. 27; 22 Ric. II. nu 46; 4 Hen. IV. nu. 41.
[4] Ib. 14 Ric. II. nu. 9.   [5] Ib. 2 Hen. VI. nu. 20.
[6] Cambridge ed. 1787.
[7] For an account of stock kept on the farms at Turvey and Barford by the Prior of St. Neot's for the Abbot of Bec, temp. Edw. I. see Gorham's *History of St. Neot's*, vol. i. p. 70.

them, their heirs and assigns, in free and common soccage, of the manor of East Greenwich.[a]

Geoffrey de Trailly was mesne lord, under the Bishop, in Chellington and Yielden. Geoffrey's descendants extended their interest under the Earls of Gloucester, and thus arose the reputed barony of Trailly, which, according to the "Testa de Nevill," comprised estates, rents, or services in Yielden, Chellington, Hinwick, Roxton, Turvey, "Lutegareshal (Ludgershall,)" Hulcote, Biddenham, Northill, and Southill. In the 16th Henry III. Eustace le Mordaunt had a law-suit with John de Trailly, but whether about premises in Turvey or elsewhere does not appear; it was adjudged against the former.[b] A fee in Turvey (under the superiority of Humphrey Duke of Buckingham) was in Alianer Trailly, temp. Henry VI.[c]

The actual occupiers of the manorial estate in early times were the De Alnetos, Daunos, or De Alnos.[d]

Agreeably to the pedigree following page 186, Turvey descended through the families of De Alno, De Ardres,[e] and Mordaunt.[f] It is stated in Halstead that

---

[a] Patent Roll 9 Jas. I. part 8, memb. 1. Dated at Westminster 8th April. From a grant of premises to Sir Allan Apsley, knt. in the 5th Charles I., it appears that William White, William Steventon, and John Perkins of London, gentlemen, were the holders of certain rents of assize in Riseley, Deene magna, Deane parva or Netherdeane, Radwell, Pertenoll, Howe, Bolnestwoodend, and Turvey. (Patent Roll 5 Charles I. part 9. Dated at "Canbury" 15 September.) Probably parcel of some other honor.

[b] Harl. 6767. "A Folio, containing the Genealogy and Arms of the noble house of Mordaunt, justified by publick Records, ancient Charters, and other Histories and authentic Proofs, by the labour of Tho. Weston, whose portrait is prefixed, well engraved, by R. White, 1682; with a supplement on the House of Alno, or Alneto. 47 pages." The greater part of this MS. is reproduced in Halstead's *Succinct Genealogies*.

[c] Esc. 38 and 39 Hen. VI. nu. 59.

[d] The De Alnos[1] were considerable benefactors to the priory of St. Neot's. Halenald de Alno gave thirteen acres of land in his lordship of Turvey to the said house, and four acres to that of Caldwell. William de Alno confirmed the above grant to St. Neot's; and Hugh de Alno made a further grant to the same in Turvey.

[e] Arms: Az. a bend betw. six mullets arg.—*Halstead*.

[f] For general historical accounts, pedigrees, and notices of this distinguished family, the reader is referred to Halstead's Succinct Genealogies. The various county histories relating to Suffolk, Bucks, Northants, Herts, Wilts, Essex, and Leicestershire. Strype's Works, v. General Index. Notes and Queries, 1st ser. vol. v. p. 441, 521; 2nd ser. vol. vii. p. 217. O'Byrne's Representative History of Great Britain and Ireland, pt. i. Bedfordshire, p. 37 (Lond. 1848). Powell's Collections (Add. MSS. 17,456). A volume in MS. by Thomas Weston (Harl. 6767). Seward's Anecdotes (Lond. 1795-7, 8vo.) Dugd. Bar.

---

[1] For a notice of this family see Collinson's *History of Somerset*, vol. ii. p. 421.

Hugh de Alno, of Turvey, living about the year 1230, died without issue, when his two sisters, Alice, wife of Eustace Le Mordaunt, and Sarah, wife of Richard de Ardres, became his coheirs, and each succeeded to a moiety of the estates. By reason of this division Turvey continued for some years under the laws and privileges of two distinct manors, the one called Mordaunt's, the other Ardres' manor, until the time of King Edward III., in whose reign they are said to have been re-united by the care and industry of Robert Mordaunt. In the meantime the heirs of Richard de Ardres and William Mordaunt held the moieties under Walter de Trailly as of the honor of Gloucester.[a]

Robert le Mordaunt and Hugh le Proud were two of the ten freeholders on De Ardres' portion. The said Hugh occupied land which had been given by an ancestor of Richard de Ardres, in the time of King John, to the Hospital of St. John of Jerusalem,[b] and paid for the same five shillings rent. In De Ardres' demesne were two carucates and an ancient park of forty acres inclosed.[c] Mordaunt's moiety—occupied by eight villans, five cotarii, and seven freeholders, including the prior of St. Neot's—comprised (*inter alia*) two water-mills, forty acres of wood inclosed, a fishery in the Ouse from "Landimareswell" to "Budewell," &c.[c]

William Mordaunt (or de Mordaunt, as it was sometimes written) in the 14th year of Edward I. purchased a manor in Chicheley, and divers messuages therein, of William, the son of Samson le Mansell, and of Galfridus de Stachden. In the two-and-twentieth of the same King's reign he had a dispute with Reginald Lord Grey about the fishing of a certain part of the river Ouse joining to the Lord Grey's lands, which, by reciprocal indenture, was accorded should be thenceforth free unto them both. His wife was Rose, daughter of Sir Ralph Wake, of Clifton. The last act of his on record we find to have been in the 11th year of Edward II., at which time he made a grant, and release, and quit-claim for ever unto the monastery of St. Neot's of all his right and claim unto three messuages, eighty-eight acres of land, and one acre of meadow in Turvey, with their appur-

---

vol. ii. p. 311. The various Peerages, more particularly Collins's, ed. 1779, vol. iii. pp. 236—61. Burke's Extinct and Dormant Peerages. Wotton's Baronetage, ed. 1741, vol. i. p. 184. Memoir of Charles Mordaunt, Earl of Peterborough, 2 vol. 1853, 8vo. Dodsley's Annual Register, 28, p. 170.

[a] Rot. Hund. 7 Edw. I. Richard de Ardres and Eustace Mordaunt are mentioned as the tenants, under the barony of Trailly, in Turvey.—Testa de Nevill, temp. Henry III., Edw. I. John de Ardres, seised of a manor in Turvey.—Esc. 35 Edw. III. nu. 73.

[b] Placita de quo warranto, temp. Edw. I. and Edw. III. pp. 6, 19.

[c] Rot. Hund.

tenances, for which he, together with his partner, Hugh de Ardres, had sued the prior of that place in the King's Court. As also of other lands and tenements which the monks of the same held of his fee, and in his fee, and which the deeds acknowledge to have been the gifts of his ancestors. Saving always to him and to his heirs, and unto Hugh de Ardres, the services due unto them.[a] In the year 1297 William Mordaunt had licence to inclose a park at Turvey, and his descendant, Robert Mordaunt, acquired the other moiety of Turvey by giving to Thomas de Ardres an estate at Shephall, in Hertfordshire, in exchange. Third in descent from Robert (living temp. Edward III. and Richard II.) was

Sir John Mordaunt, knt. (whose portrait is mentioned as being at Drayton), one of the royal commanders at the battle of Stoke. Being likewise learned in the law, he was constituted King's Serjeant in the eleventh Henry VII.; was appointed High Steward of the University of Cambridge on 6 April, 1504;[b] and held several high and lucrative offices. He was made one of the Knights of the Sword at the creation of Henry Prince of Wales. By his last will Sir John desired to be buried in St. Mary's chapel, in Turvey church. Among the objects of his bounty were the churches of Turvey, Mulsoe, and Stagsden, the friars of Bedford, the prior and canons of Newenham, and the abbot and convent of Wardon. He likewise founded a chantry in the said chapel in Turvey church, which he endowed (for the support of two priests) with the manor of Melburne, and lands, &c., in Melburne, Melreth, and Royston, co. Cambridge. The chaplains and their successors, to whom he gave a messuage in Turvey called Fyshers, were always to reside in Turvey, and were to teach grammar to the boys of the parish. His wife was Edith,[c] daughter and coheir of Sir Nicholas Latimer, knt.,

---

[a] Harl. 6767.   [b] *Athenæ Cantabrigienses*, ed. 1858.

[c] This lady appears to have been thrice married. The following is from a pedigree in Harl. 1097, f. 13:—

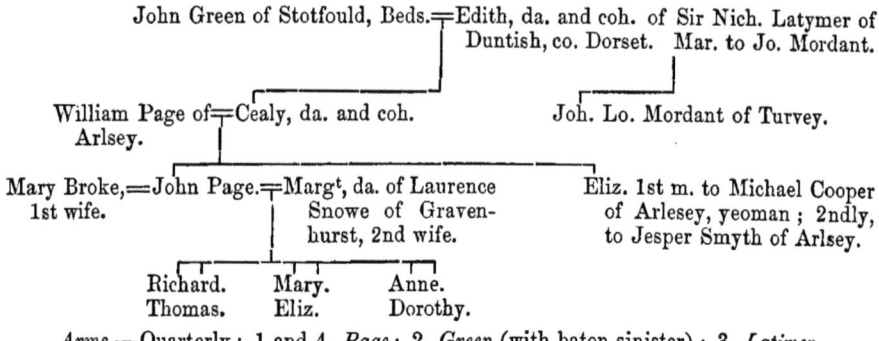

```
          John Green of Stotfould, Beds.=Edith, da. and coh. of Sir Nich. Latymer of
                                   |    Duntish, co. Dorset. Mar. to Jo. Mordant.
                   _____|_____
                  |                                 |
    William Page of=Cealy, da. and coh.      Joh. Lo. Mordant of Turvey.
        Arlsey.    |
  Mary Broke,=John Page.=Margt, da. of Laurence    Eliz. 1st m. to Michael Cooper
   1st wife.           |  Snowe of Graven-            of Arlesey, yeoman; 2ndly,
                       |  hurst, 2nd wife.            to Jesper Smyth of Arlsey.
         _____|_____
        |         |         |
     Richard.   Mary.     Anne.
     Thomas.    Eliz.     Dorothy.
```

Arms.—Quarterly: 1 and 4, *Page*; 2, *Green* (with baton sinister); 3, *Latimer*.

of Duntish, in Dorsetshire, by whom he had three sons and a daughter, viz.: John, served as sheriff in the first year of Henry VIII., knighted before 1520, and eventually summoned to Parliament as Baron Mordaunt, of Turvey, from 4th May, 1532, to 5th November, 1558; William, died without leaving issue; Robert, married Amye de Vere; and Joane, the wife of Giles Strangeways, esq. Dame Edith Mordaunt survived and married Sir Thomas Carew, of Devonshire, who (says Weston) "died valiently fighting, the fourth year of King Henry VIII., in a sea-fight upon the coast of Brittayne, being at that time captain of the noble ship called the Regent, which was burnt in the same occasion."

By an inquisition taken at Wendover, in the county of Buckingham, 4 Feb. 20 King Henry VII. it was found that Sir John Mordaunt was seised of certain premises with appurtenances in Ellesburgh, in the same county, holden of the heirs of Sir Richard Pole, knt.; that Sir John died on the 11th of September then last past; and that John Mordaunt was his son and heir, aged twenty-one years and upwards.

John Lord Mordaunt is mentioned in a letter of Richard Layton (visitor of religious houses) to Lord Cromwell about the year 1538-9. This letter, which, among other things, describes the condition of the priories of Harwold and Chicksand, is printed at length in the introductory volume of Nichols's History of Leicestershire (vol. i. part i. cxlii.) It discloses certain irregularities in those establishments, and narrates how that Lord Mordaunt and his son John persuaded the young nuns of Harwold to break up the coffer where the convent seal was, and then induced the prioress, in the presence of her "folysh young flock," to seal a writing made in Latin, Lord Mordaunt telling them that it was but a lease of a benefice impropriate with other small tenements, or words to that effect.[a]

Lord Mordaunt was a distinguished man in his day, rendering many eminent public services, and seems to have taken every opportunity to advance his own family and fortune.[b] In the 5th Henry VIII. he was a commissioner for assessing and collecting the poll-tax. In 1530 he was appointed, with others, to inquire into the landed possessions of Cardinal Wolsey; and was the first in commission, with

---

[a] In the Cotton MSS. Cleopatra E. iv. p. 130, is Lord Mordaunt's Account of his Confession to Father Forest, Feb. 23, 1538.

[b] The historian tells us that after the King's (Hen. VII.) death, John (Lord) Mordaunt applied himself wholly to the further designs of the honour and advantage of his house. King Henry VIII. granted him, by patent, the privilege of remaining covered in the royal presence, or in that of any of the judges or ministers of the realm.

other persons of rank in the county of Bedford, to prevent the enhancing the prices of corn, &c., in the year 1551, on the occasion of a great dearth of provision. He married Elizabeth Vere, descended, through the Draytons and Greenes, from the Gemys' of Stagsden,[a] by which alliance he considerably increased his estate. He also, as before mentioned in page 127, purchased Wauton's interest in Stagsden. His funeral took place at Turvey.[b]

John, son and heir of the first Lord Mordaunt, was one of the Knights of the Bath at the coronation of Queen Anne Boleyn, and succeeded his father as second baron, being summoned to Parliament 11 January, 1563.

The will of John second Lord Mordaunt is dated 16 April, 13 Elizabeth. It directs his body to be buried in Turvey church, and, after various legacies to children, servants, &c., it proceeds to the following effect:—

Item, I will that my Executors shall bestow £250 upon an Ile to be builded and made upon the South side[c] of the church of Turvey, and for a Tomb for me to be erected and set up within the said Ile.

Item, to Lady Joan my wife all that my Mansion House and all other houses, &c., situate, lying, and being in or near the Hospital of Little St. Bartholomew's, in Smithfield, within the suburbs of the City of London, for 50 years.

Executors, Lady Joan my well-beloved wife, my brother-in-law Thomas Farmer, Edward Plowden, Esqrs., and William Goodfellow my servant.

The following is from a MS. in private hands:[d]—

"The enterment of the Rt. Hon. John Lord Mordaunt of Turvey, who died at his house in London, near St. Bartholomew's Hospital, the   day of April, and from thence [was] transported to his house at Turvey[e] in Bedfordshire, and was there enterred very honourbly the 16 day of May, 1571."

---

[a] Mr. Roger Dodsworth's Collections, family of Drayton, quoted in Halstead, p. 94.

[b] In Noble's *History of the College of Arms*, p. 168, under the name of William Harvey, Clarenceux, occurs this notice: "After he became Clarenceux he injured his reputation by a disgraceful quarrel at Turvey in Bedfordshire, whilst at this funeral of Lord Mordaunt.[1] He fell so greatly under the displeasure of the Earl Marshal, that he was for some time forbidden to visit his province."

[c] The executors appear to have erected this aisle on the *north* side of the chancel.

[d] Page 109. Draft Funeral Certificate. Communicated (with other valuable notes) by Henry Gough, Esq.

[e] Turville in MS.

---

[1] This must have been in 1562.

It is narrated in Halstead's *Succinct Genealogies* that—

After the death of his first wife,[a] who left only one son for the stay of her house, called Lewis after the surname of her family, Sir John Mordaunt[b] married Joane, sister[c] of Sir John Farmer of Eston Neston, in the County of Northampton, at that time a widow, and who when she was a maid had attended upon Queen Mary then a princess. This Lady Joane had children of her own and of them a beautifull daughter, to whom the young Lewis Mordaunt as it should seem had made love, and, as it was pretended, to the passing of some engagement; her mother, therefore, greedy of such an establishment for her child, press'd hard for a proceeding unto marriage, but the young man, who had his chief dependence upon the old Lord Mordaunt, his grandfather, who was entire master of the great inheritance comprehended in the shires of Northampton and Bedford whereupon he lived at a distance from his son, durst not for all his father's commands engage in a matter of that nature without his leave and counsel, that Lord ever loving to be a master of all the interests of his family, so that when he became acquainted with his son's intentions, finding the subject far short of what he intended for his grandson both in relations and advantage, it was rejected by him with the circumstances of severe commands and menaces both to his son and grandson, which latter he recalled unto his own house and custody. Hereupon the lady, whom the disparagement of her daughter did much concern, exasperated her husband both against his father and his son Lewis, so that the father would out of displeasure have alienated from his son the Fitz Lewis's lands which were of his own mother's inheritance, and the grandfather intended to have disinherited Sir John Mordaunt of all the Mordaunts' lands, infinitely of greater consequence. At last mutual fears of general ruin made the peace, and they both concurred in marrying the young Lewis to Elizabeth, daughter of Sir Arthur Darcy.

Lewis Lord Mordaunt " was called by the Queen's summons to sit one of the Judges of the life and fortunes of that unfortunate princess Mary Queen of Scotland, unto whose sentence he did most unwillingly concur, and upon the like occasion he was again a Judge in the arraignment of Thomas Duke of Norfolk. He sat in many Parliaments, and commanded the troops of those parts assembled at the general rendezvous that were prepared against the Spanish invasion. He was also a lover of art and an encourager of learning, as also a builder, and added much to the castle at Drayton, and although he did alienate several great possessions yet it cannot be denied but what he spent was employed with honour; though he was no courtier yet he was much honoured by them all, and he had a near friendship with the Earl of Leicester and the Lord Chancellor Hatton. He lived a long and prosperous life, and departed this life at his seat of Drayton soon after the entry of King James I., on the 13th June, 1601, and was buried in the

---

[a] Ellen or Ela Fitz Lewes, otherwise Fitz Lewis.
[b] Second Baron Mordaunt.
[c] Not *daughter*, as erroneously stated in Halstead.

church of Turvey, on the 29th July next following, under a tomb of black marble."[a]

1593, October 1. Will of Lewis, third Lord Mordaunt, of this date. "To be buried in Luffwick church, where the body of Dame Elizabeth, my late wife, doth lie, if it may conveniently be so, or otherwise where it shall please God to appoint. A monument with two pictures of myself and my late wife to be made within one year. To the poor in Turvey £10; in Stagsden, Charleton, and Lawendon, £20. To my son Henry my house of Drayton with certain of the furniture, the same Henry to be executor. Trustees: my loving friends Edward Watson and John Wake, Esqrs. To the said Trustees, two parts of my manors of Carlton and Chellington, in three parts to be divided, which I lately purchased of Lord Vaux (the land, meadow, and common thereto belonging, lying in the fields of Turvey, only excepted). Also, to the same Trustees, two parts of my manor of Stagcheden, otherwise called Delwike, in three to be divided, lately by me purchased of Master William Cornwallis, Esq. and Lucy his wife, daughter and heir of Sir John Nevill, knt., Lord Latimer, deceased. Also two parts of my manor and closes of Snelson in the parish of Lavendon, co. Bucks, commonly called Snelson-Pastures, in three to be divided. Or as much of my said manors of Carleton and Chellington, Stacheden, called Delwike, and Snelson-Pastures as shall amount to two full parts of all the said manors, closes, and pastures, in three to be divided" (in order to secure the daughters' portions).

Henry Mordaunt, fourth Baron, under suspicion of being concerned in the Gunpowder Plot, was committed to the Tower, and fined by the Star-Chamber before he obtained his liberty. His will is dated 6 February, 1608, and in it he solemnly denies participation in the conspiracy with which he had been charged. He mentions his houses of Turvey and Drayton. Desires to be buried at Turvey; and names the Right Hon. Lord Compton executor. By his wife Margaret,[b] daughter of Henry Lord Compton, he had, with other issue, a son and heir,

John, who at his father's decease in 1618 became fifth Baron Mordaunt of Turvey, and was advanced to the dignity of Earl of Peterborough by letters patent

[a] Halstead.

[b] From an information to the Government of King Charles I., without date, printed in *The Discovery of the Jesuits' College at Clerkenwell*, p. 59-61, in *The Camden Miscellany*, vol. ii.

"Doctor Smith[1] liveth ordinarily in the howse of the Ladie Mordant, widow,[2] mother to the Lord Mordant, and sister to the Præsident of Wales, at Turvie in Bedfordshire, within three miles of Bedford, the howse in the midst of a parck. From thence he useth to goe to the Ladie Dormor's, in Buckinghamshire, at Winge or Ivinge, &c. &c. . . . . a daughter of the Lord Mountague is browght up with the Ladie Mordant, whom Dr. Smith sanctified with holy water and sweet oyle. Her confessor, Father Morgan," &c. &c.

[1] Richard Smith, Bishop of Chalcedon. He arrived in England in 1623.
[2] Margaret Compton.

dated 9 March, 1628. He married Elizabeth, only daughter and heir of William Howard, Lord Effingham (by Ann, daughter and heir of John second Lord St. John of Bletsoe), by which lady he had two sons and a daughter,—Henry, his successor; John, eventually elevated to the peerage, 10th July, 1659, as Baron Mordaunt, *of Rygate*, and Viscount Mordaunt, *of Avalon*, in Somersetshire; and Elizabeth, who married Thomas, son and heir of Edward Lord Howard of Escrick. The Earl of Peterborough was General of Ordnance and Colonel of a regiment of Foot in the army raised in 1642 by order of Parliament under the command of Robert Earl of Essex, and died in the same year.

About the year 1625 was the famous disputation held at Drayton[a] between the celebrated Archbishop Usher, just before he went to Ireland to take upon him the Primacy of Armagh, and a Roman Catholic priest, which is mentioned by Dr. R. Parr in these words:—

"Before the return of the said Archbishop into Ireland, I shall here mention an accident that happened about this time; to let you see that he neglected no opportunity of bringing men from the darkness of Popery into the clearer light of the Reformed Religion. I shall give you his own relation of it from a Note (which though imperfect) I find of his own hand writing: *Viz. That in November 1625 he was invited by the Lord Mordant, and his Lady, to my Lord's House at Drayton in Northamptonshire, to confer with a Priest he then kept, by the name of Beaumont, upon the points in dispute between the Church of Rome and Ours: and particularly, That the Religion maintained by Publick Authority in the Church of England was no new Religion, but the same that was taught by our Saviour and his Apostles, and ever continued in the Primitive Church during the purest times:* So far my Lord's Note. What was the issue of this Dispute we must take from the report of my Lord and Lady and other Persons of Quality there present; that this Conference held for some days, and at last ended, with that satisfaction to them both, and confusion of his Adversary, that as it confirmed the Lady in her Religion (whom her Lord, by the means of this Priest, endeavoured to pervert), so it made his Lordship so firm a convert to the Protestant Religion that he lived and died in it." (Parr's *Life of Usher*, p. 26-7.)

Henry, second Earl of Peterborough, became distinguished during the civil wars by his zeal in the royal cause. He raised a regiment at his own expense; was wounded at the battle of Newbury, and often imprisoned for his loyal exertions. He was in the rising with the Earl of Holland to release the King from his confinement; and on their defeat, though Holland was taken and beheaded, Peterborough, with his brother John, created Viscount Mordaunt of Avalon,

---

[a] Thos. Jackson, *Library of Christian Biography*, London, 1839, vol. xii. pp. 213-15. *The Life of Dr. James Usher, Archbishop of Armagh, &c.*, by Nich. Bernard, DD. Preacher to the Hon. Soc. of Gray's Inn.

escaped, but they were voted traitors to the Commonwealth and their estates were sequestered.[a] His lordship was (after the Restoration) of the Privy Council to King Charles II., and intrusted with several honourable embassies. At the coronation of King James II. he carried the sceptre with the cross, and was elected in the same year a Knight of the Garter. After the accession of William and Mary the Commons resolved (26th October, 1689) that the Earl of Peterborough and the Earl of Salisbury should be impeached for high treason, for departing from allegiance, and being reconciled to the Church of Rome; but the impeachment was dropped. His lordship married Penelope, daughter of Barnaby Earl of Thomond, by whom he had issue Elizabeth, who died unmarried, and

Mary, who became sole heiress, married, first, Henry Duke of Norfolk, from whom she was divorced in 1700, and then married Sir John Germain, Bart., but had issue by neither. Her ladyship inherited the barony of Mordaunt of Turvey at the decease of her father, but the dignity again attached to the Earldom of Peterborough at her own decease in 1705. Lady Mordaunt bequeathed her whole estate to her second husband.

John, afterwards Viscount Mordaunt,[b] the Earl's only brother, obtained great fame by his zeal in the cause of King Charles II. His lordship, after the Restoration, was constituted Constable of Windsor Castle and appointed Lord-Lieutenant and Custos Rotulorum of co. Surrey. He married Elizabeth, daughter and sole heiress of Thomas Carey, second son of Robert Earl of Monmouth, by whom he had five sons and three daughters. The Viscountess after her husband's death, which took place 5 June, 1675, appears to have resided with her children at the Bishop of London's house at Fulham. Among the Additional MSS. (Number 15,907) in the British Museum is a folio entitled "Viscountes Mordaunt's Accompt Book, by T. Weston, from 30 Nov. 1678 to 25 Dec. 1682." It contains at the beginning a letter, dated 12 Oct. 1683, from Tho. Weston to

---

[a] *History of Sequestrations* anno 1648, Add. MS. 5490, contains "A particular of the Tenants, Names, and Rents of all Papists and Delinquents' estates within the co. of Bedf. as the same were yearly let before the warrs." Rents of Lady Mordant, a papist, in Turvey, £446 3s. 4d.; and in Stagsden, £282 1s. 4d. The Earl of Peterborough compounded for his estate in 1655 for the sum of £5,106 15s.; and Charles Mordaunt paid by the hand of John Clerk £10. In the same year Elizabeth, Margaret, and Anne Mordaunt, *Recusants*, the three daughters of Henry Lord Mordaunt, paid £216 by the hand of John Manly, gent. *Bedford, Mich.* 1651. *Recovery Roll.* Erasmus Smith and Thomas Blankley, of the Manor of Turvey, and lands &c. in Turvey.—*Roll* 151.

[b] Copy of his patent (10 July, 1659).—*MS. Ashm.* 838, f. 7. There is an engraved portrait of *Lord Aviland, Baron de Rygate*, pub. 1798, by W. Richardson, York House, Strand.

the Earl of Clarendon. Some of the entries have been selected,* and are interesting as giving a few particulars of three of the sons—Harry, Lewis, and

                                Folio.

* The Accompt of Thomas Weston wth the Rt. hon^ble ye La Vicountes Mordaunt. From ye 30th November A'no 1678 To the 5th of Aprill A'no 1679 . . . 3 &c.

  Apr. 4. Paid to Thos. Dickins, Receiver for my Lord Bpp of London, 5 quarters' rent due at Chrmas last £12 10s. 0d., and for 10 acquittances, 10s. . 7 b.

Disbursments on the children their Accompt:

 For Mr. Harry Mordaunt from 30 Nov. to 5 Apr. 1679 . . . 8 b.

  Paid to Dr. Busby his New year's guift and quarteridg due at Chrmas 1678, £2 3s. 6d.

  To Mr. Knipe his New year's guift, £1 1s.

  To the Vsher his New year's guift, 10s.

 For Mr. Lewis Mordaunt, 1678-9 9

  Dec 27. Paid to Mr Robert Limpany for 15 weeks' dyet and enterteynment in order to the curing of his head £6.

  Jan. 28. For a silver spoon at his going to Eaton, 9s. 6d.

The Accompt of money rec^d by me Tho. Weston to and for the use of the Executors of the last Will and Testament of the Rt. Hon. the Lady Elizabeth, Vicountes Mordaunt, deceased, from 5 Apr. to 21 Nov. 1679. . . . . . 15 b.

  To Mr. Stevenson, Vicar of Fulham, his half year's allowance £5.

 Disbursments concerning my Lady Mordaunt's Funerall. (Total, £81 8s. 2d.) . 18

 Disbursments on Mr. Lewis Mordaunt's account . . . 44

  1680, June 26. Hire of 2 horses to Harrow on the Hill (? from Parson's Green), 4s. 6d.

  To a boy to bring back the horses, 6d. Dinner and entertainment to Mr. Robinson one of the schole masters and Mr. Winslow, 5s. 2d.

  Paid Mr. Horn, head Schole master, for his entrance, 10s.

  July 1. Paid for a silur spoon sent to him, 10s.

  July 8. 3 letters from Harrow, 6d.

  For a Bow and arrows, gloves, &c. 4s.

  July 13. To a Messenger from Harrow to make enquiry after Mr. Lewis when enticed away from schole by his Bro. Mr. Harry, 2s.

  July 23. Expences in journey to Windsor, journey to Harrow, and twice to London, to seek the two lost gents, 6s. 4d.

  Paid charges of horsmeat at London to release a hired horse Mr. Lewis left there, 2s. 4d.

  July 27. Paid hire of the same horse 10 dayes to ye owner, being a poor man living at Harrow, 15s.

  Horse hire and charges of a messenger to bring Mr. Lewis back to Harrow, 1s. 8d.

  Aug. 11. For a Greek Gramar, &c. 3s. 6d.

  Sep. 6. For paper, pens, and a history book, 3s. 2d.

  Money for his (Mr. Lewis') pocket, 2s. 6d.

Osmond—during the time of their boyhood. The eldest of these became a member of parliament, lieutenant-general in the army, and treasurer of the Ordnance; Lewis rose to the rank of brigadier-general in the army; and Osmond was slain at the battle of the Boyne.

Charles Mordaunt, created Earl of Monmouth, 9th April, 1689, succeeded his uncle Henry as third Earl of Peterborough, and at the decease of his cousin Mary, Baroness Mordaunt of Turvey, inherited that ancient dignity of the family.

The Earl was eldest son of John Viscount Mordaunt, second son of John first Earl of Peterborough. He had distinguished himself as a military character prior to the Revolution; was, upon the accession of William and Mary, sworn of the Privy Council, and made one of the Lords of the Bedchamber, and, in order to attend at their coronation as an Earl, was raised to the Earldom of Monmouth, having, the day before, been constituted First Lord Commissioner of the Treasury. Soon after the accession of Queen Anne his lordship was declared General and Commander-in-Chief of the Forces sent to Spain, in which command he acquired great military fame by the capture of Montjovi; and on 12th January, 1710-11, a vote passed the House of Lords, that during the time the Earl had command in Spain "he performed many great and eminent services;" and his lordship received the thanks of the House through the Lord Chancellor. In 1713 he was installed Knight of the Garter, and died 25 October, 1735. The Earl had married, first, Carey, daughter of Sir Alexander Fraser, of Dotes, N.B., and had issue

John Lord Mordaunt, Colonel of the Grenadier Guards at the Battle of Blen-

	Folio.
Disbursments on Mr. Osmond Mordaunt's account	45 b.
Money for his pocket on going to Eaton, 2s. 6d.	
Dec. 15. Charges of Mr. Harry Mordaunt's journey to Oxford, and of placing and setling him there, £22 17s.	52 b.
(A guinea and some clothes given to Mr. Lewis by his uncle Peterboro.; he being still at Harrow)	53
[In this year (1680) there seems to have been a sale of the furniture and effects at Fulham]	58 b.
Rec^d from Mrs. Windsor for picture of La. S^t. Jn^{os}. £8.	
[In 1681, Mr. Zac. Isham, Mr. Harry Mordaunt's tutor at Oxford, is mentioned. Lewis Mordaunt still at Harrow. In 1682, Mr. Harry Mordaunt still at Oxford, and Osmond at Eton. With reference to Lewis, who was suffering from a pain in his head, this entry occurs: *7th Oct., Fees and charges procuring his Majesties Letters and Warrant at the Admiralty Office,* £1 9s. The last account is signed Tho: Weston, Feb. 1682]	65—80

heim, 13 August, 1704, wherein he lost one of his arms. His lordship married Lady Frances Powlett, daughter of Charles, Duke of Bolton, and, dying of the small pox 6th April, 1710, left two sons; the elder of whom,

Charles Mordaunt, succeeded his grandfather as fourth Earl of Peterborough, and second Earl of Monmouth. He married, first, Mary, daughter of —— Cox, esq., of London, and had issue two daughters, the younger of whom, Mary Anastasia Grace, eventually succeeded to the Barony of Mordaunt of Turvey. The Earl married, secondly, Robiniana, daughter of Colonel Brown, and, dying in 1779, was succeeded by his only surviving son by that lady,

Charles Henry Mordaunt, fifth and last Earl of Peterborough, and third of Monmouth, born in 1758, died unmarried 1814,[a] when all his honours, except the Barony of Mordaunt of *Turvey*, became extinct. The last-named dignity devolved upon his lordship's half-sister, Lady Mary Anastasia Grace Mordaunt, as Baroness Mordaunt, at whose decease, unmarried, in 1819, it passed to Alexander Gordon, fourth Duke of Gordon, as heir-general of Charles, third Earl of Peterborough, and eventually fell into abeyance amongst his grace's five daughters or their representatives.

In the year 1786-7, Charles Henry, fifth Earl of Peterborough, sold the manor of Turvey, together with an estate in this parish, including a house now known as Turvey Abbey, to Charles Higgins, esq., sheriff of London in that year. Mr. Higgins was a native of Weston Underwood, in Buckinghamshire.[b] In 1790, at his own expense, he new-pewed the nave of the church at Turvey, and built a gallery for the singers and the children of the Sunday-school. He was never married, and dying in London[c] 29 Dec. 1792, his nephew, John Higgins, esq., succeeded under his will to the manor of Turvey, and became "of Turvey Abbey," whilst a considerable portion of the estate passed to a more distant kinsman—another John Higgins—who built Turvey House (see page 190).

Charles Longuet Higgins, esq., now of Turvey Abbey, the elder son and heir of the first John Higgins above-mentioned, was educated at Trinity College, Cambridge, where he graduated in 1830, and proceeded to the degree of M.A.,

---

[a] In 1812 the Earl's chief seat was Dantsey, Wilts.—Collins.

[b] His epitaph in the church there is attributed to the pen of the poet Cowper.—Lipscomb, Bucks, vol. iv. p. 406. A purely fabulous notice of the Higgins family will be found under the account of Clifton Reynes.—Ib. p. 115. The arms borne by this family are: Vert, three crane's heads erased arg. Crest: A griffin's head erased or, collared gu. Motto: Nihil quod obstat virtuti. According to Lipscomb the arms on the monuments at Weston Underwood are, Vert, three stork's heads erased ppr.

[c] Add. MS. 21,067, fo. 17 b.

DE ALNETO, DE ALN

(Harl. MSS. 6767, 4941 f. 12.) (Visitations of Hunts,—v. *Camden So*

Arms (Harl. 1160, fo. 44.): 1. Mordaunt, with twenty quarterings. Names of quarterings:—2. Alnot. 3. Brad
13. Drayton. 14. Mauduit. 15. *Huntington*, 16. Fitz Lewes. 17. Fitz Lewes. 18.

(For the blazon of the above and

Mordaunt, Earl of Peterborough,—Crest: In an Earl's coronet or, the bu
Supporters: Two eagles arg. armed and mer
Motto: " Nec placida contenta quiete e

The Mordaunts' ancient Crest is sometimes described as a Saracen's, and sometimes as a Negro's, head ppr. wreathed a

Eustachius de St. Ægidio or St. Giles	Osbert le Mordaunt, a Norman knight, was possessed of an estate at⊤............................¹ Radwell in Bedfordshire, by the gift of Eustace, whom he calls his brother and his lord. (Weston.)¹			William of Loweshy,
	Osbert or Osmond le=Ellen, dau. (and h ?) of Sampson Mordaunt of Radwell, Chellington, &c.² Fortis, founder of Harewold Priory.	Baldwin had land at Radwell, Beds.²		Hugh. Sir Haler Sir William de Alneto of Turvey and Maidford, 1190.
Robert le Mordaunt.	Eustace le Mordaunt,⊤Alice, eldest coh., brought with her 1197 and 1231.⁴ half the lordship of Turvey.	Hugh de Alneto of Turvey, 1230, ob. s.p.		Sarah, 2nd coh.=R. de Andre
	Agnes. (Harl. 6767.) William de Mordaunt,⁵ of Turvey, Radwell, Asthull, &c. (1245.)=Ann and Amicia, dau. of Sir Willi She m. 2ndly Ægidi			
Richard.⁷	William Mordaunt had licence (1297) to inclose a park at Turvey.=Rose, dau. of Sir Ralph Wake.			
Edward of Bucks.=Eleanor.	Maud,=William of Turvey, jun. Nich.⁷ Rich.⁷	Mary, 1st wife.⁸=Robert Mordaunt, M.P. for		
Edmund Mordaunt, esq., of Turvey. (Seised of half the manor.⊤Helen, dau. and coh. of Ralph Brock, by Margaret, dau. of Thomas Esc. 46 Edw. III, 6, and 47 Edw. III. nu. 27.) Hussey. (Brought Clifton and Shephale to her husband.)		Geoffrey, 1250.		
Robert Mordaunt, esq., of Turvey, 1372, 49=Agnes, dau. and heir of John le Strange of Ampton, Timworth, and Brokley, Suffolk, by Eliz. his wife, sister⊤T Edw. III. and 14 Rich. II. 1st husb. to Wm. Boteler of Walden, Essex. (*Vide* Gage's Hist. of Suff. p. 354.) Wid. 1432.				
Cassandra, a nun, at Elstow. (Gage.) Robert Mordaunt, esq., M.P. for Beds. 9 Hen. V. 1412.=Eliz., dau. of John Holdenby of Holde				
William Mordaunt, esq. of Turvey, temp. Edw. IV. 1447.=Margaret, dau. of John Peeke or Peck, esq., of Cople, Beds. by his				
Sir John Mordaunt, knt., of Turvey, one of the Royal commanders at the battle of Stoke, 16 June, 1484; King's=Edith, dau. and coh. of Sir Nich. Lati serjeant, 11 Hen. VII.; Just. of Chester and Chan. of the duchy of Lanc., ob. 21 Hen. VII. she was bur. in Turvey Church.				
William, of Turvey, ob. s.p. Joane, m. Giles Strangeways. Sir John Mordaunt of Turvey, Sheriff of Beds. and Bucks., 1 Her Robert, ob. s.p. v p.=Amy de Vere.⁹ from 4 May 1532, to 5 Nov. 1538—ob. 1562.				
Joan, dau. of Richard Farmer or Fermor of Easton Neston,⊤John, 2nd Baron Mordaunt, summoned=Ellen or Ella, cos. and William,=Agnes, dau. and heir Northants, a merch. of the staple at Calais; which Joan to Parliament 1563-1572, K.B. June heir of Sir Richard Fitz- 1580.¹⁰ of Chas. Booth, esq. was sist. of Sir John, of Easton Neston, knight of the car- 1553; Sheriff of Essex and Herts, Lewes, of West Thorn- of Cheshire. pet, 2 Oct. 1553, and wid. of Robt. Wilford, esq. of Kent. 1510; P. C. temp. Mary, M.P. for don, Essex. 1st wife. (a son and four daughters.) 2nd wife. (Baker, Northants. vol. 2, p. 143.) Beds, 1553-5.				
		Etheldred, ob. unm. Edmond.⁷		
Margaret, m. William Aclam of Moreby, co. York. Anne, m. Clement Tanfield of Everton. Ursula, m. Thos. Welbore of Clavering, in Essex. Lewis, M P. for co. Beds, 1562, 3rd Baron Mordaunt, summoned to Parliament 1576-1597, ki bur. in Turvey Church, honourably, 29th July; he d. at his manor house o				
Henry, 4th Baron Mordaunt, summoned to Parliament 1601-1615, suspected of being concerned in the gunpowder plot;=M was committed to the Tower; ob. 1618.				
John, 5th Baron Mordaunt, summoned to Parliament 1620-1623, advanced to the dignity of=Elizabeth, dau. and heir of Wm. Howard, Lord Effingham, Ma Earl of Peterborough 9 Mar., 1628; bur. at Turvey, 24 June, 1643.¹¹ son of Chas. Earl of Nottingham. Ant				
Henry, 6th Baron Mordaunt, 2nd Earl of Peterborough, wounded at the Battle=Penelope, dau. of Barnabas, John, b. 18 June, 1626, (*MS. Ashmole* 241); obl of Newbury. P. C. Car. II. K G., 6 Jac. II., b. Oct. 1623. (*MS. Ashmole* 241, Earl of Thomond, bur. 24 to the peerage 10 July, 1659, as Baron Mo f. 39 b, 40; 213, f. 77; 436, f. 66). ob. 19 June, 1697.¹¹ April, 1702.¹¹ Somerset; Constable of Windsor Castle—Ld.				
Elizabeth Mordaunt, ob. unm. in Mary, Baroness Mordaunt of Turvey, being eventually sole heiress, m. 1st Henry Duke of Norfolk, from whom sh the 12th year of her age. but had no issue.				
Carey, dau. of Sir=Charles, 8th Baron Mordaunt of Turvey, 3rd=Anastasia Robinson, Henry, M P., Lieut.-Gen. in the=Margaret, dau. of Anne, dau Alexander Fraser, Earl of Peterborough, 2nd Baron of Rygate, the celebrated public army, m. 2ndly Penelope dau Sir Thos. Spencer Roger Marl of Dores, N B , bur and 2nd Visct. Mordaunt of Avalon, created singer, m. 1735, 2nd and heir of Wm. Tipping, esq, of Yarnton, Oxon, esq., 1st wi 28 May, 1709, 1st Earl of Monmouth 9th April, 1689; ob. 1735, wife. and had a dau. Penelope, m. bart., 1st wife. wife.¹⁴ on his pas. to Lisbon, bur. 21 Nov., 1735. Sir Monnoux Cope, bart. Sir John M				
John, Lord Mordaunt, a Colonel in the Grenadier Guards. Died of=Frances Powlett, dau. of Henry, R.N , M.P., Henrietta.=Alexander, 2nd Duke small-pox 6 April, bur. 13 April, 1710.¹¹ Charles, Duke of Bolton, died of small-pox bur. 4 Aug. 1715.¹¹ 27 Feb., 1709, bur. Cosmo George, 3rd Duke of Gord 1 March, 1709.¹¹				
Mary, dau. of — Cox, esq.,=Charles, 9th Baron Mordaunt of Turvey, 4th Earl of Peter-=Robiniana, dau. of Colonel Mary, sister of Sc of London. 1st wife. borough, 3rd Baron of Rygate, 3rd Viscount Mordaunt Brown, 2nd wife, she was Howe, widow of of Avalon, and 2nd Earl of Monmouth, ob. 1779. 2nd cos. to her husb. Pembroke. 1st				
Frances Anne, m. Rev. Mary Anastasia Grace, b. 1738, suc. Charles Henry, 10th Baron Mordaunt of Turvey, 5th Earl of Peterborough, 4th Geor Samuel Bulkeley, D.D., eventually, on the death of her half- Baron of Rygate, 4th Viscount Mordaunt of Avalon, and 3rd Earl of Monmouth, Char of Hatfield, her lady- brother, to the barony of Mordaunt b. 1758, d. unm 1814, when all his titles but the first became extinct. His lord- Mad ship ob. s.p. v p of Turvey, d. unm. 1819. ship died and was buried, with great state, at Dauntsey in Wilts. (See New Sass Monthly Mag. for August, 1814.) Leoi				
		Poulet, d. young. A dau m. Maurice Geor Bisset, esq.		

ls, &c.) (Baker's *History of Northamptonshire*, vol. ii. p. 44.)
. 5. Bareng. 6. Brook. 7. Perott. 8. *Fodringhey*. 9. Strange. 10. Stowell. 11. Latimer. 12. Vere.
), Lovell. 20. Wauton. 21. Bardwell. N.B. Those in Italics are doubtful.
gs, see *Monuments*.)
Prince habited in cloth of gold—all ppr. and wreathed about the temples arg.

s. The motto on the tomb of Lewis 3rd Lord Mordaunt is "Lucem tuam da nobis," as also in Harl. 1160.

mesne lord of Maidford, Northants, and of Lowesby, Leic. W.I.=..................

rdets of Warwickshire.   Emmeline.=Pagan de Alneto of Turvey, H.I.

Sir Henry de Alneto, bur. in St. Neot's Priory.=Agnes, dau. of Sir William Lizures, H.I.   Herbert of Lavendon

lneto, of Turvey and Maidford, 1172.=Philippa, dau. of Sir Gilbert de Pinkeney of Weedon.   Henry.   Gerard, father of Richard, whose son
ichard Engayne,   Hugh, Prior of the Hospital of St. John of Jerusalem.   =Henry, claimed Maidford, 1202,
·1199.   Alexander, c. 1200.   living 1205.

lneto defended his right to Maidford, as great-   ... 3rd sist. and coh. (?)=Saher de Maunsell.
grandson of Pagan de Alneto, 1199, ob. s.p.

r, knt.⁶   Ric. de Ardres had a moiety of Turvey from his uncle Hugh.   *a quo* Maunsell   Gyles de Argenton.   Richard Pirott.
of Thorp Malsor,
Mansell of Cosgrove.   Cassandra Argentyne.=Rauf Pirott.

l. 1307.=Joan Bray, 2nd wife.   { Sir Lawrence Broke.=Elizabeth Pirott or Perott, dau. and h.

old Maidford,   Simon de Pinkeney, of Morton=Helewyse gave lands to=Joh. de Schelford,   Isabella,=William de   Margery,
).   Pinkney, 1214, 1st husb.   Ashby Priory.   2nd husb.   1250.   Cauz.   Eustachia, living
of Turvey,   Matilda, dau. and heir of Thomas, son of John=Sir Henry, son of Sir Hen. Greene of Green's Norton,   Ellen,   1250.
usb.   Mauduit, by Juliana dau. and h. of Dalingrigg.   by his wife, dau. and h. of Sir John Mablethorpe.   Sarah.

. secondly Robt. Tanfield of Gayton, Northants.   John Greene of Maudit, Northants.=Margaret Greene.

r or Vinter, of Crick, Northants.   Maud.   Elizabeth.   Isabella Greene, dau. and h.=...   Vere.

am, ancestor of the Mordaunts of Warwicksh., m. 1495 Anne, dau. and coh. of Thos.   Eliz. m. Sir Whiston Browne.
.untingdon of Hempstead (see Baronetage); he d. 16 Jan., 1518, bur. at Hempstead.

i to Parliament, as Baron Mordaunt of Turvey,=Elizabeth, dau. and coh. of Sir Henry Vere, knt. of Drayton and Addington,
ods.—(Fullers' Worthies.")   Northants, by Isabella his wife, dau. of Thos. Tresham.

a, dau. and coh.   Anne, m. 1st J. Rodney or   Eliz., m. Silvester   Margt. m. Ed. Fettiplace,   Winifred, m. John   Editha, m. Job.   Dorothy, m.
ohn Harding, of   Radney, esq. and 2ndly   Danvers, esq. of   esq., of Bessels Leigh,   Cheyney, of Ches-   Elmes, esq. of   Thos. More,
ling, co. Beds.   John, son and heir of   Dauntsey, Wilts.   Berks. (Joh. Denton,   ham Boys.   co. Hunts.   esq. of Had-
Sir Michael Fisher.   another husb. to Margt.)   don, Oxon.

it, esq. of Thundersley, Essex (probably the father of Humfrey who was bur. 1586.— Carlton Regis.)=Agnes Rich. (For issue see Hist. of Essex.)

. 1567, ob. 16 June, 1601,=Elizabeth, dau. of Sir Arthur Darcy, 2nd son of   Elizabeth, m. Geo. Monnoux, esq., of
ants.   Thos. Lord Darcy.   Walthamstow.

nry, Lord   Elizabeth.   Mary, m. Thos. Mansel, esq., eldest son   Katherine, m. John Heveningham, esq., eldest son of
of Sir Edw. Mansel.   Sir Arthur Heveningham or Henningham.

th.   Mary Tirringham,=James.=   ... Gostwick,   Lewis,=Mary, dau. of Sir   ... Smith,   Frances, m. Sir Thos. Neville, eldest son
1st wife.   2nd wife   wid. of Sir Robt. Throgmorton.   to Henry, Lord Bergavenny. (*Weston.*)
John Mordaunt. (*Weston.*)

by his zeal in the cause of Charles II., elevated=Elizabeth, dau. and heir of Thos.   Elizabeth, b. 6 Oct., 1627 (*MS. Ashmole* 241.) m. Thos.,
, Surrey, and Viscount Mordaunt of Avalon,   Carey, 2nd son of Robt., Earl   son and heir of Edw. Lord Howard of Escrick.
Lot. of co. Surrey, ob. 5 June, 1675.   of Monmouth.

1700, and then m. Sir John Germain, bart.,

adier,=Mary, dau. of Lieut.-Col.   Osmond, slain   Catherine, 4th dau. and=George,=Elizabeth, dau.=Elizabeth, dau.   Charlotte, m. Benj.
.   Collyer, Lieut.-Governor   at the battle   coheir of Sir Thomas   in Holy   of Sir John   of Col. Collyer.   Albin, esq.
of Jersey. 2nd wife.   of the Boyne.   Spencer, wid. of John   Orders.   D'Oyley, bart.   3rd wife.   Sophia, m. James
Dormer. 1st wife.   2nd wife.   Hamilton, esq., of
Bangor, co. Down.
liza Lucy, m. Sir Wilfred   Anne Maria, m. the Rt. Hon. Steph. Poyntz   Anna Maria, coh m.   Mary, m. Valentine Morris,   Anne, m. James
Lawson, bart.   of Midgham, Berks.   Jonathan Shipley,   esq., of Piercefield, co.   Hamilton, esq., of
Sophia, m. Sir Roger Martin, bart. of Smeeston   D.D., Bishop of St.   Monmouth.   Tollymore,
u. of Wm. Earl of Aberdeen.   Hall, in Bulmer, Essex, who d. 1762.   Asaph; left issue.   Elizabeth, m. Sir William
Milner, bart. of Nun
Appleton.
hn, a Lieut.-Col. in the army=Elizabeth, dau. of Samuel   Alexander, 4th Duke of Gordon,=Jane, dau. of Sir William
.P., m. 1st 1735, ob. s.p. 1767.   Hamilton, esq.   12th Baron Mordaunt of Turvey,   Maxwell, bart. 1st wife.
d. 17 June, 1827.

rdon, 13th Baron Mordaunt of Turvey, ob. s.p. 28 May, 1836.
, Chas. 4th Duke of Richmond, and her grandson Chas. Gordon Lennox, Duke of Richmond is senior coheir of the barony of Mordaunt of Turvey.

NOTES TO THE PEDIGREE OF MORDAUNT.

[1] Weston says:—*We cannot prove who was the wife of Osbert Mordaunt.* Her arms: Party per pale a lion rampant ducally crowned, bearing on the shoulder an escutcheon charged with three (? pellets.)

[2] Osmund le Mordaunt upon the death of his father confirmed by deeds unto his brother, Baldwin, the donation which had before been granted to him by the deceased Osbert. He moreover purchased lands in Setmanstoking of a great lord called Allan of Alno; he lived unto the days of King Henry II. Whom Osmund married is not known.—*Weston.*

[3] Baldwin Mordaunt, witness to a charter wherein Samson Fortis, a great lord in those times, granted lands in Brafield to the monastery and church of St. Peter's in Harwold.—*Ibid.*

[4] This Eustace, in the lifetime of his father, had in partage divers lands in Wahull: and he gave, under the name of Eustachius le Mordaunt de Wahull, certain lands in Turvey in pure alms to the church of St. John Baptist, and St. John the Evangelist in Caudwell, and to the canons of that place for the good of his soul, of that of Alice his wife, and of those of his ancestors and successors. After his father's decease he inherited his whole possessions; and had a suit with Gilbert Fitzwilliams in the 9th of Richard I. about a piece of land in Radwell, which was adjudged on his behalf. He granted several lands in Turvey, for their homage and service and other considerations, to William Cooke, Simon of Turvey, Reynald le Brayeur, and others; he had another suit, towards his latter end, with John de Traylly, in the 16th Henry III., which was adjudged against him; and we find him to have deceased in the 27th of that king.—*Ibid.*

[5] From the time of this William, the *le* prefixed to the surname Mordaunt is changed into *de*, as appears in old deeds. In the 29th Henry III. he paid a relief to the Lord William de la Chuche (? Zouche) and the Lady Matilda de Traylly his wife for certain lands he held; probably the same about which Eustace his father was cast in the behalf of John de Traylly. About the same time, Henry, the son of Fulk Huriell, Roger le Sock of Wybaudston, and Albreda the daughter of Robert de St. George, by several deeds, release and quit-claim to this William (under the style of William de Mordaunt, their lord) divers rights and lands; and Robert de Ardres unto the same William gives, grants, and confirms, for six marks of silver, one of his villans called Adam Pite with all his sequele and procreation, gotten and to be gotten, for ever. There passed afterwards between him and Hugh Poore, prior of St. Neots, an exchange of divers lands with advantage given by the said William in pure alms, and he is supposed to have departed this life about the 9th Edward I.—*Ibid.*

[6] Amicia de Olney brought estates in *Eashull* and *Yerdeley;* her father was one of the sons of Sir Richard Sutton, from whom the lords of Dudley did descend; he assumed the name of Olney from certain lands which he possessed by grant from Ralfe, Earl of Chester.—*Ibid.*

[7] Harl. 6767.

[8] Called by Weston *Mary of Rutland.* Arms: Az. a chev. betw. three (? lion's) faces ar.

[9] Sister to the 1st Lord Mordaunt's wife.

[10] "Anno 1587. *Bedd.* Comissioners of the peace Displaced. * * * Willm. Mordaunte, esq. Vnmeete: thoughte to be backewarde in Religion."—Lansd. 53, nu. 89, fol. 191.

[11] Turvey Register.

In the return of Gentry (Lancastrians) 12 Hen. VI. occurs the name of Robert Mordant.

The Mordaunts of Oakley descended from a younger son of the 1st baron. Arms of Edmond Mordaunt of Oakley, v. Harl. 1095. Edmund Mordaunt sat for the borough of Bedford 1553-5. Edward Mordaunt of this family served the office of sheriff of Bedford 6 James I.

12 Elizabeth, Feb. 4. Will of Katherine Okeley of Turvey.—"To be buried in the church or churchyard of Turvey. To Anne my daughter, William Balls wife, a c'tayne house in Bedford which I shall have after Mrs. Mordaunt's deccase of Okelye, w^h house I geve my daughter during life, then to Mary Ball daughter of William Ball," remainder to Elizabeth Ball: and to Robert Ball and his heirs. Testatrix also leaves a sum of money to Robert, son of William Ball.

Witnessed by Thos. Burkock, minister of Turvey.
Proved (Archd. Bedf.) 27 March 1600.

Letter from three Lords of the Council. "W. Burghley, C. Howard, Hunsdon," commanding Lady Mordante's executor to bury her suitably to her rank as a baroness, and not in a private manner. (Greenwich, 24 April, 1592).—Copy in *MS. Ashm.* 857, fo. 422. It seems the order was not attended to, for there is a note underwritten that the said lords ordered (15 May) Robert Price, a painter, to satisfy Garter for his loss in that funeral. In addition to the above, Mr. Gough has supplied the following references:—Circa 1610. Mrs. Eliz. Mordaunt of Turvey, a patient of Richard Napier.—*MS. Ashm.* 329 fo. 112; 335 fo. 186^b; also, Lady Mordaunt.—*Ibid.* 334 ff. 4, 4^b, 6^b-7, 25; Henry, son of Lady Mordaunt.—*Ibid.* 335 f. 53; and Mr. Henry Mordaunt.—*Ibid.* f. 186^b.

Nativity of "Henry, Viscount Mordaunt" (?), 16 Nov. 1621.—*MS. Ashm.* 243 f. 162.

Anne, youngest daughter of Scrope, Viscount Howe, married 8 May, 1728, to the Hon. Lewis Mordaunt.—*Burke.*

in 1834. He has served the office of sheriff for Bedfordshire, is a magistrate and deputy-lieutenant; and has for many years been chairman of the Bedford union.

Having thus traced the descent of the principal manor, it remains briefly to notice some of the ancient smaller estates.

Jn⁰ Turvey de Turvey is among the names of the gentry in this county returned by the commissioners 12 King Henry VI.ᵃ

Edward Dudley, esq., who died 1641, was seised of an estate in this parish called the manor of *Turveys*, held under the Earl of Peterborough's manor of Turvey; he left daughters—his coheirs.ᵇ In Trinity Term 1649 a fine was levied between William Dudley, armiger, querent, and John Fortescue, armiger, and Alicia his wife, and Elizabeth Dudley, deforciants, of lands in Northamptonshire and Huntingdonshire, also of two parts of the manor of Turvey, with appurtenances, and one messuage, twenty acres of arable, two acres of meadow, and ten acres of pasture, with appurtenances, in four parts divided, in Turvey, in the county of Bedford; and William paid to the deforciants eighty pounds sterling. Sir William Dudley, Knt., of Turvey, was living in 1673, according to a list of gentry of that year.

John Poley was found by inquisition, taken at Bedford 21 Oct. 6 Henry VIII., before John Mordaunt, armiger, the escheator, to have been seised of lands and premises, &c., in Clapham, Oakley, Biddenham, Turvey, and Carlton.ᶜ

ST. NEOT'S PRIORY LANDS.—The Priory of St. Neot's, as before noticed, was under the patronage of the lords of the honor of Gloucester.ᵈ Halenald, William, and Hugh de Alno, and William de Mordaunt, made or confirmed grants of lands in Turvey to the same.ᵉ In the time of King Richard the First, William le Heyr is said to have given, in pure alms, the advowson, with half a virgate of land and three messuages in Turvey, to the said priory; holden (temp. Edward I.) as of the barony of Beachamp of Bedford, and partly occupied by Hugh le Moyne, Ralph le Moyne, and Gunild *Piscator*. The prior also held thirty acres under Robert le Rowe or Reve, 4 Edward I.,

ᵃ Fuller's *Worthies*.

ᵇ Lysons. See also pedigree of Dudley under Harrold. Lysons says, "The estate came afterwards to the Mordaunts; its name (*Turveys*) has been long forgotten."

ᶜ Vide Carlton. The manor or reputed manor of *Carleton alias Pavenham* extended into this parish.

ᵈ Vide note (ᵃ), p. 174.   ᵉ Appendix [A].

and three years later is said to have been in possession of one virgate, the gift of Robert's ancestor in the preceding reign; he had, moreover, one hundred acres here (but of whom or in what way holden was not known), sixteen of which were in the hands of John de Burdeleys, and twenty (*jur. ux.*) in Alexander Bozon.[a] By deed dated 20 February, 27 King Henry VIII., John Raundes, prior, and the monks of St. Neot's, conveyed their manor, and divers lands, tenements, and hereditaments in Turvey, called or known by the name of "le pryorie," otherwise "le monkes manner," to John, Lord Mordaunt (and his heirs), who, by indenture bearing date 9 July, 5 Elizabeth, gave the same to Lewis Mordaunt.[b] Theophilus Adams and Thomas Butler, both of London, gentlemen, had a grant (27 Eliz.) of all the lands, tenements, and hereditaments, with appurtenances, in the parish of Turvey, lately or formerly pertaining to the monastery or priory of St. Neot's, to hold to them, their heirs and assigns, as of the manor of East Greenwich.[c] In the 33rd of the same reign is another grant dated "Richmond," 22 December, which makes over to William Typper and Robert Dawe, of London, gentlemen, all the lands, &c., with appurtenances, in Turvey, in the counties of Bedford and Huntingdon, or either of them, formerly belonging to the priory of St. Neot's, to hold, &c., in free and common soccage.[d] Next there is a grant,[e] 18 King James I., to Sir Henry Spiller, Knt., Robert Treswell, armiger, and Christopher Vernon, gent. (among other hereditaments), of the following in Turvey: the church with appurtenances, a moiety of certain tithes, three messuages or tenements (severally occupied by William M——, —— Thurbyn, and Hugh Suter or others), the manor of Turuey, with its rights, &c., and a capital messuage or tenement with its appurtenances, fourteen acres of pasture called "le priory of Turvey alias le priory farme in Turuey," a close of pasture called Middlehay, containing thirty acres, a close of pasture called Lyuernayle, containing twenty acres, a parcel of land called ffishers Pingle, the two lamas closes—one called Sturtleys and the other Wymonds, four acres of meadow, eighty acres of arable land lying in the open fields; which manor of Turuey, together with all and singular the premises aforesaid and the patronage of the church, formerly pertained to and were parcel of the possessions of the (lately dissolved) monastery of St. Neot's.

[a] Rot. Hund.   [b] Appendix [E].
[c] Patent Roll, 27 Eliz. part iv., memb. 29, dat. 2 August, at *Wealdhall*. This instrument recites letters patent dated *Gorhamburye*, 25 July, 12 Elizabeth, to Sir Thomas Wentworth, Knt., Lord Wentworth.
[d] Patent Roll, 33 Eliz. part i. memb. 34.
[e] Patent Roll, 18 Jas. I. part xxi. memb. 17. Given at Westminster 7th April.

NEWENHAM PRIORY LANDS.—King Henry the Third gave one hide in Turvey in pure alms, which the prior held *in capite*.[a]

HARWOLD PRIORY LANDS.—Sir Gerard Braybrook, Knt., and others held, for the prioress, in this parish, one messuage and forty acres, temp. Richard the Second.[b]

Account of free rents in Turvey belonging to the priory of St. John of Jerusalem, payable at the feasts of the Annunciation of the Blessed Virgin Mary and St. Michael, in equal portions.—Ministers' Accounts, co. Bedford, 31 and 32 King Henry VIII. nu. 114, mem. 50 D.

By whom payable.	Arising out of	Amount per annum.
Roger Morecote	One messuage with appurtenances late in the tenure of John Robyns	6d.
William Davy	One tenement with appurtenances situated in the 'Highstrete' near to the tenement of the said Roger Morecote on the east, and on the west the tenement of the Abbey of St. James. The same late in the tenure of Thomas Davy	6d.
Lord Mordaunt	One tenement with appurtenances in 'Stokkerenstrete' near to the tenement lately of Henry Harifer on the south and 'le saffren garden' of the Rector of the church of Turvey on the north. Late in the tenure of the wife of Stephen Andrewe	8d.
do.	A pasture called 'Graffoldmore' late in the tenure of the Rector of the Church of Turvey	8d.
		2s. 4d.

[a] Rot. Hund. Lysons says that Mr. Fuller purchased the tithes "which had been appropriated to the priory of St. Neot's, and after that to Newenham."
[b] Esch. 17 Rich. II. nu. 85.

ST. JAMES' ABBEY (NORTHAMPTON[a]) LANDS.—From the foregoing we learn that the tenement in Turvey belonging to the Abbey of St. James was in or near the "Highstrete."

The seat of the Mordaunts has long disappeared, and it is to be lamented that we are not in possession of an elevation of it. Near to the site is a modern farmhouse. The Hall farm is the property of William Francis Higgins, esq., and at present (1873) occupied by Mr. Thomas Finch. John, first Lord Mordaunt, mentions the *Mansion House of Turvey* in his will. The site was sold in 1786 to Mr. William Fuller, the banker, from whom it descended to Ebenezer Fuller Maitland, and was purchased by the father of the present owner in the year 1826. The moats and traces of the foundations of Turvey Hall are still visible.

The present possessor of Turvey Abbey made considerable additions to that mansion between the years 1855 and 1860; a small chamber in the uppermost storey appears to have been used as an oratory in former times.

Turvey House, a large mansion in the Italian style of architecture, was built in the year 1794, on a new site not far from the church, by John Higgins, sen., esq. The late Thomas Charles Higgins, esq., elder son of the above-named gentleman, added the top storey; he also erected a commodious residence, called Turvey Cottage, on an elevated position, commanding a delightful prospect over the River Ouse; and his brother, Lieut.-Col. W. B. Higgins, who is chairman of the Bedford and Northampton Railway Company, built the house at Picts Hill.[b] Mr. Thomas Charles Higgins was M.A. of Trinity

---

[a] In the extreme part of the west suburb of the town of Northampton was built by William Peverell, natural son to the Conqueror, before A.D. 1112, an abbey of Black canons to the honor of St. James.[1] Henry de Alneto confirmed to the church of St. James, Northampton, and to the canons of the same, lands in Turvey which had been granted by Robert, the son of Durand and others.[2] The rent in Turvey belonging to the same abbey, according to Pope Nicholas's Taxation, A.D. 1291, was 2*l*. 6*s*. 8*d*. The site of St. James' Abbey was granted 37 Henry VIII. to Nicholas Giffard.[3]

[b] A small house existed at Picts Hill previously. A family, in former times, seems to have derived its surname from this place, as we find Robert, the son of Roger de Pixill, seised of land in co. Bedf. as of the

[1] Tanner. [2] Halstead. [3] Mon. Ang.

TURVEY ABBEY (ENTRANCE FRONT.)

TURVEY ABBEY (GARDEN FRONT.)

TURVEY HOUSE.

HIGGINS.

(From the evidences of C. L. Higgins, esq, of Turvey Abbey, Parish Registers, Monuments, &c.)

Hugh Higgins, gent., of Weston Underwood, b. 1659, d. 2 Feb. 1751. =Susanna, b. 1651, d. 21 Dec. 1727.

Charles Kilpin, esq., of Hardingstone, co. Northampton, d. 30 Apr. 1717, leaving six sons and three daughters.

Ann, d. 26 July, 1750, sister of Bartholomew Clarke, esq., of Rochampton and Hardingstone, who d. 17 Oct. 1746, æt. 68, whose only dau and heiress, (by Mary Younge, his wife,) Mary, m. Sir Jacob Bouverie, afterwards Lord Folkestone. = Thomas Higgins, gent., of Weston Underwood, b. 13 June, 1681, d. 16 June, 1748.

Sarah, d. Sept. 1729.

1. William, b. 1686.
3. Susanna, b. 1693.
John Higgins, gent., of Weston Underwood, b. Feb. 1690, m. 26 Jan. 1720, d. 6 March, 1761. = 1. Ann Kilpin, b. Mar. 1689, d. 10 Jan. 1745-6.
4. Daniel, b. 1697.

Hugh, b.1708, d.1720. Thomas, d. 1721.
William, b. 1710. Sarah, b. 1714. Ellen, b. 1724, d. 1751.

2. Elizabeth Kilpin, b. June, 1706, d. 16 Sept. 1748.
Bartholomew Higgins, gent., of Weston Underwood, b. Sept. 1712, m. 25 Sept. 1739, d. 29 Nov.1778. (Monument in Weston Church.) = Susanna (widow of Joseph? Kilpin), m. 10 Aug. 1756, d. Feb. 1797. 2nd wife.

3. Bartholomew, b. Jan. 1743, d. 5 July, 1817. (Monument in Weston Church.)
4. Joseph, b. 1743.
5. William, d. 1745. Joseph, d. 1745. Ann, b. 1746, d. 1752.

1. John, b. 1724, d. 1731.
2. Charles Higgins, esq., sheriff of London, 1786-7; purchased the manor of Turvey in the same year; b. 18 April, 1727, d. 29 Dec. 1792 unmarried. (Monument in Weston Church.)
3. Bartholomew, b. 18 April, 1729, d.20 Mar.1755. = Alice Jefcott, d. 28 March, 1782.
4. William, b. 1730, d. 1743.
5. Thomas Higgins, esq., of Weston Underwood, b. 19 Oct. 1732, d. 24 May, 1794. (Monument in Weston Church.) = Mary Parrott, d. 4 June, 1791, æt. 50.

1. John Higgins, esq., of Turvey House, sheriff of Beds. 1793, d. 5 July, 1813. (Monument in Weston Church.) = Martha, dau. of Wm. Farrer, esq., of Brayfield Ho., Bucks.; d. 14 Mar. 1819.
2. Thomas, b. 1741.
Harriet, m. Maj.Gen. Scott, d. 4 Nov. 1872. Ann Maria, bap. 28 Dec.1795,[2] d. unmarried.

Sarah, b. 25 Jan. 1763, d. 3 Dec. 1802.
Theresa, dau of Benj. Longuet, esq. of Bath; b. 20 May, 1779, d. 5 Sept. 1845.[1] = John Higgins, jun., esq., of Turvey Abbey, lord of the manor of Turvey, D.L., J.P., sheriff of Beds. 1802, b. 3 May, 1768, m. 1 Nov. 1804, d. 14 Nov. 1846.[1]
Rev. Henry Hugh Higgins, M.A. = Ann Gouthwaite.
Mary, m. Rev. Edwin Horatio Steventon, M.A.
Thomas Charles Higgins, esq., of Turvey House, sheriff of Beds. 1823; b. 1797, bap. 26 Jan. 1798,[2] m. July, 1838, d. 4 Feb. 1865.[1] = Charlotte, 2nd dau of Sir Rose Price, of Trengwainton, co. Cornwall, bart., d. at Lausanne, bur. 31 Oct. 1868.[1]
William Bartholomew Higgins, esq., of Picts Hill; Lt.-Col. of Beds. Militia, D.L., J.P., served as sheriff; bap. 14, Jan. 1799.[2]

Ann, b. 1754, m. John Greaves, gent., and had a son who died unmarried, and nine daughters.

Charles Longuet Higgins, esq., M.A., of Turvey Abbey lord of the manor of Turvey; b. 30 Nov. 1806, m. 26 July, 1863. = Helen Eliza, dau. of Thomas Burgon, esq., by Catharine Margaret, only dau. of the Chev. Ambrose Herman de Casner, Austrian Consul at Smyrna.
1. William Francis Higgins, esq., of Turvey House, sheriff of Beds.1872, D.L., J.P.; b. Jan. 1845, m. 28 Jan. 1873 at Tyringham, d. there 29 Nov. 1870, æt. 41. 2nd husband. = Fanny Adela, dau. of Col. Wilby, C.B.
Wm. Backwell Tyringham, esq., of Tyringham, Bucks.; 1st husband.
2. Dennis Lambart, b. Aug. 1847.
3. Harriet Anna, m. at Turvey, Apr. 3, 1872, Richard Moon Brocklebank.
4. Emily Kathleen.
5. Louisa Blanche.

Gustavus Francis Higgins, b. at Tyringham, 18 Nov. 1873.

Charles Francis.

Roger William Giffard Tyringham, b. at Tyringham, 5 Aug. 1870. Mary Isabel Tyringham.

1. Henry Longuet. 2. Edith Ann Longuet. 3. Theresa Mary Longuet. 4. Helen Maude Longuet. 5. Charles Longuet. 6. Mildred Alice Longuet.

[1] Buried at Turvey.   [2] Turvey Register.

College, Cambridge, held the commission of the peace for Bedfordshire, Buckinghamshire, and Northamptonshire, was a deputy-lieutenant of the two former, and chairman of the Bedfordshire court of quarter sessions. He died at Leamington in 1865, when he was succeeded in the Turvey House estate by his elder son,

William Francis Higgins, esq., educated at Harrow and Pembroke College, Oxford, B.A., formerly captain in the Beds. militia. In 1872 additional ground on the northern side of Turvey House was inclosed and planted.

CHARITIES.

Table of Benefactions for the poor in the parish[a] of Turvey:

John, second Lord Mordaunt, bequeathed by will to four poor almsfolk of the parish of Turvey the sum of eight pence each weekly, payable out of land at Eastcoates, an ancient hamlet in the parish of Cardington, Beds., holden under Brasenose College, Oxford. The appointment to this charity was formerly vested in the Principal and Fellows of the said college, concurrently with the churchwardens of Turvey.

Thomas Carter, esq., by a nuncupative will in the year 1731, left £100, the interest of which is to be given annually at Christmas to the most necessitous persons in this parish, at the discretion of the minister and churchwardens. This sum is invested in the Three per Cent. Consols and the Interest is paid through the Charity Commissioners.

Dame Anne Mordaunt in the year 1791 left £100, the interest whereof is to be paid annually at Christmas to the poor inhabitants of the parish of Turvey. This sum is invested, and the interest paid, as before.

A person unknown left the sum of two pounds ten shillings, payable annually, out of land on the south-western boundary of the parish of Turvey belonging to William Jefson (or Jesson), esq., of Sutton Colefield, in the county of Warwick, and others, which it is said cannot now be identified; the distribution was to be made at Christmas to the most necessitous persons of this parish, at the discretion of the minister and churchwardens. No payment appears to have been made since 1830.

---

honor of Peverel of Dover.—Harl. 313, fo. 58. And again, Robert de Pikeshull held part of a knight's fee in Turvey *in capite*, temp. Hen. III., Ed. 1.—Testa de Nevill, p. 242.

[a] Account of Charities at Turvey as given in, according to Act of Parliament, 1786. Vide the Report of the Commissioners for the actual state of the charities of this parish in the year 1825.—*Bedfordshire*, vol. x.

Pedigree of Higgins

Compiled from Family-evidences of C. L. Higgins, esq. of Turvey

ARMS,—*On a field vert, three cranes' heads erased*

Note.—The elder branch of the Family quarters LONGUET, viz. *On a field azure, a jess or: in chief, three leopards' faces of the same:*—concerning which Family, see [Gen. Sir J. H. Lefroy's] History of the Family of LEFROY, p. 22, also pp. 69, 194.

JOHN HIGGINS, gent, of Weston Underwood, Bucks, *d.* 1661.

1. **HUGH HIGGINS** 'the elder,' gent, of Weston Underwood, *bur.* 25 Jan. 170¾.

1. **HUGH HIGGINS** 'the younger,' gent. = **Susanna**, of Weston Underwood, *b.* 1659: *d.* 2 Feb. 175⁰/₁, *æt.* 92. / *b.* 1651: *d.* 21 Dec. 1727, *æt.* 76.

Children:

1. **William H.** *bapt.* 9 May 1686.
2. **JOHN HIGGINS**, gent. of Weston Underwood, *bapt.* 15 Feb. 1690; *m.* 26 Jan. 1720: *d.* 6 Mar. 1764, *æt.* 74, *mar.* (2nd wife) Sarah, da. of Tho. H 'the younger,' 15 July 1756 (*see opposite*). = **Ann**, eld. child of Cha. Kilpin, esq.* by Ann, sister of Bartholomew Clarke, esq. of Hardingstone, whose only da. and heiress mar. Sir Jacob Bouverie, afterwards Lord Folkestone, *bapt.* 6 Mar. 1689: *d.* 10 Jan. 174¾ *æt.* 54.
3. **Susanna H.** *bapt.* 5 Dec. 1693.
4. **Daniel H.** *b.* 11 Feb. 1697: (*mar.* 29 Oct. 1727 Elizabeth Barbary, who *d.* 23 Aug. 1728?)

Children of John Higgins and Ann:

1. **John H.** *b.* 18 Apr. 1724: *d.* 3 Sep. 1734, *æt.* 10.
2. **CHARLES HIGGINS**, esq. of Turvey Abbey. Sheriff of London 1786-7. Purchased the manor of Turvey in the same year. *b.* 18 Apr. 1727: *d. unm.* 29 Dec. 1792, *æt.* 66. Mural mon. in Weston Underwood Church.
3. **Bartholomew H.** *b.* 18 Apr. 1729: *d.* 20 Mar. 1755. = **Alice Jeffcott**, *d.* 28 Mar. 1782.
4. **William H.** *b.* 9 Dec. 1730: *d.* 3 Nov. 1743, *æt.* 13.
5. **THOMAS HIGGINS**, esq. of Weston Underwood, *b.* 19 Oct. 1732: *d.* 24 May 1794, *æt.* 62. Mural mon. in Weston Underwood Church. = **Mary**, daughter of ...... Parrott, *d.* 4 June 1791, *æt.* 50. Her epitaph is by the poet Cowper.

Children of Bartholomew H. and Alice:

- **Anne H.** *b.* 4 June 1754; *mar.* John Greaves, gent. of Mark Lane, and left a large family.

Children of Thomas Higgins and Mary:

1. **Sarah H.** *b.* 25 Jan. 1763: *d.* 3 Dec. 1802. *unm.* Mural mon. in Weston Underwood Ch.
2. **JOHN HIGGINS**, esq. of Turvey Abbey, *b.* 3 May 1768: *m.* 1 Nov. 1804: *d.* 14 Nov. 1846, *æt.* 78. D.L. and J.P. High Sheriff of Beds 1801, lord of the manor of Turvey. = **Theresa**, eldest of the four daughters, coheiress, of Benj. Longuet, esq. of Louth and Bath, *b.* 20 May 1779: *d.* 5 Sep. 1845, *æt.* 66. (See the Orlebar pedigree, p. 392-3.)

Children of John Higgins and Theresa:

2. **Mary H'ggins**, *b.* 26 Feb. 1808: *mar.* (13 Oct. 1846) Rev. Edwin Horatio Steventon, M.A. of C. C. C. Camb. *s.p.*
3. **Rev. Henry Hugh Higgins**, of Rainhill, Lanc. M.A. of C. C. C. Cambridge. *b.* 28 Jan. 1814: *mar.* 3 Aug. 1852. = **Anne**, dau. of John Topper Gouthwaite, esq. B.A. of Ch. C. Camb. F.R.S. Ant. Edinb., by Anne, gt. granddaughter of Dr. Andrew Bell, *b.* 17 Oct. 1835.
1. **CHARLES LONGUET HIGGINS**, esq. of Turvey Abbey, M.A. of Trin. Coll. Cambridge, *b.* 30 Nov. 1806: *m.* 26 July 1853. D.L. and J.P. High Sheriff of Beds 1860, lord of the manor of Turvey. = **Helen Eliza**, 3rd da. of Thos. Burgon, esq. of the Brit. Mus., by Cath. Margaret, only da. of the Chev. Ambrose Herman de Cramer, Austrian consul at Smyrna, *b.* 28 May 1823.

Children of Charles Longuet Higgins and Helen Eliza:

1. **Henry Longuet H.** *b.* 31 Oct. 1853.
2. **Edith Anne Longuet H.** *b.* 31 Mar. 1855.
3. **Theresa Mary Longuet H.** *b.* 3 May 1856.
4. **Helen Maude Longuet H.** *b.* 28 Nov. 1857.
5. **Charles Longuet H.** *b.* 24 Sept. 1859.
6. **Mildred Alice Longuet H.** *b.* 2 July 1861.
7. **Francis Horace Longuet H.** *b.* 26 May 1863.

* The Arms of KILPIN are,—*Per fess argent*

NS of TURVEY.

; Wills, Monuments, and Parish Registers,—January, A.D. 1880.

[To be inserted between pp. 192-3 of Harvey's *History of Willey Hundred*, Bedfordshire.]

CREST,—*A griffin's head erased or: collared gules.*

...th; d. 22 Apr. ..., æt. 78.	2. Bartholomew Higgins, gent. (of Preston Deanery, co. Northampton?) had three children living in 1656.	3. Mary H. *mar.* ...... Sharp, and had three children.	4. Ann H. *mar.* John Lewis.	

. THOMAS HIGGINS 'the younger,' gent. of Weston Underwood, *bapt.* 13 June 1681; *d.* 16 June 1748, *æt.* 68. =Sarah, *bur.* 16 Sept. 1729.	5. Elizabeth H. *b.* 1677; *d.* 2 June 1711, *æt.* 34, *unm.*	2. Margaret H.	3. Eleanor H.	4. Mary H. *mar.* ... Neiller. three daughters living in 1702; one of them *mar.* George King.	

. BARTHOLOMEW HIGGINS, 'the elder,' gent. of Weston Underwood, *bapt.* 17 Sep. 1712; *d.* 29 Nov. 1778, *æt.* 66, *mar.* (2nd wife) Susanna, widow of Joseph (brother of Ann) Kilpin (*see opposite*) 10 Aug. 1756. She was *bur.* 22 Feb. 1797. *Mural mon. in Weston Underwood Ch.*	=Elizabeth, ninth child of Charles Kilpin, esq. (*see opposite.*) *bapt.* 2 July 1706; *m.* 25 Sep. 1739; *d.* 16 Sep. 1748, *æt.* 42.	1. Hugh H. *bapt.* 9 Nov. 1708; *d.* 12 July 1720, *æt.* 12.	2. William H. *bapt.* 25 July 1710; *bur.* 19 Oct. 1711.	4. Sarah H. *bapt.* 22 Feb. 1714; *m.* John Higgins, gent. of Weston Underwood, (*see opposite*): *d.* a widow 24 Dec. 1778, *æt.* 68.	5. Thomas H. *bapt.* 30 Mar. 1720; *bur.* 1 Apr. 1721.	6. Ellen H. ('Miss Eleanor') *bapt.* 25 Aug. 1724; *bur.* 18 Apr. 1751, *æt.* 26.

JOHN HIGGINS, esq. of Turvey House, *bapt.* 19 Nov. 1740; *m.* 1 Oct. 1793; *d.* 5 July 1813, *æt.* 73. High Sheriff of Beds 1797. *Mural mon. in Weston Underwood Ch.*	=Martha, da. of Will. Farrer, esq. of Brayfield House, *d.* 14 Mar. 1819 (*æt* 69?)	2. Thomas H. of Finsbury Sq. *bapt.* 22 Nov. 1741; *mar.* Amelia Beaty, died *s.p.* (*bur.* 15 Nov. 1801?) She was *bur.* at Newport Pagnell.	3. Bartholomew H. *bapt.* 19 Jan. 174¾; *d.* 5 July 1817, *æt.* 74½ *unm.* commemorated on his brother John's monument.	4. Joseph H. *bur.* 9 Nov. 1743. in infancy.	5. William H. *bur.* 7 May 1745. in infancy.	6. Ann H. *bapt.* 4 Sep. 1746; *bur.* 30 Apr. 1752.

THOMAS CHARLES HIGGINS, esq. of Turvey House, M.A. of Trin. Coll. Camb. *b.* 26 Dec. 1797; *m.* July 1838; *d.* 1 Feb. 1865, *æt.* 68. D.L. and J.P. High Sheriff of Beds 1823.	=Charlotte, 2nd da. of Sir Rose Price, of Trengwainton, bart. *b.* 16 May 1806; *d.* at Lausanne, 25 Oct. 1868, *æt.* 62. *Mural slab in Turvey Church.*	4. Wm. Bartholomew Higgins, esq. of Picts Hill, B.C.L. of Trin. Coll. Oxf. Lieut. Col. of Beds Militia, D.L. and J.P. High Sheriff of Beds 1845. *b.* 11 Dec. 1798; *d.* 15 Oct. 1878, *æt.* 80, *unm.* *Mural slab in Turvey ch.*	1. Harriet Higgins, *b.* 1794; *mar.* Maj. Gen. George Scott (22 May 1821); *d.* 4 Nov. 1872, *s.p.*	2. Ann Maria Higgins, *b.* 20 Nov. 1795; *d.* 28 Nov. 1838, *unm.* *Mural slab in Turvey Church.*

WILLIAM FRANCIS HIGGINS, esq. of Turvey House, M.A. of Pemb. Coll. Oxford, *b.* 5 Jan. 1845; *m.* 28 Jan. 1873. D.L. and J.P. High Sheriff of Beds 1872.	=Fanny Adela, da. of Col. Wilby C.B. and widow of Wm Backwell Tyringham, esq. who *d.* 29 Nov. 1870, *æt.* 41; and left issue as follows :—	1. Harriet Anna H. *b.* 21 Dec. 1840; *mar.* (3 Apr. 1872) Ric. Moon Brocklebank, esq.	2. Emily Kathleen H. *b.* 18 May 1843.	4. Dennis Lambert Higgins, esq. of High Littleton house, Bristol. *b.* 26 Aug. 1847.	=Theodosia Isabella, da. of Edw. Tredcroft, esq. of Warnham Court, Sussex : *b.* 26 June 1851.	5. Louisa Blanche H. *b.* 8 April 1846.

1. Gustavus Francis H. *b.* 18 Nov. 1873.	2. Adela Kathleen H. *b.* 28 Jan. 1876.	3. Mary Louisa Dorothy H. *b.* 16 Apr. 1878.	1. Mary Isabel T. *b.* 18 Aug. 1867.	2. Roger William Giffard T. *b.* 5 Aug. 1870.	1. Charles Francis H. *b.* 6 Nov. 1872.	2. Theodosia Kathleen H. *b.* 15 July 1874.	3. Alexander George H. *b.* 6 April 1876.	4. Margery Blanche H. *b.* 10 Jan. 1878.	5. Harold Dennis H. *b.* 6 Aug. 1879.

...e: in chief, an oak proper between two crescents or.

A person unknown left about an acre of land in the parish of Lavendon, in the county of Bucks, the rent of which is to be distributed at Christmas among the poor widows of the parish of Turvey, at the discretion of the minister of the said parish, in whom the bequest is vested.

Mr. John Robinson or Robeason left by will in June 1835 the sum of £50, the interest whereof is to be given annually at Christmas to the necessitous widows of Turvey at the discretion of the minister and churchwardens of the parish, who receive the interest from the Charity Commissioners.

Charles Higgins, esq., left by will in 1792 the sum of £1,000, the interest whereof is to be applied for ever towards clothing twenty poor women of the parish of Turvey. He also left £300, the interest of which is to be applied for ever towards the support of a sunday school for the parish of Turvey, provided such a sum be added by the parish as will make the stipend of the master of the said school £20 per annum.

John Higgins, esq., of Turvey Abbey, in the year 1829 purchased a piece of ground near to Great Oaks Wood, called Ball's Pasture, containing about 13 acres, and conveyed the same to Charles Longuet Higgins, esq., in trust, that so much of its annual value be applied for the use of the Church of England sunday school at Turvey as shall make up, together with the interest of the bequest of £300 from Charles Higgins, esq., above-mentioned, the sum of £20 annually for the schoolmaster for ever.

Miss Ann Maria Higgins left by will in November 1838 the sum of £700, less duty, the interest whereof is to be applied for ever towards the support of the Church of England School at Turvey. Also another sum of £700, less duty, the interest whereof is to be applied for ever towards providing the necessitous poor of Turvey with coals at Christmas. These two sums were invested in the Three per Cent. Consols, and the interest thereon, as also on the bequest of Charles Higgins. esq., is paid by the Charity Commissioners.

Advowson and Rectory.

The prior and convent of St. Neot's were possessed of the advowson of the church of Turvey under the Barony of Bedford, the donor being William le Heyr, who gave it in the time of Richard I. Such is the account given in the Hundred Rolls, seventh Edward the First; in the time of King Henry III., however, we only hear of the advowson of a moiety of the church being in the said prior and convent.ᵃ Gorham, in his *History of St. Neot's*, says that a pension was originally paid out of the rectory to the prior; but Pope Celestine III., by a Bull dated 1194, purported to *appropriate* this church to the monastery of St. Neot's.ᵇ The actual appropriation of the rectory of a portion of the parishᵃ took place in 1218, on the admission of Richard de Westun to the vicarage.ᶜ Subsequent incumbents are always styled *rectors* in the Lincoln Institution Books; and the Crown presented to the living on several occasions after the year 1344.ᵈ

The prior and convent continued to exercise the right of patrons till about the beginning of the sixteenth century, and the alienations which were then made were probably only temporary grants. At the Dissolution the advowson came to John, Lord Mordaunt,ᵉ from whom it descended to Lewis, Lord Mordaunt.ᶠ

In the 33rd of Queen Elizabeth, William Typper and Robert Dawe of London, gentlemen, had a grant (*inter alia*) of the lands, tithes, and hereditaments, with appurtenances, in Turvey, which had belonged to the priory of St. Neot's.ᵍ The appropriated tithes were granted in 1600 to the Bishop of Ely;ʰ from whom they are or were held, under lease, by Mr. Higgins of Turvey Abbey.ᵉ There is also the grant, dated 7th April, 18 King James I. (before quoted) to Sir Henry Spiller, knt., Robert Treswell, armiger, and Christopher Vernon, gentleman,

---

ᵃ Touching the appropriation (to the prior and convent of St. Neot's) of certain tithes arising out of the estates of Hugh de Alneto, William le Maunsel, and the said prior and convent in Turvey, about the year 1218, see Gorham's *History of St. Neot's*, vol. i. p. 308.

ᵇ Celestine's Bull, above mentioned, was to confirm the churches of Eynesbury and Turvey to the monks of St. Neot's, on condition that, as they (the monks) were situated close to a thoroughfare and much-frequented road, they should bestow upon all passers-by, that asked for it, meat and drink for the love of God: and declare that they would expend the revenues of the said churches for the sole use of strangers or guests. It goes on to admonish the Bishop of Lincoln, to whom it is addressed, to defend the monks in their free and undisturbed possession from deans and archdeacons, and from all the insults of men in office, and to excommunicate any one who should presume to gainsay the confirmation.—Gorham, *St. Neot's*, vol. i. p. 318.

ᶜ This vicarial decree exists also in the Institution Rolls at Lincoln, 9th of Wells; and in Bp. Wells's Ordin. Vicar. f. 26 b.—Gorham, vol. i. p. 308.

ᵈ About this time the church of the parish of Turveye, with portions of the priory of St. Neot's in the same, was estimated to be taxed at 26 marks, on the oaths of John de Wylye, William Knew, John of the Hull, Hugh de Northo, Richard de Stotker, and Robert le Wrygth.—Nonar. Inquis. p. 19. Rectory valued in the King's books at £16.

ᵉ Gorham.   ᶠ Lincoln Register.

ᵍ Patent Roll, 33 Eliz. part i. memb. 34. (Dated at Richmond, 22nd Dec.)

ʰ Pat. Rolls, 42 Eliz. p. 9.

which included the (? appropriate) tithes and advowson of the church of Turvey;[a] and another in the same reign to Sir James Ouchterlony, knt.

Henry, Earl of Peterborough, appointed to the rectory in 1669; and the advowson continued with the same family in 1764. From the Mordaunts it was purchased by Mr. Fuller, before-mentioned, from whom it passed to Miss Sarah Fuller, and from her to Ebenezer Fuller Maitland, esq., and Bethia, his wife.[b] This advowson was ultimately sold to Thomas Charles Higgins esq., father of the present patron of the living.

At the end of the second Register Book of this parish is an Account of the Rights of the Rectory and Church of Turvey, in the Archdeaconry of Bedford, made in the year 1709.

 Homstall.—The parsonage house is built with stone and covered with tiles, and contains on the ground a kitchen, a pantry, a room for brewing vessels, two butteries, and an hall, all floored with earth, the hall only is cieled; above stairs are one small room on the stair head, floor'd with boards and cieled, two other lodging rooms, a passage and a study, floor'd with boards and cieled, and a large room over the pantry and kitchen with a partition of oaken studs, floored with boards; one barn containing four bays, built with stone and covered with thatch; one hay barn containing two bays, and a stable one bay, the w^h are built with stone on one side, and are boarded next the yard, and are covered with thatch; there is a small garden or courtyard before the door, walled in with a stone wall next the street, and one other garden divided from the yard by a stone wall. The whole Homstall contains by estimation about half an acre, and is fenced round with a stone wall, and is bounded by the common highway south and west, by the Homstall of Thomas Reeve, east, and the Homstall of Roger Tucker, north.

 Gleab.—The c^h yard, which is the only gleab belonging to the rectory, contains by estimation one acre, and is fenced round with a stone wall at the charge of the parish.

 Tyths.—All manner of tyths are due to the Rect. in kind throughout the parish, except in the following cases, viz., half the tyths of grain and hay belong to the Bp. of Ely, and are of the val. of about £70 per an. Turvey Lodge containing by estimation five acres, one close of pasture called Grassie Lawn containing 52 acres, another close being part of the lawn containing 40 acres, Baxter's ground containing 26 acres, the hollow quarter 30 acres, the hill pightle 3 acres, the Lodge-quarter 8 acres, New-park close 100 acres, ploughed lawn 60 acres, little horse close 8 acres, the Hall yard 8 acres, Wood close 30 acres, Breakneck hill 40 acres, little Mansells 20 acres, great Huddicks 36 acres, little

---

[a] Pat. Roll, 18 James I., part xxi. memb. 17. (Dated at Westminster.)
[b] Lincoln Register. Gorham.

Huddicks 18 acres, Woolsey 38 acres, Horse close 30 acres, all which grounds being included within Turvey park have never paid tith since the disparking as we know of; and for the Hall wood containing 78 acres, Margets croft 14 acres, Jades pasture 12 acres, Westfield 58 acres, and Peeres ground containing 36 acres, the sum of £10 0s. 6d. is paid yearly by the Earl of Peterborough as a modus or composition. About fifty years since, Mr. Baxter being then rector, made an agreement with the parishioners for their hay and small tiths in proportion to their respective farms and estates, w^h agreement hath been confirmed from time to time ever since by the succeeding Rectors and their tenants, so that these tyths have not been taken in kind, but a sum of money hath been paid in lieu thereof by the respective occupyers of the lands in the parish, except the Midsummer ground, whereof the twentieth cock hath been always paid to the Rector in kind, and in the rest of the meadow the rector hath every twentieth pole out of the whole and hath his said proportion allotted him one year by the waterside, and another by the land, which said proportion belonging to ye Rect. contains yearly between three and four poles in breadth.

Pensions.—The Rectory besides first fruits and tenths is subject only to the payment of . . . . . to the Bp. at his triennial Visitat^n, and of 10s. 6d. to the Archdeacon yearly for procurations, and is under no obligation to maintain either bull or boar for public use.

Furniture.—The paten and cup, being all the plate belonging to the church, weigh 14 oz.; there is two linnen and one woollen cloth, and a napkin for the communion table, one pewter flagon weighing $5\frac{1}{2}$ lb., there is two books, one of them the Paraphrase of Erasmus, the other, the Defence of the Apology of the Church of England; there is one pulpit cloth and cushion. The oldest register begins 1606; in the steeple there is a ring of five bells, a Saint's bell, and a clock.

Repairs.—The church and furniture with the fence of the ch. yard, being a stone wall, are maintained at the common charge of the p'oners, the middle chancel by the Rector, and the two side chancels by the Earl of Peterborough, they being the burial place of ye family.

26 Apr. 1709. This account is just and true, we do verily believe.

       W^M. BAMFORD, Curate.
       THOS. DEXTER, ⎫
       HN. PEERES, ⎬ Ch. Wards.
       W^M. CARTER, ⎫
       JOH. HARRYSON, ⎪
       W. ODDELL,   ⎬ Parishioners.
       W^M. SKEVINGTON, ⎭

As to the commutation of the tithes[a] see Lewis's *Topographical Dictionary.*

 [a] A small rent-charge on lands in this parish belongs to the rectory of Carlton.

The old Rectory-house (page 237) was a building which had been greatly altered at different times within the present century. On 4th October, 1822, it was visited by Dr. Chalmers, who says "It is a curious house, consisting of many offsets, and intricacies, and ramifications, and the style of the rooms is highly picturesque and interesting." (*Life*, by Hanna, ii. 360).

RECTORY.

The present Rectory-house was built in 1838-9 on the site (and partly with the materials) of the former one.

List of Incumbents.

RICARDUS, SACERDOS DE TURVEIA.[a]

		Patron.
	Rogerus, Pbr.[b]	
1218	Richard de Westun[c]	St. Neot's Priory.
1227	Andrew de Croinden[c]	,,
1234	Robert de Croinden.[c] By resignation of last.	,,

Rectors.[d]

1238	Nich. de Oylle	,,
1251	Adam de Raveningham	,,

[a] Witness to charter of Henry de Alno, living temp. King Stephen or Henry II.
[b] Witness to charter of Halenald de Alno, living 1172.
[c] Gorham, *St. Neot's* (Supplement p. cxv.)
[d] Lib. Instit. apud Lincoln.

TURVEY.

	Rectors.	Patron.
1272	Rob. de Flamvil	St. Neot's Priory.
1273	Hugh de Okeburn, Subd.	,,
	Simon de Westwardon[a]	
1345	John de Warsopp. By resignation of last.[a]	Crown.
1346	John Savage. By res. of last.[a]	,,
1347	Thomas de Dersyngton[a]	
1347	Walter de Farnedale[a]	
1361	Robert de Navesby. By res of last.[a]	St. Neot's Priory.
1375[b]	Robert de Risheby[a]	Crown.
1378	John Burnet. By res. of last.[a]	,,
1381	John de Newton. By res. of last.[a]	
1391	Simon Helgey. By res of last.	Crown.
1397	Robert Wistowe.[a] By res. of last.	
	John Marshall[a]	
1404	Phillip Pope. By res. of last.	St. Neot's Priory.
1404	William Goldyng. By death of last.	,,
1414	John Appulton. By res of last.	
1419	John Cauneysh. By death of last.	St. Neot's Priory.
1420	John Halby. By death of last.	,,
1434	John Martyn. By res of last.	,,
	William Mustelwyk	
1451	John Doon. By res. of last.	St. Neot's Priory.
1457	Thomas Kyngge. By res. of last.	,,
	John Crosse. Also priest of the chantry at Turvey. Died 1517.	
1517	Robert Gostwik (called *Eestwyk* by Gorham). By death of last.	Thomas Heron, by a grant from the prior.[a]
1534	Richard Hale. By res. of last.	John, Lord Mordant.
1536	Richard Wodford. By res. of last.	,,
	Thomas Burkock	Lewis, Lord Mordaunt.
1633	William Lucas[c]	
1636	Thomas Judkin[c]	
Circa 1660	. . . Baxter[d]	
1669, July	Richard Rands.[c] Died 8 Feb. 1699.[e]	Henry, Earl of Peterborough.

[a] Gorham, *St. Neot's* (Supplement p. cxv).
[b] Some time between 1363 and 1397 Thomas Tydy held the livings of "Torvy" and "Camelton," Beds.—Bp. Buckingham's Institutions, Lincoln Register.
[c] Parish Register.   [d] Terrier.
[e] Buried in Turvey church.

TURVEY.

Date	Rectors.	Patron.
1699, Mar.	Robert Freind, M.A.	Charles, Earl of Peterborough.
1714	William Freind. (*Friend* in the Lincoln Register.)	
1745, June	Richard Hopley	James, Lord Viscount Limerick, Rt. Hon. Steph. Pointz, esq., and Charles Mordaunt, esq.
1764, June 17	Joseph Griffith, B.A., St. John's Coll. Camb. 1761. By death of last. Died 17th December, 1803, at Brompton Hall, Middlesex, buried at Peckham, Surrey. (Gent. Mag. Dec. 1803, Supplement.)	Charles, Earl of Peterborough.
1804, Feb.	Erasmus Middleton, B.D., King's Coll. Camb. By death of last. Died 25 April, 1805.[a]	Miss Sarah Fuller.
1805, July 27	Legh Richmond, M.A., Trin. Coll. Camb. 1797. By death of last. Died 8 May, 1827.[a]	,,
1827, Dec. 10	John Webster Hawksley, sen., B.A., St. John's Coll. Camb. By death of last. Also Rector of Knotting with Souldrop. Died 17 April, 1856.	Ebeneza Fuller Maitland, esq., and Bethia, his wife.
1856, May 3	William Broighton Russell, M.A., St. Cath. Coll. Camb. By death of last. Resigned Sept. 1869.	
1869	George Frederick Woodhouse Munby, M.A., Trin. Coll. Camb. By res. of last.	

Of these Rectors may be distinguished Richard Rands, who assisted in drawing up the remarkable and very rare volume of family records called "Halstead's Genealogies." (See the Appendix, page 220.) The Rands were of Radwell in Felmersham, and their pedigree is recorded in the Heralds' Visitation Books.

William Freind, rector in 1714, was son of the Rev. William Freind, Rector of Croton, Northamptonshire; he had two brothers who were celebrated men in their day. Robert,[b] the eldest, became a Prebendary of Westminster, and was Head Master of that school from 1711 to 1733.[c] John, M.D., attended the Earl of Peterborough in his campaigns in Spain, and wrote an account of the Earl's

---

[a] Buried in Turvey church.

[b] Quære, whether he was not the Robert *Freind*, Rector of Turvey, 1699. Robert *Friend*, D.D., had one daughter whom Queen Caroline took and educated, and afterwards bestowed her in marriage to one of her chaplains with a fortune of £3,000.—Add. MSS. 21,067, fo. 125.

[c] As to his works, see Watt's *Bibliotheca Britannica*, Edinburgh, 1824. Allibone's *Dictionary of British and American Authors*, London, 1859.

conduct there; he was F.R.S. and published many works:[a,b] by his will, dated 12th March, 1727, he left £100 per annum to his brother William, Rector of Turvey. On December 5, 1720, the living of "Bitlesden" (Biddlesden), Bucks, was augmented with £200 by Mr. William Freind, Rector of Turvey, and in that year the same gentleman and Mr. Archdeacon Franks gave £200 to the living of Ampthill in Bedfordshire.[c]

Of Erasmus Middleton, B.D.[b,d] there are several engraved portraits, one in *The Evangelical Magazine*, Aug. 1805, with a memoir, from which, chiefly, the following is taken. He was born, as it seems, in Lincolnshire about 1740. Early in life he attached himself to a branch of the Rev. John Wesley's connection at Horncastle. After reading some time with the Rev. Joseph Townsend, Rector of Pewsey, Wilts, he entered St. Edmund Hall, Oxford. From this society he was ejected, with five other young men, in March 1768, for methodism. (See *The Life and Times of Selina Countess of Huntingdon*, and pamphlets by Sir Richard Hill, Bart., and Dr. Nowell, also *The Shaver, a Sermon*, by John Macgowan.) Finding it impossible, on account of ecclesiastical irregularities, to obtain orders in England, he went to Ireland, where he was ordained by Dr. Trail, Bishop of Down and Connor (1765—83), soon after which he became minister of an episcopal congregation at Dalkeith in Scotland. While settled here he married Elizabeth, second daughter of Sir Gilbert Grierson, third baronet, of Lagg, co. Dumfries. In 1779, if not before, he was Lecturer of St. Benet's, Gracechurch, and of St. Helen's, Bishopsgate, London. About 1783 he became chaplain to the Countess Dowager of Crauford and Lindsay. In 1784 he is described as of King's College, Cambridge. Doubtless he obtained his degree of B.D. as a ten-year man, under the Cambridge statute of Elizabeth. Some time after 1784 he became curate to the Rev. William Romaine at St. Andrew's by the Wardrobe, and subsequently to the Hon. and Rev. William Bromley Cadogan, at Chelsea, with whom he remained till the death of that gentleman in 1797. In 1798, or thereabouts, he accepted the post of assistant to the Rev. John Davis, minister of the Broadway Chapel, St. Margaret's, Westminster (the site of which is now occupied by Christ Church). Here he remained six years. During this period he lost his wife, whose decease occurred 3 Jan. 1802. (Monumental inscription,

---

[a] Chalmers's *Biog. Dict.* Lipscomb, Bucks, vol. ii. pp. 570, 593; vol. iii. p. 282.

[b] As to his works, see Watt's *Bibliotheca Britannica*, Edinburgh, 1824. Allibone's *Dictionary of British and American Authors*, London, 1859.

[c] Willis, Bucks, p. 156. Ecton's Thesaur. (1742).

[d] See *Gent Mag.*, May 1805.

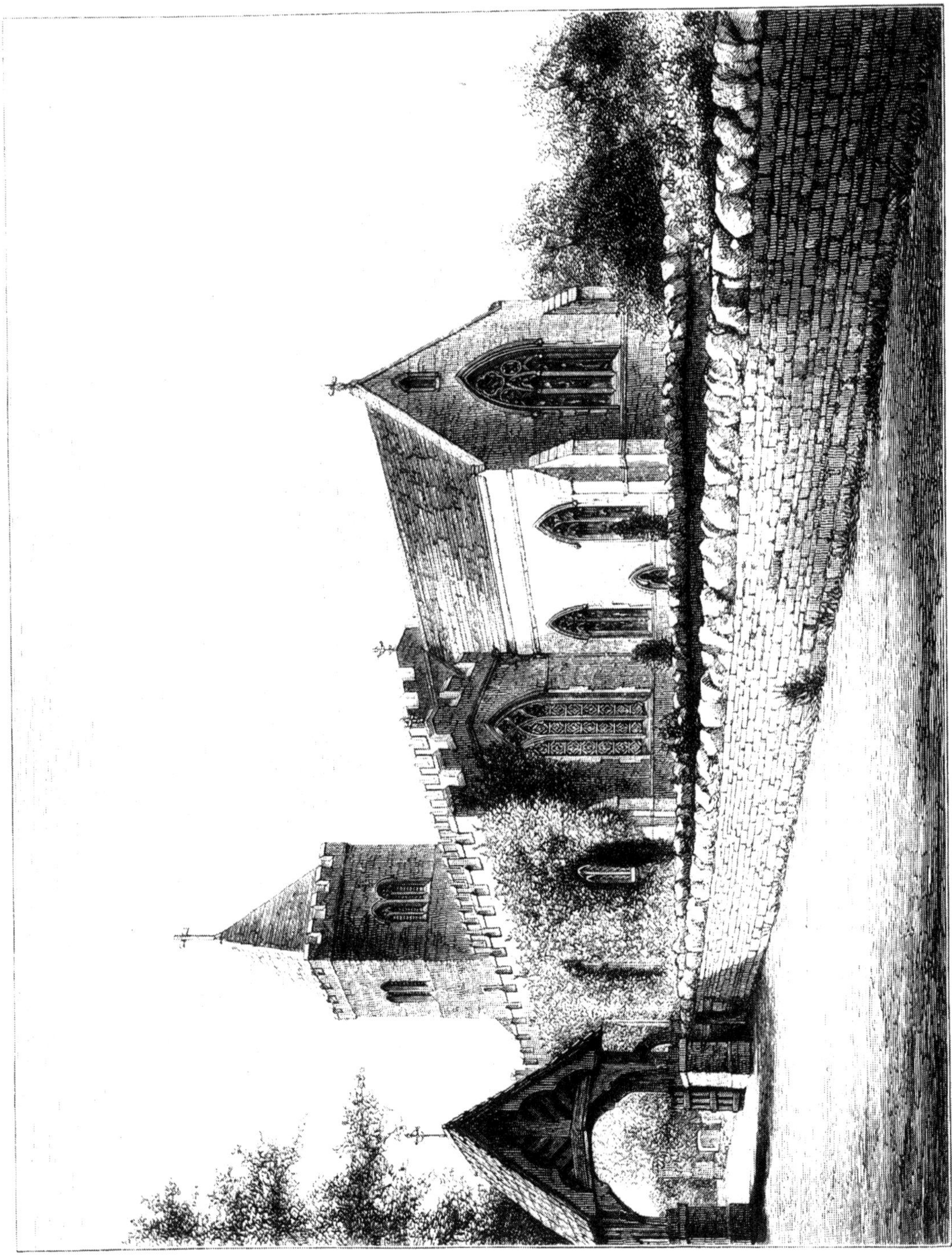

Chelsea Church). Some account of Mrs. M. will be found in Burder's *Memoirs of Pious Women.* In January 1804 he was presented by Miss Fuller to the rectory of Turvey, which he held till his death in 1805. His funeral sermon (published) was preached by the Rev. John Davies, to whom he had been curate.

A notice of Legh Richmond[a] will be found in the Gentleman's Magazine for July 1827. See also *Memoirs* by the Rev. T. S. Grimshawe (published 1828, 8vo.[b] 11th edition, 1846, 12mo.); *Scenery of the Isle of Wight; Spirit of the Pilgrims,* vol. ii. p. 213. Mr. Richmond's widow died at Clifton 11th June, 1873, in her 96th year.

The Rev. John Webster Hawksley succeeded Mr. Richmond at Turvey. He was rector of Knotting with Souldrop, Beds., and formerly vicar of Marlow, in Bucks, which last he resigned on taking Knotting. To him is ascribed an anonymous poem. He published also a sermon entitled *Christian Consolation: A Father's Funeral Discourse on the Death of a beloved Daughter, preached in a village church, Jan.* 16, 1820, 8vo. London, Ellerton and Henderson, Johnson's Court, 1820.[c]

A substantial modern lych-gate forms the entrance to the churchyard. The large and handsome parish church is dedicated to All Saints, the feast in commemoration of the dedication being kept on the Monday following the first Sunday after All Saints' Day. During the years 1852-4 the church was much enlarged and beautified under the superintendence of Mr. (now Sir) George Gilbert Scott. The work was begun on the 19th day of July in the year first mentioned, the cost being defrayed by the present much-esteemed lord of the manor, who also presented a magnificent organ to the parish, built by Hill, of Tottenham Court New Road, London. The alterations and restorations were brought to an end and completed, and the church was re-consecrated by Thomas, Bishop of Ely, on the 10th of October, 1854. In 1818 the church consisted of chancel (with north and south lateral chapels extending as far as the east end of the chancel), nave

---

[a] As to his works, see Watt and Allibone, who, however, have omitted to name the following: June 1821, "*The Gypsies' Petition*" and the "*Negro's Prayer,*" *for single voice, with an Accompaniment for Piano Forte, composed by Rev. Legh Richmond, the first and second numbers of a series of Songs of a Sacred character which are designed to be published occasionally.* Mr. Richmond is said to have left a good collection of fossils and minerals.—Add. MS. 21,067, ff. 87,211.

[b] Review of Grimshawe's *Memoir of the Rev. Legh Richmond* in Gent. Mag. Oct. 1829.

[c] Add. MS. 21,067, fo. 196.

and clerestory, north and south aisles, south porch, western tower and vestry.* At present it comprises chancel with a sacristy and organ-chamber on the north side, nave with clerestory, north and south aisles, south porch, western tower containing six bells, and a small vestry in the angle formed between the south wall of the tower and the west end of the south aisle.

The old chancel was taken down for the purpose of lengthening the nave, and the foundations for a new chancel were dug out of the churchyard. These were carried somewhat deeply, and in the excavation for that purpose more than one hundred and fifty bodies were disturbed, the greater portion of which were so much decayed that only a few of the bones remained. Whenever it was necessary to remove a coffin it was carefully placed upon a wooden frame and carried to another part of the churchyard, where a grave was prepared for its reception. It was also necessary to take down the whole of the mortuary chapel on the north side of the chancel, in order to lengthen the north aisle and provide room for the organ and the sacristy. The side windows of the chancel are of two lights with slightly varied tracery—one north and two south, the latter having a priest's door between them; these, together with the east window of three lights, are filled with stained glass from the manufactory of Messrs. Hardman of Birmingham.

The north aisle contains four windows facing north; of these, two have double lights, and two are of three lights—square-headed. The same aisle has a north door and a small western Decorated single light.

The tower is of four stages. A gilt cross is placed on the apex of its tiled pyramidal roof. Prior to 1858 it was surmounted by a weathercock bearing date 1630. In the month of July of that year the tower was struck by lightning. The belfry stage has on all sides two uniform double-light windows, below which are three square openings facing north, south, and west respectively. In the stage next below is a small western single light, and in the lowest stage are north and south lancets besides the west window. At the south-west angle of the tower is a newel staircase, approached by a doorway in the south wall of what was

---

* In the year 1842 the east window, of three lights, contained some poor modern pieces of stained glass, the only coloured glass in the church.

The north chapel had a late north door. (See a drawing and ground plan of this church (1818) among the Rev. D. T. Powell's collections.)

North aisle roof,—oak, tie-beam, plain.

North chapel roof,—wood, nearly flat, whitewashed.

South aisle roof,—oak, tie-beam, continued to the east end of south chapel.

originally part of the vestry, but which now also forms a passage to the staircase leading to the furnace for heating the church, which, together with a hot air apparatus, was constructed by Haden of Trowbridge. The remaining portion of this (the old) vestry, containing the parish chest, &c., is entered from the south aisle, and lighted by a south two-light window. A picture[a] now in the belfry at one time occupied a position above the holy table, prior to the restoration of the church, and was given to the parish by Mr. Middleton.

Both aisles exhibit gable ends east and west, instead of the usual lean-to. All the windows in the south aisle are of three lights each, viz.: three facing south and one at each end. There are small openings on either side of the porch. Like most of the neighbouring churches, the nave and aisles have the battlements, string-course, and leaden roof. The roof of the chancel is tiled, and of a high pitch.

The south porch and doorway, forming the principal entrance to the church, are good Early-English, and the door is ornamented with very rich ironwork. The porch, though prepared as if for groining, is open to the room above. Its roof dates from Scott's restoration.

The original nave of the church reached as far only as the extremity of the third arch from the tower, the old Early-English chancel arch, which was a low one, extending across the nave in that position. A door once leading to the rood loft[b] was to be seen on the south side of the nave close to the former chancel arch.

Each aisle is now separated from the nave by five pointed arches.

The clerestory (Perpendicular) contains twelve cinquefoiled double-lights, four of which were added in 1852-4, when the roof was lengthened exactly after the pattern of the original one. It was afterwards found necessary to take the whole of the roof off the nave, together with that over the north aisle. Both roofs were carefully restored and re-covered with new lead.

In consequence of the great insecurity of the foundations, it became needful to take down all the pillars and arches on both sides the nave to the tower, and the west arch and pillars also. New foundations carried down below the bottom of the disturbed soil were placed under every pillar, and they were then re-erected in their original form.

---

[a] The subject it represents is the question addressed to our Lord by St. Peter.—*St. John,* xxi. 21.

[b] The north chapel was bounded on the west side by an old loft, approached by a wooden staircase against the north wall. This loft was in the line of the ancient rood-loft, but from its clumsy construction and want of architectural character, it could scarcely have been any part of it. The chancel screen was destroyed in 1804 or 1805.

The interesting remains of two very early semicircular-headed windows were discovered on the south side of the nave, over the arches. The plaster was picked off, and they were left as little disturbed as possible. A low doorway in the wall of the tower, opening from the nave, was also found, and the weather-mold of the former high-pitched nave roof.

The various floors of the tower, having through age become much decayed and unsafe, were all taken up and relaid with sound oak plank.

The windows in the aisles are from the manufactory of the Messrs. Powell, Whitefriars, London. They are composed of quarries bearing different designs, such, for instance, as the fleur-de-lis and the oak leaf, the sacred monogram and the cross, the vine leaf and the lily, within trailing borders of leaves or flowers. The eastern window of the south aisle is copied from one of the windows in York Minster, and consists of an assemblage of geometrical forms—quatrefoils, trefoils, &c.—mostly composed of the three primitive colours.

The geometrical west window, of three lights, was the gift of William Bartholomew Higgins, of Picts' Hill, esq.

The present chancel, as mentioned above, extends considerably farther eastward than the former one: the site of the two western bays of the latter having been included in the present nave. In like manner the corresponding proportion of the site of the original north lateral chapel has been thrown into the north aisle, at the eastern extremity of which is the new organ chamber, opening into the chancel by a richly embellished screen with three cinquefoiled arches, the centre supported by two polished Purbeck marble shafts with foliated stone capitals. This chamber is covered with the old chancel roof, which was repaired and adapted to the purpose. In making these alterations two vaults belonging to the family of the Mordaunts were opened. One of the vaults contained six coffins of lead and two leaden cysts. Two of the coffins had on them the following inscriptions:—

The Right Honourable JOHN EARL of PETERBOROUGH, Baron of Turvie, Marshall-General of the Field for the Parliament forces. Lord Lieutenant of Northamptonshire Deceased the 19th of June, Anno Domini 1643, in the 43rd year of his age.

The Right Honble CHARLES EARL of PETERBOROUGH and MONMOUTH, General of the Marines, and Knight of the most noble order of the Garter, died at Lisbon, October 1735, aged 78.

The vaults were again carefully closed, and strong arches of stone were thrown over them, above which the floor of the organ chamber was placed.

The north chapel, in 1818, contained the monuments of the second and third

TURVEY.

FONT.

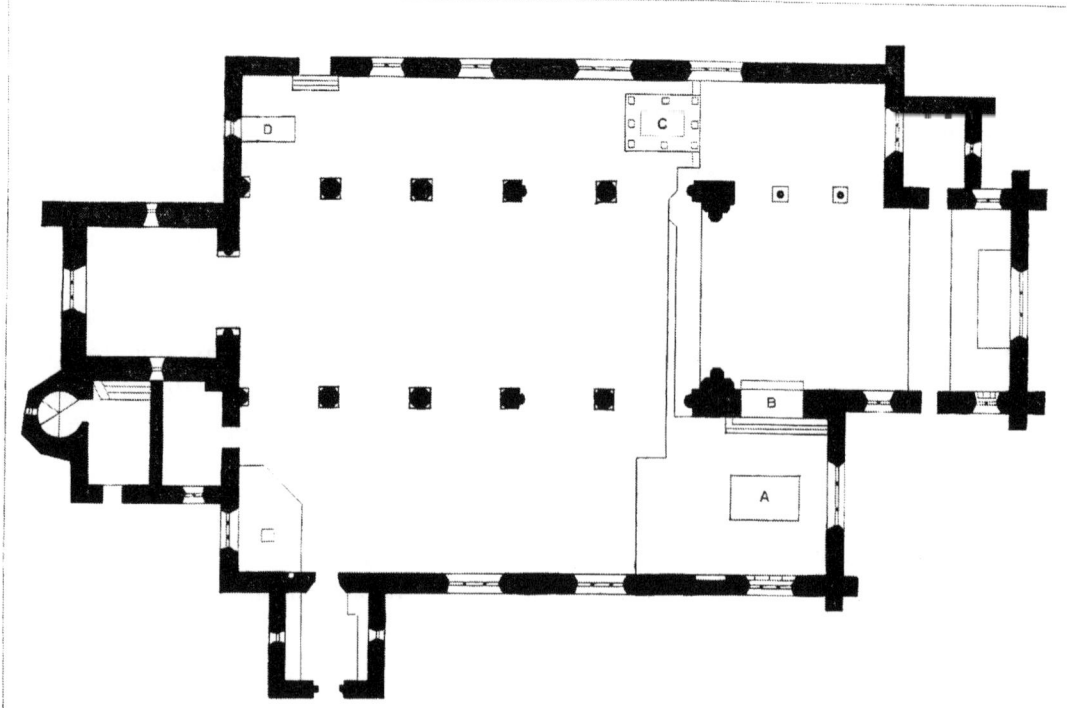

GROUND PLAN OF CHURCH.

A. Monument of Sir John Mordaunt.
B.   ,,   John, 1st Lord Mordaunt.
C. Monument of John, 2nd Lord Mordaunt.
D.   ,,   Lewis, 3rd Lord Mordaunt.

Lords Mordaunt, and that of Sir John Mordaunt, which had been removed thither from its original position between the chancel and south chapel.

At the south-west angle of the south aisle is the font, which formerly stood against one of the pillars of the nave. It is, says Gorham, probably of Norman construction, though three of the panels appear to have been chiseled out in a later period.

Westward of the south door is a circular stoup projecting from a semicircular-headed recess.

The south lateral chapel was in the eastern portion of this aisle; under its south-east window are three Early-English trefoiled sedilia with a piscina, having a dripstone continued over all, springing from three corbel heads and two masks; and west of the same window is an arched sepulchral recess. In this recess a fresco was found representing the two Mary's at the foot of the cross. It was carefully picked out, and as much preserved as possible, a glass frame was then placed over it in order that it might not sustain further injury. It is much to be regretted that a large and interesting fresco, immediately over the same arch, was destroyed.

The church and chancel are fitted with open oak seats[a] from designs by Mr. Scott, and paved with encaustic tiles from the manufactory of the Messrs. Minton. The Rev. W. B. Russell, a former rector, gave the handsome carved oak pulpit, which was made purposely for the church from a design by Mr. Scott; and Miss Gorst, of Preston, Lancashire, presented an oak lectern, also from a design by the same eminent artist. Under the tiles and flooring of the pews throughout the nave, aisles, and chancel, there is a thick covering of concrete, so that the earth beneath the church is hermetically sealed.

The chancel is reached by three steps from the nave, and the communion-table by three steps from the chancel. The upper step bears the inscription, "Jesus stood and cried, If any man thirst let him come unto me and drink." The step next below has the following: "Come unto me all ye that labour and are heavy laden, and I will give you rest." The window on the south side nearest the communion table represents, in one of the lights, the Adoration of the Wise Men; the other light represents the Flight into Egypt. The other window on the south side represents, in one compartment, Christ blessing little children; the second portion of the window represents the Sermon on the Mount. The

---

[a] About 1846 the church was wholly or in great part repewed, some ancient open seats being removed; the stoup, within the south door on the west side thereof, disappeared about this time, but has been replaced. In the year above-mentioned a large organ was erected in a western gallery. Elliott and Hill, builders.

INTERIOR OF TURVEY CHURCH

subject represented in the centre light of the east window is the Crucifixion; the left light bears as its subject our Lord's entry into Jerusalem; the compartment on the right side represents our Lord's appearance in the garden to Mary Magdalene; this window contains altogether ten figures. The window on the north side the chancel presents to us in one of the lights the Ascension, and in the other the Descent of the Holy Ghost on the day of Pentecost. The chancel roof is of oak.

The present spacious chancel-arch was built during the alterations between 1852 and 1854. In making the excavation for its foundation, on the south side, at the head of the tomb of the first Lord Mordaunt, a stone grave was found, arched at the top. There did not appear to have been any coffin. The grave was formed nearly to fit the body, and was composed of somewhat rough flat stones laid at the bottom, and others of the same kind, but smaller, set up at the sides. The arch over the top was of small rough stones laid in lime. The bones within were those of a man of more than the average stature, and there can be no doubt that they were the remains of Sir John Mordaunt, whose monument stands in the south chapel. Another body, the skin of which was still undecayed, was discovered not far from the same place, which had been interred in an ox hide. Both were carefully again closed over.

At the eastern extremity of the organ chamber is the new sacristy or vestry, communicating with the chancel by a shouldered doorway.

The alms dish, presented to the parish, was executed by A. Keith, of Westmoreland Place, from a design by Butterfield. The centre of the dish bears the the sacred monogram, with vine leaves. Round the dish is the following inscription; " + Tua sunt omnia, et quæ de manu tua accepimus dedimus tibi, peregrini enim sumus coram te sicut omnes patres nostri." On the back is the following: " + In honorem Dei et in usum ecclesiæ de Turvey : fest : pasch : A^{no} S^{tis} 1855. +"

The standards for candles, and the other modern brass-work in the church and chancel, are by Hardman of Birmingham.[a] Two candelabra, presented (1872) by Miss Baker of Turvey House, may be mentioned as worthy of especial notice.

The inscriptions on the bells are as follows:

1. G. MEARS and Co., Founders, London.
Presented to his Brother-Parishioners by Lt.-Colonel W. B. HIGGINS, of Picts' Hill, Turvey, September 1864.

2. HENREY BAGLEY made mee. 1682.

---

[a] The foregoing account of the alterations of this church, &c., is principally taken from a MS. by Charles Longuet Higgins, esq., in the custody or possession of the parish clerk of Turvey.

3. Thomas Bourton and Joseph Osmond, churchwardens, 1682.
4. R. Hopley, Rector, T. Davison, W. Skevington, churchwardens, J. Eayre, St. Neot's, fecit 1750.
5. W. and J. Taylor, Bell-founders, Oxford, Loughboro, 1839.
6. T. Battams and W. Pearson, Churchwardens. R. Taylor, St. Neot's, fecit, 1815.

The communion plate is all silver-gilt, and is as follows:

	lb. oz.
2 Chalices, weighing	. 1 2½ each
2 Flagons, ,, ...	. 3 11 ,,
1 Paten, ,, ...	. 0 10½
1 Plate, ,, ...	. 1 0

All the pieces are inscribed,

"The gift of Margaret, Daughter of the Hon[ble] Henry Mordaunt, to the Church of Turvey, 1788."

Nicasius Yetsweirt and Bartholomew Brokesbye, gentlemen, obtained a grant[a] from the crown, 12 Elizabeth (*inter alia*), of one acre of land lying in Turvey, formerly or lately in the tenure or occupation of John Stephensall or his assigns, which had been given for the purpose of sustaining a lamp in this church. To hold the same to their heirs and assigns as of the manor of East Greenwich.

Monuments[b] and Inscriptions.

South Aisle.

The Purbeck marble monument of Sir John Mordaunt and Edith his wife (*vide* Halstead, page 524) was, in the year 1810, removed from its original and proper position, in order to give room for additional seats, being then placed in the north chapel. It now stands at the east end of the south aisle, not far from the graves of the persons in whose honour it was erected. Sir John died in the year 1506, having, by his will, founded a chantry in the parish church, and

---

[a] Patent Roll, 12 Eliz. part x. memb. 23. Given at Westminster 26 Jan.

[b] See *British Traveller*; also a very interesting paper on *Turvey Church and its Monuments* read at a General Meeting of the Bedfordshire Architectural and Archæological Society, by Charles Longuet Higgins, Esq. M.A. *Reports and Papers read at the Meetings of the Architectural Societies of Yorkshire and other Counties*, vol. vi. p. 279. Vice-Admiral W. H. Smyth, writing in 1860, says: "About thirty years ago, when a worthy friend of mine was directing some repairs in Turvey church, . . . he wrote to the representative of the Mordaunt property respecting the fine tombs there . . . To this courteous and obliging application, Mr. Higgins received for answer (*piget meminisse*), that he might mend the roads with them!"—*Records of Buckinghamshire*, vol. ii. p. 180.

endowed it for the support of two chaplains. His effigy is represented in armour, over which is a robe, with the collar of SS; the effigy of his lady is in a robe and a rich coif. The inscription, now wanting, is supplied by Halstead:

> Hic jacet Dominus JOHANNES MORDAUNT, Miles, Dominus
> hujus villæ, cum Domina EDITHA Uxore ejus, filia & hærede
> Domini Nicolai Latimer, Militis; qui quidem Johannes Cancellarius
> fuit Ducatus Lancastriæ, regnante Rege Henrico Septimo, & à
> Secretioribus suis Conciliis. Multa meruit, & habuit plurima, pro
> longa & fideli servitute. Obiit tandem satur dierum, clarus
> virtute, posteritate felix, in expectatione beatissimæ Æternitatis
> . . . . . . die . . . . . Anno Domini . . . . .

In this part of the church are four brasses.[a] One represents an ecclesiastic, but the inscription is lost. Another[b] is in commemoration of a member of the Mordaunt family, as indicated by the only shield of arms remaining, viz. *Mordaunt*, impaling, quarterly 1 and 2,   ; 3 and 4, three bendlets and a canton. One of these in 1842 was in the chancel near the north-east angle, close to the wooden trap-door then leading to the Mordaunt vault. The most perfect brass of the four bears a shield of arms and the following inscription:—

> HERE LIETH Yᵉ BODY OF ALICE BERNARD, THE
> WIFE OF RICHARD BERNARD, ESQVIRE, THE
> DAVGHTER OF IOHN CHVBNOLL OF ASTWOOD,
> ESQ. WHO DEPARTED THIS LIFE Yᵉ 24ᵗʰ OF
> APRILL, 1606, BEING OF Yᵉ AGE OF LXIIIJ
> YEARES; IN REMEMBRANCE OF WHOSE VER-
> TVES & RELIGIOVS PIETY HER HVSBAND
> RICHARD BERNARD HATH LAID THIS MONVMENT.

Arms: *Bernard*, and four quarterings, impaling *Chubnoll*, quartering . . . . Dexter: 1 and 6, a bear rampant, *Bernard*; 2, three fishes naiant in pale, within a bordure engr.; 3, a bordure with ten bezants, over all a canton bearing . . . .; 4, fretty; 5, a fesse lozengy. Sinister: 1 and 4, two lions pass. guard. betw. as many flaunches, *Chubnoll* or *Chibnall*; 2 and 3, a lion rampant.

This brass was likewise in the former chancel.

Those above described are on the floor, and the two latter were drawn and

---

[a] It is said that one of these has twice been stolen.—*Notes*, communicated by Henry Gough, esq.

[b] Bearing the following legend on a scroll:
> "Quisquis eris qui transieris, sta, perlege, plora;
> Sum quod eris; fueramque quod es; p. me precor, ora."

engraved by Mr. Fisher, but only fifty copies of these (and a few other subjects) were published (in 1828); they are numbered 26 and 25 respectively in the volume of Fisher's *Extra Plates*, preserved in the Bedford General Library.

Of the fourth brass only the heraldry now remains, fastened on to a small mural stone, from which the inscription plate has disappeared. This may be seen under the window at the east end. The arms are those of a bachelor. The shield (which is surmounted by the crest fastened on an esquire's helmet) exhibits the arms of *Mordaunt* quartering *Le Strange, Brock,* and *De Alneto*.

Suspended from the sides of the eastern window are two helmets, a short sword, a pair of gauntlets, and a coronet much broken. One of the helmets has the Mordaunt crest.

Flat stone with raised white cross—

Here sleeps in peace CECILIA, the beloved Wife of Legh RICHMOND,[a] whose spirit departed hence in the Lord Aug. 3rd, 1848, Aged 27, in sure and certain hope of the resurrection to eternal life through our Lord Jesus Christ.

Mural tablet on the east wall—

In the Vault beneath, in hope of a blessed resurrection, rest the Mortal Remains of ANN MARIA HIGGINS, Second daughter of John Higgins, Esq., of Turvey House, and Martha his wife. Born Nov. xx., MDCCXCV. Died Nov. XXVIII., MDCCCXXXVIII.

On another—

✠

In Affectionate Remembrance of THOMAS CHARLES HIGGINS, of Turvey House,
who died at Leamington, February, 4th, 1865, Aged 68 years.

" He casting away his garment came to Jesus."
" Blessed is the man that considereth the poor and needy."

Also of CHARLOTTE, his dearly loved wife,
(Daughter of Sir Rose Price, of Trengwainton, Cornwall, Bart.)
She died at Lausanne, October 25th, 1868, Aged 58 [b] years. ✠ ✠

" The ornament of a meek and quiet spirit is in the sight of God of great price."
" I have waited for thy salvation, O Lord."

---

[a] Son of the Rev. Legh Richmond.
[b] This is a mistake in the inscription, it should have been 61.

Chancel.

Here, the object which at once attracts attention is the monument of alabaster, under a circular and ornamented canopy, to John, first Lord Mordaunt, and Elizabeth (Vere) his wife. An engraving of it may be seen in Halstead, page 597. By his testament bearing date 1st August, 1560, proved 1st September, 1562, Lord Mordaunt bequeathed his body to be buried in the parish church of Turvey, in the wall next above his father's tomb; appointing that the body of the Lady Elizabeth, his wife, should be removed and laid on his right side; likewise that a tomb of marble, with the images of himself and the same lady, his wife, in alabaster, should be there placed in memory of them, and upon the day of his burial one hundred marks should be distributed in alms to the poor of Turvey, Stagsden, Carlton, Chellington, Harrold, Stevington, Felmersham, Radwell, Lavendon, Brayfield, Newton Blossomville, Hardmead, Astwood, Wooton, and Cranfield; as also one hundred marks towards the church and steeple of Turvey and rough-casting the walls of the church, and for the repairing of Turvey Bridge £40. The monument has the effigies of himself and his lady; he is represented in armour with a robe; his lady is in a robe with puckered sleeves, and has the angular head-dress of the period.

Above the monument—both on the north side facing into the chancel, and on the south facing into the south aisle or chapel—are the arms, supporters, crest, and helmet (untinctured).

Arms—*Mordaunt*, with quarterings—I. A chev. betw. three estoiles, *Mordaunt*. II. Quarterly, 1 and 4, a cross flory; 2, a fesse betw. three (? martlets); 3, a fesse engr. betw. three lions pass. III. Quarterly, per pale indented, in the first and fourth quarters five lozenges conjunct. in cross. *Danne, D'Auno,* or *De Alneto*. IV. A lion ramp. billettée. V. A saltire betw. four cross-crosslets and eight (? martlets). VI. A pale of three lozenges, *Bray* or *Brey*.[a] VII. On a bend, a lure, *Brock*. VIII. A lion ramp. within a bordure. IX. A bend charged with three . . . . X. A lion ramp. and a canton charged with three (? martlets). XI. A cross lozengy, *Stowell*. XII. Quarterly, per fesse indented, in the first quarter a crescent, *Perott*. XIII. A cross lozengy, in the first quarter an eagle displ. *Argentyne*. XIV. A lion ramp. within a bordure compony, *Bryan*. XV. Three pales, over all a fesse charged with three escallops. XVI. An eagle displ. within a bordure engr. *Le Strange*. Supporters: Two eagles,[b] with wings expanded, issuing from behind the shield. Crest: The bust or head of a Negro, wreathed about the temples.

---

[a] Arms of *Bray* or *Brey*: Arg. three lozenges in pale azure.—Weston. In Harl. 1160, fo. 44, this coat appears to be assigned to *Bradston*.

[b] Represented *semée of estoiles* on the tomb of Lewis, 3rd Lord, and (formerly) on that of the 2nd Lord.

Also, facing south, another shield—

Mordaunt, with five quarterings, impaling *Vere*, with five quarterings. Dexter: 1, *Mordaunt*; 2, *De Alneto*; 3, *Brock*; 4, *Perott*; 5, *Le Strange*; 6, a cross flory, *Latimer*. Sinister: 1, Quarterly, in the first quarter a mullet, a label of three points, *Vere*; 2, a cross, *Vere*; 3, three bucks pass. *Greene*; 4, a cross engr. *Drayton*; 5, chequy, within a bordure, *Mauduit*; 6, three mullets, 2 and 1.

North Aisle.

A representation of the second Lord Mordaunt's monument is exhibited in the plate of the Interior of Turvey Church which accompanies this work; also in page 604 of Halstead. Upon this monument is Lord Mordaunt's effigy, in armour, between those of his two wives, under an open canopy supported by columns of the Doric order. John, second Baron Mordaunt, died in 1571.

On the upper part of this monument is the following heraldry:—

I. Facing west, a shield, with helmet and crest.
Arms.—*Mordaunt* and eleven quarterings. 1, Ar. a chev. between three estoiles sa. *Mordaunt*; 2, Quarterly per pale indented ar. and gu. in the first and fourth quarters a cross of the second, *De Alneto*; 3, Ar. a pale of three lozenges gu. *Bray*; 4, Ar. on a bend sa. a lure or, *Brock*; 5, Quarterly per fesse indented or and gu. in the first quarter a crescent of the second, *Perott*; 6, Gu. a cross lozengy, in the second quarter an eagle displ. ar. *Argentyne*; 7, Gu. an eagle displ. ar. within a bordure engr. or, *Le Strange*; 8, Gu. a cross flory or, *Latimer*; 9, Ar a cross gu. *Vere*; 10, Az. three bucks pass. 2 and 1, ppr. *Greene*; 11, Ar. a cross engr. gu. *Drayton*; 12, Chequy or and az. a bordure gu. *Mauduit*.

Crest.—The bust of a savage ppr. habited or, wreathed about the temples ar. and sa.

II. Facing south, a shield. *Mordaunt* and eleven quarterings, as in number I. impaling *Fitz Lewes* and five quarterings. Sinister: 1, Ar. a chev. betw. three trefoils slipped sa. *Fitz Lewes*; 2, Az. a cross between eight lions or lioncels pass. or (? *Fitz Lewes*); 3, Ar. a fesse erm. betw. two gemelles sa. *Harleston*; 4, Sa. a chev. ar. betw. three lions ramp. or (? *Willason*);[a] 5, Ar. a chev., an annulet in the dexter corner sa. *Wauton*; 6, Gu. a goat saliant (or ramp.) ar. *Bardwell*.

III. Facing east, a shield bearing the arms of *Mordaunt* only.

IV. Facing north, a shield, *Mordaunt* and eleven quarterings as before, impaling, quarterly, 1 and 4, arg. on a fesse sa. between three lion's heads erased gu. as many anchors or, *Fermor*; 2 and 3, per pale indented   a chevron between three escallops, *Browne*.

During the alterations the altar-tomb of Lewis, third Lord Mordaunt, which stood at the east end of the north chapel, was removed and placed under the window at the west end of the north aisle. This monument is figured in Halstead, page 626,[b] and an engraving of the south side was executed by Fisher, 19th September, 1823.

[a] In Harl. 1160, fo. 44, *Lovell* follows *Harleston*.
[b] In this engraving neither the arms nor the inscription are correctly represented.

On the south side (but said to be on the north, in Halstead) :—

   Pijssimæ Memoriæ Lvdovici
    Dñi Mordavnt Sacrvm
  Depositum Ludouici Dñi Mordaunt,
 Sub auitâ Fide, et certâ felicis resurrec-
 tionis spe, gloriosam Iesu Chrī Epiphaniam
     hic expectat.

On the north :—

 Vxorē Habvit Elizabethā Arthvris Darcei
 Eqvitis Avrati Filiam. Ex Qua suscepit
 Henricvm Filivm Vnicv̄ et Hæredem, Mariā
  Catharinam, et Elizabetham, Et Post
 Vitam Fæliciter et sine Qverela Perac-
 tam, svis Charvs, et Alienis, Annorvm
   Satvr et Honorvm, Æ-
    tatis svæ Anno 66°,
13° Ivnij, Anno Dñi 1601, Pie Obdormivit In Dñ.

At the head of the tomb are the arms, supporters, helmet, crest, and motto :—

Arms.—1, *Mordaunt;* 2, *De Alneto;* 3, *Brock;* 4, *Perott;* 5, *Le Strange;* 6, *Latimer;* 7, *Vere* (quarterly, gu. and or, in the first a mullet ar., on an escutcheon of the last a cross of the first); 8, *Greene;* 9, *Drayton;* 10, *Mauduit;* 11, *Fitz Lewes;* 12, *Wauton.*

Supporters and crest as before. See note (b), page 211.

Motto.—Lucem Tuam Da Nobis.

At the foot, a shield bearing *Mordaunt*, with the same quarterings, impaling *Darcy* with four quarterings.

Sinister : 1 and 6, Az. semée of cross-crosslets and three cinquefoils arg. *Darcy;* 2, ——; 3, Arg. a bend betw. six martlets sa. *Tempest;* 4, A fesse betw. three fleurs-de-lis gu. *Waddington;* 5, Gu. three goat's heads erased ar. *Gattesford.*

Mural tablets :—

    Sacred to the Memory of
 Archibald Clarke-Jervoise, Born June 4, 1833,
   died Feb. 9, 1835.—St. Matt. xix. 14.

    To the Memory of
 William Carter, of this Parish, Esqr,
  who departed this life March 18, 1728,
   in the 56th year of his Age.

Also Catherine Carter, 4th daughter of the said Wm Carter,
  who departed this Life Sept 18, 1728,
   in the 22nd year of her Age.

Also Thos. Carter, Gent.
the only surviving son of W^m, who departed this Life
April 29, 1731,
in the 28th year of his Age.

William Carter, second son of Wm Carter,
died an Infant.

The said Thos. Carter gent. gave five pounds for ever
to be distributed annually amongst the
Poorest and most needy House Keepers of this Parish.

Likewise the Body of Elizabeth Carter,
the wife of Wm Carter, Esqr,
who departed this Life August 24, 1747,
in the 73rd year of her Age.

Surmounted by arms—Sa. a talbot pass betw. three round buckles or. Crest (on helmet), a talbot's head ar.

To perpetuate the Memory of Kezia, wife of Richard Gee, ob. June 29, 17—

Also of Richard Gee, Husband of the above, who died at Horncastle, Lincolnshire, Feby 4th, 1811.

Near this Place are deposited the mortal remains of Thomas Battams and of Mary his wife.
Out of affection to their Memory this Monument is erected by their surviving children.

Sacred to the Memory of
The Rev^d. Legh Richmond, A.M.
Twenty-two years Rector of this Parish.

Endowed with superior talents,
His highest ambition was to consecrate them to the service of his God,
And hallow the attainments of the Scholar by devoting them
To the glory of his Lord and Master.
To amiableness of disposition and simplicity of character
He united Fervency of Zeal and Holiness of Life.
Eminently blending the charities of Earth with the graces of Heaven
He preached with Fidelity the grace of God in Christ Jesus,
Exemplified and adorned by his practice the Doctrines which he taught,
And after many years of unwearied Exertion and extensive usefulness,
Died, with a hope full of immortality, May 8th, 1827, Aged 55 years,
Leaving a widow and eight surviving children
To mourn the irreparable loss of an affectionate Relative,
The Parish that of a Faithful and endeared Pastor,
And the Church of God the too early removal
Of one of it's brightest ornaments.

Sacred to the Memory of SAMUEL NUGENT LEGH, eldest son of Rev^d. Legh RICHMOND, Rector of this Parish, and MARY his wife. He died at Sea on his passage homeward from India in the Month of August 1824, aged 26 years.

>Great God I own'd thy power divine
>That work'd to change this heart of mine,
>When form'd anew I learn'd to bless
>The wonders of Redeeming Grace.—Ps. lxv. 5.

Sacred to the affectionate Memory of THOMAS HENRY WILBERFORCE, second son of Rev^d. Legh RICHMOND, Rector of this Parish, and MARY his wife. He died in the Faith and Hope of the Gospel of Jesus Christ on Jany. 16, 1825, Aged eighteen years.

>It matters little at what hour of the day
>The righteous falls asleep: Death cannot come
>To him untimely who is fit to die;
>The less of this cold world the more of heaven;
>The briefer life the earlier immortality.

Also ATHERTON EDWARD, their Infant son, who died on April 25, 1821, Aged 7 Months
Them which sleep in Jesus will God bring with him.

An affectionate Memorial for LEGH BROOKE, the Infant son of the Rev^d. Legh RICHMOND and Mary his wife, died Feb^r 1, 1810, Aged 7 weeks 4 days.[a]

>This lovely Bud—so young so fair—
>Called hence by early doom,
>Just come to show how sweet a flower
>In Paradise would bloom.

Flat stones at the east end :—

>Hic Jacent Reliquiæ
>RICARDI RANDS hujus
>Ecclesiæ Rectoris
>qui 8vo Die Februarij e vitâ Decessit, Anno Domini 1699, Ætatis Suæ 63.

The Mortal Remains of The Revd ERASMUS MIDDLETON, Rector of Turvey, lie here, ob. April 25th, 1805.

On small brass in Old English letters (modern) :—

✠ Quod Mortale fuit CAROLI COMITIS de PETERBOROUGH et sex suorum avorum hoc sepulchro jacet.

Nave.

In excavating for the hot-air apparatus and for the foundations of the pillars, a large number of bodies were discovered. They appeared to have been buried

---

[a] During the time that these sheets were at press, a brass (intended for this church), in commemoration of other members of the Richmond family, was executed by Hardman.

for the most part without coffins. Nothing remained but the larger bones. Sixty bodies at least must have been so disturbed. The bones were replaced as nearly as possible in their original position. About the middle of the church was the gravestone of the Rev. E. Middleton. During the repairs the stone was broken. What remains of it was removed to the north aisle. The position of the grave is marked by a quarry of brass, with the letters E. M. A similar quarry marks Legh Richmond's grave in the chancel.

Churchyard.

In the churchyard, adjoining the southern wall of the church, is a plain altar-shaped tomb, placed there to preserve the memory of a faithful domestic at Turvey Hall, who for many years served the Mordaunt family with fidelity and zeal. The monument bears upon it a brass plate with the following inscription:

> Here lyeth JOHN RICHARDSON under this wall,
> A faithful true servant at Turvey Old Hall,
> Page to the first Lord Mordaunt of fame,
> Servant to Lewis, Lord Henry, and John:
> Payneful and careful and just to them all,
> Till death toke his lyfe.
> God have mercy of his soule.   Amen.

On the north side is the burying-place belonging to the family at Turvey Abbey; the brick wall which surrounds it is surmounted by a device in stone,— "What man is he that liveth and shall not see death?"

> In this sepulchre
> are deposited
> the mortal remains of
> THERESA,
> The beloved wife of
> JOHN HIGGINS, Esq.,
> who died
> Sept. v. MDCCCXLV.
> Aged LXVI years.
>
> JOHN HIGGINS
> of Turvey Abbey, Esqre.
> Died Nov. XIV. MDCCCXLVI.
> Aged LXXVIII. years.
> At Evening time it shall be light.—Zach. XIV. 7.

The grave of Thomas Charles Higgins, esq. is at the north-west, as also that of George William Baker, esq. (born 26 Jan. 1817), who died at Turvey House 4 July, 1870.

Names in the churchyard, 1868:

Negus, Palmer, Atterbury, Tysoe, Boulton, Skevington, Whitworth, Spencer, Sinfield, King, Wigzell, Howard, Robinson, Gardner, Wooding, Tandey, Richardson, Stock, Pinkerd, Bond, Eyles, Adams, Stewart, Finch, Vincent, Abbott, Brittain, Roe, Davison, Parker, West, Burdin, Smith, Westley, Howe, Covington, Crouchley, Battams, Johnson, Eaton, Pearson, Benbow, Bailey, Dent, Burr, Hanger, Peacock, Killingworth, Bennet, Wallinger, Paine, Cotton.

On July 18th, 1871, a new burial-ground was consecrated by the Bishop of the diocese. Afterwards public notice was issued, on the recommendation of the Inspector of Burial Grounds and with the approval of the Secretary of State for the Home Department, to the effect that on and after the 1st January, 1872, funerals would be discontinued in Turvey churchyard, except in cases where vaults or brick graves had previously existed.

In this place is buried Commander Sidmouth Stowell Skipwith, R.N., who died at Woodside, in this parish, 14 Sept. 1872.

REGISTER.[a]

"The Register before this date (1629), commencing 1606, is now wanting."
(Signed) J. W. Hawksley, Rector of Turvey and Knotting with Souldrop, 1829.

				£	s.	d.
1629 May 11.		Baptized, Ann, daughter of Wm. Sansomes and Marie his wife. (Earliest entry.)				
1647 Mar. 5.		——— Thos., son of Thos. Marshall, clerk (curate), and Anne his wife.				
1650 Dec.		——— John,				
—— Nov. 23.		Buried, Frances, children of the above Thos. and Anne Marshall.				
1655		Lewis,				
1678–1710	.	. Second Register. Collections to Briefs:—				
		July 15, 1690. For the Fire of St. Ives, in Hunts		1	0	3½
		Aug. 18, 1694. For the French Protestants		0	19	11
		,, ,, For Iniskilling, in Ireland		0	9	11
1680 June 22.		Buried, Thos. Bodenham, esq^r.				
—— June 29.		Baptized, Peter, son of Thos. Brand, gent., and Margt. his wife.				
—— Aug. 17.		Buried, Francis Brand, gent.				
1683 Mar. 10.		Baptized, Mary, daughter of Thos. Brand, gent., and Margt. his wife.				

---

[a] See list of Rectors, also the pedigrees of Mordaunt and Higgins.

1684 July 29.	Buried,	"Edith, the beautifull da. of Rob. and Ann Jeffery."	
1694 Jan. 26.	————	Thos. Brand, jun.	
1699 Feb. 11.	————	Mr. Rich. Rands, late R. of this parish.	
1706 Apr. 25.	Baptized,	Cath., daughter of Wm. Carter, gent., and Eliz. his wife.	
1709 Nov. 18.	————	Temperance, daughter of Wm. Carter, gent., and Eliz. his wife.	
1714 Nov. 18.	————	Wm., son of Wm. Carter, esqr., and Eliz. his wife.	
1719 Feb. 4.	Buried,	Fran. Baptist, gent.	
1726 Nov. 25.	————	Joh. Bray, gent.	
1728 Mar. 22.	————	Wm. Carter, esqr.	
1729 Sep. 24.	————	Rich. Tempest, esqr.	
——— Jan. 16.	————	Mary, wife of Henry Richards, of Stagsden.	
——— Jan. 18.	————	Christian Brand, gent.	
1731 Apr. 30.	————	Thos. Carter, esqr.	
1732 June 24.	Married,	John Peers and Ann Carter. (By licence.)	
1735 Jan. 2.	Buried,	William Jones, gent.	
1737 Mar. 19.	————	Peter Brand, gent.	
1740 Apr. 2.	————	Jos. Walton, gent.	
1742 Apr. 10.	————	Mrs. Susannah Brand.	
1744		Elenor, daughter of Matthew and Cælia Waling, baptized in the Romish Communion, May 1.	
1745 May 17.	Buried,	Mrs. Winifred Brand.	
1747 Aug. 26.	————	Eliz Carter, gent.	
1750 Mar. 28.	————	John Brand, gent.	
1751		[The third Register book begins.]	
1760 July 24.	Buried,	John Peers, gent., of Astwood, Bucks.	
1777		R. H. Hurst, curate.	
——— Nov. 24.	Buried,	Wm. Griffith, gent.	
1795 June 30,	————	Eliz. Granger, servant to John Higgins, Esq.	

An old inn near the bridge, called the "Three Fishes," bears date 1624, on its quaint wooden porch.

The *Tinker*, when an inn, had these lines upon its sign board:— (1842.)

The Tinker of Turvey, his Dog and his Staff,
Old Nell with her Budget, will make a Man laugh.

"Nell's Well," in this parish, was restored in 1873.

In the library of the British Museum is preserved a very rare pamphlet bearing the following title: "The Tincker of Turvey, his merry pastime, in his passing from Billingsgate to Graves-end. The Barge being freighted with mirth, and mann'd with . . . . . Trotter, the Tincker; Yerker, a cobler; Thumper, a smith, &c., and other mad-merry fellowes, euery-one of them telling his tale." London, 1630, 4to.

This was re-printed in London (privately) in 1859, in the form of an octavo volume entitled *The Tinker of Turvey; or Canterbury Tales: an early Collection of English Novels.* Edited by J. O. Halliwell.

Here are National and Infant Schools, with residences; also a reading-room and museum. The Upper School was opened 31st August, 1848; the Infant School in 1856.[a]

Assessed property (1815), £3,819. Poor-rates in 1838, £202 11s.

POPULATION.

Year.	Inhabited houses.	Number of separate occupiers.	Uninhabited houses.	Building.	Males.	Females.	Total of persons.
1801	151[b]	—	—	—	—	—	758
1831	—	—	—	—	—	—	988
1841	200	—	—	—	—	—	960
1851	—	—	—	—	—	—	1028
1861	228	275	3	1	546	547	1093
1871[c]	234	259	4	—	590	527	1117

[a] For endowments and other charities, see *Parliamentary Gazetteer*; Lewis, *Topog. Dict.*; &c.
[b] 168 families.
[c] At the time the census was taken there were about 95 railway labourers lodging in the village.

APPENDIX.

[A].

AN ANALYSIS OF CONTENTS (SO FAR AS RELATES TO TURVEY AND THE MORDAUNTS) OF THE WORK ENTITLED

SUCCINCT GENEALOGIES OF THE NOBLE AND ANCIENT HOUSES

OF

	Pages in Halstead.
Alno or de Alneto	1—15
(Including short notices of the de Ardres in pages 4, 14, and 15)	
Broc of Shephale	17—37
Latimer of Duntish	39—72
Drayton of Drayton	73—114
Mauduit of Werminster	115—147
Greene of Drayton	149—229
Vere of Addington	231—317
Fitz-Lewes of Westhornedon	319—336
Howard of Effingham	337—386
Mordaunt of Turvey	387—697

With Pedigrees of Mordaunt at the end (not paged).

By ROBERT HALSTEAD. London: Printed in the year of our Lord MD.CL.XXXV.

Of this remarkable volume only twenty or twenty-four copies were printed.

The name of Halstead is fictitious, being compiled by the then Earl of Peterborough and Mr. Rands, his chaplain. With portraits of Lord Peterborough and his wife. See *Notes and Queries*, 1st Ser. vi. 553, vii. 50.

CHARTERS AND GRANTS.

	Page in Halstead.
Paine or Paganus de Alneto of Turvey, to Richard Mansel—a tenement which Adam le Croile held	5
The same to Gerino de Sayfeild—all the tenements which Nicholas Gerin and Baldwin Ribell held in Turvey	5
Hugh de Burdet to Paine de Alneto—the town of Maydford	6
Paine de Alneto to Herbert his younger son—lands in Lavendon	6

APPENDIX.

	Page in Halstead.
Henry de Alneto to the church of St. James, Northampton, and to the canons of the same—confirmation of several lands in Turvey which had been granted by Robert, the son of Durand, and others	7
Ralphe de Kaines	7
Halenald de Alneto to the monastery of St. Neot's—lands in Turvey	8
The same to the church and canons of Caldwell—land in Turvey called *Swethmanstoching*	8
The same to Henry de Pinkney	9
Alexander de Alno [a]	9
William de Alneto (son of Halenald) to the church of St. Neot's, and to the monastery of Bec—lands in Turvey called *Muclepit*, &c.	10
William de Alnotho, lord of Turvey—confirmation of grants to St. Neot's and Bec	11
Hugh de Alno	11
Jocosa, lady of Maydford, daughter of D'Engayne, and formerly wife of William de Alneto	11
Hugh de Alnoto, son of William de Alnoto, to the monastery of St. Neot's—lands, &c. in Turvey	12
Hugh, prior of St. Neot's	12
Hugh de Alno to Gilbert Flandrensis	13
The same to Richard, the son of his sister Sarah—a moiety of his lands of Turvey	13
Eustace le Mordaunt (with consent of his brother Robert) to Alice his wife, in dower—the lands which Osmund, his father, held in Wahull, and certain services, besides a moiety of his lands of Radwell, and services	13
(Repeated)	448
The same with Alice his wife, to Reginald, the son of Simon le Brayeur, of Turvey—lands, &c. in Turvey	14
(Repeated)	448
Eustace de Sancto Ægidio, or St. Giles, to Osbert le Mordaunt, his brother—lands at Radwell	445
Osbert le Mordaunt to Baldwin le Mordaunt, his younger son—half his lands of Radwell, &c. for term of life	445
Hervey de Montemorenci, the King's Marshall of the whole of Ireland—confirmation of grants of lands to Osbert, the son of Robert	446
Osmund le Mordaunt to Baldwin his brother—confirmation of Osbert's grant of half his lands of Radwell	446
Sampson Fortis to Osmund le Mordaunt and his heirs (begotten of Helen, daughter of Sampson)—all the lands of Chillington which Robert, Sampson's father, held on the day of his death, by the service of half a knight's fee	447
William de Alno to Eustace le Mordaunt (with Alicia, William's elder sister)—half his lands, &c. of Turvey, to be held of William and his heirs, by the service of half a knight's fee	447
Eustace le Mordaunt to William, the son of Richard Cocus del Wike-end—a messuage in Turvey, for homage and service	448

---

[a] See Inscription for Alexander de Alneto, formerly in Bath Abbey.—Thynne's *Collections*, MS. Cott. Cleop. C. III. fo. 198 b.

	Philip, son of Nicholas de Turvey, to the church of All Saints at Turvey—a messuage, &c., which he had of his brother William's gift in the town of Turvey
	Eustace le Mordaunt de Wahull to the church of St. John the Baptist, and St. John the Evangelist of Caudewell, and to the canons of the same—land in Turvey
	Ralphe, Earl of Chester to William Mareschal de Sutton
	The same to Richard de Sutton—land in Olney
	John de Scot, Earl of Huntingdon, to William de Olney, son of Richard de Sutton—land in Yerdley
	William Mareschal de Sutton to Matilda . . . —a messuage in Asthull
	Richard de Ardres to William de Mordaunt—certain interests of his in the mills, waters, and fishings at Turvey
	The same to William de Mordaunt—Adam Pite, a villan
15 Edward I.	William, son of Sampson le Mansell of Turvey, to William, son of William le Mordaunt of the same, and Rose his wife—all his lands, &c., in Chicheley
22 Edward I.	Reginald de Grey and William le Mordaunt—concerning fishing in the Ouse
25 Edward I.	King Edward I. to William le Mordaunt—licence to impark the wood called Wolesey, the open field called Turvey lees, with the wood of Mancelsgrove, and other lands in the parish of Turvey. (Given at Salisbury.)
9 Edward II.	Amicia de Aubeny to William de Mordaunt her son, and to Robert, son of the same William
11 Edward II.	William de Mordaunt to the Monastery of St. Neot's—lands, &c., in Turvey
16 Edward II.	Hugh Bossard, lord of Knotting, to Robert, son of William de Mordaunt—certain homage and service in Knotting
17 Edward III.	Robert Mordaunt of Turvey to William Campion of Stacheden—all his manor of Turvey, &c.
	Alexander Bozonn of Rokesdon to Robert de Chelnestone—the manor of Rokesden, &c.
	John Oliver to Alexander Bozonn of Stacheden—his manor of Rokesden, &c.
	William Campion of Stacheden to Robert Mordaunt of Turvey and Johanna his wife—all his manor of Turvey, &c.
19 Edward III.	Robert Mordaunt of Stacheden, and Johanna le Bray his wife, to Hammon de Ibbestok of Pullokshull—*Wodecroft*
20 Edward III.	Sir Hugh Wake of Clifton, knt., to Robert Mordaunt of Turvey, and Johanna his wife, and their heirs—tenements in Clifton
27 Edward III.	Peter Carbonell
	Edmond Mordaunt and Henry de Brusselle
49 Edward III.	Robert, son and heir of Edmund Mordaunt of Turvey to John Curteys of Wimington, William Mordaunt of Wybolston, and others—his manor of Turvey, &c.
	Thomas Dardres to Robert Mordaunt of Turvey
6 Richard II.	John L'Estrange of Kimpton
	Lady Johanna Escutamore to the Abbess of Elstow, Nigel Loring lord of Chalgrave, Robert Mordaunt lord of Turvey, and Thomas Pever—certain rent
10 Richard II.	John Curteys of Wymington and William Mordaunt to Robert Mordaunt of Turvey and Agnes his wife—premises in Turvey
11 Richard II.	John L'Estrange of Brokley

APPENDIX.

Page in Halstead.

14 Richard II.	Robert Mordaunt of Turvey to Thomas Pever of Thoddington, John Curteys of Wymington, John Boteler of Stacheden, Roger Keston, Robert Brown of Turvey, and John Atte Welle, clerk—lands, &c. in co. Cambridge	475
13 Henry IV.	Robert de Mordaunt of Turvey to Thomas Pever of Toddington, Thomas Foddringey of Turvey, William Bozonn of Wootton, and William Campion, vicar of Ampthill—lands &c. in Yerdley-Hastings	478
	Other charters by the same	479-80
4 Henry V.	John Brigge sen. John Brigge, jun. and Matilda his wife, all of Turvey	480
9 Henry V.	John Dardres late of Turvey to Robert Mordaunt	485
27 Henry VI.	Robert Mordaunt of Turvey to William Mordaunt his son and Margaret, William's wife—rent, &c. in Turvey	487
	The same to William Holdenby of Isham, John Holdenby of Holdenby, John Turvey of Turvey, and John Bainton of the same—his manor called Mordaunts manor in Turvey, &c.	488
	Indenture between William Holdenby of Isham and William Mordaunt	489
9 Edward IV.	,, between Robert Tanfield of Gayton, Northants, and William Mordaunt of Turvey	491
11 Edward IV.	John Bainton of Turvey to William and John Mordaunt, John Tawe, clerk, John Faux, clerk, and William Geliott, clerk	491
21 Edward IV.	John Mordaunt of Turvey, gent. to Thomas King, parson of the moiety of the church of Turvey, John Vynter of Cardington, John Poley of Biddenham, and Richard Stevynson of Turvey —the reversion of certain premises in Turvey	493
	Deed between the same parties, by which John Mordaunt confirms to King, Vynter, Poley, and Stevynson the reversion of the manor of Botelers in Walden, Essex	494
14 Henry VII.	Edward, Duke of Buckingham to John Mordaunt of Turvey—certain premises ; also a several fishery in Brayfield	501
	Indenture between John Mordaunt of Turvey and John Tresham of Rushton (touching marriage of Vere)	501
15 Henry VII.	Thomas, prior of Caldwell, to Sir Reginald Grey, Knt. and John Mordaunt of Turvey, serjeant-at-law—the presentation to the Church of Sandy for one turn	506
17 Henry VII.	Indenture between John Mordaunt, Wistan Brown, and Humphrey Brown, his brother	506
	Indenture between Edward, Duke of Buckingham of the one part, and John Mordaunt of Turvey, gent. and William Mordaunt, his brother, of the other part—reciting that the said Duke had granted to the said John and William parcel of Gloucester fee	509
18 Henry VII.	Indenture between Henry Strangeways, esq. of the one part, and John Mordaunt of Turvey, gent. on the other part—concerning manors, lands, &c. in the counties of Stafford, Gloucester, and Dorset	511
19 Henry VII.	William, Bishop of Durham, Chancellor of Cambridge University, to Sir John Mordaunt—the place vacant by the death of Sir Roger Ormston	513
12 Henry VIII.	John Cottisford, rector of Lincoln College, Oxford, to Sir John Mordaunt of Turvey, Knt.—appointment of Sir John as chief seneschal of the manors of Skeney and Petesthoo, Bucks	540
20 Henry VIII.	Two Royal Charters	549-50
37 Henry VIII.	A grant of Deodands and other liberties in Turvey	571
1 James I.	A charter of Charles, Earl of Nottingham, Baron Howard of Effigham	630

MISCELLANEOUS DOCUMENTS, ETC.

Temp. Henry III. Rich. I.	Fine levied between John de Traylly and Eustace le Mordaunt of land, &c. in Turvey
	„ between Eustace Mordaunt and Gilbert, the son of William, of one virgate of land with appurtenances in Radwell
7 Edw. II.	„ between William Mordaunt and Thomas, son of Warin de Boses, of premises in Turvey
	Relief paid by William, son and heir of Eustace le Mordaunt, to the seneschal of William de la Chuche (Zouche) and the lady Matilda de Traylly
	Matilda, daughter of Letticia de Asthull quit-claimed to William Mordaunt, lord of Asthull and Amicia his wife, all right and claim in a certain croft in Asthull
	Henry, son of Fulk Hurel quit-claimed to William le Mordaunt, his lord, all right in a tenement in Turvey
	Albreda, daughter of Robert de St. George quit-claimed to William le Mordaunt, her lord, certain rent in Turvey
	Roger le Soc de Wibaudston resigned to William le Mordaunt de Turvey, his lord, certain rent in Turvey
	Memorandum touching Thomas de Wikeley, bailiff (in the manor of Turvey) to William de Mordaunt
	Extract from Court Rolls of Chicheley, 7 Edward III.
	Edmund Mordaunt, releases to William Mordaunt, senior, all his right and claim to certain premises in Turvey, 27 Edward III.
	Partition of Broc's lands between the coheirs
	Disputes between Edmund Mordaunt and Roger Cooke of Newton Blosseville
	Richard Dagenhale of Buckingham and Bedford to Hugh, Earl of Stafford, receipt of Relief from Robert, son and heir of Emond Mordaunt, lord of Turvey. 51 Edward III
	Families of Boteler of Walden and L'Estrange
	Thomas de Ardres and Thomas Foddringey
	Indenture between Prince Edward Duke of York, Robert Mordaunt, and Thomas Mirefield
	Records of the manor-courts of Yerdley
	Agnes Foddringey and Robert Mordaunt
	Concerning Elizabeth, the wife of Robert Mordaunt
11 Henry VII.	John Mordaunt constituted a serjeant-at-law
17 Henry VII.	Fine between Edward, Duke of Buckingham, and John and William Mordaunt, touching view of frank pledge and other liberties in Turvey
	Concession of the wardship and custody of Thomas, son and heir of John Leventhorp
19 Henry VII.	Letters Patent making Sir John Mordaunt Chancellor of the Duchy of Lancaster
	Liberties and Privileges granted from the Pope to Sir John Mordaunt
	Custody of John, son and heir of William Sayntmaur, granted to Sir John Mordaunt
19 Henry VII.	Indenture between Sir John Mordaunt, and Wistan Brown, touching the wardship of Thomas Leventhorp
21 Henry VII.	The King, to William Mordaunt and William Gascoign, the executors of the will of Sir John Mordaunt, Knt.,—the wardship of Thomas Leventhorp
1 Henry VIII.	Patent to John Mordaunt to be sheriff

APPENDIX.

		Page in Halstead.
4 Henry VIII.	Grant of a cognizance[a] to John Mordaunt, by Thomas Wryothesley, garter, and Thomas Benolt, clarenceux	526
6 Henry VIII.	An Award between the Earl of Shrewsbury and John Mordaunt concerning the manor of Drayton	528
	A Release from the Earl of Shrewsbury to John Mordaunt of all his rights concerning the manor of Drayton	530
	Patent to John Mordaunt, esq., granting several liberties, among others to be covered in the presence of the King	531
	An Act of John Lord Mordaunt, by which he does constitute his Proxies to the Parliament, the Duke of Somerset, the Lord Paulet, and the Lord Russell	573
	A Division of Lands and Tenements between the Lord Mordaunt, Sir Humphrey Brown, and others. (Not relating to the Bedfordshire estates.)	575
	The Claim and Surmise that the Lord Parre maketh for to have the Freeborde of Drayton Park to the King's use from the Lord Mordaunt	576
	An Exemplification of Depositions concerning the Freeborde of Drayton Park (temp. Edw. VI.)	582
	Extracts from Hollingshead's (p. 931, ru. 50), and Stow's (p. 610) Chronicles	599
	Causes of Disagreements between John, the second Lord Mordaunt, and his son, Lewis	605
19 Elizabeth.	A Commission for Musters within the county of Northampton to the Lord Mordaunt and others directed	607
	Extracts from Cambden (pp. 208, 413).	609
34 Elizabeth.	An Exemplification at the request of Lewis Lord Mordaunt of several Patents of Liberties granted to the manors of Drayton, Luffwick, &c.	615
45 Elizabeth.	A special Livery granted unto Henry Lord Mordaunt	627
6 James I.	Indenture Tripartite for the Settlement of the estate of Henry, Lord Mordaunt	631
17 James I.	A Pardon and Release granted to John Lord Mordaunt, of a Fine in the Star-Chamber, set upon Henry Lord Mordaunt, his father	641
3 Charles I.	The King advances John, Lord Mordaunt to the dignity of Earl of Peterborough	648
15 Charles I.	The Disafforestation of the Earl of Peterborough's lands in Northamptonshire, and grant of other Liberties thereunto	650
16 Charles I.	Patent of Lord Lieutenant of Northamptonshire to John Earl of Peterborough	660
A.D. 1640.	A Commission for constituting Deputy-Lieutenants for the co. of Northampton	662
16 Charles I.	A Commission of Array to John Earl of Peterborough	663
A.D. 1647.	A Declaration of King Charles the First against the Alienating of the lordship and priory of Rygate from Henry Earl of Peterborough	667
13 Charles II.	A Writ summoning the Earl of Peterborough to the Parliament	667
	A Commission constituting Henry Earl of Peterborough, Captain-General and Governor of Tangier	668
	Instructions for the Earl of Peterborough, General of the Army designed for Tangier	670
	Charter of King Charles II.	671
	His Majesty's Warrant for £2000, as a free gift to the Earl of Peterborough	672
A.D. 1662.	Commission by James, Duke of York and Albany to Henry, Earl of Peterborough	674
A.D. 1663.	The Earl of Teviot's Receipt of the Garrison of Tangier from the Earl of Peterborough	675

[a] This seems to have been a special grant to the individual, quite independent of the family crest.

2 H

226 TURVEY.

		Page in Halstead.
15 Charles II.	Grant of a Pension to the Earl of Peterborough of £1,000 per annum for life	675
10 Charles II.	A Commission constituting John Earl of Exeter and Henry Earl of Peterborough Lord-Lieutenants of the county of Northampton	676
A.D. 1666.	Testimony of Council for the Earl of Peterborough's having been sworn in order to the Lieutenancy	677
	A Commission from King Charles II. to raise a Company of Horse	678
A.D. 1673.	The Earl of Peterborough's Commission for being Colonel of a Regiment of Foot	680
	A Commission for the Earl of Peterborough to be Extraordinary Ambassador to the Emperor for the Marriage of the Archduchess with the Duke of York	680
	Instructions for Henry Earl of Peterborough going in quality of Ambassador Extraordinary to his Imperial Majesty	681
26 Charles II.	A Commission constituting Henry Earl of Peterborough Lord-Lieutenant of the County of Northampton	683
A.D. 1673.	Instructions for Henry Earl of Peterborough, Ambassador Extraordinary to the Court of Modena	684
	James Duke of York and Albany, Earl of Ulster, &c. Instructions for the Earl of Peterborough in his Extraordinary Embassy touching the marriage of the said Duke with the Princess of Modena	685
	The Earl of Peterborough's Pass from the King, to go Extraordinary Ambassador to Modena	687
A.D. 1674.	An Order for the Earl of Peterborough's being sworn a Privy Councillor	688
A.D. 1674.	The Earl of Peterborough's Commission for being Colonel of a Regiment of Horse	688
30 Charles II.	A Writ summoning the Earl of Peterborough to the Parliament	689
	A Commission constituting Henry Earl of Peterborough Lord Lieutenant of the county of Northampton	689
31 and 32 Charles II.	Two Writs summoning the Earl of Peterborough to Parliament	690
A.D. 1682.	An Order for the Earl of Peterborough's being sworn a Privy Councillor	692
Temp. James II.	Copy of the Oath taken by the Earl of Peterborough, as Groom of the Stole	692
1 James II.	A Writ summoning the Earl of Peterborough to Parliament	692
A.D. 1685.	An order to the Earl of Peterborough for raising the militia of the county of Northampton	694
	An order to the Earl of Peterborough for the seizing of suspected persons	694
A.D. 1685.	The Earl of Peterborough's Commission for being Colonel of a regiment of Horse	695
	The King's Warrant to discharge the Prisoners at Oxford	696
A.D. 1685.	A Patent of High Steward and Chief Bailiff to the Queen's Majesty granted to the Earl of Peterborough	696

ENGRAVINGS.

Arms of Lord Peterborough, surrounded by the Garter		387
Monument of Sir John Mordaunt		524
,, John, 1st Lord Mordaunt		597
,, John, 2nd Lord Mordaunt		604

APPENDIX. 227

	Page in Halstead.
Monument of Lewis, 3rd Lord Mordaunt	626

[NOTE.—The heraldry at the foot of this lord's monument is inaccurately represented in this engraving. The inscription also is incorrectly given, and that at present on the *south* is described as being on the *north* side of the tomb.]

Seal of Halenald Davno	9
„ William, son of Halenald Dano	10
„ Hugh Davno	12
„ Sampson Fortis	447
„ Ralphe, Earl of Chester	451
„ Reginald de Grey	457
„ Robert Mordaunt (17 Edward III. the earliest instance of the arms)	461
„ Alexander Bozonn	462
„ Edmund Mordaunt	465
„ Robert Mordaunt (49 Edward III.)	470
„ Thomas Dardres (49 Edward III.)	471
„ John Le Strange (11 Richard II.)	475
„ Robert Mordaunt (13 Henry IV.)	478
„ John Mordaunt (21 Edward IV.)	493
„ John, 1st Lord Mordaunt	596
„ John, 2nd Lord Mordaunt	603
„ Lewis, 3rd Lord Mordaunt	625
„ Charles Earl of Nottingham, Lord Howard of Effingham (1603)	631
„ Henry, 4th Lord Mordaunt (1608)	640
„ John, 1st Earl of Peterborough (1640)	663

LETTERS.

King Richard III. to John Mordaunt, gent.	494
„ „ to John Mordaunt and William Salisbury	495
King Henry VII. to John Mordaunt, gent.	495
The Prince to John Mordaunt, his Attorney	502
Lady Margaret, Countess of Richmond, the King's mother, to Sir John Mordaunt, knt.	512
King Henry VIII. to John Mordaunt (two)	527
„ „ „	532
„ „ „ (two)	533
„ „ „	536
Cardinal Wolsey to Sir John Mordaunt and Sir William Paulet, the King's counsellors	539
„ „ „ „	540
King Henry VIII. to Sir John Mordaunt and Sir William Paulet, knights (two)	548
„ to Sir John Mordaunt, knt., Master and Surveyor of the king's woods and wood-sales	549

TURVEY.

	Page in Halstead.
King Henry VIII. to Sir John Mordaunt, knt., Master and Surveyor of the King's woods and wood-sales (two)	551
,, to Sir John Mordaunt	552
,, ,, ,, ,,	553
,, to Lord Mordaunt	556
The Queen to Lord Mordaunt (25 Henry VIII.)	557
King Henry VIII. to Lord Mordaunt	559
,, ,,	560
The Queen to Lord Mordaunt	561
King Henry VIII. to Lord Mordaunt	564
,, ,,	565
Lord Mordaunt to his daughter Fettyplace	566
Margaret Fettyplace to her father, the Lord Mordaunt	567
King Henry VIII. to Lord Mordaunt (two)	568
,, ,, (34 Henry VIII.)	570
,, ,,	573
William Lord North to Lord Mordaunt	581
,, ,,	582
The Lords of the Council to Lord Mordaunt, and to Sir John Mordaunt (two)	588
,, ,, to the Sheriff and Justices of the Peace &c., of Beds. and Bucks.	589
Lord Mordaunt to Queen Mary (1553)	589
Queen Mary to Lord Mordaunt	590
,, to Lord Mordaunt, Sir John Mordaunt, Sir Edward Saunders, and Sir John Saint-John, knights	590
,, to Lord Mordaunt	591
Philip and Mary the Queen to Lord Mordaunt	592
Queen Mary to Lord Mordaunt	592
,, to Sir John Mordaunt, knt. and his Lady	600
King Henry VIII. to Sir John Mordaunt the younger	599
Lords of the Council to Lewis Lord Mordaunt (1577)	611
,, ,, ,, (two, dated in 1586 and 1587 respectively)	613
Lord Chancellor Hutton (Hatton) to Lewis, Lord Mordaunt (1587)	614
Queen Elizabeth to Lord Mordaunt (30 Eliz.)	614
King Charles I. to John Earl of Peterborough (1642)	664
Duke of Albemarle to the Earl of Peterborough (1660)	668
James Duke of York to the Earl of Peterborough (two, 1661)	673
King Charles II. (written with his own hand) to the Earl of Peterborough (1681)	674
The Earl of Arlington, Principal Secretary of State, to Henry Earl of Peterborough (1666)	677
The Lords of the Council to Henry Earl of Peterborough (1667)	678
The Earl of Arlington to Henry Earl of Peterborough (1667)	679
King James II. to the Earl of Peterborough (168⅘), commanding his attendance at the Coronation	693

APPENDIX.

Page in
Halstead.

The Duke of Norfolk to the Earl of Peterborough, intimating the King's pleasure that he should bear St. Edward's sceptre at the Coronation - - - - - - 693

The Earl of Sunderland to the Earl of Peterborough (1685), about marching his three troops to Colebrook - - - - - - - - - - 695

The Bishop of Sarum to the Earl of Peterborough (1685), intimating the King's pleasure that he attend at a Chapter of the Order of the Garter - - - - - - 696

Marriage Contracts, Settlements, etc.

10 Henry VII.	Indenture of Marriage between William Mordaunt and Anne Huntington - - -	496
14 Henry VII.	Articles of Marriage between Sir Wistan Brown and Elizabeth Mordaunt - - -	503
17 Henry VII.	Indenture between Henry Strangeways and John Mordaunt for a marriage between Gyles Strangeways *his son* and Jane the daughter of the said John - - - -	507
11 Henry VIII.	Alliance of Mordaunt and Elmes - - - - - - -	533
12 Henry VIII.	Indenture, Elmes and Mordaunt - - - - - - -	537
16 Henry VIII.	Alliance between Mordaunt and Fettyplace - - - - - -	542
16 Henry VIII.	Alliance between Mordaunt and Fisher - - - - - -	545
25 Henry VIII.	Alliance between Mordaunt and More - - - - - -	553
28 Henry VIII.	Alliance between Mordaunt and Danvers - - - - - -	557
29 Henry VIII.	,, ,, - - - - - -	561
33 Henry VIII.	Alliance between Mordaunt and Cheyne - - - - - -	569
37 Henry VIII.	,, ,, - - - - - -	572
2 Edward VI.	Articles of Agreement between the Lord Mordaunt and his son, William Mordaunt, in prospect of his marriage with Agnes Booth - - - - - - -	574
	Articles which Mr. Henry Darcy requireth to be performed for Mr. Lewis Mordaunt, concerning the Marriage of his sister - - - - - - -	607
24 Elizabeth.	Alliance of Mordaunt and Maunsell - - - - - -	611
19 James I.	A Deed of Jointure made for the Countess of Peterborough before marriage - -	643
Temp. Charles II.	The Jointure of the Countess of Peterborough in Turvey - - - -	691

Pedigrees.

Alneto - - - - - - - - - -	4B
Mordaunt of Turvey - - - - - - - - -	42B
Mordaunt of Wyboldston	
Mordaunt of Hempstead and Massingham	
Mordaunt of Oakley — Collateral branches.	
Mordaunt of Caldecot and Hill — All after page	697
Mordaunt of Hardwick	
Mordaunt Lords of Rygate	

[All the pedigrees throughout the work are illustrated with numerous engravings of coats of arms—not altogether to be accepted unchallenged. For instance, the arms for De Alno are given as a lion ramp.

ducally crowned, bearing on the shoulder an escutcheon charged with three (? martlets), whilst by Weston this coat appears to be assigned to the wife of Osbert Mordaunt, of whom he says, *we cannot prove who she was*. Again, the arms of De Olney (according to the latter authority) were Argent, a fesse, the upper part embattled az. betw. three cross-crosslets fitchée, but are represented in *Halstead* as Arg. a fesse (as before) gu. betw. six cross-crosslets fitchée.]

WILLS.

	Page in Halstead.
Sir John Mordaunt, Kt.	519
John, first Lord Mordaunt, dated 1st Aug. 1560	593
John, second Lord Mordaunt, dated 16th Apr. 13 Elizabeth	600
Lewis, third Lord Mordaunt, dated 1st Oct. 1593	619
Henry, fourth Lord Mordaunt, dated 6th Feb. 1608	639

[B].

LETTER TO CARDINAL WOLSEY.

(Cott. MSS. Titus B. I. fo. 326 or 320.)

Plesith it your good grace to be adūtised that where[as] I am informed that Sr Willm̃ Compton is depted this transitorie lyffe whos soule god pardon by whos decesse the dispoosion of his rome for the office of the   tresurer is at the kyngs grace dispoosion and at your^s And at the last voydance thereof I was so bolde to   to your good grace for the same. At whiche tyme your grace shewed me your plesure and if it had not been for   other grete urgent causes movyng your grace, your grace said that yo wold have ben good and graciouse lord to me for the same. And for asmuche as it is now voyde by his Dethe my singler trust is in yor grace that ye wyl be my singler good lord for the same at this p̃sent tyme. And also in lente last past I was at your grace at hampton Courte at whiche tyme I made sute to yor grace for to p̃ferre me to Sr Harry Wyatts rome. And your grace at that tyme showed me that yor plesure was determyned uppon Mastr Brian Tuke. And at that tyme I made further sute to yor good grace that if any suche rome or office shuld hereafter be voide by Dethe or otherwise that then yor grace wold be good lord to me for to have me in yor most gracouse remebrance at whiche tyme I founde yor grace so singler good lord to me in yor most good comfortable words that I shall never forgette your goodnesse showed to me durynge my lyffe. Trustyng now assueredly that

APPENDIX. 231

for asmuche as now this rome is thus voyde that yor grace wyl have me in yor most gracious remeberance whereby your grace shal haue my harte & my prayer. And suche pore suice as may be in me to do yor grace as feythefully and truely as the most humble sūnt that app'teynith or belongith to yor good grace. And for the manyfold benefites that I haue founde in yor good grace and dayly do fynde. And that my singler trust is that I shal fynde at this p̃sent tyme for the said rome of Wiltm and do trust also in yor grace of cotynuance of the same. Where[as] I cannot des[erve] yor goodnesse showed unto me in tyme past nor am not of power ne abilite for to recompense the same—that notw^tstanding as one of yor most humble & true sūnts consideryng yor graciouse goodnesse in sundry wise shewed unto me and on my behalffe, and also havyng in remeberance yor most graciouse & blessed   dispoosion for the   of yor Colege in Oxford. And the goodnesse that thereby shal hereafter ensue & folow for the   of lernyng. And for many other good   that hereafter shal grow, arise, & folow, by reasons of the said good Acte don I shal humbly besech yor grace to accepte & take of me toward the   & augmentacn of that good dede fyve hundred marks to dispose the same to the said Colegge or otherwise as it shal plese yor grace for to order the same whiche money yor grace shal have. And also my true harte & prayer duryng my lyffe. And if it be yor graces plesure that I shal geve to the kyngs grace one hundred pounds for his graciouse goodnesse to be shewed to me therein I shal be content therew^t. And to stand to yor graces plesure how   yor grace to ordyr me for the same. ffurthermore and it lyke yor grace I am also informed that G. Browghton is dep̃ted this transitorie lyff whos soule God pardon. And that by his dethe his too sisters whiche be tendr & yonge of age shuld be his heires as I am informed wherein also I beseche yor grace to be my good & graciouse lord that if yor grace be mynded to departe w^t them or any of them for any money that it myght lyke yor grace that I myght haue the p̃ferrence of them before any other. And if it shal stande as yor graciouse plesure at this my humble sute for to graunte me the same yor graces plesure therein   I shal acordyngly   my selff to geve attendance bffore yor grace or bffore yor most honable Councell for the opteyning of them for my yonger sonnes consideryng that a good parte of theire lands lyeth in the Counte of Bedford wherein I do dwelle and was borne my Selffe and yor grace beyng so singler graciouse lord to me I shal geve unto yor grace too hundred pounds for to have the p̃ferrence of them more than any other man lyvyng shal geve. And where as I have no redie money nor am not of power ne abilitie to pay redie money in hande considering suche grette charge as yor grace do know that I have had in byeing of the heire of S. Ric. ffitzlewes and also for dyvers mariages for my doughters whiche I doute not but that yor grace of yor goodnesse will right well consider the same accordyngē. That notw^tstandyng your grace beyng so plesed I shal geve unto yor grace   or too suche as yor grace shal be plesed w^t whiche shall amounte to suche somes of money as your grace wyl be plesed to take for the same. And for the   of them. And also for Sr Willm. Compton's rome I wold accordyng to my dewtie haue come myselffe for to haue made my humble sute unto yor grace but onely that I dare not p̃sume or be so bold to come to yor grace consideryng this   of   so dyversly beyng   . And yor graces plesure before not   and also at the tyme of   to me of the   I was before in   the kynges grace wood w^tin the fforest of Rokynghm wherein dayly the kyngs grace sufferethe grete losse as yor grace shal hereafter know ffurther the especialls thereof al be it I am sorry for to se it so farre oute of ordyr whiche

me thus rudely & boldely to wryte to yor grace w^t my rude hand my pore mynde & entent for that I dare not come my selff to show it to yor grace humbly besechyng yor grace to accepte & take my assuered sūice that I bere to yow in harte more better than I can expresse the same here in wrytyng. And if it shal stande w^t yor graces plesure that I shal come to yor grace my selff yor graciouse plesure so known at any tyme I shal accordyng to my dewtie repayre to yor grace accordyngly. And for the knowlegge of yor graces plesure my sūnt (Tringham) hereof shal dayly geve his attendance bffore your grace unto the tyme that yor plesure be ffurther known in that behalff. Also most lowly besechyng yor grace for to take [no] displesure to me for this my bolde and playne wrytyng to yor grace and for the expressing of my mynde so rudely to yor grace I have no ffrende to speke to yor grace for me but onely I must trust to your graciouse goodnesse and to do that I myselff for to have yor good and graciouse favo^r to the whiche I do trust assuredly as knoweth my lord who ev^r p̃sve yor most noble grace to his plesure. Wreten the second day of July by the rude hande of yor most humble and lowly sūnt.

I trust yor grace of yor goodnesse wyl burne this Letter.

(Signed)   JOHN MORDAUNT.

In the Cottonian MS. Vespasian F. XIII. Art. 211, fo. 158, is a letter addressed by *John Mordaunt* (Lord Mordaunt) *To the Ryght Worshipfull Thomas Cromwell, Esquer*, concerning a debt of Lord Mordaunt's due to Government.

[C].

ABSTRACT OF INQUISITION TAKEN AT BEDFORD, 30TH SEPTEMBER, 6 ELIZABETH (NUMBER 6), AFTER THE DEATH OF SIR JOHN MORDAUNT, LORD MORDAUNT.

He was seised in fee of the manors of Turvey and Stacheden, with appurtenances in the co. of Bedford, and of the manors of Grenes and Wydowsons alias Wydowsons Hall manor, with appurtenances in Stotfold in the said county, and of the manor of Carlyles in Roxston and Bereford; and of and in 220 messuages, 100 cottages, 100 tofts, 6 water-mills, 3 horse-mills, 20 dove-cotes, 220 gardens, 6,000 acres of land, 450 acres of meadow, 6,000 acres of pasture, 1,000 acres of wood, 40 pounds of rent, 10lbs. pepper, 10lbs. cummin, 100 capons, 100 hens, and 20 geese in Turvey, Stachedon, Carleton, Stevington, Bromham, Wotton, Wotton Pillynge, Bedford, Elnestowe, Stotfold, Eyworthe, Astwyke, Cardyngton, Wylshamstede, West Cotton, East Cotton, Roxton, Bereford, Renhold, Temmysford, Collesden, Charleston a!s Chalton, Kempston, Cranfilde, Holcott, Felmersham, Radwell, Wybyston, Wylden, and Colworthe. Also of and in the advowson of the church of Turvey, and the advowson of the vicarage of Stacheden. Also of a free fishery in the water of Ouse. And in the third part of 10 messuages, 8 cottages, 10 tofts, &c. in Chalton als Chalston, Tuddyngton, Chargrave, and Sondon, with appurtenances in the aforesaid county.[a]

By an Indenture, shown to the Jurors at the taking of the Inquisition, it would seem that a portion of the above-named manors, &c., was settled on Louis Mordaunt for the term of his natural life. And as to the residue of the same to the use of the aforesaid John Lord Mordaunt for the term of his life.

Here follow provisions, impossible to make out clearly, by reason of the obliteration of the document, but relating (*inter alios*) to Lady Ela Mordaunt, deceased, late wife of the said Lord Mordaunt, and cousin and heir of Richard Fitzlewis; and to Joan, Lord Mordaunt's second wife.

It is further recited that estates were settled on the heir-male of Lewis Mordaunt,—remainder to the 2nd, 3rd, 4th, 5th, 6th, 7th, and 8th sons of the then Lord Mordaunt in tail male,—remainder to William Mordaunt, esq. second son of John Lord Mordaunt, for the term of his life,—remainder to Edmund, son of the said William, in tail male,—remainder to the second son of the said William—with provisions (as before) to sons up to the 8th son of the said William,—remainder to George Mordaunt (3rd son of John Mordaunt) for term of his life,—remainder to the several sons of George to the 8th son in tail male,—remainder to the right heirs of the said John Lord Mordaunt. And in default of such heirs, then as to the manor of Turvey, and other premises in Turvey, with appurtenances, to Robert Mordaunt of Hempstede, in tail male,—remainder to the said John Lord Mordaunt in tail male,—remainder to the right heirs of the said Lewis Mordaunt for ever. And in default of male heirs of the said John as to all and singular the premises specified (except the manor of, and other premises in, Turvey) to the said John and his heirs—remainder to the right heirs of Lewis Mordaunt for ever. And further, the Jurors said that long before the date of the aforesaid Indentures the manor of Westhorndon, co. Essex, was of the inheritance of Richard Fitzlewis, Knt. and descended to the said Ela Mordaunt, deceased, late wife of Lord Mordaunt, who was seised of the said manor in fee for two years before the date of the said Indentures, and also that the said Lord Mordaunt within the space of six months after the Feast of St. Andrew the Apostle, next after the date of the Indentures shown to the Jury, had not conveyed or assured the said manor of Westhorndon to Robert Throkmorton, John Cheynie, and Thomas Nicolls, and their heirs, and that each of the said Robert, John, and Thomas lived for the space of seven months next following the said Feast of St. Andrew. And, further, they said that Lewis Mordaunt, in the lifetime of John Lord Mordaunt, deceased, took to wife a certain Elizabeth Darcy, daughter of Arthur Darcy, Knt.; and further, that there was a manor in Stacheden, known as well by the name of Gymces as by that of Stacheden, and another manor in Stacheden, known as well by the name of Bozones as by the name of the manor of Stacheden; and by the aforesaid Indentures, and by an Act of Parliament, 4 Feb., 27 Henry VIII., John Lord Mordaunt, in the brief named, was seised of and in the said manor of Turvey and

[a] Some part of these premises appears to have been vested in Sir Robert Throkmorton, Knt., John Cheynie, Esq., and Thomas Nycolls, gent., probably as Trustees. The parchment containing the Inquisition is much mutilated.

Stacheden, and other premises, in Turvey and Stacheden, for term of his life—remainder to Lewis Mordaunt for term of his life And by virtue of the said premises, after the marriage had and solemnised between the said Lewis and Elizabeth, the said Lewis was seised of and in the manor of Grenes and Wydowsons, als Wydowsons Hall manor, and of Carlyles, and of and in all and singular the premises in Stotfold, Bedford, and Elnestowe aforesaid, &c., parcel of the premises of which John Mordaunt, Knt. (father of the said John in the brief named), at any time of his life was seised in any state in Bereford, Roxston, and Colworthe, co. Bedford, with appurtenances. And after the decease of Lewis, the same to remain to the wife of said Lewis in recompense of parcel of the Jointure of such wife appertaining and belonging. And the aforesaid John Lord Mordaunt, in said brief named, was seised of and in the manor of Rowsberie, als Wotton Pyllynge, co. Bedford, with appurtenances, and of and in the moiety of . . . . Throkmortons, in Roxston, &c., for term of life, with remainder to Lewis for his life, and after his death to any wife of said Lewis who survived him for and in recompense of the whole Jointure of such wife—remainder to the heir-male of Lewis. And further, John Lord Mordaunt, in the said brief named, was seised in fee of and in 3 messuages, 60 acres of land, one acre of meadow, 12 acres of pasture, and 1 acre of wood, &c., lately purchased of John Jeffrey ; and of 2 acres of pasture in Turvey, with appurtenances, lately purchased of William Byllyngton ; and of 1 messuage, 2 acres of land in Turvey, lately purchased of Henry Stevenson ; and also of 40 acres of land and 3 acres of pasture in Carleton, lately purchased of   of 1 messuage, 60 acres of land, 2 acres of meadow, and 2 acres of pasture, in Roxston, lately purchased of William Hunt, gent. ; and of 40 acres of land and 2 acres of meadow in Roxston, lately purchased of George FitzJeffrey, gent. And thus being seised, the said John Lord Mordaunt enfeoffed the aforesaid Thomas Nycolls and a certain Henry Edwards, to the use of John Lord Mordaunt (in the brief named) for life, and after his death to the sole use of Lewis. Remainder to the sole use of the heir-male of the said John Lord Mordaunt—remainder to the right heirs of Lewis for ever. And further, the Jurors found that the aforesaid moiety of the manor of Throckmortons in Roxston was held of the Queen *in capite* by the service of half a fortieth part of a knight's fee. But of whom or in what way the residue of the premises were held the Jurors were wholly ignorant.

The said John Lord Mordaunt in the brief named died 18 August, 4 Eliz. (1562), and the aforesaid John (Lord Mordaunt) was his son and next heir, aged 50 years and upwards. Lewis Mordaunt from the time of the death of the said John Lord Mordaunt received the outgoings and profits of certain premises in the said county ; and John Lord Mordaunt in the brief named was not seised on the day of his death of any other estate or inheritance, or in any other lands, tenements, or hereditaments in the said county.

[D].

Letter from Lewis Mordaunt to the Earl of Sussex.

(MS. Cott. Vesp. F. xii. fo. 173.)

My very good Lord whereas I was once a suter vnto yor L. ffor the office of Deputie Justice in the countie of Bedf. vnder yor L. wch so I Did thinke hadd byne voyde at that tyme by the Death of the Lord cheiffe Justice wch ffell out otherwise then the report was. Yt pleasede yor L. at that tyme to graunt me my request ffor the wch I cannot but give vnto you most heartie thankes, and to rest at yor L. comanndement in any thinge yt pleaseth you to comannde me. My request vnto yor L. nowe is That it would please you to have me nowe in remembrance ffor the same, ffor that he is Departede out of this lyffe this p̃sent Day beinge the xvjth of September, wherfore I thought good to advertise yor L. of the same for that I woulde be verie loth to be p̃vented. I was likewise given to vnderstande by my brother Mr. Edwarde Darcey that yor L. shoulde write vnto me about certaine disorderly huntinge in Tickforde Parke. Yf it were so assuredlie I receivede no letter ffrom yo^u as at my comeinge to London yor L. shall further vnderstande, when I mynde to wayte vppon yo^u and to let you vnderstand of all the matter, Thus beinge bolde of yor L. as of my especiall good L. I leve yo^u to the pleasure of the Almightie. ffrom my house Drayton this xvjth of September 1574.

Yo^r Lo. most assurede to comannde

(Signed)　　Lewes Mordaunt.

To the right honorable his singler good Lord the Eale (*sic*) of Sussex, Lord Chamberlayne of the Quenes Maiesties most honorable housold.

[E].

The inquisition after the death of Lewis Lord Mordaunt, taken at Bedford on the 23rd day of March, in the 44th of Queen Elizabeth, recites that Sir John Lord Mordaunt, the grandfather, had been seised of estates in Collesden, Roxden als' Roxton, Chalsterne, Wiboston, Bereford, and Colmorth, and of view of frank-pledge in Collesden, and of a free fishery in the Ouse, which he purchased of Francis Fitzgefferye; also of the manor of Bereford, &c., and of rents and view of frank-pledge in the same places and in Ronhall, with a several fishery in the Ouse, in Roxton, and Bereford, which he purchased of the said Francis, and of Leonard Fitzgefferye;

also of a moiety of Throgmorton's manor in Roxton, and the whole of its water and river, and the whole of the pasture in Roxton called 'le Ray,' granted by Letters Patent dated June 29, 1 Mary, to the same Sir John Lord Mordaunt, his heirs and assigns for ever. That the same John Lord Mordaunt, by deed 3 & 4 Philip and Mary, vested all his manors, &c., in Roxton, Collesden, Chalsterne, Bereford, Westcotten, and Wilshamstedd, in the hands of trustees, viz., Thomas Denton, William Mordaunte, and George Mordaunte, armigers, and Ewan Quicke, clerk, their heirs and assigns, to his own use during life, remainder to John (Lord) Mordaunt, his son, to the heirs male of Lewis Lord Mordaunt, to the said William and his heirs male, to the said George and his heirs male, to Robert Mordaunt of Hempstedd, in the county of Essex, and his heirs male, to the right heirs of the said George. That John Lord Mordaunt died at Turvey 18th August, 4 Elizabeth, seised of hereditaments in Turvey, which he purchased of a certain John Jefferie; of two acres of pasture with appurtenances in the same, purchased of William Billington; of one messuage, two acres of land with appurtenances, in the same, purchased of Henry Stevenson; of forty acres of land and three acres of pasture, with appurtenances, in Carleton, purchased of Richard Michell; of a messuage, sixty acres of land, two acres of meadow, and two acres of pasture, with appurtenances, in Roxton, purchased of William Hunte, gentleman; of forty acres of land and two acres of meadow, with appurtenances, in the same, purchased of George Fitzgefferie, gentleman; and that he enfeoffed therewith Thomas Nicolls, gentlemen, and Henry Edwardes, to his own use for term of life, remainder to Lewis, Lord Mordaunt, and his heirs male, to the heirs male of John Lord Mordaunt, to the right heirs of Lewis, Lord Mordaunt. That John Raundes, prior of the (lately dissolved) monastery of St. Neot's, in the county of Huntingdon, and the monks of the same place, by one assent and consent, for them, their heirs, successors, &c., by deed dated 20th February, 27th King Henry VIII., under their common seal, conveyed their manor and divers lands, tenements, and hereditaments in Turvey called or known by the name of "le pryorie," otherwise "le monkes manner," in Turvey aforesaid, to John Lord Mordaunt and his heirs and that John Lord Mordaunt, by indenture bearing date 9th July, 5 Queen Elizabeth, gave the same to Lewis Mordaunt. That the latter, on the day of his death, was seised in fee of and in the manors of Carleton and Chellington, in the county of Bedford, with their appurtenances, and of the advowsons of the churches of the same, which he purchased of William Vauxe, Lord Harowden and Henry Vauxe, son and heir apparent of William; of thirty acres of wood, with appurtenances, in Carleton, which he purchased of Thomas Adams; of a certain manor in Stagedon called or known by the name of the manor of Stagedon alias Dilwicke, in Stachedon; of lands, tenements, and hereditaments, and of view of frank-pledge, with appurtenances, in Stachedon, als Stagedon and Turvey, which he purchased of William Cornewallis and Lucy his wife; of a messuage and garden, sixty acres of land, two acres of meadow, sixteen acres of pasture, and three acres of wood, with appurtenances, in Stagdon and Bromham, which he purchased of George Goodfellowe; of a close called "Saunders," and a piece of woodland called "longehedge," also another piece adjacent to the same, two and a half acres of land, and another close called "longe close," lying and being in Carleton, which he purchased of William Hall; of three messuages, &c., in Turvey, late "murcotts," and of all those lands &c. pertaining to the same in

Turvey, which he purchased of Edmund Wallys and Elizabeth his wife; of twenty acres of pasture and two acres of wood, with appurtenances, in Stagedon and Steventon, which he purchased of Robert Hatley, gentleman; of all the lands, &c., in Stagedon, with appurtenances, called or known by the name of "Duxfordes," which he purchased of William Goodfellowe, deceased: of a moiety of one messuage and certain premises, with appurtenances, in Carleton, Chellington, Steventon, and Turvey, which he purchased of George Mordaunt, armiger; and of three closes in Wotton, in the county of Bedford, called or known by the name of "les coppie closes," which he purchased of Thomas Bedells, gentleman. The jurors also found that the same nobleman, at the same time, was seised in demesne as of fee (and Henry, next Lord Mordaunt, as free tenant) of and in the manor of Carmynoes, with appurtenances, and of premises, rents, &c., in Northill als Norrill, Over caldcote, Nether caldcote, Beiston, Ickwell, Sandy, and Begleswade, in the county of Bedford, purchased of George Mordaunt and Cecilia his wife; and that his interest descended to Henry, his son and heir. That the manors of Carleton, Chellington, Stagedon als Dilwicke, Carmynoes, the advowsons of Carleton and Chellington, the premises aforesaid, purchased of William and Lucy Cornewallis, and those purchased of George and Cecilia Mordaunt, were held *in capite* by military service; but of whom or by what service the other lands and premises were held the jurors were ignorant. That the whole was of the clear annual value of one hundred marks. That the said Sir Lewis (late) Lord Mordaunt died on the 16th day of June then last past, and the said Henry (then) Lord Mordaunt was his son and heir, aged thirty-three years and upwards. And the same Lewis held no other manors, lands, or tenements in demesne, nor services in the county of Bedford, on the day of his death.

Among the jurors' signatures to the Inquisition occur the names of David faldo, Robert Carter, and Thomas ffrancklin.

THE OLD RECTORY HOUSE AT TURVEY.
From a Sketch by the Rev. J. W. Burgon, B.D., Fellow of Oriel College, Oxford.

SUPPLEMENTAL ADDITIONS TO THE HISTORY OF TURVEY.

Page 186.—There is an omission in the paragraph beginning "In the year 1786-7." Instead of the statement at the close, "whilst a considerable portion of the estate, &c.," it should have been *first* stated that at the sale of the Peterborough estates in 1786 the second allotment in Turvey, consisting of five farms and including the famous "Tinker" public-house, was purchased by W. Farrer, esq., of Brayfield House, Bucks., and immediately afterwards from him by John Higgins, esq., *senior* (see Higgins Pedigree), who in 1792 built the residence known as Turvey House (see p. 190) now in possession of his grandson.

Page 190.—In the description of Turvey House it would be more correct to state that having been built by John Higgins, esq., senior, it was afterwards twice altered by his successor, the late T. C. Higgins, esq., who besides adding the top storey changed its style into the present Italian exterior.

The eldest surviving member of this branch of the Higgins family is Lieut.-Col. Higgins. He was educated at Rugby, and afterwards entered Trinity College, Oxford, where he took the degree of B.C.L., served the office of Sheriff in 1845, and is a Magistrate and Deputy Lieutenant for Beds. and Bucks. His residence, "Picts Hill," was formerly spelt Pix-hill. (Vide p. 190, note b.)

Page 191.—With reference to the Higgins pedigree it may be mentioned that Thomas Higgins, of Weston Underwood (as appears from the Register of Baptisms there), was the son of Hugh Higgins and Elizabeth his wife.

Page 193.—At the end of the account of the Charities for "bequest" read "bequests": and it should be added that Miss A. M. Higgins made a donation of the first organ introduced into the Church, which was afterwards supplemented by the large and admirable instrument erected at a later period by Mr. C. L. Higgins: she also left by will 1000£ towards the re-building of the Rectory during the Rev. W. B. Russell's curacy.

Page 199.—The patron who presented the Rev. W. B. Russell was T. C. Higgins, esq., and the Rev. G. F. W. Munby was presented by the Trustees of W. F. Higgins, esq.

Page 201.—The Rev. William Breighton Russell, who had been curate of the parish for some years, succeeded the Rev. J. W. Hawksley and resigned, to the great regret of the inhabitants, in 1869.

Page 206.—Paragraph 4, after "the Rev. W. B. Russell" for "a former rector" read "at that time rector."

Page 207.—6th line from foot, for "of Turvey House" read "then residing at Turvey House."

Page 209.—*Dele* Note a.

CARLTON.

Carlentone.—The lands of this parish were formerly much intermixed with Chellington; but under an act of inclosure, in 1801, a distinct boundary was established.[a] The date of the Award is 1806. On the north-west the river Ouse divides this parish from Harrold; on the north-east it is bounded by Chellington; on the south-east by Pavenham; and on the south by Stevington and Turvey.

The dowager Countess Cowper, Miss Trevor of Tingrith, and Crewe Alston, esq., are the principal landowners.

There was no manor here at the time of the great survey, but the lands of Carlton were parcelled out to the Bishop of Baieux,[b] Nigel de Albini,[c] Osbern

---

[a] Acreage, according to the valuation for the Union, 1470A. 2R. 26P.

Amongst the Rev. T. O. Marsh's collections is a note to the effect that in 1809 four acres and two roods in Ovenstead furlong, valued on the inclosure at £4 17s. 8d. per annum, let for one year at £21, to plant potatoes.

[b] *Baieux Fee.*[1] (The land of the Bishop of Baieux.) In the hundred of Wilga, two socmen hold in Carlentone one hide and one virgate of Herbert, son of Ivo, and he of the Bishop. There is land for a plough-team and a-half which are there. Pasture for one plough-team. The whole worth twenty-six shillings and eight pence—when he received it and in the time of King Edward thirty shillings. The same who now hold this land, held and were able to give and sell it. (Domesday, p. 209 b.) This fee was in all probability the origin of part of the Pabenhams' estate here. (Vide pages 114 and 250.)

[c] *Nigel de Albingi Fee.*[2] *Honor of Cainhoe.* (The land of Nigel de Albingi.) In the hundred of Wilge, Chetel holds of Nigel one hide and a third part of one hide in Carlentone. There is land for one plough-team and a-half which are there. And there are three villans and two bordars. Pasture for a plough-team and a-half. Worth twenty shillings—when he received it ten shillings; in the time of King Edward fifteen shillings. Golderon, a man of Leuenot, held this land and could give it to whom he would.

In the same place, Bernardus holds of Nigel one hide and half a virgate. There is land for a plough-team and a-half, and they are there, together with five bordars. There is pasture for one plough-team; and one mill of thirteen shillings and four pence. Worth forty shillings—when he received it twenty shillings;

---

[1] Vide Stagsden, p. 113, and Turvey, p. 170.   [2] Vide Turvey, p. 170.

(piscator),ᵃ and the King's bailiffs and almoners;ᵇ and were afterwards, as was usual, annexed to certain honors.ᶜ

The second of those above-named possessed the most considerable estate, which was divided into two parts, containing together two hides and a third of one hide and half a virgate.

in the time of King Edward thirty shillings. Three socmen held this land and were able to give it to whom they wished. (Domesday, p. 214 b.)

ᵃ *Osbernus piscator Fee*.[1] (The land of Osbernus piscator in Wilge hundred.) In Carlentone the same Osbernus holds of the King one hide and one virgate and a-half. There is land for two plough-teams. In demesne is one plough-land, and two villans have another. There are four bordars. Pasture for two plough-teams. Worth and hath been worth twenty shillings. Goduinus frambolt, a thane of King Edward, held and was able to sell this land. (Domesday, p. 216 b.)

ᵇ The land of the King's bailiffs and almoners. Chelbertus holds in Carlentone, in Wilge hundred, three virgates and a-half. The land is for one plough-team which is there, with two villans, and three bordars. Pasture for one plough-team. Worth ten shillings—when he received it two—(*duas ores*); in the time of King Edward ten shillings. Of this land the same tenant, who was a man of Queen Eddith, held one virgate and was able to give it. The remainder was in the hands of Alli, a thane of King Edward. (Domesday, p. 218 b.)

ᶜ Out of fees above noted, or mentioned under adjoining parishes, arose also the following:—

BEDFORD BARONY LANDS.—Part of Carlton was annexed to the barony of Bedford, at least as early as the reign of Henry III.;[2] and it was at length divided into severalties in the same manner as Stagsden.[3]

Under William de Beauchamp, various proportions of knight's fees in Sharnbrook and Carlton were in the hands of Peter de Loring, Galfridus son of Pagan, William Malherbe, Henry de Sharnebroc, and Robert de Montibus.[2]

In the 7th King Edward the First, John Malherbe, Henry de Sharnebroc, and John de Montibus were the head tenants in Carlton. The first of these held his lands of William de Monchensi, to whose purparty attached view of frank-pledge. The second, holding of John de Pateshulle (under Roger le Strange on the part of Roger de Mowbray), was in possession of a capital messuage, his demesne comprised half a virgate, and the prior of Caldwell is named among his free tenants; Galfridus de Karlton, also one of Henry's tenants, held land under John Malherbe. The portion of John de Montibus was holden of Ralph Paganell (*jur. ux.*), and a Nicholas de Montibus was one of John's tenants.[4]

BOULOGNE HONOR LANDS.—Another fee in this parish was annexed to the honor of Boulogne and passed with Stevington to Baldwin Wake, among whose tenants were Ralph Pirot and Henry de Lega.[5]

CALDWELL PRIORY LANDS.—One virgate of land here, parcel of Bedford barony, was given to this

---

[1] Vide Sharnbrook.
[2] Testa de Nevill, p. 248 b.
[3] Page 115; see also pp. 32, 36 *note* ᵉ.
[4] Rot. Hund.
[5] Rot. Hund.

The family of de Lega or de la Legh appear to have been connected with this parish in the time of King John, *vide* p. 252.

Henry de la Legh, temp. Edward III. was summoned to show whereon he founded his claim to certain rights and privileges in his manor of Carlton.—Abbrev. Placit. p. 52, ro. 1. Placita de quo warranto, ro. 27.

The barony of Cainhoe, of which Nigel de Albini's estate in this parish was afterwards member,[a] appears to have descended uninterruptedly in the male line to John (or, according to some authorities, Robert) De Albini or Daubeny.[b] About the time of Henry III. or Edward I. it was in three coheiresses or their representatives,[c] viz., Isabella, who married firstly William de Hocton or Houton, and secondly Drogo de Pratellis; Johanna, wife of Ceffrey de Beauchamp; and Asceline, wife of Ralph de St. Amand. Johanna died without leaving issue, and consequently her share was divided. From Isabella descended Peter de St. Cruce, Thomas de Norton, Brian Saffrey, John Biddyng,[d] and Roger Dakeny; and from Asceline, the Barons St. Amand,[e] a title which passed eventually through the family of Braybrooke to that of Beauchamp.[f] Some of the lands of the honor of Cainhoe appear to have been sold to John Cheyny, chevalier, in the reign of King Edward III.[g]

The Pirots[h] were tenants in this parish under the Barons of Cainhoe.

[a] Rot. Hund.

[b] Dugdale's *Bar.* vol. i. p. 131. Lipscomb's *Bucks*, vol. i. p. 455.

[c] Testa de Nevill, p. 250b

[d] Also written Giddyng and Budyk.

[e] Placita de quo warranto, temp Edwd. III. Dugd. Bar. vol. i. p. 131. Abbrev. Rot. Orig. 9, 10, and 47 Edw. III. pp. 101, 108, 328. Esc. 36 Edw. III. nu. 42; 47 Edw. III. nu. 73.

[f] For an account of the Barons St. Amand see Burke's *Dormant and Extinct Peerages.* Vide Beauchamp's pedigree under Biddenham.

[g] Abbrev. Rot. Orig. 37 Edw. III. p. 278, ro. 35.

[h] Also spelt Pyrot, Perot, Perrot, &c.

They held Towersey, Bucks, under the family of Albini at least from the reign of Henry II.—Lipscomb, Bucks, vol. i. p. 456.

In this county we find them holding land in Pulloxhill, in the time of King John, which land is

house, in pure alms, by an ancestor of the family of de Sharnebroc, in the time of King Henry III.; in the following reign it was occupied by John Hareng, with his tenants, at an annual rent of twelve pence.[1] John Day and others (for the prior) held a messuage and tenements in Carlton, Chellington, Pavenham, Clapham, and Bedford.[2]

ST. BARTHOLOMEW'S PRIORY LANDS.—Hugh de la More of Carlton, for the prior and canons of St. Bartholomew of "Smythefeld," London, held lands and tenements in Carleton, Beds., and Asserberge, Essex; also in Hendon and Stanmore, Middlesex.[3]

[1] Rot. Hund.

[2] Esc. 22 Edw. IV. nu. 64.

[3] Esc. 32 Edw. III. nu. 78. It is at least remarkable that a John de Carleton was Prior of St. Bartholomew's (elected 1356).

In the 44th and 45th King Henry III. Ralph Pirot had a suit with John de Grey concerning tenements in Carlton and Turvey, when it appears that the former recovered two water-mills, a fishery, and other appurtenances in Carlton.[a] According to the "Testa de Nevill" he held four fees in the counties of Bedford and Bucks, as of the honor of Cainhoe; half under the superiority of Isabella (wife of William de Houton) and half under Ralph de St. Amand.[b] Under Almaric de St. Amand, Ralph Pirot held all the lands in Carlton (in two parts divided), which were parcel of Cainhoe barony. The one part, which Ralph held by the service of a knight's fee, comprised a demesne of one carucate and the site of a water-mill; appendant to the same was a fishery *in common* in the Ouse and the advowson of the church; he had four villans, and this part was occupied by upwards of twelve freeholders, including John de Pabenham, Walter Trailly, and the Prioress of Harwold.[c] The Abbot of St. James', Northampton, Henry de la Leye, and other freeholders occupied the second part of Pirot's estate.[d]

The ancient family of Vaux *of Harrowden*[e] possessed a manor or manors in Carlton and Chellington,[f] at least from the time of Edward IV. They matched with the Lucys and Cheynes, the latter family being descended from

---

mentioned in the succeeding reign as parcel of the honor of Cainhoe.—Abbrev. Placit. p. 95, ro. 5; Testa de Nevill, p. 250b. Land in Radwell Beds, was held of Ralph Pirot by military service.—Abbrev. Placit. 18 Edw. I.

Other feudatories or tenants under the barony of Cainhoe: Hugh de Lacy, seised of a manor in Cainhoe.—Esc. 9 Edw. I. nu. 15. In the reign of King Edward III. Gerard de Braybrok, chevalier, and Edm. de Morteyn of Marston.

Persons bearing this surname were possessed of estates in Cambridgeshire, Essex, Kent, Northants, Oxon, Herts, and Wilts.—Rot. Lit. Claus. 16 John, vol. i. p. 177b; 1 Hen. III. p 325 and p 327; 7 Hen. III. p. 554b. Esc. 36 Hen. III. nu. 37. Abbrev. Placit. 56 Hen. III. p. 180, ro. 3. Testa de Nevill, p. 219. Esc. 33. Edw. I. nu. 100. Abbrev. Placit. 8 Edw. II. p. 320, ro. 10. Esc. 8 Edw II. nu. 7. Inq. ad quod damnum, 9 Edw. II. nu. 136. Rot. Orig. 3 Edw. III. Esc. 3 Edw. III. nu. 49; 4 Edw. III. nu. 31; 11 Edw. III. nu. 35; 44 Edw. III. nu. 52.

[a] Abbrev. Placit. p. 152-3, ro. 15.

[b] Testa de Nevill, p. 250b. A Ralph Pirot gave land to Woburn Abbey.—Placita de quo warranto.

[c] Premises in Carlton—parcel of Harwold Priory—were held, for the prioress, by Sir Gerard Braybrook and others.—Esc. 16 Rich II. nu. 75.

[d] Rot. Hund.

[e] Vide Chellington. See also Lipscomb's *Bucks*, vol. i. p. 271; Bridges's *Northants*, vol. ii. p 103; Clutterbuck's *Herts*, vol. iii. p. 80; Nichols's *Leicestershire*, vol. iii. part ii. p. 1129; *Herald and Genealogist*, vol. iii. p. 515.

[f] Part of the Trailly's estate in these parishes. (See page 249; also under Chellington and Pavenham.)

Thomas Pabenham, mentioned in page 248. William Vaux, armiger, afterwards knighted, presented to Chellington Church before 1462. Sir William married Maud, daughter of Sir Geoffrey Lucy, knt., of Brecknock,[a] by whom he had a son,

Sir William Vaux, knt., (cousin, and one of the heirs of Sir William Lucy, knt.,[b]) who adhered to King Henry VI., and was slain at the battle of Tewkesbury. He was seised of manors in Chellington and Carlton, of the advowson of the church of the former parish, of a moiety of manors in Clapham and Oakley, and of estates in the counties of Warwick, Bucks, Leicester, Cambridge, Berks, and Northampton.[c]

Nicholas Vaux, son and heir of the last-named Sir William, was despoiled of his estates in virtue of an Act of Attainder passed against his father, 1463, and the whole or greater part, including the Carlton and Chellington portion, was granted by King Edward IV. to

Sir Ralph Hastings, knt., esquire of the body to his Majesty and keeper of the lions in the Tower. He was younger brother to William, Lord Hastings, K.G., beheaded in the Tower 13 June, 1483, with whom he was at one time joint Constable of Rockingham Castle.[d] Sir Ralph presented twice to Chellington Church and once to Carlton, and was styled "of Harrowden." He died without male issue, but had seven daughters, Florence, married to Edward Lord Grey de Wilton; Lady Norwich; Isabel, married to Sir John Dyve, knt., of Bromham; Maud, first wife of Sir John Longueville, knt.; Lady Gresley; Lady Elton; and Lady Harcourt.

In the first King Henry VII., the Act of Attainder passed against Sir William Vaux was totally reversed, and his son above-named, then a knight, was restored to all the possessions of which he had been deprived.[e] Sir Nicholas Vaux (who presented several times to this church) was highly distinguished as a statesman and a warrior, and was much in favour with Henry VII. and Henry VIII.; by the latter he was summoned to parliament as Baron Vaux of Harrowden, the 27th of April 1523, but died in May in the fifteenth of that King's reign. Two

---

[a] Harl. 1184, fo. 146; Add. MS. 5523, fo. 68. But compare Baker, Lipscomb, and Clutterbuck.

[b] Clutterbuck's *Herts*, vol. i. pp. 393-5. This family of Lucy possessed (*inter alia*) Potsgrove, Wodecrofte, and "Gledene," in this county; held Dallington in Northamptonshire of the Abbot of Peterborough, and premises in Cublington, Bucks, of the honor of Gloucester.

[c] See the pedigree under Chellington.   [d] Edmondson's *Bar.* vol. ii. p. 93.

[e] Sir Nicholas Vaux was the owner of certain lands and tenements called *Giddyngs*, holden of Sir Thomas Lucy's manor of Carlton.—Carlton Manor Rolls, 8 and 9 Henry VIII.

years later, by an inquisition taken at Cranfield in this county, 28 August, before Richard Rothall, armiger, the escheator, it was found that Nicholas Vaux, knight, Lord Vaux, on the day of his death was seised of manors in Clapham, Oakley, Chellington, Carlton, Bromham, Woodcrofte, and Luton with appurtenances, and that by virtue of a deed of feoffment, bearing date the last day of February, 3 Henry VIII., Sir William Parr, knt., deceased, Thomas Lovell, Robert Mathewe, Roger Gyfford, Edmund Newenham, John Chauncy, and Thomas Aylmer were trustees of the same to certain uses specified. That the manor, lands, and tenements, in Oakley and Clapham were holden of the King as of his honor of Wallingford, and were worth x li. vi s. per annum; the manor and premises in Chellington and Carlton of the King as of the hundred of Willey for a yearly rent of xij d. for all service, and worth by the year x li. xj s.; the tenements and premises in Bromham of Sir John Dyve, knt., and worth iij s.; and the premises in Woodcrofte and Luton of the King by the service of a twenty-fourth part of a knight's fee. That Thomas Vaux was son and heir of the said Lord Vaux, and that in prospect of a marriage intended to be solemnized between the said Thomas Vaux and Elizabeth Cheyne, Lord Vaux entered into an agreement[a] with Lady Anne Cheyne, the mother, whereby the said Thomas and Elizabeth should, in the event of their marriage, have all and singular the premises, &c. in Clapham, Oakley, Chellington, Carlton, and Bromham for the term of their lives, and the longer life of the two. On the 25th April, 15 King Henry VIII. Thomas Vaux

---

[a] At a later period confirmed and settled by Parliament, 27 Hen. VIII. cap. 30. (A.D. 1535–6).

An Acte conc'nyng the assur{a}unce of c'ten Londs to the Lady Elizabeth Vaulx in recompence of her Joynture.

I. Recital of sale of the Manor of Grenes Norton (to the Kings Highnes by Sir Nicholas Vaux Lord Harrowdon) which had been settled on Elizabeth the wife of Sir Thomas Vaux Lord H.

The Kyng's Highnes is contentid that it be enacted by his Royale assent and by thassent of his Lordes sp'uall and temporal and the Comyns in this p'sent parliament assembled and by auctoritie of the same, that the seid Thomas Lorde Harrowdon and the seid Lady Elizabeth nowe his wyfe shall have holde and enjoye to theym and their assignes for t'me of their two lyves and the lenger liver of theym withoute impechement of waste of the seid nowe Lorde Harrowdon (inter alia). The Manours or Lordships of Clopham Okely Carleton Chillyngton and Bromeham with all their Members and appurtenaunces in the Countie of Bed';——which late were the seid Syr Nicholas Vaux Knyght late Lorde Harrowdon in possession rev'sion or use, the remaynder therof after the decesses of the seid nowe Lorde Harrowdon and the seid Lady Elizabeth hys wyfe to William Vaux nowe sonne and heire apparaunte of the seid Thomas Lorde Harrowdon and to the heires males of the bodie of the same William Vaux lawfully begoten; The remaynder for defaute of suche Issue to the heires males of the bodye of the seid Thomas nowe Lorde Harrowdon betweyne hym and the seid Ladye Elizabeth his wyff lawfully begoten, The remaynder therof for default of suche yssue to the heires of the bodye of the seid Thomas Lorde Harrowdon lawfully begoten;

was fourteen years old, and afterwards on arriving at the appointed age he married the said Elizabeth when she was sixteen years of age and upwards. And the Inquisition finds further that Nicholas Lord Vaux made and declared his last will (*inter alia*) in these words :—

Item, I wylle thatt myn executo^{rs} founde amortes in moche harrowden a chauntre of oon p̃ste to syng in the pysshe churche there ⁊ the seyd p̃ste ⁊ his successo^{rs}; to be endowed for their salary w^t londs ⁊ teñts of the yerely value of Eyght Pounds Itm, I bequeyth to my Doughto^r Margarete to her marriage ffyve hundreth Pounds to be payed when she shall come ⁊ be of the age of xv yere; yf she be marryed by the aduyse of myn executo^{rs}; or any of them. Also, I bequeythe to my Doughto^{rs}; Brygett ⁊ Mawde ⁊ euy of them ffyve hundreth Poundes to be payed toward their marriage in lyke mañ So that aswell my seyd Doughto^r Bryget as my seyd Doughto^r Mawde be orderyd in their marryage by myn executo^{rs}; or by oon of them. And yf yt fortune any of my seyd Doughto^{rs}; to be marryed w^towt the assent of myn executo^{rs}; that then all suche bequeste of money to her oonly that so doth marrye shall be voyde. Itm, I wylle that my son Wyllm̃ haue oon Thowsand Pounds ⁊ the same M^l li. to rest in the hands of myn executo^r ĩ tyll londs ⁊ teñts by them may be ffound to be purchesyd to the yerely value of oon hundreth marks clerelye aboue all chargs or ells to purchesse hym a Wyffe that may dyspend Too hundreth marks of inherytūnce by yere ⁊ aboue And I wyll that my Son Strange be payed oon Thowsand Marks Accordyng to the coueñnts of marryage at the daye as they shall growe, so that in no wyse I renne in no fforfeture for lack of payment. And in lyke wise oon other Thowsand Marks to be payed accordyng to the coueñnts of marriage between me ⁊ S. Robt Throgmarton for payment wherof there is ffourty pounds of my londs bounden ⁊ to be forfeyted for the non payment of the same. Itm, I bequeyth to my Son Throgmarton ⁊ to my Doughto^r Kateryne his wyffe oon hundreth pounds. Item, I wyll that my ffeoffeez ⁊ all other psones seased of all my mañs londs ⁊ teñts w^tyn the Realme of Englond ⁊ euy oon of them shall stand ⁊ be seased of all my seyd mañs londs ⁊ teñts ⁊ of euy pcell of them to the vse of this my last wylle ⁊

The remaynder therof further for default of suche issue to the right heires of the said Thomas now Lorde Harrowdon for ever.

II. Bargains and Grants hereafter to be made by Lord Harrowdon shall be void after his Death.

III. Saving of Rights.

IV. All Bargains and Sales made by Lord Harrowdon since the Acknowledgment of a certain Recognisance declared void after his Death.

V. Provyded alwey that this acte nor anythyng therin conteyned shalbe in any wyse hurtfull or p'judycyall unto S Will'm Parre Knyght his executours or assignes, for one annuytie or yerely rent of xl. pounds st'lyng which the seid Syr Will'm claymeth to have yerely goyng out of the seid Lordshipps Mano^{rs} Londs Ten'ts and Hereditaments or any p'cell therof, by reason of a graunte therof made unto the seid Sir Will'm by the seid Thomas Vaulx Knyght now Lorde Harrowdon ; but that the same Sir Will'm and his assignes shall and may have take & r'ceyve the seid annuytie or yerely Rent in lyke man' fourme facyon and condyc'on as yf this acte hadde nev' be hadde or made, anythyng in this acte to the contrary in any wyse notw^tstondyng.—*The Statutes of the Realm*, vol. iii. pp. 579, 580.

Testament. And that my seyd ffeoffeez ⁊ eu̅y of them suffer myn executoᵘˢ; to take levye r̅ceyve all the yssuez ⁊ pfetts of the seyd londs to ⁊ for the pformaunce of thys my last wylle ⁊ Testament.

Thomas, second Lord Vaux, who had married Elizabeth, daughter and heiress of Sir Thomas Cheyne, knt., of Irthlingborough, Pavenham, &c.,ᵃ presented to the livings of Chellington and Farndish. He was succeeded by his only son

William, Lord Vaux, several times convicted of recusancy, and as often imprisoned and fined.

His son and heir apparent, Henry Vaux, joined with his father in selling the said manors of Carlton and Chellington, together with the advowsons of the churches of the same,ᵇ to Lewis, Lord Mordaunt.

Carlton Hall farm, now the property of Lady Cowper (Baroness Lucas in her own right), was acquired by purchase from the Peterborough family.

The Poleysᶜ and Staysmores or Staresmores were feoffees under the Vaux family.

John Poley was possessed of six messuages, three hundred acres of arable land, twenty acres of meadow, twenty acres of wood, and twenty shillings rent with appurtenances in Clapham, Oakley, Biddenham, Turvey, and Carlton, which he conveyed to John Mordaunt, William Gascoign, armiger, and William Cowp in trust to the uses of his will. The premises in Biddenham he held of John Dyve, armiger, for three shillings rent; those in this parish, of Sir Nicholas Vaux, knt., for a rent of five shillings in lieu of all service; lands and tenements in Clapham and Oakley, called "Gilberts, Martens, ffitz Richards, Dollys, hennys, Emmes lands," of John Fitz Jeffery at fourteen shillings and eight pence rent; and the remaining premises in Clapham and Oakley, of Sir Nicholas Vaux, knt., for suit instead of service. His tenements in Biddenham were worth forty shillings; in Clapham and Oakley, fourteen pounds; in Carlton, twenty shillings. John Poley died 20th December, 5 Henry VIII., leaving a son and heir, John Poley, then aged twenty-four years and upwards.ᵈ

An inquisitionᵉ taken at Woburn 4 Oct. 20 Henry VIII. before John ffaldoe, finds that William Staysmore, armiger, who died 10 May in the same year, was seised of manors in Hockliffe and Carlton with appurtenances; and of one messuage, eighty acres of arable land, twelve acres of meadow, ten of pasture, and

---

ᵃ Vide Chellington and Pavenham.
ᵇ Turvey, Appendix [E].   ᶜ Vide Biddenham, p. 8.
ᵈ Inq. p. m. taken at Bedford, 21 Oct. 6 Hen. VIII., before John Mordaunt, armiger. Part 1, nu. 164.
ᵉ Chanc. Inq. p. m. 20 Hen. VIII. nu. 134.

ten of wood in Stagsden and Bromham called Monyshyll. That on the 8th November, 23 Henry VII. the same William enfeoffed with his said estates Walter Leeson, ar., Edmund Ryugeley, gent., and John Hyll, yeoman, in trust to the use of John Staysmore his son and heir-apparent, and Mary, John's wife, and their heirs. After Mary's death, viz., on the 2nd May, 10 Henry VIII. these estates were re-settled on the said John and the heirs of his body, remainder to the said William Staysmore and his heirs. John survived his father, and was upwards of forty at the date of the Inquisition. His manor in Hockliffe, holden of the Prior of St. Peter of Dunstable for two shillings rent, was worth six pounds; the manor in Carlton with its appurtenances was held of Nicholas, Lord Vaux, *as of his manor of Carlton*, and worth four marks; and the other premises, held of Sir Thomas Bedyngfeld, knt., were worth four marks. Two years after the above-recited Inquisition, John Staysmore levied a fine of the manor of Carlton.[a]

The tenement known as Staysmore, occupied at one time by Charles Bithrey, of Fishers,[b] belonged to Mr. Palmer, an American merchant, who sold it to Thomas Battams. The latter pulled down the old house, and near its site erected a new one about the year 1805. Mr. George Battams, the grandson of the said Thomas Battams, sold it, with other lands, to the late Earl de Grey, who was also the owner of Carlton Hall farm.

[a] Indenture of mortgage between Francis Reynolds and Ralphe Lee. This document also contains the following names: Edmund ffetiplace, 1533-4; William Cobb, esq., 1611; Thomas Reynolds, 1611; Thomas Wells, 1665; Vincent Goddard, 1668; Gedeon ffisher, 1668; —— Greatbach, 1678; William Bythrey,[1] 1680; Thomas Brand, 1688; Charles Cutts, 1688.

[b] *Fishers* or *Fishes*, the property (1873-4) of W. Talbot Wallace, esq., possibly derived its name from *Osbernus piscator*.

A respectable family surnamed Fisher formerly resident in this parish are mentioned in an early list of gentry of the county,[2] and their pedigree is preserved in the Harleian collection of MSS., number 1531, fo. 155:—

Thomas Fisher of Worcester=Eliz. Parker.

John Fisher.	Anne Fisher, m. — Thompson.	Wm. Fisher of Hounslow, Dep. Auditor for the north. =Alice, dau. of Anthony Keane, of Wellingborough, Northants.
Wm. Fisher, s.p. 1639. Thos. Fisher, s.p. MS. Marsh.	Gedeon Fisher, of Carlton, Beds. = Anne, dau. of ...Darell.	Jasper Fisher, D.D., rector of Wilden, 1639. = Eliz. dau. of Wm. Sams of Bursted, Essex.	Elizabeth Fisher, wife of Thos. White, of the manor of Caldecutt in co. ——.

[1] In the time of Queen Elizabeth, William Bytheray, Richard Mychell, and William Longworte, were freeholders in this parish.—Lansd. 5, fo. 27.   [2] Lansd. 854.

MANOR OF CARLTON *alias* PABENHAM.—The family of Pabenham, or de Pabenham,[a] whose pedigree will be more appropriately placed under Pavenham (from whence they derived their surname), were possessed of one-fifth part of a knight's fee here *in capite*, and were freeholders under Ralph Pirot as mentioned above. Early in the thirteenth century their estate also comprised manors and lands in Wilden, Pavenham, Hinwick, and Harrold. In Wilden they held as of the honor of Peverel of Dover, in Pavenham and Hinwick of the barony of Beauchamp of Bedford, and in Harrold (under the De Greys) as of the honor of Huntingdon.[b]

John Pabenham, the first of the name on record, was living in the time of King Henry III. He married Alianora, daughter and coheiress of William de St. Remigius, who had part of Wilden for her fortune. His own estate consisted of manors in Carlton, Pavenham, and Hinwick.[c] His demesne here contained three virgates and a-half, and he had an inclosed wood of twenty acres.[d] His grandson,

John Pabenham, senior (son of John), had livery of the whole of St. Remigius's estate in Wilden, as next heir to John Ridell, only child of Agnes the other daughter of William de St. Remigius. He was knight of the shire for the county of Bedford about 1307, and sheriff of Beds. and Bucks. 1314. In the 5th Edward the Second he obtained a grant of free-warren in Hinwick, Harrold, Wilden, and Pavenham; and in the following year had licence to impark his woods, &c., in Wilden; as also in this parish and in Harrold, being within the King's forest.[e] His lands in Harrold, containing five virgates, appear to have been part of his father's possessions; he also had a manor in Farndish and an estate in Huntingdonshire. Sir John was father of John Pabenham, junr., of whom we treat, and, probably, also of Thomas Pabenham who inherited the Farndish, Hinwick, and Harrold portion of the estates, together with part of Pavenham and Wilden. Thomas was moreover possessed of lands, &c., in Northamptonshire.[e]

John Pabenham, junior, who represented the county in parliament, had for his portion manors or lands in Carlton, Wilden, Stanford, Pavenham, Emberton, Corneye, Bissmede, and Olney.[e] By his wife, who was the daughter of James de

[a] Lipscomb's *Bucks*, vol. iv. p. 375; Baker's *Northants*, vol. i. p. 714.
[b] Rot. Hund. Harl. 313, ff. 38b, 48b, 58.
[c] See the pedigree under Pavenham.
[d] Rot. Hund.
[e] Lysons.

la Planch, he had three sons, John the eldest died without leaving issue; James, heir to his brother; and Edward, rector of Wilden. The eldest son,

John Pabenham, chevalier, was found, by Inquisition, to have been seised of the manor of Wilden, and it was also found that his brother James (afterwards knighted) was his next heir.

Sir James Pabenham, knt., was seised of premises in Wilden and Carlton.[a] He married Katherine, daughter of Walter Trailly, sister of John Trailly, and, in her issue, heir or coheir of John's grandson, Reginald Trailly, who possessed an interest in Northill, Ravensden, Wootton, Carlton,[b] Chellington,[b] and Yielden. The issue of this great alliance was an only daughter, who became the wife of Sir William Hugeford, knt.; by some authorities[c] she is said to have borne the same Christian name as her mother, but in legal records she is called Mary and Margery.

Mary, the wife of Sir William Hugeford,[d] was seised of Wilden manor as of the honor of Peverel, of a tenement in Carlton called Pabenham, of De la Hoo manor in Wootton—parcel of Bedford barony, and of two parts of the manor of Ravensden. The two latter were parcel of the Traillys' possessions and were inherited upon the decease of Reginald above-named.

Margery, daughter and heir of William, son of Sir William Hugeford,[e] died seised of the manor and advowson of Wilden, of a toft and premises in Carlton called Pabenham, of two parts of the manors of De la Hoo and Ravensden, and of estates in Cambridgeshire, Salop, and the Marches of Wales.[f]

Alice, described as *the daughter of Margery, the daughter of James, the son of John Pabenham*,[g] was possessed of a manor in Haversham, Bucks. She was married to Sir Thomas Lucy, knt., of Charlecote, in the county of Warwick, who, conjointly with the said Alice his wife, held the manor of Wilden *in capite* by the service of half a knight's fee, and a wood called Carlton Park *in capite* by the service of one-eighth part of a knight's fee.[h] Alice married another husband,

[a] Rot. Orig. 23 Edw. III. ro. 11; Esc. 34 Edw. III. nu. 16.

[b] Afterwards in the Vaux family, *vide ante;* and under Chellington.
The Vaux estate in these two parishes was holden as of the hundred of Willey, whilst the paramouncy of the Pabenham's Carlton property was annexed to the honor of Dover.

[c] Harl. 1100, fo. 10; 1167, fo. 1; 1563 fo. 24.

[d] Esc. 10 Hen. IV. nu. 39.

[e] Dugdale's *History of Warwickshire*, vol. i. p. 504 b, 507.

[f] Esc. 1 Hen. V. nu. 44.

[g] Esc. 36 Hen. VI. nu. 35a. [h] Harl. 34.

Richard Archer,[a] by whom the following estates were enjoyed: the manor and advowson of Wilden, Ravensden alias Traillys manor, Hoo manor in Wootton, Carlton manor called Pabenhams, and lands in Salop.[b]

In the second King Edward IV., which was some nine or ten years before Richard Archer's name occurs in connection with the family estates, William Lucy, armiger, *heir to Alice, late wife of Thomas Lucy*, held the manor and advowson of Wilden of the King by the service of a knight's fee; and likewise the manor of Carlton called Pabenhams, together with a certain wood called Carlton Park, pertaining to the said manor by the service of a fifth part of a knight's fee.[c] This William Lucy was, 2 King Henry VI., upon the death of Elizabeth,[d] widow of Sir John Clinton, knt., found cousin and heir to her; viz., son of Alice Hugeford, daughter of Margerie, daughter of James Pabenham, son of Joan, sister of William, father of William, father to the said Elizabeth.[e]

By an Inquisition[f] taken at Bedford on the 23rd Sept., 8 Henry the Seventh, it was found that Sir William Lucy, knt., died on the third day of the previous month of July, seised of the manor and advowson of Wilden which he held by the service of half a knight's fee; of the manor of Carlton with its appurtenances, holden of the King as of the honor of Dover, by the service of one-fifth part of a knight's fee, the same being worth 30s.; of the manor of Traillys in Ravensden, held of the barony of Bedford, formerly belonging to Sir John Traill, knt.; of four messuages, eighty acres of arable land, six acres of meadow, ten acres of pasture, and 20s. rent, with appurtenances in Bolnhurst, Collesden, " Colworth " (? Colmworth), and Wootton, held of the Abbot of Peterborough; also of one messuage, sixty acres of arable land, six acres of meadow, ten acres of pasture, with appurtenances in Wilden and Ravensden, held of the Abbot of Peterborough and called Abbot's tenement. And that Edmund Lucy, jun., was his son and heir, aged twenty-eight years and upwards.

Another Inquisition,[g] taken at Bedford 5th January, 21st of the same reign, in the presence of Sir John Fisher, knt., Sir John St. John, knt., and Walter Luke

---

[a] Harl. 1100, fo. 10.   [b] Esc. 11 Edw. IV. nu. 39.

[c] MS. in the General Library, Bedford.

[d] According to the pedigree in Lipscomb's *History of Buckinghamshire*, vol. iv. p. 187, this Elizabeth, who was the daughter and eventual heiress of Wm. de la Planch, married four times, viz.: first to Robt. Lord Grey of Rotherfield; secondly, Sir John Clinton; thirdly, Sir John Birmingham; and, fourthly, Sir John Russell.

[e] Dugdale's *History of Warwickshire*, vol. i p. 504 b, 507.

[f] Chanc. Inq. p.m 8 Hen. VII. nu. 89.   [g] Chanc. Inq. p.m. 21 Hen. VII. nu. 29.

DE LA PLANCH, PABENHAM

Arms: LUCY. Gu. semée of cross-crosslets, three luces hauriant ar. HUGEFORD or HUGFORD.[3] An eagle displayed. M[ ]
HAVERSHAM.[3] A fesse between six cross-crosslet[ ]

[Lucy quarters: *Furches, Hugeford, Middleton,* [ ]

Geoffrey de Trailly.[1]

John Trailly of Chellington

William Trailly, presented to Ch[ ]

Sir Walter Trailly, knt.,[2] presented
Feudatory of the hon. of Glou[ ]
Hinwick, &c. (Rot. Hund. an[ ]

James de la Planch.[3]=Maud de Haversham.[4]

Joh. de la Planch, s.p.[4]　　Sir William de la Planch.[5]=Hawise.[4]　　Joan de la Planch.=John Pabenham, jun.,

William de la Planch.[5]=Elizabeth, dau. of Roger Hilary.[4]　　Walter, son of Sir William de Hugeford or Hugford, knt.[5]=... dau. and heir of

Two other daughters.[4]　Elizabeth de la Planch, m. Sir John Clinton, knt., (to whom she was 2nd wife),[12] her heir was found to be William Lucy, the son of Sir Thomas L. and Alice (Hugeford.)[5]　　Sir William Hugeford, knt.[5]=... Pabenham, dau[ ] tenement in [ ]

Sir Thomas Lucy, knt., of Charlecote, co. Warwick.[3][6]=Alice Hugeford;[3][6] m. 2ndly (within 8 weeks after the death of Sir Thomas Lucy) Richard Archer, ar., of ... in Tamworth, co. Warwick. Richard Archer was lord of the manor of *Carlton alias Pabenham.*　　William Hugeford.[6]

1st hus. Seised of Carlton Park.

Margery Hugefor[ ] of a toft and pr[ ]

William Lucy, esq.,[6] lord of=Eleanor, dau. of Reginald, Lord Grey de Ruthyn. (This Lord Grey was seised *int. al.* of manors in Thurleigh
Carlton alias Pabenham.　Brogburgh, Northwode, and Flyte in Bedfordshire.—(Dugd. Bar. i. 716.)

Margaret, dau. of John Brecknock.=Sir William Lucy, knt., of Charlecote,[6] lord of=Alesia Hambury.[10]　Sir Edmund Lucy,=Eleanor, dau. and
　Wilden, Carlton, &c.　　2nd wife.　　2nd husb.　(*Trumpingt*[ ]

Sir Ri[ ]

Edmund Lucy, esq., of Charlecote,[6]=Johanna (*Anna,* Harl. 1167, fo. 1.) dau. of　Humphrey Lucy.　Rose Lucy, m. 1st. John Poultney; 2ndly
lord of Wilden.　Sir Richard Ludlow, knt. Remarried　Richard Lucy.　　John Brasbridge or Braconbridge.
　to Richard Hungerford.

Sir Thomas Lucy, knt., of Charlecote, lord of Carlton, &c., left his estate=Elizabeth, dau. of Sir Richard Empson.=George Catesby, ar. 1st. husb.
at Bickering, Segenhoe, and Ridgmount, co. Beds., to Edmund Lucy,
his second son.[6]　　*a quo* Robert Catesby the conspirator.
　　(Baker's *Northants,* vol. i. p. 245.)

William Lucy, esq.,=Anne, dau. of Richard Farmer of London.　Sister to Lady Mordaunt　Edmund Lu[ ]
of Charlecote.[6]　　and to Sir John Farmer or Fermor, who married Maud, dau. of
　　Sir Nicholas (Lord) Vaux [9]

Sir Thomas Lucy, knt., of Charlecote;[6] (the *Justice Shallow* of Shakspeare.)=Joyce, dau. and heir of Sir Thomas Acton, k[ ]

a quo Lucy of Charlecote.
See Dugdale's *History of Warwickshire,* Burke's *Landed Gentry, &c.*

---

[1] Domesday.　　[2] Lincoln Register.
[4] Lipscomb's *Buckinghamshire,* vol. iv. p. 187; Nichols's *Leicestershire,* vol. iv. p. 102; Gage's
[5] Dugdale's *Warwickshire,* vol. i. p. 504 *b*.　　[6] *Ibid.* and pp 505, 507.
[8] Harl. 1563, fo. 24.　　[9] Harl. 890, fo. 4.
[11] Inq. taken at Bedford 17 February, 2 Henry VIII.　Harl. 1100 fo. 10.　Compare Dyve's Pedig[ ]
On the 2nd November (the year not mentioned) a warrant issued for certain rents, &c., to be
appoints to seize for his use all the Castles, Lordships, &c., in Beds. and Bucks., which belo[ ]
William Norreys, Sir William Stonere, Sir Thomas St. Leidger, Sir Richard Enderby of [ ]
(Amand), knts., Walter Hungerford and John Cheney, esqs.—Harl. 433, ff. 121, 124.
[12] Dugdale's *Baronage,* i. 529.

William Lucy of Elstow, presented twice to the church of C[ ]
Exchequer Record.　Concerning William Lucy, esq., to sh[ ]

RAILLY, HUGEFORD, AND LUCY.

[Between p. 250 and 251

ETON.³ A buck's head cabossed. PABENHAM.³ Barry of six, on a bend three mullets. DE LA PLANCH.³ Billettée, a lion rampant.
TRAILLY.³ A cross engrailed between four martlets.

nham, De la Planch, Haversham, Trailly, Acton, &c.]

sc. 41 Hen. III)

gton Rectory, temp. Hen. III.—Edw. I.²

Chellington Rectory, temp. Edw I.²
t in Biddenham, Turvey, Chellington,
brev. Placit. 15 Edw. I.)

'. of Pavenham, Wilden, Carlton, &c.⁷

illiam Midleton of Midleton, Salop.³ — Sir James Pabenham of Wilden and Carlton.=Katherine Trailly.³ — John Trailly.³ ... =Elizabeth.

id heir. Seised (int. al.) of a — Sir John Trailly, knt.³ Attorney-General of England; in conjunction=Johanna, dau. of Sir Thomas Aylesbury,
ton, called Pabenham.   with Nicholas Westerdale presented to the ch. of Chellington,   knt., in conjunction with other persons
                             temp. Edw. III.—Rich. II.² Seised of manors in Northill,   presented to the ch. of Carlton, temp.
                             Wottonhoo, Yielden, Chellington and Carlton; of the advowson   Hen. IV.²
                             of Northill, and of Lands, &c. in Ravensden, and in Cambridge-
                             shire and Northants. (Esc. 1 Hen. IV. nu. 42.)

au. and heir.⁶ Seised (int. al.) — Reginald Trailly, esq., ob. s.p.³ Seised of the manor and advowson of Northill, of
es in Carlton called Pabenham.   manors in Ravensden, Wottonhoo, Carlton, Yielden, Chellington; and of lands in
dington, Harrold, Wrest,   Cambridgeshire. (Esc. 3 Hen. IV. nu. 37.)

r of Walter Throgmorton. Richard Lucy.   Elizabeth.   Agnes, m. .... Holdenby, and had a dau. and heir, Elizabeth Holdenby,
Harl. 1167, fol. 110.)   m. to Henry Hutton.⁸
=
d Enderby, knt., 1st husb.¹⁰ ¹¹.
                          John Enderby.¹¹= ...
Edward Lucy.
William Lucy.   Alianora Enderby, heir to her grandmother, aged 9 years, 2 Hen. VIII. (The manors of Thernecot and Beston held
Mary Lucy.   to the use of Alianore Lucy for life,—remainder to John Enderby, of Edworth and Stratton, and his heirs.)¹¹

       Edmund Lucy.   Radigunda Lucy.
                          Anne Lucy, who had a life interest in Wilden, m. .... Lee, or Leigh of Leigh, and had a dau., Elinor Leigh, m. to
                              Henry Mackwilliams.⁸

       Thomas Lucy.   Anne (*Agnes*, Harl. 1167, fo. 1) m. Thomas Harbert.¹⁰
                          Radigunda, m. .... Betts of co. Southampton.⁸ ¹⁰
                          Barbara, m. Richard Tracey of co. Gloucester.¹⁰

   Thomas Lucy.   Elizabeth, m. William Fuller.¹⁰
   Edward Lucy, m. .... dau. of West of Yorkshire.¹⁰   Mary, m. Christopher Halles.¹⁰
   Timothy Lucy, m. and had a son Thomas Lucy, who   Jane, m. George Verney, son of Sir Richard Verney.⁸ ¹⁰
       m. .... Boughton.⁹   Martha.
   William Lucy.   Jocosa.
   Richard Lucy.

³ Harl. 1163.
lk; Wright's *Essex* (under Theydon Boys).
           ⁷ *Vide* Pavenham.
           ¹⁰ Harl. 1167, fo. 1 and 110.
nder Bromham.
to Thomas Fowler, the King's full trusty Squire, Gentleman Hussher of his Chamber, whom the King
to his Rebel Traitors Henry Stafford late Duke of Buckingham, Thomas late Marquis of Dorset, Sir
m, Sir John Done, Sir Thomas de la Mere, Sir Roger Toketts, Sir Richard Beauchamp de St. Emaint

gton. temp. Henry VI. Edw. IV. (Lincoln Register.)

—the King's Justices finds that Edmund Lucy, armiger, died on the feast of St. Andrew the Apostle in the 11th year of the same King's reign. Edmund was seised of the manor and advowson of Wilden, and he conveyed an interest in the same to Trustees for the benefit of his daughter Anne during her lifetime. Thomas Lucy was his son and heir aged nine years.

From the Carlton-manor Court Rolls we learn that Sir Thomas Lucy, knt., held his court here on the 14th June, 8 King Henry VIII. and again on the 18th July in the following year; he was seised of part of the Traillys' inheritance and of the reversion of Wilden. Sir Thomas married Elizabeth,[a] sister of Thomas and John Empson, widow of George Catesby, armiger. In his Will he names his sons, Thomas and Edmund, and his uncle, Humphrey, and appoints as executors, Elizabeth his wife and John Cole, clerk. This manor he held in the same way as his grandfather Sir William had done, but it had increased to 40s. value; Wootton-hoo was held by him under Peterborough Abbey; the manor of Wilden of the honor of Peverel by the service of half a knight's fee; the manor of Ravensden, and Abbot's tenement in Wilden and Ravensden, were held as in the time of his grandfather. Sir Thomas Lucy had moreover an interest in the manor of Sharpenhoe, and certain premises in Sharpenhoe, Bekeryng, Segenhoe, and Ridgmont, subordinate to his kinsman, the Earl of Kent. He died 4th Sept. 16 or 17 Henry the Eighth, at which time William, his son and heir, was fifteen years old and upwards.[b]

On or about 8th December, 36 Queen Elizabeth, Thomas Adams conveyed the manor of *Carlton alias Pavenham*[c] to William Goddard, armiger,[d] whose son and heir Vincent Goddard was found, on Inquisition taken at Bedford 6th June, 13 James I., to be a lunatic. In this instrument William Goddard's estate is set forth. It comprised the said manor with its rights, members, and appurtenances in Carlton, Pavenham, Chellington, and Turvey, also four messuages, one barn, two gardens, two hundred acres of arable land, twelve acres of meadow,

---

[a] Daughter of Sir Richard Empson, of Easton Neston. From her descended two notorious persons, viz., Robert Catesby, the conspirator, by her first husband; and, by her second husband, Sir Thomas Lucy, who built the present manor-house at Charlecote near Stratford-on-Avon, whom the poet has satirized under the character of *Justice Shallow*.

[b] Escheator's Inq. Bedford and Bucks, 16-17 Henry VIII. memb. 3.

[c] MS. Cooper.

[d] Arms of Goddard or Godard: Quarterly, 1 and 4, A chev. vair betw. three crescents; 2 and 3, Az. a fess lozengy betw. three partridge's heads erased or.—Harl. 4600, fo. 85.

Goddard of Carleton in a List of Gentry of the county.—Lansd. 854. See also Nichols's *Leicestershire*, vol. iii. p. 170.

forty acres of pasture, four acres of wood, 5s. rent, two capons, and appurtenances in the said four parishes, all of which (holden of the King by military service, and worth seven pounds) were purchased of Thomas Adams; a manor in Felmersham, and one hundred and ten acres of arable, eighteen of meadow, and six of pasture, with appurtenances in Felmersham, holden of the King as of his hundred of Willey for suit of court and 6s. 8d. rent, and worth five pounds, purchased of John Harvye, armiger; and two messuages, two acres of meadow, and two of pasture, with appurtenances in Carlton and Chellington, holden of the King as of his hundred of Willey for suit of court and 1d. rent, and worth ten shillings, purchased of William Hall, gentleman. By indenture bearing date 1st July, 43 Elizabeth, the manor and premises purchased of Adams were settled on Vincent Goddard and Edith his wife, and their heirs, remainder to the right heirs of William Goddard; the manor in Felmersham and premises purchased of Harvye and Hall, to the use of the said William Goddard during the term of his natural life, and afterwards to the use of Johanna, the wife of the said William for life, remainder to Vincent in tail male, remainder to the right heirs of William Goddard. Johanna Goddard died here in her husband's lifetime, and Vincent survived his father and became possessed of the whole of the family estate. He married Edith, daughter of Nicholas Pawlett, armiger, of Mynty, in the county of Gloucester, and had a son and heir, William Goddard, jun., aged twelve years seven months and six days at the date of the Inquisition.

On or about 4th August, 2 Queen Anne, the manor or reputed manor of *Carlton alias Pavenham* was sold by the Goddard family to William Steph, who about 1st September, 1714, for the sum of £154, sold it to William Weald, and Mr. Weald, the Coroner, to Sir Rowland Alston, Bart., of Odell.[a]

---

[a] MS. Cooper.

Advowson and Rectory.

This advowson was appendant to the Cainhoe barony lands of Carlton.[a]

In the time of King John it appears that Gerinus de Lega had the right of presentation to this church.[b] It was afterwards in the Pirots. The advowson, at a later period, attended the Traillys' estate, and subsequently that of the Vaux's. By the last-named family it was sold, with the advowson of Chellington, to the Mordaunts. In 1605 Lord Mordaunt was patron of both livings, and Bernardge Turnor in 1683.[c] Early in the last century both advowsons became the property of Lord Trevor. By Act of Parliament, 1769, this rectory was consolidated with that of Chellington, since which time the advowson of the united benefices has passed with the Bromham estate.

About the year 1345 this church was rated at seven marks on the testimony of John Heryng, John Cudding, Stephen Abbot, John of the More, John Fitz John, clerk, and John de Rislee, all of this parish.[d] Its value in the King's books is £15 6s. 8d. This rectory, as stated above, was united to that of Chellington in 1769, and in 1804-5 the tithes were commuted for land and money payments.[e]

RECTORY.

The Rectory-house, of stone, was built, during the incumbency of Mr. Ellman, on the site of the old one.

[a] Rot. Hund.   [b] Abbrev. Placit. p 52.   [c] Lincoln Register.
[d] Nonar. Inquis. p. 19.   [e] Lewis.

RECTORS.[a]

		Patrons.
1258—1279	Thos. Pyrot, subdeacon. By death of last.	Sir Ralph Pyrot, knt.
1280—1289	Richard de . . ., subdeacon. By res. of last.	,,
1290—1299	Gilbert de Pouly. Succeeded by Reginald de St. Ebys	Prior and Canons of St. ——
1398—1404	John Chyld John Gevelden, Pbr. By death of last. Also rect. of Chellington.	Johanna, late the wife of Sir John Traylly, knt., daughter of Sir Thos. Aylesbury, knt., John Goldyngton, William Bosom, Joh. Hyne, rect. of Chellington, and Joh. Morteyn.
1456—1470	John Sumter John Smyth. By death of last. John Dee. By death of last.	John Chapman, of Western Underwode, Bucks. Ralph Hastings.
94	Thomas . . .	Nicholas Vaux.
1514—1520	John Sherard	Sir Nicholas Vause, Knt.
1521—1546	William Lane. By res. of last. Thomas Poley. By death of last.	Nicholas Vaux. (Lord Harrowden.) Joh. Mordant of Turvey, and C. . . . Mody of Pavenham.
15—	Thomas Wells. Also rect. of Chellington. Died 5 Aug. 1642.[b]	
1642	Richard Pargiter	
1657, May 1	Thomas Greatbach. Bur. 19 Jan. 1683.	
1683	Joseph Chaderton. By death of last. Also rect. of Chellington. Bur. 30 Apr. 1720.	
1720, June 25	Benjamin Rogers.[b] By death of last.	Lord Trevor.

Rectors of *Carlton cum Chellington* since the livings were consolidated by Act of Parliament, 1769.

William Hooper, M.A.,[c] appointed rector of Chellington in May 1769, on cession of Samuel Rogers; became incumbent of *Carlton cum Chellington* after the death of Benjamin Rogers. — Lord Trevor.

---

[a] Lib. Instit. apud Lincoln.　　　[b] Buried at Carlton.
[c] Buried at Chellington on Sunday, 16 Nov. 1828.
Died, 9th Nov. 1828, at Harpur Place, Bedford, Rev. W Hooper, M.A., in the 87th year of his age; for upwards of sixty years rector of Chellington, and upwards of fifty-seven years rector of Carlton. He

CARLTON.

	Rectors of *Carlton cum Chellington*.	Patrons.
1828—9	Henry John Ellman. By death of last. Died 3 Feb. 1862.	
1862	William Sweet Escott, M.A., formerly Fellow of New. Coll. Oxon. By death of last.	Trustees.

Thomas Wells, rector of this parish and of Chellington, is remarkable as having lived to the great age of "about a hundred," to quote the words of his inscription in the chancel.

The Rev. Benjamin Rogers, M.A., of Sidney College, Cambridge, a native of Bedford, born Oct. 2, 1686, began life under very straitened circumstances, and was for some years second master of the Free Grammar School, Bedford, to which he was appointed by New College, Oxford. He had been educated at the same school, having first attended it March 30, 1693, and was admitted at Sidney College July 5, 1702; ordained a deacon at Buckden, and priest at London, 1712. He wrote the long Latin inscription on the tomb of his friend Nicholas Aspinal, A.M., head master of the said school, who died 1727, and was buried in St. Peter's Churchyard, Bedford. In 1712 he was presented by Thomas Lord Trevor to the vicarage of Stagsden, which he resigned in 1720, on his appointment to this living. He died here 12th Sept. 1771, in the eighty-sixth year of his age, having been rector of the parish for upwards of fifty years. Mr. Rogers kept a diary[a] of remarkable circumstances, &c., which furnished particulars for this notice. One of his sons, the Rev. Samuel Rogers, several years rector of Chellington, of whom a brief memoir will be found under the account of that parish, has sometimes been mistakenly identified with the poet of the same name.

The church is said to be dedicated to St. Mary; but the feast is on the Sunday after St. Bartholomew.

There was, a few years ago, a design for pulling down this church and that of Chellington and building one between them; happily the idea has been abandoned.

The south aisle of this church has two Decorated windows—one facing south and the other east, also a small lancet in the south wall westward of the porch. The north aisle is lighted by two Decorated three-light windows and by a western lancet; both aisles have Decorated doors.

The north and south elevations of the clerestory exactly correspond.

was educated at the Charter House, and Ch. Ch. Oxon., and was for many years a useful magistrate for the county of Bedford. Add. MS. 21,067, fo. 154; Gent. Mag., April, 1829.

[a] In possession of Mr. Walton.

The belfry stage of the tower is Perpendicular and contains four uniform windows. Its substructure exhibits two small windows[*] and other traces of Saxon or early Norman work. A lancet, a pointed window of two lights, and a plain door of Domestic type have been inserted in the west front.

The chancel also contains some very ancient masonry, particularly on the north side, where may be seen the remains of a semicircular-headed window[*] and "herring-bone work" below it. Besides the windows on the south and east, shown in the engraving, it has on the north a large modern square-headed wooden window of three lights, a single light opposite to the one on the south and corresponding in character, and a pointed two-light window placed above a small door, the latter being similar to the west door.

On either side the nave are three Early-English or early Decorated arches of the character so common in this district; those on the south side are supported on octagonal piers, those on the north on two clustered of four round shafts and one small octagonal pier; the eastern arch on the north side of the nave does not extend to the east wall, but in the space thus formed a portion of another arch is inserted, forming a curious arrangement. The imposts at the ends of the arcades are, so to speak, counterchanged. The font is said to be Transition-Norman.

At the west end of the south aisle is an original fire-place and chimney of the fourteenth century.

There are some good open seats in the church.

The chancel-screen, though mutilated, is *in situ*, and there are remains of a staircase on the south side. The chancel-arch, like that of Stagsden, springs from the side walls. Within the rails is a trefoiled piscina with an ogee arch; and there is a square opening opposite. On the south side of the chancel is a closed-up pointed archway. This formerly communicated with a chapel the site of which may still be traced.

BELLS.

1st. Bell. D.
    Praise the Lord. 1602.
3rd. Bell. B.
    × Sanctæ Marthæ.

2nd. Bell. C sharp. (Re-cast 1868.)
    Chandler made me. 1659.
4th. Bell. A.
    In multis annis resonet campana Johannes.

---

[*] Discovered 1871-2.

CARLTON CHURCH

CARLTON.

FONT.

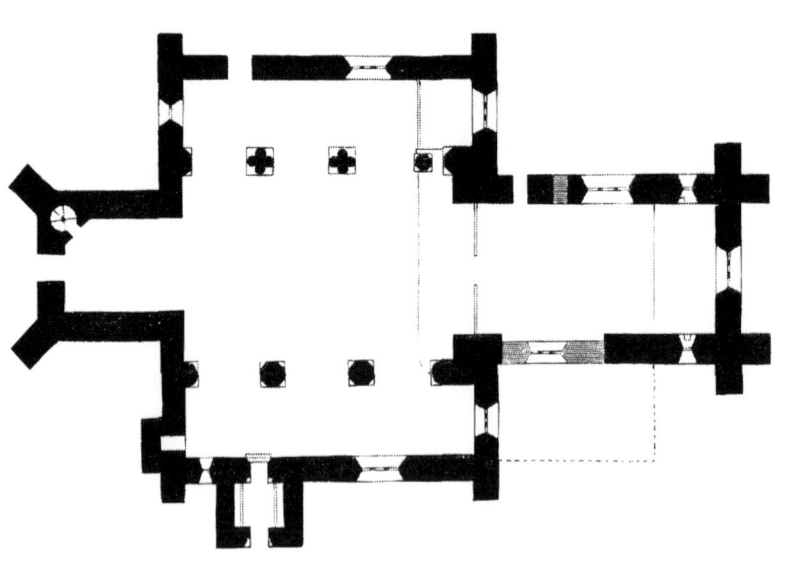

GROUND PLAN OF CHURCH.

Inscriptions.

Chancel.

A small brass against the south wall bears the following:—

> JOANE GODDARD.
> HERE LYETH HIR CORPS ENTOMBED WHICH WAS EVER
> FROM INFANCIE TO AGE A DYING LYVER;
> HER BODIE HERE DOTH LYE, NOE MASSIE STONE
> ENTOMBES HIR SOVLE, HIR SOVLE IS GODWARD GONE.
> WHO GODWARD LIVES WITH GOD SHALL LIVE AND REST,
> THEN IS HIR SOVLE ENTOMBD IN ABRAMS BREST.
> 1610.
> Then let not man defer to ye last howr;
> Repentance is of God, not in man's powre.

Flat stones:—

Here Lies Mr. Tho. Wells who Lived Parson of Carlton and Chellington About Threescore and Ten Years, and Died Aug. 5, 1642, Aged About A Hundred.

Thomas Great Bach, gent., of London, April 23, 166—, aged 64.[a]

John and Thomas, sons of Thomas Great Bach, rector of Carlton, and Mary his wife. The former buried here Dec. 12, 1672; the latter Dec. 20, 1675, aged 16.[a]

—— Bithrey, 1770.

Underneath lieth ye Body of Jane, wife of Benj. Rogers, Rect^r of this Parish, by whom he had Issue 6 Sons and 5 Daughters, of which 4 died in Infancy, 2, viz. Mary & Paul, at Bedford, & are buried in St. Paul's Chyard, & 2 here, viz. Jane & another Paul, & lie under this Stone, ye rest survivd her. She died Augst ye 25th, 1742, in ye 53rd year of her Age.

Underneath this stone is deposited the Mortal part of ye Revd Benjn Rogers, 50 years Rector of this Parish. Whose extensive Learning, Unaffected Piety, and Strict Integrity, Deservedly gained him ye Admiration, Esteem, and Love of all who knew him. He changed this life for a Better one, The 12° Day of Septr. in ye year of Redemption 1771, Aged 85 years. To whose memory this stone is Inscribed as a token of his Duty by his son, John Rogers.

To the Memory of the Revd H. J. Ellman, who was Rector of the Parishes of Carlton and Chellington 34 years. Died Feb. 3rd, 1862. Aged 62 years.

Names in the churchyard:

Battams, Lord, Eady, Bodington, Bond, Walenger, Walton, Rogers (John, gent., 1787), Palmer, King, Brown, Lett, Eyles, Ibbott, Skevington, Wright, Faulkner, Bithrey (gent., 1787), Hannah, Steff, Coopper, Covington, Gilpin, Horn.

The churchyard also contains the base of a cross and two flat coffin-slabs with crosses.

[a] Original in Latin, *imperfect*.

CARLTON.

REGISTER.

1554 Aug. 13.	Baptized,	Rosa, daughter of James Butcher. (Earliest entry.)
1569 Aug.	———	F . . . Harrington, daughter of Sir William Clerke.
1579 Sept.	Married,	William Goddard, gent., and Joan Vaux.
1580	Baptized,	Richard, son of William Goddard, gent.
1581 Sept. 8.	———	Parees, daughter of William Goddard.
1584 May 4.	———	. . . . . Goddard.
1585 July 2.	———	Robert, son of William Goddard.
1586 Feb. 8.	Buried,	Humfrey, son of Edmund Mordant, gent.
1587 May 1.	Baptized,	John, son of William Goddard, gent.
1596 Jan. 30.	———	John, son of Laurence Percy.
1604 Feb. 20.	Buried,	Vincent, son of Vincent Goddard.
—— Sept. 24.	Married,	John Marshall and . . . . . Goddard.[a]
1605 June 3.	Baptized,	Thomas, son of Vincent Goddard.
1607 April 9.	Buried,	Thomas, son of Vincent Goddard.
1610 Feb. 24.	———	Johanna, wife of William Goddard, gent.
1612		(An entry relating to Goddard.)
1613 June 17.	Baptized,	Barnardishton, daughter of William Fish, ar.
1614 April 0.	Buried,	William Goddard, gent.
1630	———	Humphrey Goddard.
1633	Baptized,	Johanna, daughter of William Goddard.
1657 Jan. 15.	Buried,	Henry Manning, gent.
1659 March 24.	———	William, son of Vincent Goddard.
1660 April 26.	Baptized,	Thomas, son of Thomas Great-Bach, rector of Carlton. (Born March 31.)
1665 April 23.	Buried,	Thomas Great-Bach, gent., of London.
1666 July 19.	Baptized,	John Bithrey, son of John and Elizabeth Goddard.
—— Nov. 3.	Buried,	James, son of William Goddard.
1668 July 31.	———	Malcolm Ferris, gent.
1670 Sept. 16.	———	Edith, wife of Vincent Goddard.
1672 Dec. 19.	———	Maria, daughter of Thomas Great-Bach, rector of Carlton.
1675 Dec. 20.	———	Thomas, son of Thomas Great-Bach, rector of Carlton.
1676 April 22.	Baptized,	Francisca, daughter of John Alston.
—— Aug. 8.	Buried,	Elizabeth, daughter of James Goddard.
1683 Jan. 17.	———	Thomas Great-Bach, rector of Carlton.
1685 Nov. 23.	Married,	Thomas Boddington and Ann Great-Bach.
1693 Mar. 31.	Baptized,	Joseph, son of Joseph Chaderton, rector. (Born March 15.)
1694 Aug. 31.	Baptized,	Mary, daughter of Joseph Chaderton, rector, and Elizabeth his wife. (Buried, Sept. 15.)
1695	Married,	Francis Bletsoe and Judith Bithrey.

---

[a] William Godard of Carlton, c. 1600 ?
Verney=John Marshall.   Vis. Hunt. (Camden Soc.). p. 34.

1698 Nov. 30.	Buried,	Vincent Goddard, gent.	
1702 Dec. 14.	——	William Boteler, esquire.	
1706 May 1.	——	John Atkins, esquire.	
—— May 29.		Mary De-Barr, granddaughter to Widow Atkins.	
1720 April 30.	Buried,	Mr. Joseph Chaderton, rector of this parish and Chellington.	
1721 April 4.	Baptized,	Mary, daughter of Benjamin Rogers, rector of this parish, and Jane his wife.	
—— Sept. 7.	Buried,	Judith, wife of Francis Bletsoe of Harold.	
1722 Aug. 17 & 20.		Jane, daughter of Benjamin Rogers, rector of Carlton, and Jane his wife, baptized privately and publicly.	
1723 Nov. 25.	Baptized,	Jane, daughter of Benjamin Rogers, rector, and Jane his wife.	
1727 June 15.	——	Paul, son of Benjamin Rogers and Jane. (Buried June 16.)	
1728 Aug. 9.	Buried,	Mrs. Eliz. Chaderton, widow of Joseph Chaderton, rector.	
—— Oct. 7.	Baptized,	John, son of Benjamin Rogers and Jane his wife.	
1730 Nov. 3.	Buried,	John Melson (Jockey).	
1740 Oct. 16.	Married,	Rev. Mr. Oliver St. John Cooper, rector of Tilbrooke, and Mss Judith Orlebar of this parish, spinster. (By licence.)	
1742 Aug. 27.	Buried,	Jane, wife of Benjamin Rogers, rector of this parish.	
1744 Mar. 4.	Married,	The Rev. Mr. Sawyer Smith and Mss Diana Orlebar. (By licence.)	
—— Mar. 7.	——	John Marsh, of the parish of St. Paul, Bedford, attorney-at-law, and Mss Ursula Orlebar of this parish. (By licence.)	
1771 Sept. 15.	Buried,	Rev. Mr. Ben. Rogers, late rector of this parish.	
1826 Aug. 19.	——	Thomas Johnson, aged 92.	
—— Dec. 17.	——	John Whiting, aged 90. (Bedridden 14 years.)	
1828 May 18.	——	Mary Maxy, aged 90 years.	

A family surnamed Stokes, of Carlton, bore for arms : A bend between six pick-axes.—Harl. 1531.

"Jeromie Byrte of Carleton, Inholder," left by will, dated 20 October, 1599, proved 22 May, 1600, "to every poore Cotager of Carleton vj d. Item to the longe bridge soe muche as shall repayre & make good the broken Arche that hath the hole in yt. Item to my Mother lands in Marston, after to Edward Byrte, my son." Witness, Thos. Wells.

On Sunday morning, 7th Jan. 1798, a violent hurricane blew down an oak which was planted here by Moses Aaron of Sharnbrook circa 1698; it measured four yards and a-half just above ground. It stood by a pond and was not very firmly planted.[a]

In the village is a parochial school for the children of Carlton and Chellington. Also a large place of worship for Particular Baptists;[b] it bears date 1760, and has a burial-ground adjoining.

Assessed property (1815), £1,497. Poor-rates in 1837, £37.

[a] MS. Marsh.

[b] Enlarged shortly before 1861. Anti-pædobaptist meeting.—One existed here between 1717 and 1729. It is mentioned in a list drawn up at that period by Dr. John Evans and preserved in Dr. Williams's Library—printed in T. S. James's *History of the Litigation and Legislation,* &c.

Population.[a]

Year.	Inhabited houses.	Number of separate occupiers.	Uninhabited houses.	Building.	Males.	Females.	Total of persons.
1801	87[b]	—	6	—	—	—	376
1831	87	—	—	—	—	—	424
1841	—	—	—	—	—	—	444
1851	—	—	—	—	—	—	432
1861	109	119	2	—	236	234	470
1871	114	119	—	—	267	258	525

[a] In December, 1720, there were 74 families, 36 of which were Dissenters.—MS. Marsh.

[b] 89 families.

CHELLINGTON,

Chelvynton, or Chelwinton,[a] is separated from Harrold and Odell by the River Ouse on the north, it is bounded on the east by Felmersham, south by Pavenham, and west by Carlton.

In the Award, mentioned under the account of the last-named parish, the quantity *to be awarded* in Carlton and Chellington together is put down 1,483 A. 3 R. 13 P., but the whole amount of acreage according to the valuation for the union is

	A.	R.	P.
Carlton	1,470	2	26
Chellington	527	0	12
	1,997	2	38

Miss Trevor, of Tingrith, in this county, is the principal landowner and lady of the manor.[b]

The village is so united with the adjoining parish of Carlton as to be considered little more than a hamlet of that place and is so designated in the Hundred Rolls.

It has been said that, before the marriage Act, several people used to come from London to be married here on account of this being an obscure village,[c] but the entries in the parish register do not bear out the statement.

This place is not *named* in Domesday Book, but there can be little or no doubt that it was included in a manor (which probably extended into the parishes of Carlton and Felmersham) belonging to the Bishop of Coutance, and to which no name is attached in the record of the great survey.

Manor. Coutance Fee,[d] *Honor of Gloucester.*[e] (The land of the Bishop of

---

[a] Rot. Hund. Placita de quo warranto. Nonar. Inquis.
The name is also found with the variations, Chillington, Chylynton, Chilvynton, Chelinton, &c.
[b] Crewe Alston, esq. owns a large water meadow, and there are a few other small freeholders.
[c] MS. Marsh.   [d] Vide Turvey.   [e] Vide Biddenham.

Coutance.) In the hundred of Wilga Goisfridus de Tralgi holds four hides of the bishop. There is land for five plough-teams; in demesne are two plough-teams, and the villans have three. There are fourteen villans, and five bordars, and four servi. Pasture for four plough-teams. Worth and hath been worth one hundred shillings. Turbertus, a man of King Edward, held this manor, and was able to sell it. The bishop acquired this land in exchange for Bledone, as his men testify.—Domesday, p. 210.

The history of the descent of the paramouncy of Chellington is the same as that of the bishop's interest in Turvey, and, as parcel of the honor of Gloucester, is traceable through the De Clares, Audleys, and Staffords, down to Humphrey Duke of Buckingham.[a]

The mesne lordship, also like Turvey, was annexed to the barony of Trailly.

The Traillys, as before stated, possessed extensive estates and flourished under the auspices of the Earls of Gloucester.

In the year 1211 Walter de Trailly was assessed to the scutage for Scotland for two knight's fees, under the honor of Warden; in 1216 the sheriff of Beds and Bucks was commanded to deliver all his (Walter's) lands within his bailiwick to Ralph de Beauchamp. In 1224 the wardship of the lands of Walter Trailly, a *minor*, with benefit of marriage, was committed to the Earl of Gloucester. In 1231 William de Hobrey was appointed guardian to Walter Trailly.[b]

Brian Fitz Alan and Thomas de Huse held a fee in Chellington and Hinwick, under the same family, as of the honor of Gloucester, temp. Henry III.—Edward I.[c]

About the same time the mesne lordship of the manor of Chellington was in John de Trailly,[d] and a John de Strayley (so written in the *Cal. Inq. p. m.*, probably a misprint) was seised of land and other hereditaments here.[e]

According to the Hundred Rolls, seventh Edward the First, Walter de Trailly held *Chelvynton, a hamlet of the vill of Karlton*, of the Earl of Gloucester as of the honor of Gloucester, by the service of half a knight's fee. The usufructuary interest, with the exception of the advowson of the church, was in Philip Burnel (for term of life) and others. To the church (rectory) belonged a messuage with a croft and three roods of land, which the parson held in demesne. Of the free

---

[a] For references to the evidence, see note (a) in page 174, and notes (b), (c), (d), (e), in page 3.
[b] Lipscomb's *Buckinghamshire*, vol. iv. p. 111. See also Harl. 313, fo. 48b, 58.
[c] Testa de Nevill, p. 248b.   [d] Esc. 41 Hen. III. nu. 28.
[e] Ib. 1 Edw. I. nu. 14.

tenants or freeholders, Nor̃ fil. Walter held one virgate of land at four shillings rent, which was applied to the sustaining of a lamp in the church or chancel. John de Cowe held a virgate and a half of Walter at one penny per annum, and had in demesne a capital messuage with a fishery in half the river Ouse from Harrold bridge to Odell ford. Half a virgate at two shillings rent was in the hands of Galfridus de Carlton, with his tenants; and another half virgate at the same rent was in possession of Richard de Ponte; both holdings being under the superiority of Walter Trailly. And Roger Abbot was tenant of a messuage for which he paid one penny a year. The same Walter appears to have been seised of the manor of Chellington until about the seventeenth or eighteenth year of King Edward's reign,[a] when (probably at his death) his lands were committed to Henry de Bray, the King's escheator.[b]

John, the son of Walter Trailly, was possessed of 11^{li} 1^s 4^d rent, &c. in this place;[c] and a John Trailly was found seised of this manor in the time of King Edward III.[d]

During that King's reign Walter Trailly was summoned to show by what right he claimed view of frank-pledge and other privileges in Chellington, on which occasion he appears to have paid a fine to the King for the same.[e]

On the authority of a pedigree in the Harleian collection, number 1163, John Trailly (the brother of Katherine, wife of Sir James Pabenham)[f] was, by Elizabeth his wife, father of

Sir John Trailly, knt., Attorney-General of England, lord of Carlton, Chellington, &c. in the fourteenth century. He married Johanna, daughter of Sir Thomas Aylesbury, knt. (who survived him), by whom he had an only son and heir,

Reginald Trailly, esq., with whom ended the male line of the family, he dying, a few years after his father, without leaving issue.[f]

From Sir John Trailly's time down to the purchase of *Carlton and Chellington* by Lewis Lord Mordaunt the manorial history has been anticipated under Carlton.[g] A pedigree of the Vaux family, the intermediate possessors, is annexed.

[a] Esc. 18 Edw. I. nu. 54.
[b] Lipscomb's *Buckinghamshire*, vol. iv. p. 111.
[c] Esc. 32 Edw. I. nu. 37.
[d] Ib. 34 Edw. III. nu. 65.
[e] Placita de quo warranto, p. 27.
[f] See the pedigree under Carlton.
[g] Vide pages 242-6.

A considerable part of the Traillys' Bedfordshire estate appears to have been divided between the families of Lucy and Vaux. The Traillys' interest in Carlton and Chellington passed to the latter, but there was, apparently, an interval when the Lucys were in possession, or had set up a claim to the manors

VAUX.[12]

Arms: [10][11] Chequy, or and gu. (another, ar. and gu.), on a chevron azure three roses or.

Vaux quarters: *Thureng, Grene or Greene, Mahlethorp, Harrowden, Lucy, Chambers, Cheyne or Cheyny, Aire, Pabenham, Engaine, Remston or Rempston, Helmbridge (or Berkeing), Loudham.*

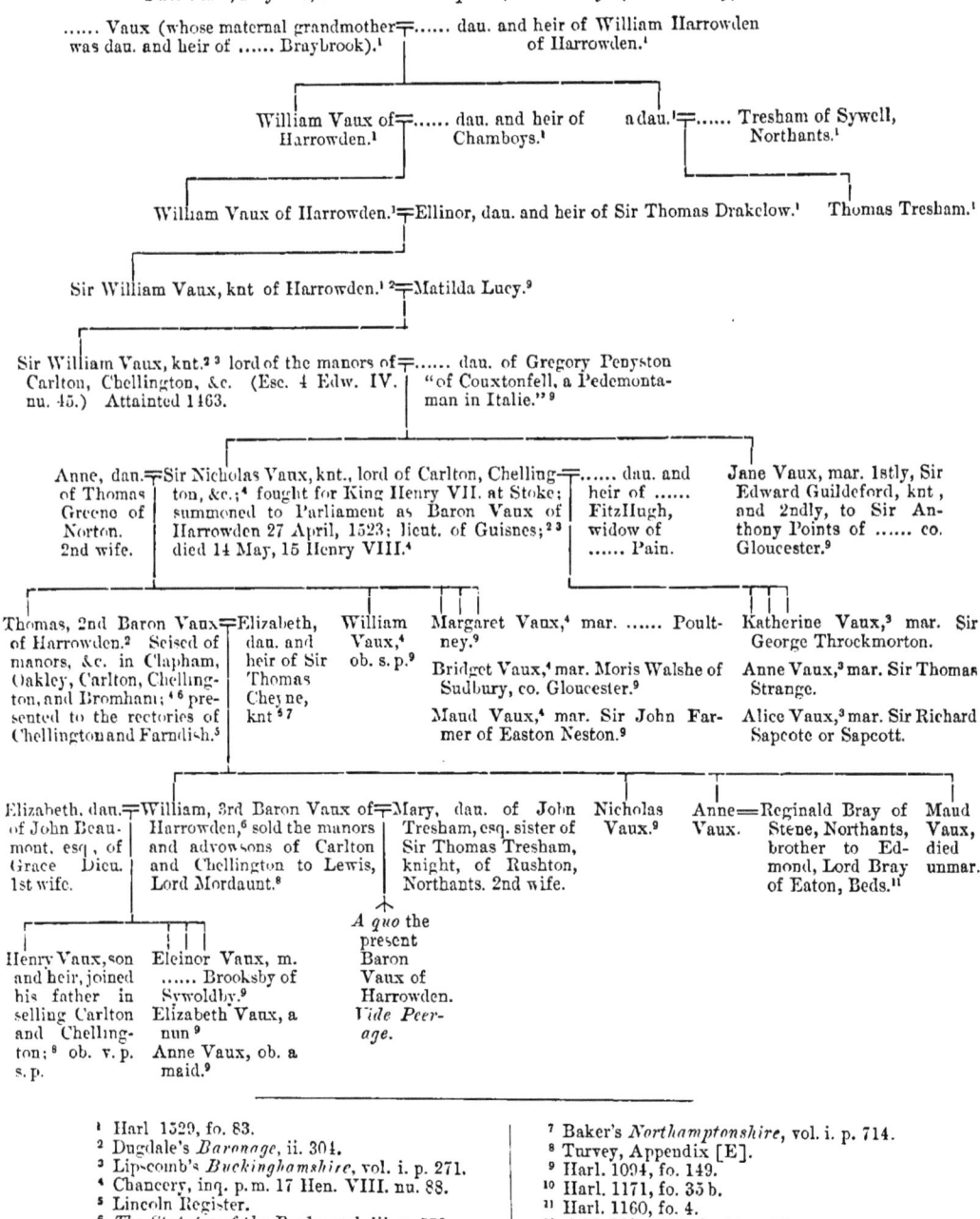

...... Vaux (whose maternal grandmother was dau. and heir of ...... Braybrook).[1] = ... dau. and heir of William Harrowden of Harrowden.[1]

William Vaux of Harrowden.[1] = ... dau. and heir of Chamboys.[1]

a dau.[1] = ... Tresham of Sywell, Northants.[1]

William Vaux of Harrowden.[1] = Ellinor, dau. and heir of Sir Thomas Drakelow.[1]

Thomas Tresham.[1]

Sir William Vaux, knt. of Harrowden.[1] [2] = Matilda Lucy.[9]

Sir William Vaux, knt.[2][3] lord of the manors of Carlton, Chellington, &c. (Esc. 4 Edw. IV. nu. 45.) Attainted 1463. = ... dau. of Gregory Penyston "of Couxtonfell, a Pedemonta-man in Italie."[9]

Anne, dau. of Thomas Greene of Norton. 2nd wife. = Sir Nicholas Vaux, knt., lord of Carlton, Chellington, &c.;[4] fought for King Henry VII. at Stoke; summoned to Parliament as Baron Vaux of Harrowden 27 April, 1523; lieut. of Guisnes;[2][3] died 14 May, 15 Henry VIII.[4] = ... dau. and heir of ...... FitzHugh, widow of ...... Pain.

Jane Vaux, mar. 1stly, Sir Edward Guildeford, knt., and 2ndly, to Sir Anthony Points of ...... co. Gloucester.[9]

Thomas, 2nd Baron Vaux of Harrowden.[2] Seised of manors, &c. in Clapham, Oakley, Carlton, Chellington, and Bromham;[4][6] presented to the rectories of Chellington and Farndish.[5] = Elizabeth, dau. and heir of Sir Thomas Cheyne, knt.[5][7]

William Vaux,[4] ob. s. p.[9]

Margaret Vaux,[4] mar. ...... Poultney.[9]

Bridget Vaux,[4] mar. Moris Walshe of Sudbury, co. Gloucester.[9]

Maud Vaux,[4] mar. Sir John Farmer of Easton Neston.[9]

Katherine Vaux,[3] mar. Sir George Throckmorton.

Anne Vaux,[3] mar. Sir Thomas Strange.

Alice Vaux,[3] mar. Sir Richard Sapcote or Sapcott.

Elizabeth, dau. of John Beaumont, esq, of Grace Dieu. 1st wife. = William, 3rd Baron Vaux of Harrowden,[6] sold the manors and advowsons of Carlton and Chellington to Lewis, Lord Mordaunt.[8] = Mary, dau. of John Tresham, esq. sister of Sir Thomas Tresham, knight, of Rushton, Northants. 2nd wife.

Nicholas Vaux.[9]

Anne = Reginald Bray of Stene, Northants, brother to Edmond, Lord Bray of Eaton, Beds.[11]

Maud Vaux, died unmar.

Henry Vaux, son and heir, joined his father in selling Carlton and Chellington;[8] ob. v. p. s. p.

Eleinor Vaux, m. ...... Brooksby of Sywoldby.[9]

Elizabeth Vaux, a nun.[9]

Anne Vaux, ob. a maid.[9]

A quo the present Baron Vaux of Harrowden. *Vide Peerage.*

---

[1] Harl. 1529, fo. 83.
[2] Dugdale's *Baronage*, ii. 304.
[3] Lipscomb's *Buckinghamshire*, vol. i. p. 271.
[4] Chancery, inq. p. m. 17 Hen. VIII. nu. 88.
[5] Lincoln Register.
[6] *The Statutes of the Realm*, vol. iii. p. 579.
[7] Baker's *Northamptonshire*, vol. i. p. 714.
[8] Turvey, Appendix [E].
[9] Harl. 1094, fo. 149.
[10] Harl. 1171, fo. 35 b.
[11] Harl. 1160, fo. 4.
[12] Add. MS. 5523, fo. 64 or 68.

The manor and advowson of Chellington, together with the principal part of the estate, passed subsequently, by purchase, to the Trevors of Bromham. The advowson having been merged in that of Carlton, is treated of under the account of that parish.

In 1806 Thomas, second Viscount Hampden, was in possession of this estate, and it came eventually to Robert Trevor, esq., who married Mary, daughter of the Rev. Edmond Williamson, rector of Milbrook in this county (by Mary Tipping,[a] his second wife), by whom he had issue three daughters and coheirs, one only of whom survives.

---

[a] Vide note (a) in page 136, and note (b), page 132.

---

of *Carlton and Chellington*. (See notes to the pedigree under Carlton.) Possibly some design on the part of Sir William Vaux to save his estates may supply the explanation of the circumstance.

Information respecting other early proprietors of land, &c. in this parish, so far as has been ascertained, is of the most fragmentary description.

In the 32nd Henry III. there appears to have been a dispute, touching a free tenement in " Chylynton," between William Giffard and John, son of John, son of Galfridus.[1]

Michael, younger son of the lord of Wahul or Wodehull, is styled " of Chellington." Michael was father of Simon de Wahul, of Chellington, who had a son Walter de Wahul.[2] Towards the end of King Edward the Third's reign Elizabeth and Alianora, the daughters and heirs of John de Wodhull, chevalier, were found seised of land, &c. here.[3]

Robert de Insula possessed an interest in this place.[4]

William Haile, of " Chellingdon," occurs in the list of gentry returned by the Commissioners 12 King Henry VI.[5]

A messuage and land, &c., in the hands of John Day about the year 1481, were parcel of the possessions of Caldwell Priory.[6]

Thomas Smythe, a freeholder here in the time of Queen Elizabeth.[7]

" Simon Hale, of Chillington, gent." (In a list of nobility and gentry of the county of Bedford, 1673.)

---

[1] Esc. 32 Hen. III. nu. 31.
[2] MS. Wood.
[3] Esc. 50 Edw. III. nu. 69.
[4] Ib. 42 Edw. III. nu. 53.
About a century earlier Brian de Insula was holding land in this county as of the honor of Leicester. (Harl. 313, fo. 48b, 58.)
[5] Fuller's *Worthies*.
[6] Esc. 21 Edw. IV. nu. 64.
[7] Lansd. 5, fo. 27.

It has been stated on good authority[a] that Sir Robert Darling, knight, whose tomb may be seen near the south-east corner of the chancel here, used, as a boy, to keep cows on Chellington hill. When of proper age he put himself apprentice to a lapidary, and by diligence acquired at length a large fortune. In 1767 he served as sheriff of London and Middlesex, and the following year was elected member of parliament for Wendover, as the colleague of Edmund Burke, esq.,[b] the eminent statesman and orator. He does not appear to have married, and died in the year 1770, aged 55.

Mr. Marsh has left on record the name of another successful individual, a native of this village:—

Mr. Henry Sharp, of mean parentage, who, by his industry and marriage, acquired an independent fortune. By his will he gave to the poor parishioners of Chellington the Interest of 100*l.* in Three per Cent. stock, to be distributed annually at Christmas. In youth he followed the humble occupation of an huxter. He died at Silsoe, in this county, in 1791 or 1792.[a]

Advowson and Rectory.

Until after or about the time that Chellington came into the possession of the Trevors this advowson appears to have attended the manor; it will not therefore be necessary to do more than refer the reader to the names of Patrons to be found under the list of *Rectors*, and to the later account of the advowson, under Carlton, in page 253.

In reference to the conjecture embodied in note ([g]) at pages 265 and 267, attention may be called to the fact that a William Lucy, of Elstow, presented twice to this rectory just before the Vaux estates were granted to Sir Ralph Hastings.

The following is the substance of a Return made in the reign of King Edward III.:—

"John de Rysle, William de Rysle, William Hadd, Walter Godwyne, John Waker, and John de Flaundres, parishioners of Chellington, being sworn before the Prior of Dunstable, Simon Croyser, and his Fellows: Say that the church of Chellington does not pay tax on account of its poorness. Nevertheless, the ninth part of the sheaves, of the fleeces, and of the lambs in the fourteenth year of the present King Edward's reign was worth forty shillings and not more, because most of the lands of the same parish lay in the same year uncultivated

---

[a] Add. MS. 21,067, fo. 62 b. 98.   [b] Lipscomb's *Buckinghamshire*, vol. ii. p. 479.

on account of the poverty of the parishioners, and the land in the same place does not bear except scantily poor wheat, and the two-teethed sheep and the lambs almost all died. They say also that there were not in the same village citizens, burgesses, nor any others possessed of chattels dwelling there in the same year."[a]

The value of the rectory in the King's books is £10.

The rector of *Carlton-cum-Chellington* has 78 A. 2 R. 3 P. of glebe in this parish.

RECTORS.[b]

		Patrons.
1220—1234	Joh. de Winthorn	
	William	
1258—1279	Hugh de Gyvelden, subdeacon. By death of last.	W. . . . de Trayly.
1280—1299	Hugh de Givelden, subdeacon.	Sir Walter Trayli, knt.
1363—1397	Joh. Boteler	
	Joh. Smalfelowe, Pbr. By res. of last.	Sir John Trailly, knt.
	Galfridus Dyue or Dyne	
	John Hyne. By death of last.	Nich. Westerdale and Sir Joh. Trayle, knt., Attorney-Gen¹. for England.
1398—1404	John F. . . . . alias Gevelden, Pbr. Also rect. of Carlton.	Johanna, late the wife of Sir John Trailly, knt., and others.
	John Hyne	
1420—1429	Robt. Hyne. By res. of last.	
1450—1470	Robert Cole	Willm. Vaux, armiger.
	John Chapman. By death of last.	Wm. Lucy, of Elnestowe.
	John Wynge, a Carmelite.	,,
	John Wynet	Rad. Hastings, armiger.
	William Smyth	Rad. Hastings, of Harowdon.
1521—1546	. . . . Kyng	
	Brian Wright. By death of last.	Thos. Lord Vaux, of Harowdon.
	Robt. Alyn. By res. of last.	Lord Vaux, of Harrowden.
	Richard Hall. By death of last.	,,
	William Lathus. By res. of last.	,,
	Thomas Wells. Also rect. of Carlton.[c]	
1642	Thos. Chaderton[c]	
1680	Joseph Chaderton. Also rect. of Carlton.[c]	
1720	Robert Richards.[c] Chaplain to Thos Ld. Trevor. Also vic. of Bromham.	
1758, March	Samuel Rogers.[c] By death of last.	Lord Trevor.

For subsequent Rectors see Carlton, p. 254.

---

[a] Nonar. Inquis. p. 21.　　[b] Lib. Instit. apud Lincoln.　　[c] Parish Register.

Samuel Rogers, A.M., born at Carlton, received his early training from a parish schoolmaster named Bordley; and was afterwards sent to Oakham School, where he remained from 1745 to 1752, and from thence to Emmanuel College, Cambridge. In March 1758 he was instituted to this living, which he resigned, in 1768, for Brampton Ash or Dingley, Northants., on presentation of Earl Spencer, to whom he was chaplain; and on 3rd May, 1777, was instituted to the valuable living of Husbands Bosworth, Leicestershire.[a] He published two volumes of Poems, 8vo. 1782,[b] printed at Bath, having previously published a volume of Poems (many of them satirical) in a much earlier period of his life, and was the supposed author of one or two anonymous pamphlets.[c] He lived some years at Chellington, and kept a grammar school. At this school Thomas Orlebar Marsh was a pupil when very young. From Mr. Rogers' poems in 1782 it appears that he had been preceptor to the Hon. William Cockayne of Rushton, son to Charles, Viscount Cullen; he was also at one time head master of the Northampton grammar school. There is an indifferent print of him in his Poems, 1782. He married Miss Catherine Peers, but died without issue,[d] in the Close at Salisbury in July, 1790.[e]

The church, dedicated to St. Nicholas, stands on Chellington Hill, and forms an interesting feature in the landscape.[f]

The fabric consists of a nave and clerestory, aisles, south porch, chancel, and western tower supporting a broach spire, and has portions of Early English and Decorated work.

---

[a] Nichols's *Leicestershire*, vol. ii. part 2, p. 468.
[b] Among these is an epitaph to his father.
[c] Mr. Marsh mentions having seen, in 1824, a MS. poem of his called "the Journey."
[d] Add. MS. 21,067, ff. 109, 134, 200.
[e] Gent. Mag. Aug. 1790, vol. 60, part 2, p. 767.
[f] A view of Harrold from Chellington churchyard (showing a small portion of the north aisle of this church) drawn by T. Hearne, F.S.A., engraved by Wm. Byrne, F.S.A., was published in London, 1 Jan. 1803.

Chellington Church stands by itself in a field at a considerable distance from the village, and there is a local tradition that the village was formerly near the church. The probability is, however, that in choosing its site, the founder of the church was guided principally by the position of his manor-place.

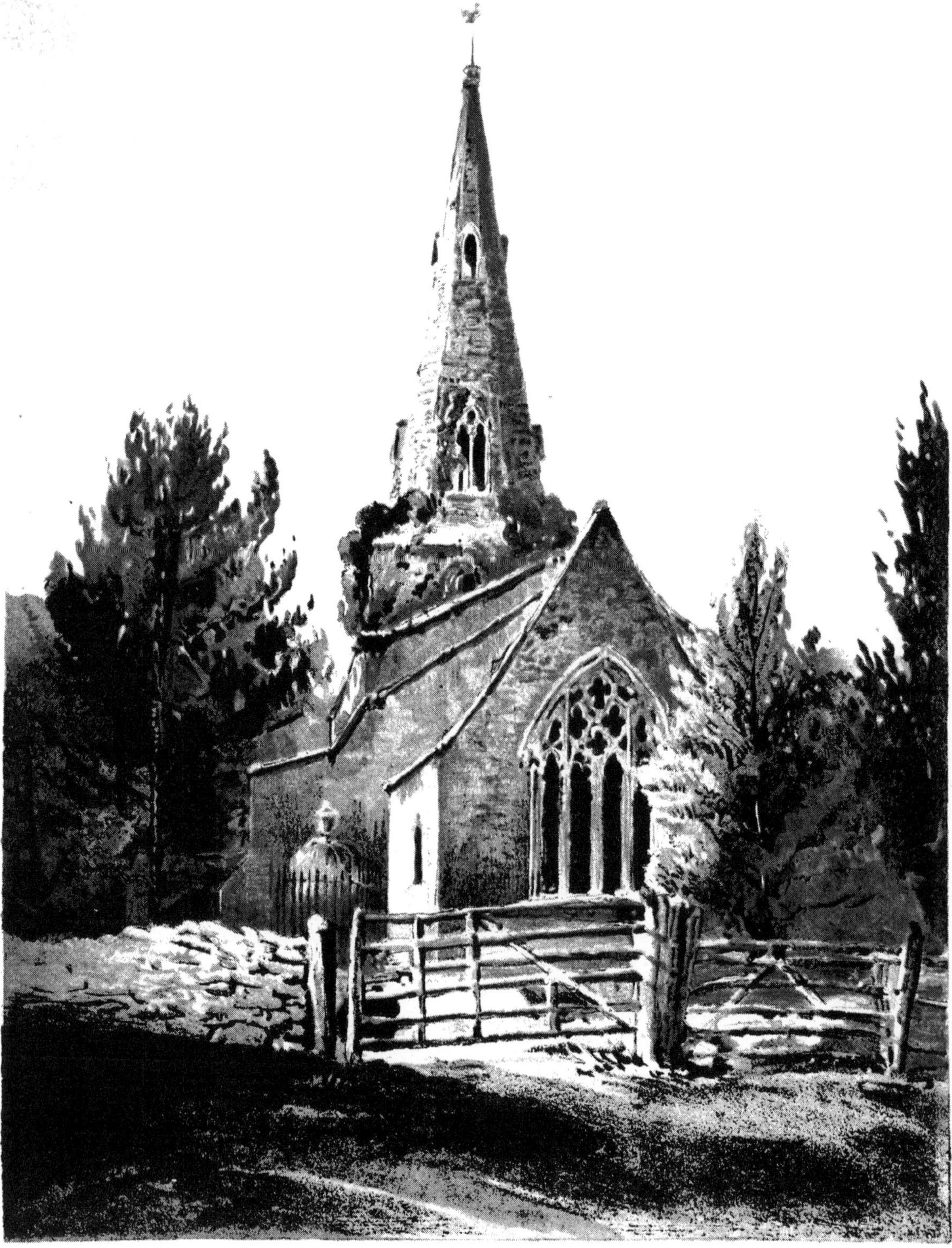

CHELLASTON CHURCH, SOUTH-EAST VIEW.

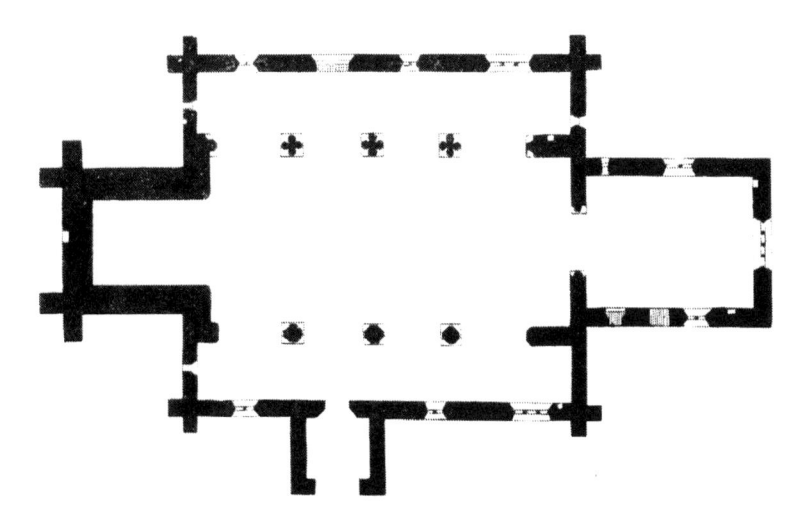

GROUND PLAN OF CHURCH.

In 1869 it underwent considerable repairs and renovation, the expense being defrayed by the late Lord Dynevor, the ladies of the manor, and the parishioners. Plaster was removed from pillars and arches, the stonework pointed, a new roof placed over the clerestory, the floor laid down with red and black tiles, open seats of stained deal were introduced, and an obstruction in the west arch was removed. At the same time the rector did some substantial repairs to the roof and some other portions of the chancel.

The chancel has a north and a south Decorated two-light window with flamboyant tracery. A low side window and priest's doorway on the south are blocked up, but a small window opposite to and corresponding with the former has been re-opened by the present rector. The east window is Transition from Decorated to Perpendicular.

The south aisle contains three Decorated windows and doorway, and a lancet at the west end. The north aisle has also three Decorated windows, a lancet at each end, and a good Early English doorway (closed up) with a row of tooth ornament in the head, and above is the weather-mold of a porch, now destroyed. Both aisles have a cornice of masks.

The nave is lighted by six uniform clerestory windows.

The tower and spire are Decorated; the former divided into four stages by string-courses. In the western face of the lowest stage is a large but low cinquefoiled niche; next above is the west window (pointed) of two lights; the belfry stage contains on each side a two-light window of uniform design. The steeple was repaired in 1824.

The nave has four arches on either side. Those on the south have octagonal piers; those on the north, cluster of four shafts with Decorated moulded capitals and bases. The west arch is well proportioned and has a drip-stone springing from corbel heads. A drip-stone is continued over the south face of the arches on the north side of the nave.

Each aisle contains a piscina. Remains of steps to the rood-loft may be seen in the south aisle. At the west end of the north aisle was formerly a large plain fireplace; this was removed during the recent repairs. The font, attached to the westernmost pillar of the south aisle, is Early English; its bason circular. At the east end of each aisle is the upper part of a pointed-arched recess; that in the north aisle, together with the north-east window, carrying a drip-stone.

The chancel is approached under an Early English arch with moulded capitals and round shafts, and having a drip-stone over its west face. In the head of

2 P

the east window are some fragments of ancient glass,ª put up about the year 1846 or 1848 by the then rector. There are no altar-rails. In the east wall, near the north-east angle, is a recess and a projecting stone; there is likewise a piscina (with a shelf) in the usual position. The chancel roof was renewed in 1863.

Bells.

1st. Bell. E flat.
    John Hodson made me. 165-.

2nd. Bell. D.
    Pray-e the Lord. 1630.

3rd. Bell. C.
    W. Atton—Robert Thorn made me. 1611.

4th. Bell. B flat. T. × D.
    Sancta Katerina
    Ora pro nobis.

On the parish chest are carved these characters:

    R B
    1667
    I M
    G

Font.

ª The following heraldry was formerly in the church:—

    In the east window: Or, a cross pattée gu. Barry of six argent and azure.

    In an upper window of the north aisle: Or, a cross gu. between four martlets, a plate for difference (? Trailly.)

    In a clerestory window, north: Gu. seven lozenges (or mascles?) conjoined. 3, 2, 1. erm.

Unfortunately the reference to the manuscript from which the above was taken has been overlooked.

Inscriptions.

Chancel.

Eliz. sole offspring of Wm Hooper, M.A., Rector of this parish, died 18th Augt 1811, æt. 46. Samuel Hooper Adams, her eldest son, Attorney-at-Law, died æt. 25. Elizabeth, wife of Wm Hooper, M.A., Rector, ob. Feby 1807, æt. 64. Revd William Hooper, M.A., Rector of Carlton-cum-Chellington for 61 years, ob. 9th Novr 1828, æt. 86. Elizabeth and Samuel Adams, his daughter and grandson.

In the Nave and South Aisle.

Martha, wife of Charles Wright, ob. 5th Feby 1737, æt. 72. Charles Right (*sic*), ob. 12th Septr 1727, æt. 67.

Catharine Darling, 1733.

William Chaderton, A.M., died 1 May, 1724, aged 34. Revd Thos. Chaderton, A.M., Feb. 1735, aged 48. . . . Chaderton, widow of Revd Thos. C., March, 1754, aged 68.

Here lies interrd the Body of Judith Bamford, the daughter of William and Mary Bamford, Gent., who departed this life Sepr 5th, 1751, aged 37 years.

In Memory of Robert Bamford, son of Mary and William Bamford. And Mary, his wife, who died April 4th, 1766. Aged 48 years.

In the Churchyard.

Jane Hooper, widow of Revd Wm Hooper, formerly Rector of this parish, died 20th Apr. 1840, aged 76.

In Memory of Sr Robert Darling, Knight, son of Mr John Darling, late of this Parish, who departed this life Aug^st 4th, 1770, aged 55 years; he served Sheriff of the City of London and County of Middlesex in the year 1767, one of his Majesty's Justices of the Peace for the said County, and Member of Parliament for Wendover in the Co. of Bucks.

Arms: A chevron erm. between three ewers.

Crest: (On helmet and wreath) a demi (? lion) rampant.

REGISTER.[a]

1567 Oct. 12.	Baptized,	Mary Simes, daughter of Roger. (Earliest entry.)
1650 June 4.	——	Jos., son, of Thos. and Mary Chaderton.
1665 April 3.	Married,	Graveley Waple and Mary Chaderton.
1683 July 28.	Buried,	Thos. Chaderton, rector, "in sheep's wooll onely as was attested by affidavit under hand of Dr. Dillingham."
1688 May 1.	Baptized,	Thomas, son of Joseph and Eliz. Chaderton.
1699 Mar. 17.	Buried,	Mary Chaderton, widow.
1711 June 8.	Baptized,	Robert, son of John and Cath. Darlin.
1715 Aug. 25.	Married,	Thomas Orlebar of Henwick, gent., and M⁽ˢˢ⁾ Judith Boteler of Carlton.
1724 May 3.	Buried,	William, son of Rev⁽ᵈ⁾ Mr. Jos. Chaderton late rector of this parish.
1735 Feb. 11.	——	Rev⁽ᵈ⁾ Mr. Thos. Chaderton.
1753 Mar 12.	——	Ursula Chaderton, gent.
1764—9		John Hutchinson, curate.
1770 Aug. 4.	Buried,	Sir Robert Darling, knt.

In the cover of the old register book is the following memorandum:—

Mr. Tho. Wells mention⁽ᵈ⁾ in Carlton Regist. as Rect. of y⁽ᵗ⁾ p. in y⁽ᵉ⁾ year 1554 when that Book was bought is also mentioned in y⁽ᵉ⁾ regist⁽ʳ⁾ as bur⁽ᵈ⁾ on y⁽ᵉ⁾ 7⁽ᵗʰ⁾ Aug., 1640 (but y⁽ʳᵉ⁾ is reason to think this Thos. Wells was a Layman), in Carlton Regis. he is s⁽ᵈ⁾ to have been bur. Aug. 5, 1642, and therefore seems to have been Rect⁽ʳ⁾ of this p. also w⁽ᶜʰ⁾ if he was he seems to have been suc⁽ᵈ⁾ by Mr. Thos. Chaderton, father of M⁽ʳ⁾ Jos. Chaderton, who was bur. July 28, 1680, and was suc⁽ᵈ⁾ by his son, M⁽ʳ⁾ Jos. Chaderton, who the same year suc⁽ᵈ⁾ M⁽ʳ⁾. Great-Bach in the Rectory of Carlton, & was bur. 1720, Apr. 30, & suc⁽ᵈ⁾ by M⁽ʳ⁾. Rob⁽ᵗ⁾. Richards, Vic. of Brumham, & Chaplain to y⁽ᵉ⁾ Rt. Hon. Thos. Lord Trevor, B. of Brumham.

1799, July 25, a shepherd named Thole or Tole was killed by lightening on Chellington hill.[b]

Assessed Property (1815), £622.   Poor rates in 1837, £14.

POPULATION.

Year.	Inhabited houses	Number of separate occupiers.	Uninhabited houses.	Building.	Males.	Females.	Total of persons
1801	24[c]	—	1	—	—	—	112
1831	—	—	—	—	—	—	119
1841	—	—	—	—	—	—	125
1861	30	36	—	—	72	64	136
1871	26	33	6	—	49	55	104

[a] See also pedigree of Boteler under Biddenham.   [b] MS. Marsh.   [c] 26 families.

www.ingramcontent.com/pod-product-compliance
Ingram Content Group UK Ltd.
Pitfield, Milton Keynes, MK11 3LW, UK
UKHW051422100825
7319UKWH00026B/872